Mob
Travel Guide

New York City

ExxonMobil
Travel Publications

Maps by
🏵 RAND McNALLY

Acknowledgements

We gratefully acknowledge the help of our representatives for their efficient and perceptive inspections of the lodging and dining establishments listed; the establishments' proprietors for their cooperation in showing their facilities and providing information about them; and the many users of previous editions who have taken the time to share their experiences.

Mobil Travel Guide is also grateful to all the highly talented writers who contributed entries to this book.

Maps Copyright © 2004 Rand McNally & Company

Printing Acknowledgement: North American Corporation of Illinois

www.mobiltravelguide.com

ISBN: 0-7627-2882-5

Manufactured in the United States of America.

10 9 8 7 6 5 4 3 2 1

Contents

MAP SYMBOLS

Symbol	Description
Free limited-access highway	Interstate highway
New — under construction	
Toll limited-access highway	U.S. highway
New — under construction	
Other multilane highway	State or provincial highway
Principal highway	Other highway
Other through highway	Miles between arrows
	One mile or less not shown
Other road	Interchanges and interchange numbers
Unpaved road	Time zone boundary
Ferry	

Urbanized area in state maps; in city maps
Separate cities within metro area

National capital; state capital; cities; towns
(size of type indicates relative population)

U.S. or Canadian National Park

State/Provincial Park or Recreation Area

National Forest or Grassland, city park

Point of interest

Hospital, medical center

Continental divide

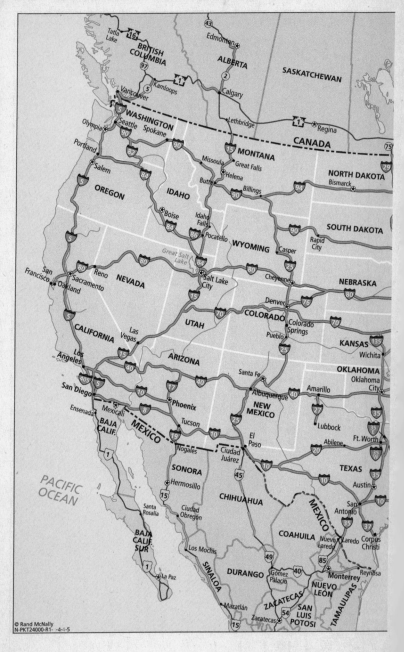

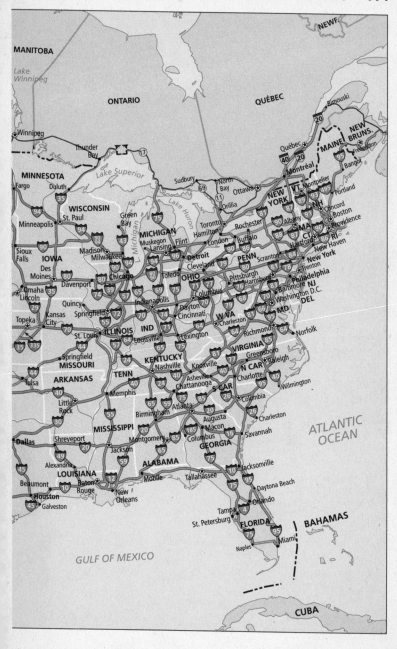

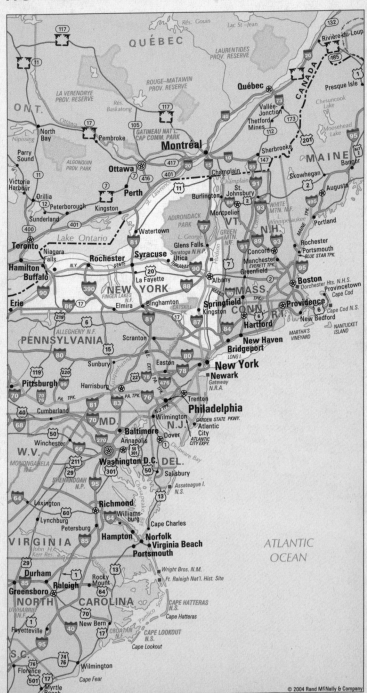

© 2004 Rand McNally & Company

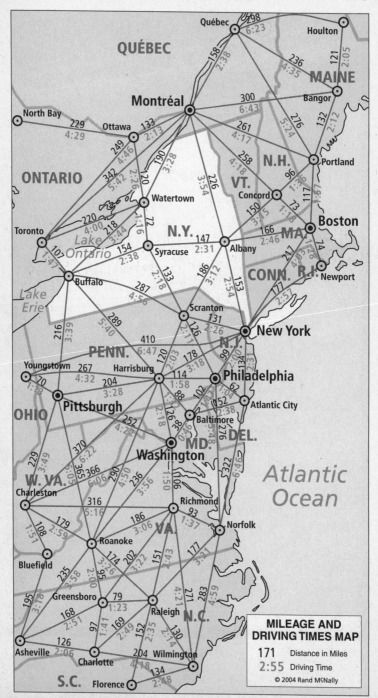

MILEAGE AND DRIVING TIMES MAP

171   Distance in Miles

2:55   Driving Time

© 2004 Rand McNally

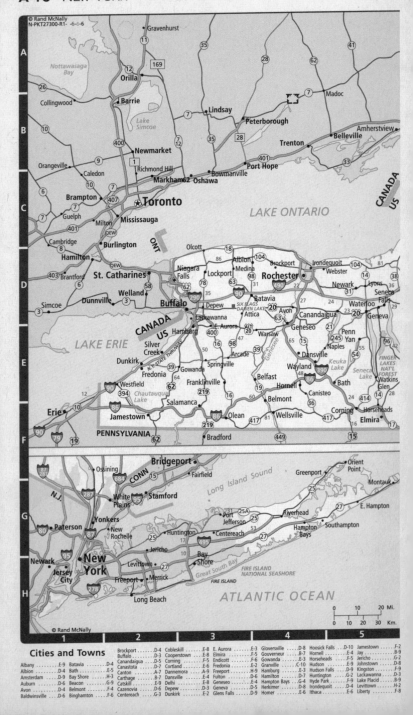

Cities and Towns

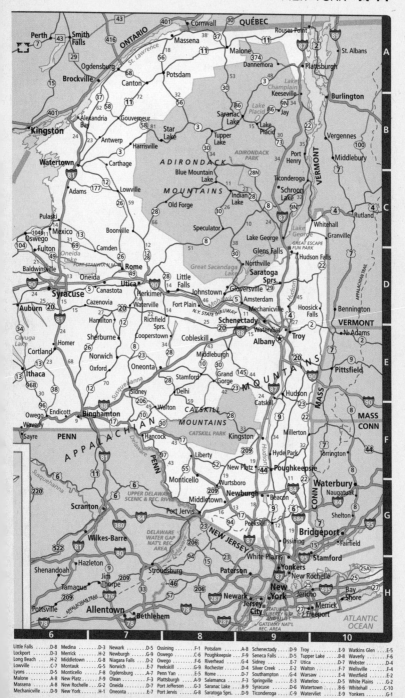

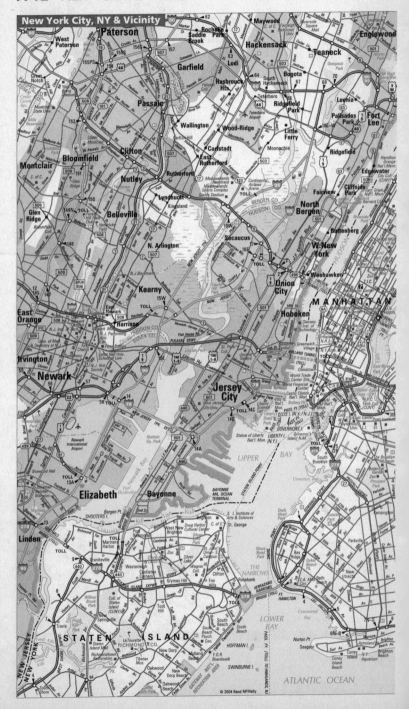

New York City, NY & Vicinity

© 2004 Rand McNally

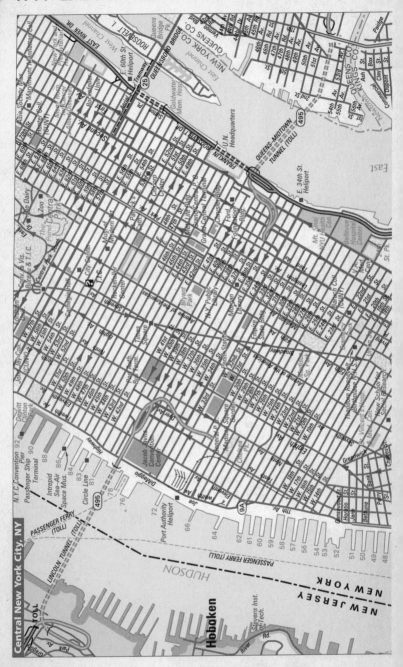

Central New York City, NY

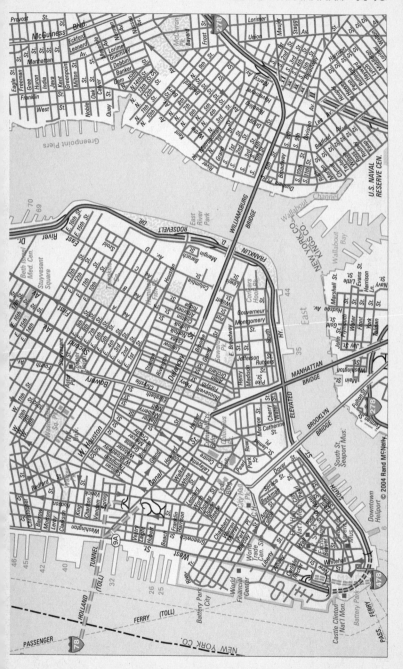

© 2004 Rand McNally

Manhattan and Bronx, NY

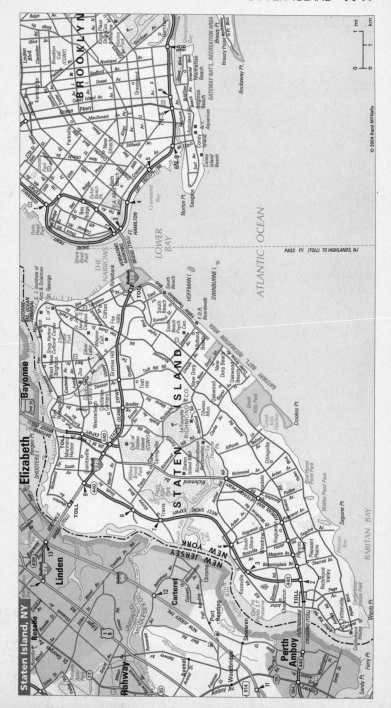

Staten Island, NY

© 2004 Rand McNally

Brooklyn and Queens, NY

© 2004 Rand McNally

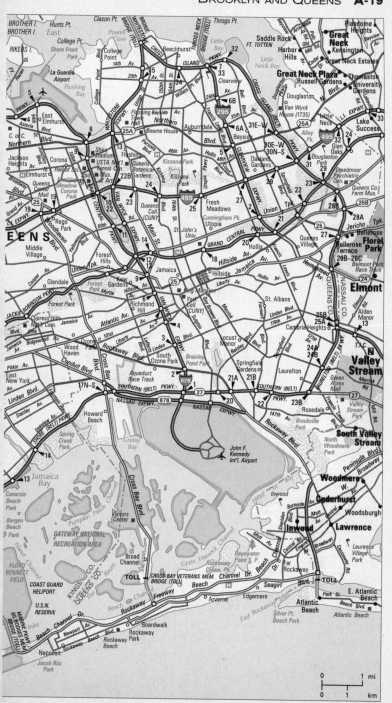

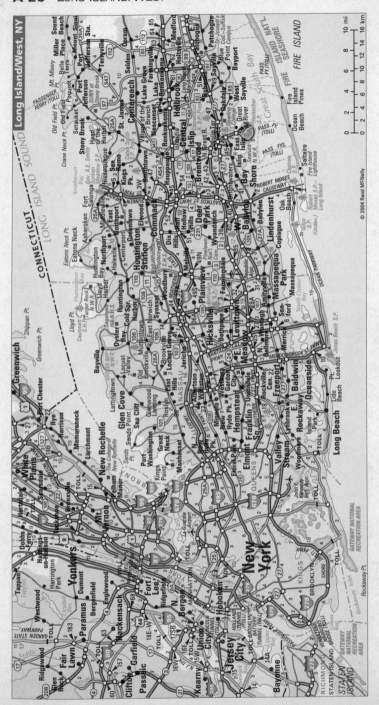

© 2004 Rand McNally

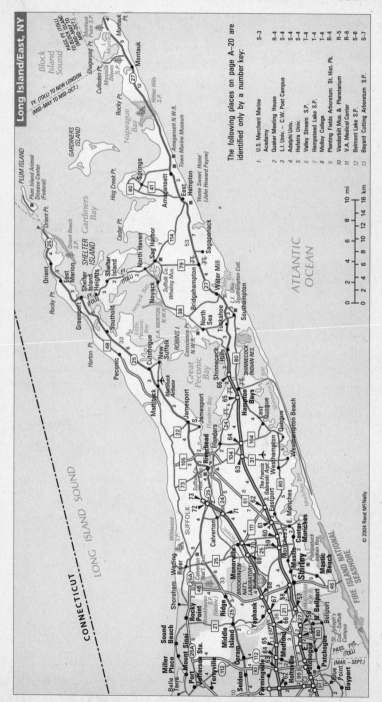

Long Island/East, NY

The following places on page A-20 are identified only by a number key:

1	U.S. Merchant Marine Academy	S-3
2	Quaker Meeting House	R-4
3	L.I. Univ. – C.W. Post Campus	S-4
4	Adelphi Univ.	S-4
5	Hofstra Univ.	T-4
6	Valley Stream S.P.	T-4
7	Hempstead Lake S.P.	T-4
8	Molloy College	R-4
9	Planting Fields Arboretum St. Hist. Pk.	
10	Vanderbilt Mus. & Planetarium	R-5
11	V.A. Medical Center	R-6
12	Belmont Lake S.P.	S-6
13	Bayard Cutting Arboretum S.P.	S-7

© 2004 Rand McNally

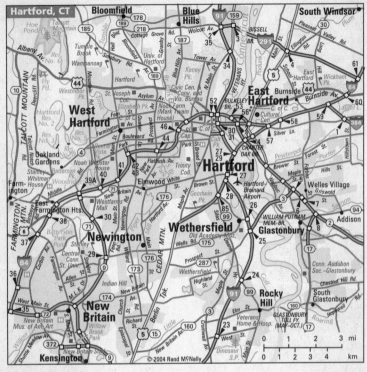

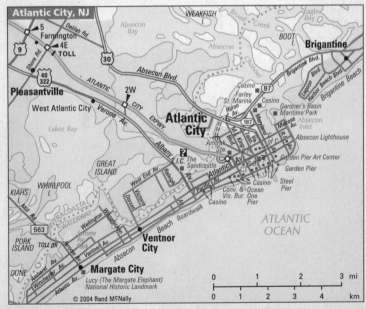

Cape Cod, MA & Vicinity

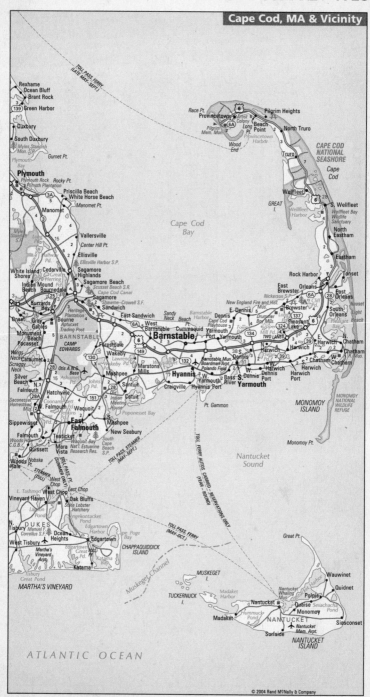

Rexhame
Ocean Bluff
Brant Rock
139 Green Harbor
Duxbury
South Duxbury
Myles Standish
Mon. S.R.
Gurnet Pt.
Plymouth
Bay
Plymouth
Plymouth Rock
Plimoth Plantation
Rocky Pt.
3A
Priscilla Beach
White Horse Beach
Manomet
Manomet Pt.
Myles
Standish
S.F.
Long
Pd.
Vallersville
Center Hill Pt.
Ellisville
White Island
Shores
Cedarville
Great
Herring
Pd.
Ellisville Harbor S.P.
Sagamore Highlands
Sagamore Beach
Indian Mound
Beach
Bournedale
Scusset Beach S.R.
Cape Cod Canal
Burzards
Bay
25
Sagamore
Shawme-Crowell S.F.
Heritage
Plantation
Sandwich
Onset
Gray
Gables
Bourne
Aptucxet
Trading Post
Monument
Beach
Pocasset
East Sandwich
West
Barnstable
6A
Cummaquid
CAMP
EDWARDS
Forestdale
Wakeby
Wings
Neck
Catamet
130
Lawrence
Lakeby Pd.
149
Scraggy
Neck
Silver
Beach
Otis A.N.G.
Base
Mashpee
Marstons
Mills
132
Barnstable Mun.
Falmouth
Hatchville
28A
Ashumet
Pd.
Johns
Pd.
151
Santuit
Old
Indian
Meeting
House
Cotuit
Saconesset
Homestead
Mus.
W. Falmouth
Coonamessett
Jenkins
Pd.
Waquoit
S.
Mashpee
Poponesset Bay
Pt. Gammon
Sippewisset
East
Falmouth
New Seabury
Falmouth
Woods Hole
C.G.B.
Quissett
Mara
Vista
Waquoit Bay
Nat'l Estuarine
Research Res.
South
Cape
Beach
S.P.
Nobska Pt.
Woods
Hole
STEAMER
(TOLL)
West Chop
West Chop
Vineyard Haven
L. Tashmoo
East Chop
Oak Bluffs
State Lobster
Hatchery
Lagoon
Pond
Sengekontacket
Pond
N.
Tisbury
DUKES
Manuel F.
Correllus S.F.
Ocean
Heights
Edgartown
Edgartown
Harbor
Cape Poge
Bay
West Tisbury
Martha's
Vineyard
Arpt.
Edgartown
Great
Pd.
CHAPPAQUIDDICK
ISLAND
Katama
Bay
Tisbury
Great Pond
West Tisbury
Katama
MARTHA'S VINEYARD

Race Pt.
Provincetown
Pilgrim
Mem. Mon.
6
Artist
Colony
6A
Long
Pt.
Pilgrim Heights
Beach
Point
North Truro
Wood
End
Provincetown
Harbor
7
Truro
Truro
CAPE COD
NATIONAL
SEASHORE
Cape
Cod
Wellfleet
28
GREAT
I.
Wellfleet
Harbor
S. Wellfleet
Wellfleet Bay
Wildlife
Sanctuary
North
Eastham
Rock Harbor
Eastham
East
Brewster
Nickerson S.P.
Orleans
28
Nauset
Light
East
Orleans
New England Fire and Hist.
Mus.
E. Dennis
6A
Cliff
Brewster
South
Orleans
Nauset
Light
Beach
Dennis
Sandy
Neck
Beach
Barnstable
Harbor
Cape Cod
Playhouse
Drummer
Boy Mus.
137
Pleasant
Lake
6
N.
Harwich
Chatham
Yarmouth
Port
Yarmouth
134
Follins
Stony
Brook
Mill Pd.
124
TWO LAKES
Harwich
39
Harwich
Chatham
Lt. Mus.
Barnstable
Barnstable Mun.
Boardman Arpt.
Polando Field
38 S.
Dennis
Harwich
39
Chatham
W.
Chatham
Hyannis
W.
Yarmouth
S.
Dennis
Dennis
Port
Harwich
Port
Chatham
Craigville
Hyannis Port
Yarmouth
Bass
River
Harwich
Port
MONOMOY
ISLAND
MONOMOY
NATIONAL
WILDLIFE
REFUGE
Monomoy Pt.

Cape Cod
Bay

TOLL FERRY AUTOS CARRIED RESERVATIONS ONLY
(YEAR ROUND)

TOLL PASS STEAMER
(MAY-SEPT.)

STEAMER FLY
(SUMMER ONLY)

TOLL PASS FLY
(SUMMER ONLY)

TOLL PASS FERRY
(MAY-OCT.)

Nantucket
Sound

Great Pt.

MUSKEGET
I.

TUCKERNUCK
I.

Muskeget Channel

Madaket
Harbor

Nantucket
Whaling Mus.

Nantucket

Quaise

Wauwinet

Quidnet

Polpis

Sesachacha
Pond

Monomoy

Madaket

Hummock
Pond

NANTUCKET

Nantucket
Mem. Arpt.

Surfside

Siasconset

NANTUCKET
ISLAND

ATLANTIC OCEAN

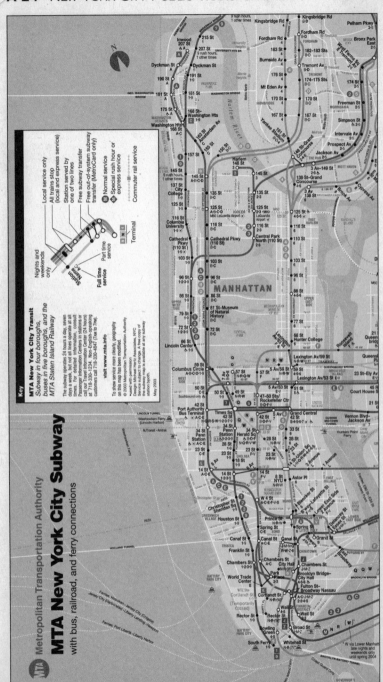

Metropolitan Transportation Authority

MTA New York City Subway

with bus, railroad, and ferry connections

Making road trips easy is our driving ambition.

Come and see how easy and convenient our Exxon and Mobil locations are. Before you head off for your next road trip, stop into your local Exxon or Mobil retailer and fill up on the essentials: film, batteries, cold soda for your thirst, salty snacks and candy for your hunger and, of course, automotive services and quality fuels. With over 16,000 locations nationwide, we make it effortless.

And don't forget to use your *Speedpass*™ to get back on the road even faster. After all, getting there is half the fun. How do we know? We're drivers too.

We're drivers too.

I know the long way home is shorter today.

You no longer have to listen to traffic reports telling you you're stuck in traffic. With mMode only from AT&T Wireless, you can see the real-time traffic data the radio stations use right on the screen of your phone. And if you want to take another route, getting driving directions with mMode is just as easy.

Call 1 866 reachout,® go to attwireless.com/mMode, or visit any AT&T Wireless Store for more information.

reachout® with mMode™

on the wireless service America trusts™

Meet The Stars
Mobil 2004 *Five-Star* Award Winners

LODGINGS

California
The Beverly Hills Hotel, *Beverly Hills*
Chateau du Sureau, *Oakhurst*
Four Seasons, San Francisco,
 San Francisco
Hotel Bel-Air, *Los Angeles*
The Peninsula Beverly Hills,
 Beverly Hills
Raffles L'Ermitage Beverly Hills,
 Beverly Hills
The Ritz-Carlton San Francisco,
 San Francisco

Colorado
The Broadmoor, *Colorado Springs*
The Little Nell, *Aspen*

Connecticut
The Mayflower Inn, *Washington*

Florida
Four Seasons Resort Palm Beach,
 Palm Beach
The Ritz-Carlton, Naples, *Naples*
The Ritz-Carlton, Palm Beach,
 Palm Beach

Georgia
Four Seasons Hotel Atlanta, *Atlanta*
The Lodge at Sea Island Golf Club,
 Sea Island

Illinois
Four Seasons Hotel Chicago, *Chicago*
Peninsula Chicago, *Chicago*
**The Ritz-Carlton, A Four Seasons
 Hotel,** *Chicago*

Massachusetts
Four Seasons Hotel Boston, *Boston*
Blantyre, *Lenox*

New York
Four Seasons Hotel New York,
 Manhattan
The Point, *Saranac Lake*
**The Ritz-Carlton New York Central
 Park,** *Manhattan*
The St. Regis, *Manhattan*

North Carolina
Fearrington House, *Pittsboro*

South Carolina
Woodlands Resort and Inn, *Summerville*

Texas
The Mansion on Turtle Creek, *Dallas*

Vermont
Twin Farms, *Woodstock*

Virginia
The Inn at Little Washington,
 Washington
The Jefferson Hotel, *Richmond*

RESTAURANTS

California
**The Dining Room at The Ritz-Carlton
 San Francisco,** *San Francisco*
The French Laundry, *Yountville*
Gary Danko, *San Francisco*

Georgia
The Dining Room, *Atlanta*
Seeger's, *Atlanta*

Illinois
Charlie Trotter's, *Chicago*
Trio, *Evanston*

New York
Alain Ducasse, *Manhattan*
Jean Georges, *Manhattan*

Ohio
Maisonette, *Cincinnati*

Pennsylvania
Le Bec-Fin, *Philadelphia*

South Carolina
The Dining Room at Woodlands,
 Summerville

Virginia
The Inn at Little Washington,
 Washington

The Mobil Travel Guide has been rating establishments since 1958. Each establishment awarded the Mobil Five-Star rating is "one of the best in the country."

Welcome

Dear Traveler,

Since its inception in 1958, Mobil Travel Guide has served as a trusted advisor to auto travelers in search of value in lodging, dining, and destinations. Now in its 46th year, the Mobil Travel Guide is the hallmark of our ExxonMobil family of travel publications, and we're proud to offer an array of products and services from our Mobil, Exxon, and Esso brands in North America to facilitate life on the road.

Whether you're looking for business or pleasure venues, our nationwide network of independent, professional evaluators offers their expertise on thousands of travel options, allowing you to plan a quick family getaway, a full-service business meeting, or an unforgettable Five-Star celebration.

Your feedback is important to us as we strive to improve our product offerings and better meet today's travel needs. Whether you travel once a week or once a year, please take the time to contact us at www.mobil travelguide.com. We hope to hear from you soon.

Best wishes for safe and enjoyable travels.

Lee R Raymond

Lee R. Raymond
Chairman and CEO
Exxon Mobil Corporation

A Word to Our Readers

Travelers are on the roads in great numbers these days. They're exploring the country on day trips, weekend getaways, business trips, and extended family vacations, visiting major cities and small towns along the way. Because time is precious and the travel industry is ever-changing, having accurate, reliable travel information at your fingertips is critical. Mobil Travel Guide has been providing invaluable insight to travelers for more than 45 years, and we are committed to continuing this service well into the future.

The Mobil Corporation (known as Exxon Mobil Corporation since a 1999 merger) began producing the Mobil Travel Guide books in 1958, following the introduction of the US highway system in 1956. The first edition covered only five southwestern states. Since then, our books have become the premier travel guides in North America, covering the 48 contiguous states and Canada. Now, ExxonMobil presents the newest editions to our travel guides: city travel planners. We also recently introduced road atlases and specialty publications, a robust new Web site, as well as the first fully integrated, auto-centric travel support program called MobilCompanion, the driving force in travel.

Since its founding, Mobil Travel Guide has served as an advocate for travelers seeking knowledge about hotels, restaurants, and places to visit. Based on an objective process, we make recommendations to our customers that we believe will enhance the quality and value of their travel experiences. Our trusted Mobil One- to Five-Star rating system is the oldest and most respected lodging and restaurant inspection and rating program in North America. Most hoteliers, restaurateurs, and industry observers favorably regard the rigor of our inspection program and understand the prestige and benefits that come with receiving a Mobil star rating.

The Mobil Travel Guide process of rating each establishment includes:
- Unannounced facility inspections
- Incognito service evaluations for Mobil Four- and Five-Star properties
- A review of unsolicited comments from the general public
- Senior management oversight

For each property, more than 450 attributes, including cleanliness, physical facilities, employee attitude, and courtesy, are measured and evaluated to produce a mathematically derived score, which is then blended with the other elements to form an overall score. These quantifiable scores allow comparative analysis among properties and form the basis that Mobil Travel Guide uses to assign its Mobil One- to Five-Star ratings.

This process focuses largely on guest expectations, guest experience, and consistency of service, not just physical facilities and amenities. It is fundamentally a relative rating system that rewards those properties that continually strive for and achieve excellence each year. Indeed, the very best properties are consistently raising the bar for those that wish to compete with them. These properties proactively respond to consumers' needs even in today's uncertain times.

Only facilities that meet Mobil Travel Guide's standards earn the privilege of being listed in the guide. Deteriorating, poorly managed establishments are deleted. A Mobil Travel Guide listing constitutes a positive quality recommendation; every listing is an accolade, a recognition of achievement. Our Mobil One- to Five-Star rating system highlights its level of service. Extensive in-house research is constantly underway to determine new additions to our lists.

- The Mobil Five-Star Award indicates that a property is one of the very best in the country and consistently provides gracious and courteous service, superlative quality in its facility, and a unique ambience. The lodgings and restaurants at the Mobil Five-Star level consistently and proactively respond to consumers' needs and continue their commitment to excellence, doing so with grace and perseverance.

- Also highly regarded is the Mobil Four-Star Award, which honors properties for outstanding achievement in overall facility and for providing very strong service levels in all areas. These award winners provide a distinctive experience for the ever-demanding and sophisticated consumer.

- The Mobil Three-Star Award recognizes an excellent property that provides full services and amenities. This category ranges from exceptional hotels with limited services to elegant restaurants with a less-formal atmosphere.

- A Mobil Two-Star property is a clean and comfortable establishment that has expanded amenities or a distinctive environment. A Mobil Two-Star property is an excellent place to stay or dine.

- A Mobil One-Star property is limited in its amenities and services but focuses on providing a value experience while meeting travelers' expectations. The property can be expected to be clean, comfortable, and convenient.

Allow us to emphasize that we do not charge establishments for inclusion in our guides. We have no relationship with any of the businesses and attractions we list and act only as a consumer advocate. In essence, we do the investigative legwork so that you won't have to.

Keep in mind, too, that the hospitality business is ever-changing. Restaurants and lodgings—particularly small chains and stand-alone establishments—change management or even go out of business with surprising quickness. Although we make every effort to double-check information during our annual updates, we nevertheless recommend that you call ahead to make sure the place you've selected is still open and offers all the amenities you're looking for. We've provided phone numbers; when available, we also list fax numbers and Web site addresses.

We hope that your travels are enjoyable and relaxing and that our books help you get the most out of every trip you take. If any aspect of your accommodation, dining, or sightseeing experience motivates you to comment, please drop us a line. We depend a great deal on our readers' remarks, so you can be assured that we will read your comments and assimilate them into our research. General comments about our books are also welcome. You can write to us at Mobil Travel Guide, 1460 Renaissance Dr, Suite 401, Park Ridge, IL 60068, or send an e-mail to info@mobiltravelguide.com.

Take your Mobil Travel Guide books along on every trip you take. We're confident that you'll be pleased with their convenience, ease of use, and breadth of dependable coverage.

Happy travels!

How to Use This Book

The Mobil Travel Guide City Guides are designed for ease of use. The book begins with a general introduction that provides a geographical and historical orientation to the state and gives basic statewide tourist information, from climate to highway information to seatbelt laws. The remainder is devoted to the featured city, as well as neighboring towns and nearby tourist destinations.

The following sections explain the wealth of information you'll find in this book: information about the city and its neighborhoods, things to see and do there, and where to stay and eat.

Maps

At the front of this book in the full-color section, we have provided a US and a state map as well as detailed city maps to help you find your way around. You'll find a key to the map symbols on the Contents page at the beginning of the map section.

Driving and Walking Tours

The driving tours that we include are usually day trips that make for interesting side excursions, although they can be longer. They offer you a way to get off the beaten path and visit an area that travelers often overlook. These trips frequently cover areas of natural beauty or historical significance.

Each walking tour focuses on a particularly interesting area of the city. Again, these tours can provide a break from everyday tourist attractions, and they often include places to stop for meals or snacks.

What to See and Do

The Mobil Travel Guide offers information about nearly 20,000 museums, art galleries, amusement parks, historic sites, national and state parks, ski areas, and many other types of attractions. A white star on a black background ★ signals that the attraction is a must-see—one of the best in the area. Because municipal parks, public tennis courts, swimming pools, and small educational institutions are common to most cities, they generally are not mentioned.

In an attraction's description, you'll find the months, days, and, in some cases, hours of operation; the address/directions, telephone number, and Web site (if there is one); and the admission price category. We use the following ranges for admission fees:

⚬ **FREE**
⚬ **$** = Up to $5
⚬ **$$** = $5.01-$10
⚬ **$$$** = $10.01-$15
⚬ **$$$$** = Over $15

Special Events

Special events are either annual events that last only a short time, such as festivals and fairs, or longer, seasonal events such as horseracing, summer theater and concerts, and professional sports. The Mobil Travel Guide Special Events listings also include infrequently occurring occasions that mark certain dates or events, such as centennials and other commemorative celebrations.

Side Trips

We recognize that your travels don't always end where a city's boundaries fall, so we've included some side trips that technically fall outside the scope of this book but that travelers frequently visit when they come to this city. Nearby national parks, other major cities, and major tourist draws fall into this category. We have broken the side trips into three categories: day trips (less than a three-hour drive); overnight stays (between a three- and five-hour drive); and weekend excursions (more than a five-hour drive). You'll find the side trips at the end of the listings.

Lodging and Restaurant Listings

Lodgings and restaurants are listed under the city or town in which they are located. Lodgings and restaurants located within 5 miles of a major commercial airport are listed under a separate "Airport Area" heading that follows the city section.

LODGINGS

Travelers have different wants and needs when it comes to accommodations. To help you pinpoint properties that meet your particular needs, each lodging property is classified by type according to the following characteristics:

⚬ **Motels/Motor Lodges.** These accommodations are in low-rise structures with rooms that are easily accessible to parking, which is usually free. Properties have small, functional lobbies, and guests enter their rooms from the outdoors. Service is often limited, and dining may not be offered in lower-rated motels. Shops and businesses are generally found only in higher-rated properties, as are bellstaff, room service, and restaurants serving three meals daily.

⚬ **Hotels.** A hotel is an establishment that provides lodging in a clean, comfortable environment. Guests can expect private bathrooms as well as some measure of guest services, such as luggage assistance, room service, and daily maid service.

⊙ **Resorts.** A resort is an establishment that provides lodging in a facility that is typically located on a larger piece of land. Recreational activities are emphasized and often include golf, spa, and tennis. Guests can expect more than one food and beverage establishment on the property, which aims to provide a variety of food choices at a variety of price points.

⊙ **All Suites.** In an All Suites property, guest accommodations consist of two rooms: a bedroom and a living room. Higher-rated properties offer facilities and services comparable to regular hotels.

⊙ **B&Bs/Small Inns.** The hotel alternative for those who prefer the comforts of home and a personal touch. It may be a structure of historic significance and often is located in an interesting setting. Breakfast is usually included and often is treated as a special occasion. Cocktails and refreshments may be served in the late afternoon or evening. Rooms are often individually decorated, but telephones, televisions, and private bathrooms may not be available in every room.

⊙ **Extended Stay.** These hotels specialize in stays of three days or more and usually offer weekly room rates. Service is often limited, and dining may not be offered at lower-rated properties.

⊙ **Casino Hotels.** Casino hotels incorporate areas that offer games of chance such as blackjack, poker, and slot machines and are found only in states where gambling is legal. These hotels offer a wide range of services and amenities comparable to regular hotels.

Because most lodgings offer the following features and services, information about them does not appear in the listings unless exceptions exist:

⊙ Year-round operation with a single rate structure

⊙ Major credit cards accepted (note that Exxon or Mobil Corporation credit cards cannot be used to pay for room or other charges)

⊙ Air-conditioning and heat, often with individual room controls

⊙ Bathroom with tub and/or shower in each room

⊙ Cable television

⊙ Cots and cribs available

⊙ Daily maid service

⊙ Elevators

⊙ In-room telephones

Each lodging listing gives the name, address/location (when no street address is available), phone number(s), fax number, and total number of guest rooms. Also included are details on business, luxury, recreational, and dining facilities on the property or nearby. A key to the symbols at the end of each listing can be found on the inside front cover of this book.

For every property, we also provide pricing information. Because lodging rates change frequently, we opt to list a pricing category rather than specific prices. The pricing categories break down as follows:

- **$** = Up to $150
- **$$** = $151-$250
- **$$$** = $251-$350
- **$$$$** = $351 and up

All prices quoted by the Mobil Travel Guide are in effect at the time of publication; however, prices cannot be guaranteed. In some locations, short-term price variations may exist because of special events or holidays. Certain resorts have complicated rate structures that vary with the time of year; always confirm rates when making your plans.

RESTAURANTS

All dining establishments listed in our books have a full kitchen and offer table service and a complete menu. Parking on or near the premises, in a lot or garage, is assumed. If parking is not available, we note that fact in the listing.

Each listing also gives the cuisine type, address (or directions if no street address is available), phone and fax numbers, Web site (if available), meals served, days of operation (if not open daily year-round), reservation policy, and pricing category. We also indicate if a children's menu is offered. The price categories are defined as follows per diner and assume that you order an appetizer, an entrée, and one drink:

- **$** = $15 and under
- **$$** = $16-$35
- **$$$** = $36-$85
- **$$$$** = $86 and up

QUALITY RATINGS

The Mobil Travel Guide has been rating lodgings and restaurants in the United States since the first edition was published in 1958. For years, the guide was the only source of such ratings, and it remains among the few guidebooks to rate restaurants across the country and in Canada.

All listed establishments have been inspected by experienced field representatives and/or evaluated by a senior staff member. Our ratings are based on detailed inspection reports of the individual properties, on written evaluations of staff members who stay and dine anonymously, and on an extensive review of reader comments. Rating categories reflect both the features a property offers and its quality in relation to similar establishments.

Here are the definitions for the Mobil star ratings for lodgings:

✪ ★ : A Mobil One-Star lodging is a limited-service hotel, motel, or inn that is considered a clean, comfortable, and reliable establishment.

✪ ★ ★ : A Mobil Two-Star lodging is considered a clean, comfortable, and reliable establishment that has expanded amenities, such as a full-service restaurant on the premises.

✪ ★ ★ ★ : A Mobil Three-Star lodging is well appointed, with a full-service restaurant and expanded amenities, such as a fitness center, golf course, tennis courts, 24-hour room service, and optional turn-down service.

✪ ★ ★ ★ ★ : A Mobil Four-Star lodging provides a luxury experience with expanded amenities in a distinctive environment. Services may include, but are not limited to, automatic turndown service, 24-hour room service, and valet parking.

✪ ★ ★ ★ ★ ★ : A Mobil Five-Star lodging provides consistently superlative service in an exceptionally distinctive luxury environment, with expanded services. Attention to detail is evident throughout the hotel, resort, or inn, from bed linens to staff uniforms.

The Mobil star ratings for restaurants are defined as follows:

✪ ★ : A Mobil One-Star restaurant provides a distinctive experience through culinary specialty, local flair, or individual atmosphere.

✪ ★ ★ : A Mobil Two-Star restaurant serves fresh food in a clean setting with efficient service. Value is considered in this category, as is family friendliness.

✪ ★ ★ ★ : A Mobil Three-Star restaurant has good food, warm and skillful service, and enjoyable décor.

✪ ★ ★ ★ ★ : A Mobil Four-Star restaurant provides professional service, distinctive presentations, and wonderful food.

✪ ★ ★ ★ ★ ★ : A Mobil Five-Star restaurant offers one of few flawless dining experiences in the country. These establishments consistently provide their guests with exceptional food, superlative service, elegant décor, and exquisite presentations of each detail surrounding a meal.

TERMS AND ABBREVIATIONS IN LISTINGS

The following terms and abbreviations are used throughout the Mobil Travel Guide lodging and restaurant listings to indicate which amenities and services are available at each establishment. We've done our best to provide accurate and up-to-date information, but things do change, so if a particular feature is essential to you, please contact the establishment directly to make sure that it is available.

Complete meal Soup and/or salad, entrée, and dessert, plus a non-alcoholic beverage.

Continental breakfast Usually coffee and a roll or doughnut.

D Followed by a price, indicates the room rate for a double room—two people in one room in one or two beds (the charge may be higher for two double beds).

Each additional The extra charge for each additional person beyond the stated number of persons.

In-room modem link Every guest room has a connection for a modem that's separate from the main phone line.

Kitchen(s) A kitchen or kitchenette that contains a stove or microwave, sink, and refrigerator and is either part of the room or a separate, adjoining room. If the kitchen is not fully equipped, the listing will indicate "no equipment" or "some equipment."

Laundry service Either coin-operated laundry facilities or overnight valet service is available.

Luxury level A special section of a lodging, spanning at least an entire floor, that offers increased luxury accommodations. Management must provide no less than three of these four services: separate check-in and check-out, concierge, private lounge, and private elevator service (with key access). Complimentary breakfast and snacks are commonly offered.

Movies Prerecorded videos are available for rental or check-out.

Prix fixe A full, multicourse meal for a stated price; usually available at finer restaurants.

Valet parking An attendant is available to park and retrieve your car.

VCR VCRs are present in all guest rooms.

VCR available VCRs are available for hookup in guest rooms.

Special Information for Travelers with Disabilities

The Mobil Travel Guide Ⓓ symbol indicates establishments that are at least partially accessible to people with mobility problems. Our criteria for accessibility are unique to our publications. Please do not confuse them with the universal symbol for wheelchair accessibility.

When the Ⓓ symbol follows a listing, the establishment is equipped with facilities to accommodate people using wheelchairs or crutches or otherwise needing easy access to doorways and rest rooms. Travelers with severe mobility problems or with hearing or visual impairments may or may not find the facilities they need. Always phone ahead to make sure that an establishment can meet your needs.

All lodgings bearing our D symbol have the following facilities:

- ISA-designated parking near access ramps
- Level or ramped entryways to buildings
- Swinging building entryway doors a minimum of 39 inches wide
- Public rest rooms on the main level with space to operate a wheelchair and handrails at commode areas
- Elevator(s) equipped with grab bars and lowered control buttons
- Restaurant(s) with accessible doorway(s), rest rooms with space to operate a wheelchair, and handrails at commode areas
- Guest room entryways that are at least 39 inches wide
- Low-pile carpet in rooms
- Telephones at bedside and in the bathroom
- Beds placed at wheelchair height
- Bathrooms with a minimum doorway width of 3 feet
- Bath with an open sink (no cabinet) and room to operate a wheelchair
- Handrails at commode areas and in the tub
- Wheelchair-accessible peepholes in room entry door
- Wheelchair-accessible closet rods and shelves

All restaurants bearing our D symbol offer the following facilities:

- ISA-designated parking beside access ramps
- Level or ramped front entryways to the building
- Tables that accommodate wheelchairs
- Main-floor rest rooms with an entryway that's at least 3 feet wide
- Rest rooms with space to operate a wheelchair and handrails at commode areas

Making the Most of Your Trip

A few hardy souls might look back with fondness on a trip during which the car broke down, leaving them stranded for three days, or a vacation that cost twice what it was supposed to. For most travelers, though, the best trips are those that are safe, smooth, and within budget. To help you make your trip the best it can be, we've assembled a few tips and resources.

Saving Money

ON LODGING

Many hotels and motels offer discounts—for senior citizens, business travelers, families, you name it. It never hurts to ask—politely, that is. Sometimes, especially in the late afternoon, desk clerks are instructed to fill beds, and you might be offered a lower rate or a nicer room to entice you to stay. Simply ask the reservation agent for the best rate available. Also, make sure to try both the toll-free number and the local number. You may be able to get a lower rate from one than the other.

Becoming a member of MobilCompanion will entitle you to discounted rates at many well-known hotels around the country. For more information, call 877/785-6788 or visit www.mobilcompanion.com.

Timing your trip right can cut your lodging costs as well. Look for bargains on stays over multiple nights, in the off-season, and on weekdays or weekends, depending on the location. Many hotels in major metropolitan areas, for example, have special weekend packages that offer considerable savings on rooms; they may include breakfast, cocktails, and dinner discounts.

Another way to save money is to choose accommodations that give you more than just a standard room. Rooms with kitchen facilities enable you to cook some meals yourself, reducing your restaurant costs. A suite might save money for two couples traveling together. Even hotel luxury levels can provide good value, as many include breakfast or cocktails in the price of a room.

State and city taxes, as well as special room taxes, can increase your room rate by as much as 25 percent per day. We are unable to include information about taxes in our listings, but we strongly urge you to ask about taxes when making reservations so that you understand the total cost of your lodgings before you book.

Watch out for telephone-usage charges that hotels frequently impose on long-distance, credit-card, and other calls. Before phoning from your room, read the information given to you at check-in, and then be sure to review your bill carefully when checking out. You won't be expected to pay for charges that the hotel didn't spell out. Consider using your cell phone if you have one; or, if public telephones are available in the hotel lobby, your cost savings may outweigh the inconvenience of using them.

Here are some additional ways to save on lodgings:

○ Stay in B&B accommodations; they're generally less expensive than standard hotel rooms, and the complimentary breakfasts cut down on food costs.

○ If you're traveling with children, find lodgings at which kids stay free.

○ When visiting a major city, stay just outside the city limits; these rooms are usually less expensive than those in downtown locations.

○ Consider visiting national parks during the low season, when prices of lodgings near the parks drop 25 percent or more.

○ When calling a hotel, ask whether it is running any special promotions or if any discounts are available; many times reservationists are told not to volunteer deals unless specifically asked about them.

○ Check for hotel packages; some offer nightly rates that include a rental car or discounts on major attractions.

ON DINING

There are several ways to get a less expensive meal at a more expensive restaurant. Early-bird dinners are popular in many parts of the country and offer considerable savings. If you're interested in sampling a Mobil Four- or Five-Star establishment, consider going at lunchtime. Although the prices are probably still relatively high at midday, they may be half of those at dinner, and you'll experience the same ambience, service, and cuisine.

As a member of MobilCompanion, you can enroll in iDine. This program earns you up to 20 percent cash back at more than 1,900 restaurants on meals purchased with the credit card you register; the rebate appears on your credit card bill. For more information about MobilCompanion and iDine, call 877/785-6788 or go to www.mobilcompanion.com.

ON ENTERTAINMENT

Although some national parks, monuments, seashores, historic sites, and recreation areas may be used free of charge, others charge an entrance fee (ranging from $1 to $6 per person or $5 to $20 per carload) and/or a usage fee for special services and facilities. If you plan to make several visits to national recreation areas, consider one of the following money-saving programs offered by the National Park Service:

○ **National Parks Pass.** This annual pass is good for entrance to any national park that charges an entrance fee. If the park charges a per-vehicle fee, the pass holder and any accompanying passengers in a private noncommercial vehicle may enter. If the park charges a per-person fee, the pass applies to the holder's spouse, children, and parents as well as the holder. It is valid for entrance fees only; it does not cover parking, camping, or other fees. You can purchase a National Parks Pass in person at any national park where an entrance fee is charged; by mail from the National Park Foundation, PO Box 34108, Washington, DC 20043-4108; by calling 888/GO-PARKS; or at www.nationalparks.org. The cost is $50.

○ **Golden Eagle.** When affixed to a National Parks Pass, this sticker, available to people who are between 17 and 61 years of age, extends coverage to sites managed by the US Fish and Wildlife Service, the US Forest Service, and the Bureau of Land Management. It is good until the National Parks Pass to which it is affixed expires and does not cover usage fees. You can purchase one at National Park Service, Fish and Wildlife Service, and Bureau of Land Management fee stations. The cost is $15.

○ **Golden Age Passport.** Available to citizens and permanent US residents 62 and older, this passport is a lifetime entrance permit to fee-charging national recreation areas. The fee exemption extends to those accompanying the permit holder in a private noncommercial vehicle or, in the case of walk-in facilities, to the holder's spouse and children. The passport also entitles the holder to a 50 percent discount on federal usage fees charged in park areas, but not on concessions. Golden Age Passports must be obtained in person and are available at most National Park Service units that charge an entrance fee. The applicant must show proof of age, such as a driver's license or birth certificate (Medicare cards are not acceptable proof). The cost is $10.

○ **Golden Access Passport.** Issued to citizens and permanent US residents who are physically disabled or visually impaired, this passport is a free lifetime entrance permit to fee-charging national recreation areas. The fee exemption extends to those accompanying the permit holder in a private noncommercial vehicle or, in the case of walk-in facilities, to the holder's spouse and children. The passport also entitles the holder to a 50 percent discount on usage fees charged in park areas, but not on concessions. Golden Access Passports must be obtained in person and are available at most National Park Service units that charge an entrance fee. Proof of eligibility to receive federal benefits (under programs such as Disability Retirement, Compensation for Military Service-Connected Disability, and the Coal Mine Safety and Health Act) is required, or an affidavit must be signed attesting to eligibility.

A money-saving move in several large cities is to purchase a CityPass. If you plan to visit several museums and other major attractions, CityPass is a terrific option because it gets you into several sites for one substantially reduced price. Currently, CityPass is available in Boston, Chicago, Hollywood, New York, Philadelphia, San Francisco, Seattle, and southern California (which includes Disneyland, SeaWorld, and the San Diego Zoo). For more information or to buy one, call 888/330-5008 or visit www.citypass.net. You can also buy a CityPass from any participating CityPass attraction.

Here are some additional ways to save on entertainment and shopping:

- Check with your hotel's concierge for various coupons and special offers; they often have two-for-one tickets for area attractions and coupons for discounts at area stores and restaurants.

- Purchase same-day concert or theater tickets for half-price through the local cheap-tickets outlet, such as TKTS in New York City or Hot Tix in Chicago.

- Visit museums on their free or "by donation" days, when you can pay what you wish rather than a specific admission fee.

ON TRANSPORTATION

Transportation is a big part of any vacation budget. Here are some ways to reduce your costs:

- If you're renting a car, shop early over the Internet; you can book a car during the low season for less, even if you'll be using it in the high season.

- Rental car discounts are often available if you rent for one week or longer and reserve in advance.

- Get the best gas mileage out of your vehicle by making sure that it's properly tuned up and keeping your tires properly inflated. If your tires need to be replaced, you can save money on a new set of Michelins by becoming a member of MobilCompanion.

- Travel at moderate speeds on the open road; higher speeds require more gasoline.

- Fill the tank before you return your rental car; rental companies charge to refill the tank and do so at prices of up to 50 percent more than at local gas stations.

- Make a checklist of travel essentials and purchase them before you leave; don't get stuck buying expensive sunscreen at your hotel or overpriced film at the airport.

FOR SENIOR CITIZENS

Look for the senior-citizen discount symbol **SC** in this book's lodging and restaurant listings. Always call ahead to confirm that a discount is being offered, and be sure to carry proof of age. At places not listed in this book, it never hurts to ask if a senior-citizen discount is offered. Additional information for mature travelers is available from the American Association of Retired Persons (AARP), 601 E St NW, Washington, DC 20049; phone 202/434-2277; www.aarp.org.

Tipping

Tips are expressions of appreciation for good service. However, you are never obligated to tip if you receive poor service.

IN HOTELS

- Door attendants usually get $1 for hailing a cab.
- Bellstaff expect $2 per bag.
- Concierges are tipped according to the service they perform. Tipping is not mandatory when you've asked for suggestions on sightseeing or restaurants or for help in making dining reservations. However, a tip of $5 is appropriate when a concierge books you a table at a restaurant known to be difficult to get into. For obtaining theater or sporting event tickets, $5 to $10 is expected.
- Maids should be tipped $1 to $2 per day. Hand your tip directly to the maid, or leave it with a note saying that the money has been left expressly for the maid.

IN RESTAURANTS

Before tipping, carefully review your check for any gratuity or service charge that is already included in your bill. If you're in doubt, ask your server.

- Coffee shop and counter service waitstaff usually receive 15 percent of the bill, before sales tax.
- In full-service restaurants, tip 18 percent of the bill, before sales tax.
- In fine restaurants, where gratuities are shared among a larger staff, 18 to 20 percent is appropriate.
- In most cases, the maitre d' is tipped only if the service has been extraordinary, and only on the way out. At upscale properties in major metropolitan areas, $20 is the minimum.
- If there is a wine steward, tip $20 for exemplary service and beyond, or more if the wine was decanted or the bottle was very expensive.
- Tip $1 to $2 per coat at the coat check.

AT AIRPORTS

Curbside luggage handlers expect $1 per bag. Car-rental shuttle drivers who help with your luggage appreciate a $1 or $2 tip.

Staying Safe

The best way to deal with emergencies is to avoid them in the first place. However, unforeseen situations do happen, so you should be prepared for them.

IN YOUR CAR

Before you head out on a road trip, make sure that your car has been serviced and is in good working order. Change the oil, check the battery and belts, make sure that your windshield washer fluid is full and your tires are properly inflated (which can also improve your gas mileage). Other inspections recommended by the vehicle's manufacturer should also be made.

Next, be sure you have the tools and equipment needed to deal with a routine breakdown:

- Jack
- Spare tire
- Lug wrench
- Repair kit
- Emergency tools
- Jumper cables
- Spare fan belt
- Fuses
- Flares and/or reflectors
- Flashlight
- First-aid kit
- In winter, a windshield scraper and snow shovel

Many emergency supplies are sold in special packages that include the essentials you need to stay safe in the event of a breakdown.

Also bring all appropriate and up-to-date documentation—licenses, registration, and insurance cards—and know what your insurance covers. Bring an extra set of keys, too, just in case.

En route, always buckle up! In most states, wearing a seatbelt is required by law.

If your car does break down, do the following:

- Get out of traffic as soon as possible—pull well off the road.
- Raise the hood and turn on your emergency flashers or tie a white cloth to the roadside door handle or antenna.
- Stay in your car.
- Use flares or reflectors to keep your vehicle from being hit.

If you are a member of MobilCompanion, remember that En Route Support is always ready to help when you need it. Just give us a call and we'll locate and dispatch an emergency roadside service to assist you, as well as provide you with significant savings on the service.

IN YOUR HOTEL OR MOTEL

Chances are slim that you will encounter a hotel or motel fire, but you can protect yourself by doing the following:

- Once you've checked in, make sure that the smoke detector in your room is working properly.
- Find the property's fire safety instructions, usually posted on the inside of the room door.
- Locate the fire extinguishers and at least two fire exits.
- Never use an elevator in a fire.

For personal security, use the peephole in your room door and make sure that anyone claiming to be a hotel employee can show proper identification. Call the front desk if you feel threatened at any time.

PROTECTING AGAINST THEFT

To guard against theft wherever you go:

- Don't bring anything of more value than you need.
- If you do bring valuables, leave them at your hotel rather than in your car.
- If you bring something very expensive, lock it in a safe. Many hotels put one in each room; others will store your valuables in the hotel's safe.
- Don't carry more money than you need. Use traveler's checks and credit cards or visit cash machines to withdraw more cash when you run out.

For Travelers with Disabilities

To get the kind of service you need and have a right to expect, don't hesitate when making a reservation to question the management about the availability of accessible rooms, parking, entrances, restaurants, lounges, or any other facilities that are important to you, and confirm what is meant by "accessible."

The Mobil Travel Guide **D** symbol indicates establishments that are at least partially accessible to people with special mobility needs (people using wheelchairs or crutches or otherwise needing easy access to buildings and rooms). Keep in mind that our criteria for accessibility are unique to our publication and should not be confused with the universal symbol for wheelchair accessibility. Further information about these criteria can be found in the earlier section "How to Use This Book."

A thorough listing of published material for travelers with disabilities is available from the Disability Bookshop, Twin Peaks Press, Box 129, Vancouver, WA 98666; phone 360/694-2462; disabilitybookshop.virtual ave.net. Another reliable organization is the Society for Accessible Travel & Hospitality (SATH), 347 Fifth Ave, Suite 610, New York, NY 10016; phone 212/447-7284; www.sath.org.

Important Toll-Free Numbers and Online Information

Hotels and Motels

Adams Mark 800/444-2326
www.adamsmark.com
AmericInn 800/634-3444
www.americinn.com
AmeriHost Inn Hotels 800/434-5800
www.amerihostinn.com
Amerisuites 800/833-1516
www.amerisuites.com
Baymont Inns 877/BAYMONT
www.baymontinns.com
Best Inns & Suites 800/237-8466
www.bestinn.com
Best Value Inns 888/315-BEST
www.bestvalueinn.com
Best Western International 800/WESTERN
www.bestwestern.com
Budget Host Inn 800/BUDHOST
www.budgethost.com
Candlewood Suites 888/CANDLEWOOD
www.candlewoodsuites.com
Clarion Hotels 800/252-7466
www.choicehotels.com
Comfort Inns and Suites 800/252-7466
www.choicehotels.com
Country Hearth Inns 800/848-5767
www.countryhearth.com
Country Inns & Suites 800/456-4000
www.countryinns.com
Courtyard by Marriott 888/236-2427
www.courtyard.com
Cross Country Inn 800/621-1429
www.crosscountryinns.com
Crowne Plaza Hotels and Resorts 800/227-6963
www.crowneplaza.com
Days Inn 800/544-8313
www.daysinn.com

Delta Hotels 800/268-1133
www.deltahotels.com
Destination Hotels & Resorts 800/434-7347
www.destinationhotels.com
Doubletree Hotels 800/222-8733
www.doubletree.com
Drury Inns 800/378-7946
www.druryinn.com
Econolodge 800/553-2666
www.econolodge.com
Economy Inns of America 800/826-0778
www.innsofamerica.com
Embassy Suites 800/362-2779
www.embassysuites.com
ExelInns of America 800/FOREXEL
www.exelinns.com
Extended StayAmerica 800/EXTSTAY
www.extstay.com
Fairfield Inn by Marriott 888/236-2427
www.fairfieldinn.com
Fairmont Hotels 800/441-1414
www.fairmont.com
Four Points by Sheraton 888/625-5144
www.starwood.com
Four Seasons 800/545-4000
www.fourseasons.com
Hampton Inn/Hampton Inn and Suites 800/426-7866
www.hamptoninn.com
Hard Rock Hotels, Resorts and Casinos 800/HRDROCK
www.hardrock.com
Harrah's Entertainment 800/HARRAHS
www.harrahs.com
Harvey Hotels 800/922-9222
www.bristolhotels.com
Hawthorn Suites 800/527-1133
www.hawthorn.com
Hilton Hotels and Resorts (US) 800/774-1500
www.hilton.com
Holiday Inn Express 800/HOLIDAY
www.sixcontinentshotel.com
Holiday Inn Hotels and Resorts 800/HOLIDAY
www.holiday-inn.com

Homestead Studio Suites 888/782-9473
www.stayhsd.com
Homewood Suites 800/225-5466
www.homewoodsuites.com
Howard Johnson 800/406-1411
www.hojo.com
Hyatt 800/633-7313
www.hyatt.com
Ian Schrager .... Contact individual hotel
www.ianschragerhotels.com
Inter-Continental 888/567-8725
www.intercontinental.com
Joie de Vivre 800/738-7477
www.jdvhospitality.com
Kimpton Hotels 888/546-7866
www.kimptongroup.com
Knights Inn 800/843-5644
www.knightsinn.com
La Quinta 800/531-5900
www.laquinta.com
Le Meridien 800/543-4300
www.lemeridien.com
Leading Hotels of the World 800/223-6800
www.lhw.com
Loews Hotels 800/235-6397
www.loewshotels.com
MainStay Suites 800/660-6246
www.choicehotels.com
Mandarin Oriental 800/526-6566
www.mandarin-oriental.com
Marriott Conference Centers 888/236-2427
www.conferencecenters.com
Marriott Hotels, Resorts, and Suites 888/236-2427
www.marriott.com
Marriott Vacation Club International 800/845-5279
www.marriott.com/vacationclub
Microtel Inns & Suites 800/771-7171
www.microtelinn.com
Millennium & Copthorne Hotels 866/866-8086
www.mill-cop.com
Motel 6 .... 800/4MOTEL6
www.motel6.com

Omni Hotels 800/843-6664
www.omnihotels.com
Pan Pacific Hotels and Resorts 800/327-8585
www.panpac.com
Park Inn & Park Plaza 888/201-1801
www.parkhtls.com
The Peninsula Group . . . . Contact individual hotel
www.peninsula.com
Preferred Hotels & Resorts Worldwide 800/323-7500
www.preferredhotels.com
Quality Inn 800/228-5151
www.qualityinn.com
Radisson Hotels 800/333-3333
www.radisson.com
Raffles International Hotels and Resorts 800/637-9477
www.raffles.com
Ramada International 888/298-2054
www.ramada.com
Ramada Plazas, Limiteds, and Inns 800/2RAMADA
www.ramadahotels.com
Red Lion Inns 800/733-5466
www.redlion.com
Red Roof Inns 800/733-7663
www.redroof.com
Regal Hotels 800/222-8888
www.regal-hotels.com
Regent International 800/545-4000
www.regenthotels.com
Relais & Chateaux 800/735-2478
www.relaischateaux.com
Renaissance Hotels 888/236-2427
www.renaissancehotels.com
Residence Inns 888/236-2427
www.residenceinn.com
Ritz-Carlton 800/241-3333
www.ritzcarlton.com
Rockresorts 888/FORROCKS
www.rockresorts.com
Rodeway Inns 800/228-2000
www.rodeway.com
Rosewood Hotels & Resorts 888/767-3966
www.rosewood-hotels.com

Scottish Inn 800/251-1962
www.bookroomsnow.com
Select Inn 800/641-1000
www.selectinn.com
Sheraton 888/625-5144
www.sheraton.com
Shilo Inns 800/222-2244
www.shiloinns.com
Shoney's Inns 800/552-4667
www.shoneysinn.com
Signature/Jameson Inns 800/822-5252
www.jamesoninns.com
Sleep Inns 800/453-3746
www.sleepinn.com
Small Luxury Hotels of the World 800/525-4800
www.slh.com
Sofitel 800/763-4835
www.sofitel.com
SpringHill Suites 888/236-2427
www.springhillsuites.com
SRS Worldhotels 800/223-5652
www.srs-worldhotels.com
St. Regis Luxury Collection 888/625-5144
www.stregis.com
Staybridge Suites by Holiday Inn 800/238-8000
www.staybridge.com
Summerfield Suites by Wyndham 800/833-4353
www.summerfieldsuites.com
Summit International 800/457-4000
www.summithotels.com
Super 8 Motels 800/800-8000
www.super8.com
The Sutton Place Hotels 866/378-8866
www.suttonplace.com
Swissotel 800/637-9477
www.swissotel.com
TownePlace Suites 888/236-2427
www.towneplace.com
Travelodge 800/578-7878
www.travelodge.com
Universal 800/23LOEWS
www.loewshotel.com

Vagabond Inns 800/522-1555
www.vagabondinns.com
W Hotels 888/625-5144
www.whotels.com
Wellesley Inn and Suites 800/444-8888
www.wellesleyinnandsuites.com
WestCoast Hotels 800/325-4000
www.westcoasthotels.com
Westin Hotels & Resorts 800/937-8461
www.westin.com
Wingate Inns 800/228-1000
www.wingateinns.com
Woodfin Suite Hotels 800/966-3346
www.woodfinsuitehotels.com
Wyndham Hotels & Resorts 800/996-3426
www.wyndham.com

Airlines

Air Canada 888/247-2262
www.aircanada.ca
Alaska 800/252-7522
www.alaskaair.com
American 800/433-7300
www.aa.com
America West 800/235-9292
www.americawest.com
ATA 800/435-9282
www.ata.com
British Airways 800/247-9297
www.british-airways.com
Continental 800/523-3273
www.flycontinental.com
Delta 800/221-1212
www.delta-air.com
Island Air 800/323-3345
www.islandair.com
Mesa 800/637-2247
www.mesa-air.com
Northwest 800/225-2525
www.nwa.com
Southwest 800/435-9792
www.southwest.com

United 800/241-6522
www.ual.com
US Airways 800/428-4322
www.usairways.com

Car Rentals
Advantage 800/777-5500
www.arac.com
Alamo 800/327-9633
www.goalamo.com
Allstate 800/634-6186
www.bnm.com/as.htm
Avis 800/831-2847
www.avis.com
Budget 800/527-0700
www.budgetrentacar.com
Dollar 800/800-4000
www.dollarcar.com
Enterprise 800/325-8007
www.pickenterprise.com
Hertz 800/654-3131
www.hertz.com
National 800/227-7368
www.nationalcar.com
Payless 800/729-5377
www.800-payless.com
Rent-A-Wreck.com 800/535-1391
www.rent-a-wreck.com
Sears 800/527-0770
www.budget.com
Thrifty 800/847-4389
www.thrifty.com

Four-Star and Five-Star Establishments in New York City

★ ★ ★ ★ ★ Lodgings
Four Seasons Hotel New York
The Ritz-Carlton New York
 Central Park
The St. Regis

★ ★ ★ ★ ★ Restaurants
Alain Ducasse
Jean Georges

★ ★ ★ ★ Lodgings
The Carlyle
The Lowell
Mercer Hotel
The New York Palace
The Peninsula
The Pierre New York, A Four
 Seasons Hotel
The Regency Hotel
The Regent Wall Street
The Ritz-Carlton New York
 Battery Park
The Stanhope, A Park Hyatt Hotel
Trump International Hotel
 & Tower

★ ★ ★ ★ Restaurants
Aureole
Bouley
Daniel
Danube
The Four Seasons Restaurant
Gotham Bar and Grill
Gramercy Tavern
Kuruma Zushi
La Caravelle
La Grenouille
Le Bernardin
Le Cirque 2000
Lutece
March
Oceana
Picholine
RM
Sugiyama
Veritas

New York

The largest of the north-eastern states, New York stretches from the Great Lakes to the Atlantic. The falls at Niagara; the gorge of the Genesee, the "Grand Canyon" of the East; the Finger Lakes, carved by glaciers; the Thousand Islands of the St. Lawrence; the Catskills, where Rip Van Winkle is said to have slept for 20 years; the white sand beaches of Long Island; the lakes and forested peaks of the Adirondacks; and the stately traprock bluffs along the Hudson—these are a few of the features that attract millions of tourists and vacationers every year.

Population: 17,990,456
Area: 54,471 square miles
Elevation: 0-5,344 feet
Peak: Mount Marcy (Essex County)
Entered Union: Eleventh of original 13 states (July 26, 1788)
Capital: Albany
Motto: Ever upward
Nickname: Empire State
Flower: Rose
Bird: Bluebird
Tree: Sugar Maple
Fair: August-September in Syracuse
Time Zone: Eastern
Website: www.iloveny.state.ny.us

Industry grew because water power was available; trade and farming grew because of the Erie Canal and its many branches. The state has given the nation four native-born presidents (Van Buren, Fillmore, and both Roosevelts) and two who built their careers here (Cleveland and Arthur).

In addition to being a delightful state in which to tour or vacation, New York has New York City, one of the great cosmopolitan centers of the world.

Governor DeWitt Clinton envisioned a canal extending from the Hudson River at Albany to Buffalo to develop the state and give needed aid to its western farmers. Started in 1817 and finished in 1825, the Erie Canal became the gateway to the West and was the greatest engineering work of its time, reducing the cost of freight between Buffalo and New York City from $100 to $5 a ton. Enlarged and rerouted, it is now part of the New York State Canal system, 527 miles used mainly for recreational boating.

When Giovanni da Verrazano entered New York Harbor in 1524, the Native Americans of the state were at constant war with one another. But around 1570, under Dekanawidah and Hiawatha, they formed the

Iroquois Confederacy (the first League of Nations) and began to live in peace. They were known as the Five Nations and called themselves the "Men of Men."

In 1609, Samuel de Champlain explored the valley of the lake that bears his name, and Henry Hudson sailed up the river that bears his. There was a trading post at Fort Nassau (Albany) in 1614. New Amsterdam (now New York City) was founded in 1625.

Wars with the Native Americans and French kept the area in turmoil until after 1763. During the Revolution, New York's eastern part was a seesaw of military action and occupation. After the war, Washington was inaugurated president in 1789, and the seat of federal government was established in New York City. As late as 1825, much of New York's central area was swampy wilderness.

When to Go/Climate

New York State is large, and the weather is varied. The northern and western parts of the state experience more extreme temperatures—cold, snowy winters and cool summers. Winters are long, especially near the Great Lakes. The Adirondacks, too, can have frigid winters, but fall foliage is magnificent, and summer temperatures and humidity are ideal. Spring thunderstorms frequently travel the Hudson River Valley, and summers here, as well as in New York City and its environs, are hot and humid.

AVERAGE HIGH/LOW TEMPERATURES (°F)

New York City

Jan 38/25	**May** 72/54	**Sept** 76/60
Feb 40/27	**June** 80/63	**Oct** 65/50
Mar 50/35	**July** 85/68	**Nov** 54/41
Apr 61/44	**Aug** 84/67	**Dec** 43/31

Parks and Recreation

Water-related activities, hiking, riding, various other sports, picnicking and visitor centers, as well as camping, are available in many of New York's parks and recreation areas. There are more than 200 outdoor state recreation facilities, including state parks, forest preserves, and similar areas. For information about recreation areas within the Adirondack and Catskill forest preserves, contact the Department of Environmental Conservation, 50 Wolf Rd, Albany 12233-4790; phone 518/457-2500. For information about other state parks and recreation areas, contact Office of Parks, Recreation and Historic Preservation, Albany 12238; phone 518/474-0456. The state also provides funds for maintenance of 7,300 miles of trails for snowmobiling. Reservations for all state-operated campgrounds and cabins can be made by calling 800/456-CAMP. There is a fee for boat launching at some state parks. Pets on leash where allowed. The basic fee for camping is $13/night; additional charges for amenities and hookups (electric and sewer). Call or write for detailed information about individual parks.

FISHING AND HUNTING

New York state offers excellent fishing and hunting opportunities, with a wide variety of lengthy seasons. Write or phone for detailed information about fees and regulations. Contact the NYS Department of Environmental Conservation, License Sales Office-Room 151, 50 Wolf Rd, Albany 12233-4790, phone 518/457-3521, for the most current fees and a mail-order license application and fishing/hunting regulations guides. *The Conservationist* is the department's official illustrated bimonthly periodical on New York State natural resources; contact PO Box 1500, Latham, NY 12110-9983 for a subscription ($10 per year).

Driving Information

Safety belts are mandatory for all persons in the front seat of a vehicle. Children under 16 years of age must be in an approved passenger restraint anywhere in the vehicle; ages 4-9 may use a regulation safety belt; age 3 and under must use an approved child safety seat. For more information, phone 518/474-5111.

INTERSTATE HIGHWAY SYSTEM

The following alphabetical listing of New York towns shows that these cities are within 10 miles of the indicated interstate highways. Check a highway map for the nearest exit.

Highway Number	Cities/Towns within 10 Miles
Interstate 81	Alexandria Bay, Binghamton, Clayton, Cortland, Syracuse, Watertown.
Interstate 84	Brewster, Fishkill, Middletown, Newburgh, Port Jervis.
Interstate 87	Albany, Bolton Landing, Catskill, Diamond Point (Lake George Area), Glens Falls, Hartsdale, Hudson, Kingston, Lake George Village, Lake Luzerne, Monroe, Newburgh, New Paltz, New York City, Nyack, Plattsburgh, Poughkeepsie, Rouses Point, Saratoga Springs, Saugerties, Schroon Lake, Spring Valley, Stony Point, Tarrytown, Troy, Warrensburg, Woodstock, Yonkers.
Interstate 88	Bainbridge, Binghamton, Oneonta.
Interstate 90	Albany, Amsterdam, Auburn, Batavia, Buffalo, Canaan, Canajoharie, Canandaigua, Canastota, Dunkirk, Geneva, Herkimer, Ilion, Johnstown, Oneida, Palmyra, Rochester, Rome, Schenectady, Seneca Falls, Syracuse, Troy, Utica, Victor, Waterloo.
Interstate 95	Mamaroneck, White Plains.

Additional Visitor Information

The *I Love New York Winter Travel & Ski Guide* and the *I Love New York Travel Guide* (covering upstate New York, Long Island, and New York City) may be obtained from the State Department of Economic Development, Division of Tourism, PO Box 2603, Albany 12220-0603; phone 518/474-4116 or 800/CALL-NYS; www.iloveny.com.

Calendar Highlights

MARCH

St. Patrick's Day Parade *(Manhattan). Along Fifth Ave.* New York's biggest parade; approximately 100,000 marchers.

APRIL

Central New York Maple Festival *(Cortland). Phone 607/849-3812.* A variety of events showing the process of making maple syrup; also arts and crafts, hay rides, and entertainment.

MAY

Tulip Festival *(Albany). Washington Park. Phone 518/434-2032.* Three-day event includes the crowning of the Tulip Queen, as well as arts, crafts, food, vendors, children's rides, and entertainment. Over 50,000 tulips throughout the park.

JULY

Stone House Day *(Kingston). In Hurley. Phone 845/331-4121.* Tour of ten privately owned colonial stone houses led by costumed guides; old Hurley Reformed Church and burying ground; antique show; re-creation of American Revolution military encampment; and country fair.

Rochester Music Fest *(Rochester). Brown Square Park. Phone 800/677-7282.* Three-day celebration of American music. Nationally and internationally known jazz, blues, country, and folk musicians.

AUGUST

Erie County Fair *(Buffalo). Phone 716/649-3900.* One of the oldest and largest fairs in the nation. Entertainment, rides, games, exhibits, agricultural and livestock shows.

US Open *(Queens). Box office phone 718/760-6200.* One of the bigger tennis tournaments of the year.

New York State Fair *(Syracuse). State Fairgrounds. Phone 315/487-7711.* The only state fair in New York. Agricultural, animal, and commercial exhibits; midway concerts.

SEPTEMBER

Adirondack Canoe Classic *(Saranac Lake). Phone Chamber of Commerce 518/891-1990 or 800/347-1992.* 90-mile race from Old Forge to Saranac Lake for canoes, kayaks, and guideboats.

NOVEMBER

NYC Marathon *(Manhattan). Phone 212/423-2249.* Major city marathon with more than 25,000 runners.

Macy's Thanksgiving Day Parade *(Manhattan). Down Broadway to 34th St, from W 77th St and Central Park W. Phone Macy's Special Events, 212/494-4495.* Floats, balloons, television and movie stars.

Festival of Lights *(Niagara Falls). Downtown. Phone 716/285-2400.* Colored lights, animated displays, decorations, and entertainment. Lighting of the Christmas tree.

ADIRONDACK PARK

From Albany, take Route 9 north to Glens Falls and 9N to Lake George Village. Described as "the most queenly of American lakes," Lake George is 44 square miles of deep blue water dotted with 225 islands; opportunities for water recreation abound in this vacation mecca. Fresh powder awaits winter travelers north on Route 28 at the Gore Mountain Ski Area in North Creek.

Farther north on 28 is Adirondack Park, which is bordered by Lake Champlain on the east, the Black River on the west, the St. Lawrence River on the north, and the Mohawk River valley on the south. At 6 million acres, Adirondack State Park is the largest US Park outside of Alaska (9,000 square miles). Six million acres—that's the size of New Jersey and Rhode Island combined. Just imagine the recreational opportunities available—you could spend days here and not even scratch the surface of all there is to see and do. Whitewater raft on the Hudson, Moose, or Black rivers. Climb one of the 46 peaks in the Adirondack Range. Feeling adventurous? Have a go at Mount Marcy, also known as "Cloud Splitter," which is the highest peak in the range at 5,344 feet. Not a climber? Try canoeing, fishing, or mountain biking instead.

Be sure to make time for a visit to Enchanted Forest/Water Safari (off Route 28 in Old Forge; phone 315/369-6145)—especially if you are traveling with children. After all, there's no better place to spend a hot day than at New York's largest water theme park. Challenging adventure slides are sure to be a hit with older kids, while Tadpole

Hole and Pygmy Pond keep the tots cool and happy. Enchanted Forest entertains with the Treetop Skyride and the Enchanted Forest Railroad, and Magical Escapades offers such distractions as bumper cars, a Ferris wheel, and tilt-a-whirl. If that's not enough excitement for one day, stop next door at Calypso's Cove where you will find miniature golf, go-karts, batting cages, bumper boats, and an arcade.

The next stop is Blue Mountain Lake. Take the 3-mile trail to the summit of Blue Mountain (3,800 feet) for spectacular views of Adirondack Park. Then head to the Adirondack Museum for a taste of Adirondack history and modes of life. Housed in 20 buildings on 30 acres, the museum also showcases one of the best boat collections in the world, including sail canoes, steamboats, and the famous Adirondack guide boat.

Head south on 28 back to Lake George. Take 9N to Bolton Landing and Ticonderoga, home of Fort Mt. Hope and Fort Ticonderoga (1755). Head south on 22 to Whitehall, then follow the Champlain Canal and Hudson River down Route 4. Stop in Saratoga Springs to visit Saratoga National Historical Park, the National Museum of Horse Racing and Hall of Fame, and Saratoga Spa State Park. Continue on Route 4 to return to Albany. **(Approximately 280 miles)**

ESCAPE TO LONG ISLAND

Long Island is a world unto itself—especially off the Long Island Expressway. A mix of city sophistication and rural simplicity, Long Island is a playground for New Yorkers, who find the state parks, wildlife sanctuaries, and small towns refreshing. From New York City, take Southern Parkway 27 to Freeport, then Meadowbrook Parkway south. Stop and visit the beautiful white beaches of Jones Beach State Park for some fun in the sun. Unwind by swimming in the cool waters of the Atlantic, fishing, boating, exploring the nature and bike trails, golfing, or playing softball or shuffleboard. Then continue east on the Parkway along the Atlantic Ocean to JFK Wildlife Sanctuary, Cedar Beach in Gilgo Beach State Park, and Oak Beach. Cross over Robert Moses Bridge for a trip to Robert Moses State Park, located on the western end of Fire Island National Seashore. The pristine white-sand beach located here features such amenities as restrooms, showers, lifeguards, concession, and picnic areas. Camping is available farther east at Watch Hill. Ranger-led interpretive canoe programs and nature walks begin at the Watch Hill visitor center. Stop in at the picturesque Fire Island Light Station to visit the ground-floor museum, which houses exhibits on shipwrecks and offshore rescues. (The lighthouse can be toured if reservations are made in advance.) From there, backtrack across the bridge to Robert Moses Causeway. Take 27A east to Bay Shore to visit 690-acre Bayard Cutting Arboretum. Continue through Islip and East Islip back to 27 (Sunrise Expressway), connecting with 27A again to Shinnecock Indian Reservation and Southampton.

One of the oldest English settlements in New York, Southampton was settled in 1640 by colonists from Massachusetts. Today, it is a blue-blood resort, with old, established homes and swanky boutiques along Job's Lane and Main Street and luxurious beach cottages and Victorian gingerbread mansions. Tour The Olde Halsey House, the oldest English frame house in New York. Parrish Art Museum features 19th- and 20th-century American art, as well as Japanese woodblock prints and changing exhibits. Southampton Historical Museum includes a fantastic collection of Indian artifacts.

Continue on to East Hampton, a fashionable resort town with lots to see and do. Take a guided tour of the 1806 windmill at Hook Mill; visit the Guild Hall Museum for a look at regional art; explore Historic Mulford Farm, a living history farm museum with costumed interpreters; or make an appointment to tour Jackson Pollock's home and studio. The nearby town of Amagansett is home to the Town Marine Museum—sure to be a hit with the anglers in your family. Exhibits explore commercial and sportfishing, whaling, fishing techniques, and underwater archeology. At the very tip of Long Island is Montauk, home to Hither Hills State Park and Montauk Point State Park. Be sure to tour the Montauk Point Lighthouse Museum before taking the Long Island Expressway back to Manhattan. **(Approximately 275 miles)**

EXPLORING THE FINGER LAKES REGION

This scenic, rolling region is marked by 11 finger-shaped lakes, named for the tribes of the Six Nations of Iroquois. According to Native American legend, the lakes were formed when God placed his hands on some of the most beautiful land ever created. The landscape features dazzling waterfalls, wild gorges and glens spanned by trestle bridges, steep hills and fairy-tale valleys, spring-fed lakes, sand beaches, and richly forested state parks. Area recreational opportunities include fascinating hiking and boating and fishing on all 11 lakes.

The towns of the Finger Lakes region have a penchant for classical Greek and Latin names—Romulus, Homer, Etna, Ovid, Camillus, Marcellus, Sparta, Sempronius, Vesper, Scipioville—suggesting rural sophistication and architectural flamboyance. The public buildings and mansions on the wide, shady streets of Ithaca, Skaneateles, Seneca Falls, Penn Yan, Geneva, and Canandaigua celebrate every architectural fad from 1840-1910, including Greek and Gothic revival, Italianate, Georgian, Federal, Queen Anne, Richardsonian

Romanesque, Beaux Arts, and Art Deco styles. If architecture isn't your thing, you can attend wine tastings and festivals at local vineyards or learn everything there is to know about enology (the science of winemaking) and viticulture (grape harvesting, fermentation, bottling, riddling racks, French oak barrels, tartrates, and yeasts) by taking the vineyard tours.

From Rochester, head south on Route 96 to Canandaigua, where you will find Sonnenberg Gardens and Mansion and Finger Lakes Race Track. Spend some time exploring the 50-acre estate at Sonnenberg, which includes the 40-room mansion, 9 formal gardens, ponds, and a green house conservatory. Continue east on Route 5 to Geneva, which is located on Seneca Lake, the deepest and widest of the Finger Lakes. Seneca Lake is known for its large concentration of lake trout, so this is a great place to cast your fishing lines into the water. If you are traveling over Memorial Day weekend, you'll catch the National Trout Derby here. Otherwise, head to Seneca Lake State Park, where the kids can take a swim or play at the playground while you try to catch the evening's dinner. From there, follow Route 14 south along Seneca Lake to Penn Yan for a look at the local architecture. The Windmill Farm and Craft Market, where Mennonites arrive in horse and buggy to sell farm produce and hand-made crafts, is also worth a stop. Children will enjoy Fullager Farms Family Farm and Petting Zoo, a working dairy farm that offers such diversions as pony rides, hay rides, and a petting zoo. Farther south on Route 14 is scenic Watkins Glen. Take some time to explore Watkins Glen Gorge, a glacier-made chasm complete with waterfalls. Several foot trails trace the rim of the gorge; stairs and bridges allow you to explore the inside of the chasm. Along the same lines, the nearby town of Montour Falls features 156-foot Chequaga Falls. If you are looking to do more fishing, stop at Catharine Creek where rainbow trout are abundant. From Watkins Glen, head south on 224 and north on 13 to Ithaca on picturesque Cayuga Lake. Visit Cornell Plantations Botanical Gardens, Sapsucker Woods Bird Sanctuary, and Moosewood Cafe. Those traveling with children might want to check out the Sciencenter, home to over 100 hands-on science exhibits. Talk a walk along Sagan Planetwalk, an outdoor scale model of the solar system located on the grounds of Sciencenter—it stretches for almost a mile! Children and adults alike will enjoy a visit to Fall Creek Gorge; the falls here stand almost as high as those at Niagara. This is a good place to pause for a scenic picnic. Round out your tour of the Finger Lakes Region by taking 348/90 north and 20 west to Seneca Falls. The big draw here is the Women's Rights National Historic Park, which honors such women's rights activists as Elizabeth Cady Stanton, Amelia Bloomer, Lucretia Mott, and Susan B. Anthony. Return to Rochester via 20 west and 96 west. **(Approximately 220 miles)**

THE THOUSAND ISLANDS

From Syracuse, cross the Erie Canal on Route 48. Follow the Oswego Canal route (48 to 481) to the Fort Ontario State Historical Site, where you can explore military life as it was in the 1860s. For more history, head next to the H. Lee White Marine Museum. Continuing on, take 104 east to Mexico Bay, then follow 3 north to Sackets Harbor and Sackets Harbor Battlefield State Historical Site. In nearby Watertown, visit the Sci-Tech Center, a hands-on science museum sure to be a hit with the kids. Ever wonder how maple syrup is made? A visit to the American Maple Museum should answer all your questions about this sweet, sticky stuff. Continue on 12E to Clayton, where three state parks offer swimming, fishing, boating, and camping. Stop in at the Thousand Islands Museum to learn more about the history of this scenic region. The Antique Boat Museum may be of interest to the nautically minded in your group; the Antique Boat Show takes place here in August.

Our last stop is Alexandria Bay and the Thousand Islands. Described by French explorer Count Frontenac as "a Fairyland, that neither pen nor tongue of man may even attempt to describe," these 1,793-odd islands and islets, some only big enough to hold an American flag and others several acres in size, lie along the world's longest unprotected international border. When the International Boundary Commission divided up the islands (1817-1822), Canada got roughly 2/3 of them. The United States got the larger islands, including Wellesley and Grindstone, as well as the deep-water channel to Lake Ontario and the other Great Lakes.

Each of the Thousand Islands in the St. Lawrence River is a little kingdom with a story. On Zavikon, you can see the shortest international bridge in the world. Only 10 meters long, the bridge connects a Canadian cottage with an American flag on a pole. On Heart Island, you can tour the melancholy ruins of the half-finished Boldt Castle. Self-made millionaire George Boldt began building the $2,500,000 castle as a gift for his beloved young wife in the 1890s; he abandoned it to ruin when she died in 1904.

What better way to experience the Thousand Islands than out on the water? Boat tours and canoe expeditions explore the sheltered natural wonders of the islands. Sailboat charters and scuba dives are available to see the many shipwrecks off Kingston, including the Horace Tabor (1867), a 46-meter sailboat built in Michigan, and the Steamer Comet (1848), a 337-ton paddlewheeler built in Portsmouth.

On land, visit the Aqua Zoo (phone 315/482-5771), a privately owned aquarium that displays hundreds of varieties of marine life, including piranhas, alligators, and sharks-oh my! Head up into the air with a hot-air balloon or helicopter ride for gorgeous aerial views of the islands. **(Approximately 215 miles)**

New York City

Settled 1615 **Pop** 8,008,278 **Elev** 410 ft

Information New York City Convention & Visitors Bureau, 810 Seventh Ave, New York, NY 10019

Web www.nycvisit.com

New York is the nation's most populous city, the capital of finance, business, communications, theater, and much more. It may not be the center of the universe, but it does occupy a central place in the world's imagination. Certainly, in one way or another, New York affects the lives of nearly every American. While other cities have everything that New York has—from symphonies to slums—no other city has quite the style or sheer abundance. Nowhere are things done in such a grandly American way as in New York City.

Giovanni da Verrazano was the first European to glimpse Manhattan Island (1524), but the area was not explored until 1609, when Henry Hudson sailed up the river that was later named for him, searching for a passage to India. Adriaen Block arrived here in 1613, and the first trading post was established by the Dutch West India Company two years later. Peter Minuit is said to have bought the island from Native Americans for $24 worth of beads and trinkets in 1626, when New Amsterdam was founded—the biggest real estate bargain in history.

City Fun Facts

1. Gennaro Lombardi opened the first pizzeria in the country in New York City in 1895.

2. Downtown Manhattan was the nation's first capital.

3. As late as the 1840s, thousands of pigs roamed Wall Street to consume garbage– an early sanitation system.

4. The New York Stock Exchange began in 1792 when 24 brokers met under a buttonwood tree facing 68 Wall Street.

5. New York was the first state to require license plates on automobiles.

6. The nation's largest public Halloween parade is the Greenwich Village Halloween Parade.

7. Macy's, the world's largest store, covers 2.1 million square feet of space and stocks over 500,000 different items.

8. Babe Ruth hit his first home run in Yankee Stadium in the first game ever played there.

9. There are 6,374.6 miles of streets in New York City.

In 1664, the Dutch surrendered to a British fleet and the town was renamed New York in honor of the Duke of York. One of the earliest tests of independence occurred here in 1734 when John Peter Zenger, publisher and editor of the *New York Weekly-Journal,* was charged with seditious libel and jailed for making anti-government remarks. Following the Battle of Long Island in 1776, the British occupied the city through the Revolution, until 1783.

On the balcony of Federal Hall at Wall Street, April 30, 1789, George Washington was inaugurated as the first president of the United States, and for a time New York was the country's capital.

When the Erie Canal opened in 1825, New York City expanded vastly as a port. It has since consistently maintained its leadership. In 1898, Manhattan merged with Brooklyn, the Bronx, Queens, and Staten Island. In the next half-century several million immigrants entered the United States here, providing the city with the supply of labor needed for its growth into a major metropolis. Each wave of immigrants has brought new customs, culture, and life, which makes New York City the varied metropolis it is today.

New York continues to capitalize on its image as the Big Apple, attracting more than 39 million visitors each year, and its major attractions continue to thrive in style. These, of course, are centered in Manhattan; however, vacationers should not overlook the wealth of sights and activities the other boroughs have to offer. Brooklyn has Coney Island, the New York Aquarium, the superb Brooklyn History Museum, Brooklyn Botanic Garden, Brooklyn Children's Museum, and the famous landmark Brooklyn Bridge. The Bronx is noted for its excellent Botanical Garden and Zoo and Yankee Stadium. Flushing Meadows-Corona Park, in Queens, was the site of two World's Fairs; nearby is Shea Stadium, home of the New York Mets. Uncrowded Staten Island has Richmond Town Restoration, a re-creation of 18th-century New York, rural farmland, beaches, salt marshes, and wildlife preserves.

Weather

The average mean temperatures for New York are 34°F in winter; 52°F in spring; 75°F in summer; and 58°F in fall. In summer the temperature is rarely above 90°F, but the humidity can be high. In winter the temperature is rarely lower than 10°F but has gone as low as -14°F. Average mean temperatures are listed from surveys taken at the National Weather Bureau station in Central Park.

Theater

New York is the theatrical headquarters of the United States, and theater here is an experience not to be missed. Broadway, a 36-square-block area (41st to 53rd streets and 6th to 9th avenues), offers standard full-scale plays and musicals, more than 30 of them on any particular evening. Off-Broadway, not confined to one area, is less expensive and more experimental, giving new talent a chance at exposure and established talent an opportunity to try new and different projects, such as the New York Shakespeare Festival (see SEASONAL EVENTS). Even less expensive and more daring is off-off-Broadway, consisting of dozens of small theaters in storefronts, lofts, and cellars, producing every imaginable type of theater.

There are a number of ways to obtain tickets, ranging from taking a pre-arranged package theater tour to walking up to the box office an hour before curtain for returned and unclaimed tickets. TicketMaster outlets (phone 212/307-7171), hotel theater desks, and ticket brokers will have tickets to several shows for the box office price plus a service charge. All Broadway theaters accept phone reservations charged to major credit cards. An On Stage Hotline can be reached at 212/768-1818.

The Times Square Ticket Center (a booth with large banners proclaiming "TKTS") at 47th St & Broadway has same-day tickets at half-price for most shows (daily) and for matinees (Wed, Sat, Sun). Same-day half-price tickets to music and dance events may be obtained at the Music & Dance Booth, at 42nd St & Avenue of the Americas in Bryant Park. *The New Yorker* and *New York* magazines carry extensive listings of the week's entertainment; the Friday edition of *The New York Times* also reports weekend availability of tickets.

Additional Visitor Information
Contact the New York Convention and Visitors Bureau, 810 7th Ave, 10019; 212/484-1222. The bureau has free maps, "twofers" to Broadway shows, bulletins, and brochures on attractions, events, shopping, restaurants, and hotels. For events of the week, visitors should get copies of *The New Yorker* and *New York* magazines and *The New York Times.*

Transportation

AIRPORTS
LaGuardia, in Queens 8 miles northeast of Manhattan; **Kennedy International,** in Queens 15 miles southeast of Manhattan (for both, see QUEENS—LAGUARDIA & JFK INTERNATIONAL AIRPORT AREAS); **Newark International,** 16 miles southwest of Manhattan in New Jersey.

CAR RENTAL AGENCIES
See IMPORTANT TOLL-FREE NUMBERS.

PUBLIC TRANSPORTATION
Subway and elevated trains, buses (New York City Transit Authority), phone 718/330-3322 or 718/330-1234. The subway system, which carries more than 4 million people on weekdays, covers every borough except Staten Island, which has its own transportation system. Maps of the system are posted at every station and on every car.

RAIL PASSENGER SERVICE
Amtrak 800/872-7245.

Driving in New York
Vehicular traffic is heaviest during weekday rush hours and on both week-days and weekends between Thanksgiving and Christmas week—a period of almost continuous rush hour. Most Manhattan avenues and streets are

one-way. To assist tourists in finding cross streets nearest avenue addresses, telephone books and several tourist guides contain address locator tables. Because New York traffic is very heavy and parking is both scarce and expensive, many visitors find taxis more convenient and economical than driving.

Sightseeing Tours

For travelers desiring a general overview of the city, a variety of sightseeing tours are available using various forms of transportation (see WHAT TO SEE AND DO under individual neighborhoods).

MUSEUMS OF NEW YORK

New York is a city of museums. Almost everywhere you go, from the stately Upper East Side of Manhattan to the leafy reaches of Staten Island, you stumble upon them. Some are renowned world-wide: the Metropolitan Museum of Art, the Museum of Modern Art, the Museum of Natural History, the Guggenheim. Others are known only to enthusiasts: the Isamu Noguchi Garden Museum, the Tibetan Museum, the New York City Fire Museum, the Lower East Side Tenement Museum.

On these pages, find a guide to some of the city's most important, interesting, and/or offbeat museums, arranged by subject matter. If you're short on time, the must-sees are the Metropolitan Museum of Art, the Museum of Modern Art, and the American Museum of Natural History. Following not far behind are the Guggenheim, the Whitney, the Brooklyn Museum of Art, the Studio Museum in Harlem, the Cooper-Hewitt, the National Museum of the American Indian, and the Frick Collection.

Many of New York's major museums are packed with visitors on the weekends, especially in the afternoons or early evenings, because many are open late on Fridays and Saturdays. To avoid the crowds, come during the week or on weekend mornings.

MAJOR ART MUSEUMS

Any guide to the Big Apple's museums must start with that most venerable, enormous, and glorious of institutions, the **Metropolitan Museum of Art** (1000 Fifth Avenue, at 82nd Street; phone 212/535-7710). Housed behind an impressive Beaux Arts façade designed by Robert Morris Hunt, the museum holds collections of everything from Egyptian sarcophagi to contemporary American paintings. Equally important, it hosts at least two or three major temporary exhibits at any give time.

Founded in 1870, the Met centers on the Great Hall, a vast entrance room with a stately staircase leading to the second floor. Here you'll find the European Paintings galleries, one of the Met's most important collections. Housed in about 20 rooms are works by such masters as Rembrandt, Breughel, Rubens, Botticelli, Goya, and El Greco. Next door are the impressive 19th-century European Galleries, housing works by more modern masters such as van Gogh, Gauguin, Seurat, and Renoir.

Three sides of the Met's original buildings are flanked by modern glass wings. At the back is the Robert Lehman Collection, containing an exhibit of 19th-century French paintings, among other things. On the south side are the Rockefeller and Acheson Wings, the first holding a South Pacific collection-everything from totem poles to canoes-the second, 20th-century art. On the north side, find the Sacker Wing, best known for its 15th-century-BC Temple of Dendur, carved in faded hieroglyphics, and the American Wing, housing exhaustive galleries of decorative arts and paintings by the likes of Thomas Eakins and John Singer Sargent.

The Met's Egyptian collection is one of the largest in the world and a must-stop for history buffs. The Islamic art collection and the new South and Southeast Asian art collection are also among the world's finest. To see the museum's medieval collection, travel north to the **Cloisters** (Fort Tyron Park, 190th Street at Overlook Terrace; phone 212/923-3700). Situated high on a hill with great views of the Hudson River, the Cloisters are housed in a reconstructed medieval monastery that incorporates the actual remains of four medieval cloisters.

The second stop for any serious art lover should be the **Museum of Modern Art** (11 West 53rd Street, between Fifth and Sixth avenues; phone 212/708-9480). Currently in the midst of major expansion (not to be completed until late 2004), the museum houses 100,000 paintings, sculptures, drawings, prints, and photographs and presents first-rate films—mostly classic, foreign, and experimental—in its comfortable basement auditorium.

Major temporary exhibits usually dominate the museum's first and basement floors, whereas the permanent collections are housed above. On the second floor, find such masterpieces as Cezanne's *The Bather* and van Gogh's *Starry Night,* along with entire rooms devoted to Mondrian, Pollock, Matisse, and Monet's *Water Lilies.* Also on the second floor is a superb photography exhibit. The third floor houses prints and illustrated books, and the fourth, architectural drawings and design objects. A jazz concert series is held in the museum's outdoor sculpture garden in the summer.

Another essential stop for modern art lovers is the **Solomon R. Guggenheim Museum** (1071 Fifth Avenue, at 88th Street; phone

212/423-3500). Housed in a circular building designed by Frank Lloyd Wright in 1959, the main gallery is a gentle multileveled spiral circling around a central atrium. The exhibits, all major temporary shows featuring 20th- or 21st-century artists, start at the top of the spiral and wind their way down.

Next door to the main gallery is a rotunda, housing the small but stunning Justin K. Thannhauser Collection, which includes works by such artists as Picasso, Cezanne, Modigliani, and Seurat. A ten-story tower also abuts the main gallery to the back; here, find a mix of temporary and permanent exhibits and an outdoor sculpture garden. This museum boasts a second branch in SoHo, the **Guggenheim Museum SoHo** (575 Broadway, at Prince Street; phone 212/423-3500), which usually houses the work of younger and more cutting-edge artists.

Not far from the Guggenheim is the **Whitney Museum of American Art** (Madison Avenue, at 75th Street; phone 212/570-3676). Most of the exhibits here are temporary and feature the work of one major American artist such as Edward Hopper, Jasper Johns, or Jean-Michel Basquiat. The museum is also known for its superb permanent collection and for its controversial "Biennial" show, presented every two years to showcase the latest work of contemporary American artists.

A few blocks south of the Whitney, find the hushed **Frick Collection** (1 East 70th Street, at Fifth Avenue; phone 212/288-0700). The museum is housed in a lovely 1914 mansion, the former home of 19th-century industrialist Henry Clay Frick, built around a peaceful courtyard. Renowned for its permanent European art collection, the Frick boasts masterpieces by Breughel, El Greco, Vermeer, Rembrandt, and many others. Near the entrance is the Jean-Honore Fragonard Room, where all four walls are covered with *The Progress of Love,* a mural commissioned by Louis XV.

A few blocks north of the Metropolitan beckons another museum housed in a former mansion: the **Cooper-Hewitt National Design Museum** (2 East 91st Street, at Fifth Avenue; phone 212/849-8400). Once home to the 19th-century industrialist Andrew Carnegie, the 64-room building is now a branch of the Smithsonian Institution dedicated to design and the decorative arts. The exhibits are temporary and focus on such subjects as ceramics, furniture, textiles, and metalwork. Out back is a romantic garden, where concerts are sometimes presented.

The **Studio Museum of Harlem** (144 West 125th Street, between Lenox Avenue and Adam Clayton Powell Boulevard; phone 212/864-4500) is located in Harlem. Founded in 1968, the museum is the "principal center for the study of Black Art in America," spread out over several well-lit floors of a turn-of-the-century building.

The permanent exhibit features works by such masters as Romare Bearden, James VanDerZee, and Jacob Lawrence; temporary exhibits present a mix of both world-renowned and emerging artists. The Studio is also known for its lively lecture and concert series, presented September through May.

Although often overlooked by tourists, the **Brooklyn Museum of Art** (200 Eastern Parkway, at Washington; phone 718/638-5000) is one of the city's foremost art institutions. Similar to the Metropolitan in some ways, it is housed in a lovely Beaux Arts building, with collections spanning virtually the entire history of art. Highlights include a large Egyptian wing, a superb Native American collection, and a major permanent assemblage of contemporary art. In addition to staging some of the more unusual and controversial exhibits in town, the museum also hosts a "First Saturday" series (the first Saturday of every month, 5-11 pm) featuring free concerts, performances, films, dances, and dance lessons.

SMALLER ART MUSEUMS

In addition to the behemoths above, New York City is home to scores of smaller art museums, many of which are unique gems. No matter where your art interests lie, you're bound to find something that speaks to you.

Photography buffs won't want to miss the **International Center of Photography,** recently relocated from the Upper East Side to Midtown (1133 Sixth Avenue, at 43rd Street; phone 212/768-4682). In these spacious galleries, you'll find changing exhibits featuring everyone from Weegee (Arthur Fellig) to Anne Lebovitz.

Meanwhile, sculpture fans will want to visit the **Isamu Noguchi Garden Museum** in Long Island City, Queens (32-37 Vernon Boulevard, at 33rd Road; phone 718/204-7088), just a short trip from Manhattan. Housed in the sculptor's former studio, complete with an outdoor sculpture garden, the museum is filled with Noguchi stone, metal, and woodwork. The museum is open only from April through October, so you will have to time your visit accordingly.

In Murray Hill, find the **Pierpont Morgan Library** (29 East 36th Street, at Madison Avenue; phone 212/685-0610), housed in an elegant neoclassic mansion that was once financier John Pierpont Morgan's personal library and art museum. The library holds a priceless collection of illuminated manuscripts and Old Master drawings; compelling traveling exhibits are frequently on display as well.

In SoHo, the **New Museum of Contemporary Art** (583 Broadway, between Houston and Prince streets; phone 212/219-1222) hosts experimental and conceptual works by contemporary artists from all over the world. Also a premier center for art on the cutting edge is the **P.S. 1 Contemporary Art Center** in Long Island City, Queens (22-25 Jackson Avenue, at 46th Street). On the Upper West Side, the **Museum of American Folk Art** (2 Columbus Avenue, between 65th and 66th streets; phone 212/595-9533) showcases everything from quilts and weathervanes to painting and sculpture; admission is always free.

HISTORY MUSEUMS

A good introduction to the history of the Big Apple can be found at the **Museum of the City of New York** (Fifth Avenue, between 103rd and 104th streets; phone 212/534-1672), an eclectic establishment filled with a vast permanent collection of paintings and photographs, maps and prints, Broadway memorabilia and old model ships. Housed in a sprawling neo-Georgian building, the museum also hosts an interesting series of temporary exhibits on such subjects as Duke Ellington or stickball.

Also devoted to the history of New York is the **New York Historical Society** (2 West 77th Street, at Central Park West; phone 212/873-3400), which recently reawakened after years of inactivity due to financial troubles. Spread out over many high-ceilinged rooms, the society presents temporary exhibits on everything from the legendary Stock Club—frequented by everyone from Frank Sinatra to JFK—to the small African-American communities that once dotted Central Park.

To find out more about immigration history, visit the **Ellis Island Museum,** a trip that is usually made via ferry, in conjunction with a jaunt to the **Statue of Liberty** (for information, call the Circle Line Ferry at 212/269-5755; the ferries leave from Battery Park in Lower Manhattan). The primary point of entry for immigrants to the United States from 1892 to 1924, Ellis Island is a castlelike building, all red-brick towers and white domes, that now houses multiple exhibits on the immigrant experience, along with photographs, films, and taped oral histories. To avoid the crowds that flock here, especially during the summer, arrive first thing in the morning.

Related in theme to Ellis Island is the **Lower East Side Tenement Museum** (97 Orchard Street, between Delancey and Broome streets; phone 212/431-0233; visits by guided tour only, reservations recommended). Deliberately dark and oppressive, the museum re-creates early immigrant life in Manhattan.

The **South Street Seaport Museum** is not so much a museum as it is an 11-block historic district, located in Lower Manhattan where Fulton Street meets the East River. A thriving port during the 19th century, the now-restored area is filled with commercial shops and restaurants, along with dozens of historic buildings—a boat-building shop, a former counting house—and a few historic sailing ships. The ships and some of the buildings require an entrance ticket that can be purchased at the Visitor Center (on Schermerhorn Row, an extension of Fulton Street; phone 212/748-8600).

In the East Village, find the **Merchant's House Museum** (29 East 4th Street, near the Bowery; phone 212/777-1089). This classic Greek Revival home is furnished exactly as it was in 1835, when merchant Seabury Tredwell and his family lived here.

Near Gramercy Park presides **Theodore Roosevelt's Birthplace** (28 East 20th Street, near Broadway; phone 212/260-1616), a handsome four-story brownstone that is an exact replica of the original. Now administered by the National Park Service, the museum houses the largest collection of Roosevelt memorabilia in the country.

CULTURAL MUSEUMS

As befits a city made up of many peoples, New York is home to a number of museums that focus on the culture of one country or area of the world. Some of these are major, professionally assembled institutions; others are small and homespun.

In lower Manhattan, find the George Gustav Heye Center of the **National Museum of the American Indian** (1 Bowling Green, at State Street and Battery Place; phone 212/668-6624), a branch of the Smithsonian Institution. Housed in a stunning 1907 Beaux Arts building designed by Cass Gilbert, the museum holds some of the country's finest Native American art and artifacts, ranging in date of origin from 3200 BC to the 20th century. Admission is always free.

Also in Lower Manhattan is the **Museum of Jewish Heritage** (18 First Place, at Battery Park, Battery Park City; phone 212/968-1800), built in the shape of a hexagon, symbolic of the Star of David. Opened in 1997, the museum features thousands of moving pho-tographs, cultural artifacts, and archival films documenting the Holocaust and the resilience of the Jewish community.

A second Jewish museum, this one devoted to the arts, culture, and history, can be found on the Upper East Side. Housed in a mag-nificent French Gothic mansion, the **Jewish Museum** (1109 Fifth Avenue, at 92nd Street, 212/423-3200) holds an outstanding perma-nent collection of ceremonial objects and artifacts while also host-ing many major exhibits on everything from "The Dreyfus Affair" to painter Marc Chagall.

Also on the Upper East Side, find the **Asia Society** (502 Park Avenue, at 59th Street; phone 212/517-2742) and **El Museo del Barrio** (1230 Fifth Avenue, between 104th and 105th streets; phone 212/831-

7272). The former presents first-rate temporary exhibits, concerts, films and lectures on various aspects of Asian culture and history. The latter features changing exhibits on both contemporary and historic subjects and houses a superb permanent collection of *Santos de Palo,* or carved wooden saints.

In Harlem is the **African American Wax Museum** (318 West 115th Street, between Manhattan Avenue and Frederick Douglass Boulevard; phone 212/678-7818; by appointment only), a tiny private place created and run by Haitian-born artist Raven Chanticleer. The museum is filled with wax figures of famous African Americans— Frederick Douglass, Josephine Baker, Nelson Mandela—as well as Chanticleer's own paintings and sculptures.

The **Museum of the Chinese in the Americas** in Chinatown (70 Mulberry Street, at Bayard Street, second floor; phone 212/619-4785) is a small but fascinating place, filled with photographs, mementos, and poetry culled from nearly two decades of research in the community. Women's roles, religion, and Chinese laundries are among the subjects covered in the exhibits.

On Staten Island, find the **Jacques Marchais Museum of Tibetan Art** (338 Lighthouse Avenue, at Windsor; phone 718/987-3500). Perched on a steep hill with views of the Atlantic Ocean, the museum houses the collection of Jacqueline Norman Klauber, who became fascinated with Tibet as a child. Highlights of the exhibit include a series of bright-colored masks and a large collection of golden *thangkas,* or religious images.

NATURAL HISTORY, SCIENCE, AND TECHNOLOGY MUSEUMS

The must-stop in this category is the enormous **American Museum of Natural History** (Central Park West at 79th Street; phone 212/769-5100), one of the city's greatest museums. Always filled with hundreds of shouting, enthusiastic kids, the museum went through a major renovation in the late 1990s and is now filled with many state-of-the-art exhibits.

At the heart of the museum are approximately 100 dinosaur skeletons, some housed in the soaring, not-to-be-missed Theodore Roosevelt Memorial Hall. Other highlights include the Mammals Wing, the Hall of Human Biology and Evolution, the Hall of Primitive Vertebrates, and the museum's many dioramas and exhibits devoted to native peoples around the world. Adjoining the museum to the north is the spanking new **Rose Center for Earth and Science,** featuring a planetarium with a Zeiss sky projector capable of projecting 9,100 stars as viewed from Earth.

The city's top pure science museum is the **New York Hall of Science** (47-01 111th Street; phone 718/699-0005), located in Flushing Meadows-Corona Park, Queens—best reached from Manhattan via the 7 subway. Housed in a dramatic building with undulating walls, the museum is packed with hands-on exhibits for kids and features a large Science Playground out back, where kids can learn about the laws of physics.

Docked at Pier 86 on the western edge of Manhattan is the **Intrepid Sea-Air-Space Museum** (West 46th Street at 12th Avenue; phone 212/245-0072). A former World War II aircraft carrier, the museum is now devoted to military history and includes lots of child-friendly hands-on exhibits. Small aircraft and space capsules are strewn here and there, and exhibits focus on such subjects as satellite communication and spaceship design.

Also in Midtown is the **Museum of Television and Radio** (25 West 52nd Street, between Fifth and Sixth avenues; phone 212/621-6800), where you can watch your favorite old television show, listen to a classic radio broadcast, or research a pop-culture question. The museum also offers traditional exhibits on such subjects as the history of animation. Be sure to arrive early if you plan to visit on the weekend and want to use one of the museum's 96 semiprivate televisions or radio consoles.

MUSEUMS FOR KIDS

In addition to the natural history, science, and technology museums, children might also enjoy visiting the **Children's Museum of Manhattan** on the Upper West Side (212 West 83rd Street, between Broadway and Amsterdam Avenue; phone 212/721-1223) or the **Children's Museum of the Arts in SoHo** (182 Lafayette Street, between Broome and Grand streets; phone 212/274-0986). In the former, aimed at ages 2 to 10, kids can draw and paint, play at being newscasters, or explore the ever-changing play areas; the latter features an "Artists' Studio," where youngsters can try their hand at sand painting, origami, sculpture, and beadwork.

Although not, strictly speaking, a children's museum, the **New York City Fire Museum** in SoHo (278 Spring Street, between Varick and Houston; phone 212/691-1303) has great appeal for kids. Housed in an actual firehouse that was used up until 1959, the museum is filled with fire engines new and old, helmets and uniforms, hoses, and lifesaving nets. Retired firefighters take visitors through the museum, reciting fascinating tidbits of fire-fighting history along the way. This museum has been a particularly poignant stop since the terrorist attacks of 2001 reminded New Yorkers—and all Americans—what heroes firefighters are.

Curious kids will like the **Sony Wonder Technology Lab** (56th Street between Madison and Fifth Avenues; phone 212/833-8100; reservations strongly suggested), an interactive museum that teaches the wonders of communication and technology. Learn how a CD produces sound, and mix your own song. Design your own video game in the Image Lab. Or, learn the about the science of robotics through b. b. Wonderbot, a high-tech puppet that guides visitors through the museum, and is able to interact with them through cameras and sensors. The museum also holds many special events as well as free movie screenings. Call or visit the web site (wondertechlab.sony.com) for more information.

For children who dream about becoming a police officer when they grow up, the **New York City Police Museum** (100 Old Slip; phone 212/480-3100) in Lower Manhattan is surely a place they'll want to visit. Located in a historic building that was the home of the NYPD's 1st Precinct until 1973, the museum holds one of the largest collections of police memorabilia in the United States. The exhibits, which include uniforms, badges, firearms, squad cars, and photos, tell the story of these New York heroes, and trace the development of police work through the years.

Older kids might enjoy a visit to the **Forbes Magazine Galleries** in Greenwich Village (62 Fifth Avenue, near 12th Street; phone 212/206-5548). Housing the collections of the idiosyncratic media tycoon Malcolm Forbes, the museum includes exhibits of more than 500 toy boats, 12,000 toy soldiers, about a dozen Fabergé eggs, and numerous historical documents relating to American history. Admission is free.

New York City Professional Sports

Although Madison Square Garden is home to the Knicks, the Liberty, and the Rangers, the island of Manhattan just isn't big enough to accommodate the rest of New York's nine professional sports teams. If you're a sports nut, look here for various teams to cheer on while you're in the Big Apple.

MetroStars (MLS). *Giants Stadium. 50 NJ 120, East Rutherford, NJ (07073). New Jersey Tpke exit 16 W. Phone 201/583-7000. www.metrostars.com.* Soccer is still an up-and-coming professional sport in the US, but that doesn't mean you should expect anything less from these pros than you would from athletes in any other sport. Tickets are plentiful and should put you close to the action.

New York Giants (NFL). *The Meadowlands. 50 NJ 120, East Rutherford, NJ (07073). New Jersey Tpke exit 16 W. Phone 201/935-8111. www.giants.com.* The Giants made an improbable run to the Super Bowl in 2000 before losing to the Baltimore Ravens. The team has had sporadic success throughout the 1980s and '90s (including winning two Super Bowls) and still shares its stadium with the New York Jets.

New York Islanders (NHL). *Nassau Coliseum. 650 5th Ave, Uniondale (10019). Phone 800/882-4753. www.newyorkislanders.com.* The Islanders were the dominant team in the early 1980s, winning three Stanley Cups in a row from 1980 to 1982. Players like Mike Bossy have not come along since, but the team has picked up key free agents and continues to thrill fans on Long Island.

New York Jets (NFL). *The Meadowlands. 50 NJ 120, East Rutherford, NJ (07073). Phone 516/560-8100. www.newyorkjets.com.* The Jets began their tenure in the NFL with a bang, when "Broadway Joe" Namath guaranteed victory over the Baltimore Colts in Super Bowl III and then pulled off the feat. They now share their stadium with the New York Giants.

New York Knicks (NBA). *Madison Square Garden. Two Pennsylvania Plaza (10121). Phone 212/465-5867. www.nyknicks.com.* In the past, Knicks tickets have been nearly impossible to get because corporations and season ticket holders have snatched them up, but, depending on the team's current performance, you may be able to snag a couple of seats this season. Remember to be on the lookout for celebrities—Woody Allen and Spike Lee often attend games.

New York Liberty (WNBA). *Madison Square Garden. Two Pennsylvania Plaza (10121). Phone 212/564-WNBA. www.nyliberty.com.* The Liberty have been one of the more consistent WNBA teams despite no longer boasting the talents of original players like Rebecca Lobo. The team draws as well as any in the league, thanks in large part to playing in easily accessible Madison Square Garden.

New York Mets (MLB). *Shea Stadium. 123-01 Roosevelt Ave, Flushing (11368). Phone 718/507-6387. www.mets.com.* Although the Mets may not have as long and colorful a history as the Yankees, they are nonetheless a fun team to watch and offer baseball lovers a great spring or summer afternoon's or evening's experience. Tickets are usually easy to get, except for the annual match-up against the Yankees.

New York Rangers (NHL). *Madison Square Garden. Two Pennsylvania Plaza (10121). Phone 212/465-6741. www.newyorkrangers.com.* If you love the thrill of ice hockey—as well as the colorful fights that break out between players and the screaming, cursing fans on the sidelines—try to catch the popular New York Rangers in action. Because the team has done so well over the years, getting tickets has become very difficult. Buy yours months in advance if you can. Avoid the temptation to buy overpriced (or worse, counterfeit) tickets from the numerous scalpers who sell their wares in front of the Garden before each game. If you just can't get tickets but still want to experience live hockey while you're visiting New York, opt for a short commute to see either the New York Islanders (631/888-9000 for tickets) or the New Jersey Devils (201/935-6050 for tickets).

New York Yankees (MLB). *Yankee Stadium. E 161st St at River Ave, Bronx (10451). Phone 718/293-6000. www.yankees.com.* If you're a baseball fan and you're visiting New York City during the summer, you owe it to yourself to catch a Yankees game in the "House That Ruth Built." Watching the Bronx Bombers—a team that has won four World Series since 1996—is the quintessential New York experience.

NYC Marathon

Staten Island side of the Verrazano-Narrows Bridge (10024). Phone 212/860-4455. www.nyrrc.org. What event attracts more than 2 million spectators, 30,000 participants from every corner of the globe, and 12,000 volunteers? None other than the grueling 26.2-mile New York City Marathon. Whether you're an experienced runner or a diehard couch potato, to stand on the sidelines and cheer on these amazing men and women during the world's largest marathon is a thrilling and rewarding experience. The event begins on the Staten Island side of the Verrazano-Narrows Bridge, goes through all five boroughs of the city, and finishes up by Tavern on the Green restaurant in Central Park. Bring your camera, pack some bagels and coffee, and get ready to clap and holler. You'll feel really inspired afterward. First Sun in Nov.

Manhattan

When most people think of New York City, they think of Manhattan. When the first colonists arrived in 1626, Manhattan was a rugged, wooded island inhabited only by a small band of Native Americans at its northern end. A mere three and a half centuries later, it has become our most concentrated definition of the word "city." Only 12 1/2 miles long and 2 1/2 miles wide at its widest point, it is the center of American culture, communications, and business, containing an enormous variety of restaurants, shops, museums, and entertainment. Many superlatives are needed to describe Manhattan— it has the largest banks, several of the finest streets and avenues, one of the greatest city parks (Central Park), an incredible skyline, the greatest theater district, and the most sophisticated of almost everything. If Manhattanites sometimes forget that there is more to America than this tiny island, perhaps they may be forgiven. Their island is unique.

In this book, we have divided Manhattan into the following neighborhoods: Upper West Side/Harlem, Upper East Side, Midtown, Midtown East, Midtown West, Greenwich Village/SoHo, East Village/Lower East Side, and Lower Manhattan.

Upper West Side/Harlem

Primarily residential, the **Upper West Side** has traditionally been known as the liberal-leaning home of writers, intellectuals, musicians, dancers, doctors, lawyers, and other upper-middle-class professionals. A mix of ornate 19th-century landmarks, pre-World War II apartment buildings, and tenement houses, the Upper West Side stretches from 57th Street north to 110th Street and from Fifth Avenue west to the Hudson River. At its eastern border, between Fifth Avenue and Central Park West and 59th and 110th streets, Central Park sprawls out in a vast and beautifully landscaped expanse of green.

Anchoring the neighborhood to the south is one of its best-known addresses—the Lincoln Center for the Performing Arts (Broadway, between 62nd and 66th streets), which presents about 3,000 cultural events a year. Centering on a large, circular fountain, the 14-acre complex is home to such renowned institutions as the Metropolitan Opera House and Avery Fisher Hall. Many free outdoor concerts are presented on the plaza during the summer.

Directly across from Lincoln Center beckons a row of attractive restaurants and cafés, many with outdoor seating in summer. The Museum of American Folk Art (Broadway, between 65th and 66th streets), one of the city's smaller and more unusual museums, is also here. Another dozen or so blocks farther north, the Museum of Natural History (Central Park West, at 79th Street) is packed with everything from more than 100 dinosaur skeletons to artifacts from peoples around the world. Adjoining the museum on its north side is the state-of-the-art Rose Center for Earth and Space. Completed in 2000, the center is instantly recognizable for its unusual glass architecture revealing a globe within a triangle.

The Upper West Side didn't begin developing until the late 1800s, when a grand apartment building called the Dakota was built at what is now the corner of Central Park West and 72nd Street. At the time, the building was so far north of the rest of the city that New Yorkers said it was as remote as the state of Dakota—hence the name. Still standing today, the Dakota has been home to many celebrities, including Lauren Bacall, Gilda Radner, Boris Karloff, and John Lennon, who was fatally shot outside the building on December 8, 1980. In Central Park, directly across the street from the Dakota, is Strawberry Fields, a teardrop-shaped acre of land that Yoko Ono had landscaped in her husband's memory.

Central Park can be entered at major intersections all along Central Park West. Near the park's southern end, find Tavern on the Green (near Central Park West and 67th Street), a glittering extravaganza of a restaurant packed with mirrors and chandeliers. A bit farther north, find an odd-shaped body of water simply known as "The Lake" (between 72nd and 77th streets); rowboats can be rented at the Loeb Boathouse at the lake's eastern edge.

Stretching from 110th to 168th streets, between the Harlem and Hudson rivers, **Harlem** is in the midst of a renaissance. After years of being known primarily for its grinding poverty, drugs, and despair, the historic African American neighborhood is sprucing itself up, attracting mainstream businesses such as Starbucks and Ben & Jerry's, and becoming home once again to the middle class—African American and white.

Harlem can be divided in two: West/Central Harlem, which is primarily African American, and East Harlem, home to many Latinos and a smaller number of Italians. Between 110th and 125th streets west of Morningside Park is Morningside Heights, where Columbia University is located. Washington Heights, north of 155th Street, is home to Fort Tyron Park and the Cloisters, which houses the medieval collection of the Metropolitan Museum of Art.

First a farming community and then an affluent white suburb, Harlem began attracting African American residents after the construction of the IRT subway in 1901, and soon became the nation's premier African American neighborhood. The Harlem Renaissance boomed during the 1920s and 1930s, attracting writers and intellectuals such as Langston Hughes and W. E. B. DuBois, and the streets were packed with nightclubs, dance halls, and jazz clubs. Everything changed, however, with the Depression, when poverty took a strong hold that continues in many parts of the neighborhood today. When exploring Harlem, it's best to stick to the main thoroughfares.

The heart of Harlem is 125th Street, where you'll find a new Magic Johnson Theater complex, several restaurants and sweet shops offering soul food and baked goods, and the famed Apollo Theater (253 West 125th Street). Nearly every major jazz, blues, R&B, and soul artist to come along performed here, and the theater still presents its famed Amateur Night every Wednesday. Just down the street from the Apollo is the Studio Museum of Harlem (144 West 125th Street), a first-class fine arts institution spread over several floors of a turn-of-the-century building.

Another Harlem landmark is the Schomburg Center for Research in Black Culture (Lenox Avenue at 135th Street), founded by Arthur C. Schomburg, a Puerto Rican of African descent who was told as a child that his race had no history. Although primarily a library, the center also houses a large exhibit area where a wide array of changing exhibits is presented.

Not far from Columbia University, which is centered on Broadway and 116th Street, the Cathedral of St. John the Divine (Amsterdam Avenue at 112th Street), is the world's largest Gothic cathedral, said to be big enough to fit both Notre Dame and Chartres inside. Another major attraction nearby is Grant's Tomb (122nd Street at Riverside Drive), an imposing mausoleum sitting high on a bluff overlooking the Hudson.

What to See and Do

African American Wax Museum. *318 W 115th St (10026). Between Manhattan Ave and Frederick Douglass Blvd in Harlem. Phone 212/678-7818.* This tiny private place, created and run by Haitian-born artist Raven Chanticleer, is filled with wax figures of famous African Americans such as Frederick Douglass, Josephine Baker, and Nelson Mandela, as well as Chanticleer's own paintings and sculptures. (By appointment only) **DONATION**

American Bible Society Gallery/Library. *1865 Broadway (10023). Phone 212/408-1500. www.americanbible.org/gallery.* Changing exhibits run the gamut from stained glass in American art and architecture to the impact of the Bible on the world to religious folk art in Guatemala. Special events include lectures, workshops, and symposia. (Mon, Tues, Wed, Fri 10 am-6 pm; Thurs 10 am-7 pm; Sat 10 am-5 pm; closed holidays) **FREE**

⭐ **American Museum of Natural History.** *79th St and Central Park W (10024). Phone 212/769-5100; 212/769-5200. www.amnh.org.* Kids love this behemoth of a museum. Among its 36 million specimens are at least 100 dinosaur skeletons, including a huge Tyrannosaurus Rex whose serrated teeth alone measure 6 inches long. You may prefer to stroll through a roomful of free-flying butterflies or examine the 563-carat Star of India sapphire. Expect to be blown away by the 3-year-old Rose Center for Earth and Space and the Hayden Planetarium. The Planetarium Space Show is only 30 minutes long, but it's dazzling. Narrated by the likes of Tom Hanks and Harrison Ford, it uses the world's largest, most powerful projector, the Zeiss Mark IX, which was built to the museum's specifications. The show is one of unparalleled sophistication, accuracy, and excitement. Seating is limited, so choose a day for the museum and order tickets in advance. (Daily; closed Thanksgiving, Dec 25) **$$$$**

Hayden Planetarium at the Rose Center for Earth and Space. *Phone 212/769-5100. www.amnh.org/rose/haydenplanetarium.html.* Located in the four-block-long American Museum of Natural History, this exciting new planetarium will transport you to new galaxies. The planetarium is a huge sphere housed in a glass box several stories high. In the top part of the sphere is the Space Theater, which presents the awesome Space Show, a feat of sight and sound. The bottom part, called the Big Bang, re-creates the first moments of the universe in a multisensory format narrated by author and poet Maya Angelou. This is fun for the whole family that will leave everyone breathless. The admission price includes entrance to the Museum of Natural History and the rest of the Rose Center for Earth and Space, which features exhibits that cover cosmic evolution, discoveries in astrophysics, and the sizes of the universe's various heavenly bodies. (Daily; closed Thanksgiving, Dec 25) **$$$$**

Cathedral Church of St. John the Divine. *1047 Amsterdam Ave (10025). Phone 212/316-7540. www.stjohndivine.org.* Episcopal. Under construction since 1892. When completed, this will be the largest Gothic cathedral in the world, 601 feet long and 124 feet high. Bronze doors of the central portal represent scenes from the Old and New Testaments. The great rose window, 40 feet in diameter, is made up of more than 10,000 pieces of glass. Cathedral contains tapestry, painting, and sculpture collection. The cathedral and five other buildings are on 13 acres with park and garden areas, including the Biblical Garden. No parking provided. (Daily; tours Tues-Sat; also Sun following last morning service; no tours religious holidays) **$$**

Central Park. (see Midtown West)

Bicycle rentals at Loeb Boathouse. *Park Dr N and E 72nd St (10023). Phone 212/517-2233. www.nyctourist.com.* Central Park is an 843-acre oasis of calm in an otherwise chaotic city. Rent a bike for yourself and the kids and enjoy a ride through this sprawling mix of winding paths, meadows, lakes, and ponds. Take in the sight of dog walkers, kids playing softball, joggers—and an occasional homeless person. The park especially comes alive on the weekends in summer.

Children's Museum of Manhattan. *212 W 83rd St (10024). Phone 212/721-1234. www.cmom.org.* Hands-on exhibits for children 2-10; kids can draw and paint, learn crafts, play at being newscasters, listen to stories, or explore changing play areas. (June-Labor Day, Tues-Sun; closed holidays) **$$$**

City College of New York. *160 Convent Ave (10031). Phone 212/650-7000. www.ccny.cuny.edu.* (1847) 11,000 students. One of the nation's best-known municipal colleges and the oldest in the city university system. Alumni include eight Nobel laureates, Supreme Court Justice Felix Frankfurter, and authors Upton Sinclair, Paddy Chayefsky, and Bernard Malamud. Tours (Mon-Thurs, by appointment).

Claremont Riding Academy. *175 W 89th St (10024). Phone 212/724-5100. www.potomachorse.com/clarmont.htm.* Come to the oldest continuously operated stable in the United States to take a private or group lesson, or rent a horse and go for an unescorted walk, trot, or canter on Central Park's bridle paths. Escorted rides also are available for those with riding experience. Book as early as you can. Viewing the action from atop a beautiful horse on a mild, sunny day in the park can be quite peaceful—and is quite popular. (Daily; closed Dec 25) **$$$$**

⭐ **The Cloisters.** *In Fort Tryon Park, off Henry Hudson Pkwy, 1 exit N of George Washington Bridge. Phone 212/923-3700. www.netmuseum.org.* To escape the often frantic pace of the city, take the A train to Fort Tryon Park in Upper Manhattan where The Cloisters, the medieval branch of the Metropolitan Museum, perches peacefully on a bluff overlooking the Hudson River. Funded in large part by John D. Rockefeller Jr., The Cloisters houses an extraordinary collection of sculpture, illuminated manuscripts, stained glass, ivory, and precious metalwork, as well as the famed Unicorn tapestries. The architectural setting is as remarkable as its contents. Five cloisters (quadrangles enclosed by a roofed arcade), a chapter house, and chapels were taken from monasteries in France and Spain and reassembled stone by stone. In the Bonnefont Cloister, catch the spicy fragrance of the herb garden and take time to meditate; the sublime view of the Hudson Valley is always pristine. Donor Rockefeller also purchased the land across the river and restricted development there. (Tues-Sun; closed Jan 1, Thanksgiving, Dec 25) **$$$$**

Columbia University. *Broadway and 116th St. Phone 212/854-1754. www.columbia.edu.* (1754) 19,000 students. This Ivy League university was originally King's College; classes were conducted in the vestry room of Trinity Church. King's College still exists as Columbia College, with 3,000 students. The campus has more than 62 buildings, including Low Memorial Library, the administration building (which has the Rotunda and the Sackler Collection of Chinese Ceramics), and Butler Library, with more than 5 million volumes. The university numbers Alexander Hamilton, Gouverneur Morris, and John Jay among its early graduates and Nicholas Murray Butler, Dwight D. Eisenhower, and Andrew W. Cordier among its former presidents. Barnard College (1889), 2,300 women, and Teachers College (1887), 5,000 students, are affiliated with Columbia. Multilingual guided tours. (Mon-Fri except holidays and final exam period) **FREE**

The Dakota. *1 W 72nd St at Central Park W (10024).* The first and most famous of the lavish apartment houses on Central Park West, The Dakota got its name because it was considered so far west that New Yorkers joked that it might as well be in the Dakotas. Planned as a turreted, chateaulike structure, it was then embellished with Wild West ornamentation. It has been the home of many celebrities, including Judy Garland, Boris Karloff, and John Lennon and Yoko Ono. On December 8, 1980, The Dakota earned its tragic claim to fame when Lennon was shot and killed by a crazed fan at its gate. Five years later, Yoko Ono—who still resides here—had a section of Central Park visible from The Dakota landscaped with foliage and a mosaic with the title of Lennon's song, *Imagine.* Today, that area is known as Strawberry Fields.

Dyckman House Park and Museum. *4881 Broadway, at 204th St. Phone 212/304-9422.* (circa 1784) Only 18th-century Dutch farmhouse still on Manhattan Island. Built by William Dyckman; refurnished with some original Dyckman pieces and others of the period. Replica of British officers' hut on landscaped grounds; smokehouse; garden. (Tues-Sun; closed holidays) Children only with adult. **FREE**

Fordham University. *60th St and Columbus Ave (10023). Across from St. Paul's Church. Phone 212/636-6000. www.fordham.edu.* Private Jesuit university founded in 1841. Other campuses are located in the Bronx and Tarrytown.

General Grant National Memorial. *122nd St and Riverside Dr (10027). Phone 212/666-1640. www.nps.gov/gegr.* President and Mrs. Ulysses S. Grant are entombed here. (Daily; closed holidays)

Hamilton Grange National Memorial. *287 Convent Ave, at W 141st St. Phone 212/283-5154.* (1802) Federal-style residence of Alexander Hamilton. (Wed-Sun) **FREE**

Jewish Theological Seminary of America. *3080 Broadway at 122nd St. Phone 212/678-8000. www.jtsa.edu.* Extensive collection of Judaica; rare book room; courtyard with sculpture by Jacques Lipchitz. Special programs. Kosher cafeteria. Tours available. (Mon-Fri, Sun; closed holidays)

Lincoln Center for the Performing Arts. *70 Lincoln Center Plaza (10023). Phone 212/546-2656. www.lincolncenter.org.* The approach of curtain time at The Met is a glittering New York moment. People hurry across Lincoln Plaza and disappear under the ten-story marble arches that front the Opera House. The lobby empties, director James Levine raises his baton, and the overture begins. The Metropolitan Opera House, at the heart of Lincoln Center, is home to one of the world's greatest opera companies and the renowned American Ballet. At the right side of the square is Avery Fisher Hall, where Lorin Maazel conducts the New York Philharmonic and an impressive roster of guest artists perform. The Philharmonic's Mostly Mozart Festival in August and frequent Young People's Concerts for children are perennial favorites. Opposite is the New York State Theater, shared by the New York City Opera and the New York City Ballet, especially famous for its beloved holiday classic, Balanchine's *The Nutcracker*. In addition to the three main buildings, the 14-acre campus contains a multitude of other venues, including the Vivian Beaumont Theater, which presents Broadway plays; Alice Tully Hall, home of the Chamber Music Society and the New York Film Festival; and the world-famous Juilliard School. Damrosch Park and its band shell offer many free summer programs, including folk, jazz, and classical concerts. To get the big picture, take a Lincoln Center Guided Tour (212/875-5350), which includes stops at viewing booths when rehearsals are in session. (Daily; closed major holidays) **$$$**

Lincoln Center Guided Tours. *70 Lincoln Center Plaza (10023). Phone 212/ 875-5350 (reservations). www.lincolncenter.org.* Includes the Metropolitan Opera House, New York State Theater, and Avery Fisher Hall. The Tour Desk is located on the Concourse Level, downstairs from the Plaza. (Daily; no tours holidays). **$$**

Live TV shows. *For information regarding the availability of regular and/or standby tickets, contact NBC's ticket office at 30 Rockefeller Plaza, 10112 (phone 212/664-4000); CBS at 524 W 57th St, 10019 (phone 212/975-2476); or ABC at 77 W 66th St, 10023 (phone 212/456-7777).* On the day of the show, the New York Convention and Visitors Bureau at 2 Columbus Circle often has tickets for out-of-town visitors on a first-come, first-served basis. Except for NBC productions, many hotels can get tickets for guests with reasonable notice. (To see an important production, write four to six weeks in advance; the number of tickets is usually limited.) Most shows restricted to people over 18.

Metropolitan Opera Company. *Metropolitan Opera House, Lincoln Center, Broadway and 64th St (10023). Take the #1 or #9 subway to the 66th St stop. Phone 212/362-6000. www.metopera.org.* This is undoubtedly one of the world's leading opera companies. Some of the top performers can be seen on the massive, very impressive stage of the Metropolitan Opera House. Tickets go on sale in the March for the upcoming season, so book in advance. While prices can be high, it is worth spending the money on the best seats you can get if you are a true opera aficionado. When the lights go down, the curtain opens, and the orchestra begins playing, you will feel like you have been transported to another world. Attending the Metropolitan Opera also gives you a chance to get really dressed up and feel like a star yourself. Add an elegant dinner beforehand at a nearby Upper West Side restaurant and drinks afterwards at a lounge or piano bar and you may have the perfect evening. (Sept-May) **$$$$**

Morris-Jumel Mansion. *65 Jumel Terrace (10032). Phone 212/923-8008.* (1765) Built by Colonel Roger and Mary Philipse Morris, this was George Washington's headquarters in 1776 and later became a British command post and Hessian headquarters. Purchased by French merchant Stephen Jumel in 1810, house was the scene of the marriage of his widow, Madame Eliza Jumel, to Aaron Burr in 1833. The mansion is the only remaining colonial residence in Manhattan. Period furnishings. (Wed-Sun; closed holidays) **$$**

New York Historical Society. *2 W 77th St at Central Park W (10024). Phone 212/873-3400. www.nyhistory.org.* This monument to the history of the city recently reawakened after years of inactivity due to financial troubles. Spread out over many high-ceilinged rooms, the society presents temporary exhibits on everything from the legendary Stork Club—frequented by everyone from Frank Sinatra to JFK—to the small African-American communities that once dotted Central Park. The Henry Luce III Center for the Study of American culture features 40,000 objects, including George Washington's camp bed at Valley Forge to the world's largest collection of Tiffany lamps, as well as a nice collection of paintings, sculpture, furniture, and decorative objects. (Tues-Sun 11 am-6 pm) **$$**

New York Public Library for the Performing Arts. *40 Lincoln Center Plaza. Phone 212/870-1630.* Books, phonograph record collection; exhibits and research library on music, theater, and dance; concerts, films, dance recitals. **FREE**

Riverside Park. *W 72nd St to W 159th St along the Hudson River.* This city park, on the Upper West Side, offers a pleasant, bucolic setting that's even more laid back than Central Park. The long, narrow, breezy park has a promenade for bike riders between West 72nd and West 110th streets designed for those who want to take a nice, easy ride at a slow pace. Bike rentals are available at the nearby Toga Bike Shop (110 West End Ave, 212/799-9625). For even more relaxation, the 79th Street Boat Basin provides a quiet respite for walking on the river's edge. There's also a nearby café that's open in summer. The park offers some sightseeing in the way of Grant's Tomb, a towering granite tomb that is one of the world's largest mausoleums. It holds the remains of president Ulysses S. Grant and his wife, Julia—a must-see for Civil War history buffs. **FREE**

Schomburg Center for Research in Black Culture. *515 Malcolm X Blvd, at 135th St. Phone 212/491-2200.* The center's collection covers every phase of black activity wherever black people have lived in significant numbers. Books, manuscripts, periodicals, art, and audiovisual materials. **FREE**

The Studio Museum in Harlem. *144 W 125th St (10027). Phone 212/864-4500. www.studiomuseuminharlem.org.* Founded in 1968, this museum is the "principal center for the study of Black art in America," spread out over several well-lit floors of a turn-of-the-century building. The permanent exhibit features works by such masters as Romare Bearden, James

VanDerZee, and Jacob Lawrence; temporary exhibits present a mixture of both world-renowned and emerging artists. The Studio is also known for its lively lecture and concert series, presented September through May. (Wed-Fri noon-6 pm, Sat 10 am-6 pm, Sun noon-6 pm; closed Mon, Tues, and major holidays) **$$**

Washington Heights Museum Group. *Broadway and 155th St (10032).* (Audubon Terrace) Clustered around a central plaza and accessible from Broadway, this group includes the American Geographical Society and the American Academy and Institute of Arts and Letters, as well as the

> **American Numismatic Society.** *Phone 212/234-3130. www.amnumsoc.org.* Society headquarters; numismatic library; "World of Coins" exhibit; changing exhibits. (Tues-Fri; closed holidays) **FREE**

> **Hispanic Society of America.** *Phone 212/926-2234. www.hispanicsociety.org.* Art of the Iberian Peninsula from prehistoric times to present. Paintings, sculpture, ceramics, drawings, etchings, lithographs, textiles, and metal-work. (Tues-Sun; closed holidays) **FREE**

Yeshiva University. *500 W 185th St (10033). Phone 212/960-5400. www.yu.edu.* (1886) 6,300 students. America's oldest and largest university under Jewish auspices. Zysmon Hall, historic main building, has elaborate stone facade and Byzantine domes. Mendel Gottesman Library houses many specialized collections (academic year, Mon-Fri, Sun; closed holidays, Jewish holidays; tours by appointment). On campus is

> **Yeshiva University Museum.** *2520 Amsterdam Ave (10033). Phone 212/ 294-8330. www.yu.edu/museum.* Teaching museum devoted to Jewish art, architecture, history, and culture has permanent exhibits, including scale models of synagogues from the 3rd to 19th centuries; reproduction of frescoes from the Dura-Europos Synagogue; ceremonial objects, rare books; audiovisual presentations; theater; changing exhibits. (Academic year, Tues-Thurs, Sun; closed major holidays, Jewish holidays) **$$$**

Zabar's. *2245 Broadway (10024). Phone 212/787-2000. www.zabars.com.* Zabar's is one of those places that makes New York the yummy place that it is. This second-generation gourmet food market, considered sacred by those who enjoy fine eating, has graced Manhattan's Upper West Side since 1934. Occupying close to one city block and employing 250 people, Zabar's sells sinful breads and pastries, meats, cheeses, smoked fish, condiments, and cookware. The shop's babka (Russian coffee cake) makes life worth living. Since Zabar's is one of the rare establishments in New York that's open every day of the year, you can treat your taste buds anytime you like. Forget diets and just enjoy. (Daily)

Special Events

Christmas Star Show. *Hayden Planetarium, 79th St and Central Park W (10024). Phone 212/769-5920.* Late Nov-early Jan.

New York Shakespeare Festival & Shakespeare in the Park. *81st St and Central Park W or 79th St and Fifth Ave (10024). Phone 212/539-8750. www.centralpark.org.* At the 2,000-seat outdoor Delacorte Theater in Central

Park, near W 81st St. Tues-Sun. Free tickets are distributed on the day of the performance. June-Sept.

The Nutcracker. *New York State Theater. 20 Lincoln Center (10023). Phone 212/870-5570. www.nycballet.com.* Taking your child (and yourself!) to the New York City Ballet's performance of *The Nutcracker* is one of those magical events that both tourists and New Yorkers love to take in during the colorful, festive Christmas season. This fantasy story of the Mouse King and little Clara has delighted children for many years. The New York Ballet's version of this classic is sure to please, with renowned dancers, some of the most appealing young performers, beautiful music by Tchaikovsky, and luscious sets and costumes. No ballet lover should miss a performance of *The Nutcracker* while visiting New York City during Christmas. Dec.

Summer Events in Central Park and Lincoln Center. *Broadway and 64th St (Lincoln Center) (10023). Events held throughout the park and at Lincoln Center. Take the #1 or #9 subway to the 66th Street stop to get to Lincoln Center. Phone 212/546-2656 (Lincoln Center). www.centralpark.org.* The city comes alive in summer with a plethora of wonderful, free cultural events that run the gamut and appeal to all ages. Central Park hosts a variety of musical performances by the New York Philharmonic and the Metropolitan Opera Co. In addition, its SummerStage (212/360-2777) attracts a mix of pop, blues, and rock stars. At nearby Lincoln Center, free concerts and dance performances are held during August at its Damrosch Park outdoor area. All these events, coupled with brunch or a casual picnic in the park, are a great, budget-conscious way to spend a warm, sunny day in the Big Apple. (Daily)

Hotels

★ ★ **HOTEL BEACON.** *2130 Broadway at 75th St (10023). Phone 212/787-1100; toll-free 800/572-4969; fax 212/724-0839. www.beaconhotel.com.* 241 rooms. Check-out noon. TV; VCR available. Laundry services. Health club privileges. Parking. **$$**

⊡ ⊠ 🆂🅲

★ ★ **MAYFLOWER ON THE PARK.** *15 Central Park W (10023). Phone 212/265-0060; toll-free 800/223-4164; fax 212/265-0227. www.mayflower hotelny.com.* 365 rooms, 18 story. Pets accepted. Check-out noon, check-in 3 pm. TV; cable (premium). In-room modem link. Restaurant, bar. Room service. In-house fitness room. Valet parking. Concierge. **$$$**

🔾 🐾 ⊠

★ ★ ★ ★ **TRUMP INTERNATIONAL HOTEL & TOWER.** *1 Central Park W (10023). Phone 212/299-1000; toll-free 888/448-7867; fax 212/299-1150. www.trumpintl.com.* Occupying an enviable site across from Central Park on Manhattan's Upper West Side, the 52-story Trump International Hotel & Tower makes guests feel like they are on top of the world. The lobby's warm brass tones and polished marble welcome visitors to the world of Trump, where attention to detail results in perfection and everyone feels like a tycoon. The rooms and suites are elegantly decorated with a contemporary

European flavor, while the floor-to-ceiling windows focus attention on the mesmerizing views of Central Park framed by the impressive skyline. The Personal Attaché service ensures that all guests are properly coddled, while the extensive fitness center caters to exercise enthusiasts. All suites and most rooms are complete with kitchens, and in-room chefs are available to craft memorable dining experiences. Room service is world-class and created by one of New York's top chefs, Jean-Georges Vongerichten, whose Five-Star restaurant, Jean-Georges (see), is located here. *Secret Inspector's Notes:* Dinner at Jean-Georges is the one component of this hotel not to be missed. It is one of the finest dining experiences you'll find. 168 rooms, 52 story. Pets accepted. Check-out noon, check-in 4 pm. Valet parking. TV; cable (premium), VCR available. In-room modem link. Restaurant, bar. Room service. Babysitting services available. In-house fitness room, sauna, steam room, massage, spa. Indoor pool. Business center. Concierge. **$$$$**

D 🛏 🏊 🧍 🚭 🏃

Restaurants

★ ★ ★ **CAFÉ DES ARTISTES.** *1 W 67th St (10023). Phone 212/877-3500; fax 212/877-7754. www.cafedesartistesnyc.com.* Café des Artistes is a timeless New York City classic. Originally fashioned after the English Ordinary, a cozy bistro with a limited menu based on food available in the market, the Café was a regular meeting place where local artists in the neighborhood would come together to discuss their creative works. Today, the restaurant remains an old-guard favorite for its luxurious, sophisticated setting, impeccable service, and menu of up-to-the-minute, yet approachable, seasonal, French bistro fare. While elegant in its art-filled décor, the restaurant's menu does not try too hard, over-flourish, or over-think things. The kitchen stays true to its roots, offering satisfying French food like steak frites, rack of lamb, oysters, and goujonettes. Country French menu. Closed Dec 25. Dinner, Sat, Sun brunch. Bar. Jacket required (after 5 pm). **$$$**

★ ★ **CAFÉ LUXEMBOURG.** *200 W 70th St (10023). Phone 212/873-7411; fax 212/721-6854. www.cafelux.com.* American, French menu. Dinner. Bar. Near Lincoln Center. **$$$**

D

★ **CARMINE'S.** *2450 Broadway (10024). Phone 212/362-2200; fax 212/362-0742. www.carminesnyc.com.* Southern Italian menu. Lunch, dinner. Bar. Dining room, originally a hotel ballroom, is re-creation of 1940s neighborhood Italian restaurant. Outdoor seating. **$$$**

D SC

★ ★ **FIORELLO'S ROMAN CAFE.** *1900 Broadway (10023). Phone 212/595-5330; fax 212/496-2471. www.cafefiorello.com.* Italian menu. Closed Dec 25. Lunch, dinner, late night, Sat, Sun brunch. Bar. Glass-front Italian trattoria with contemporary art; antipasto bar. Casual attire. Reservations required. Outdoor seating. Totally nonsmoking. **$$$**

D

★ ★ ★ **GABRIEL'S.** *11 W 60th St (10023). Phone 212/956-4600; fax 212/ 956-2309. www.gabrielsbarandrest.com.* The dining room is comfortable but sophisticated and provides good service. Italian menu. Closed Sun; holidays. Lunch, dinner. Bar. Casual attire. **$$$**

D

★ ★ ★ ★ ★ **JEAN GEORGES.** *1 Central Park W (10023). Phone 212/299-3900; fax 212/299-3914. www.trumpintl.com.* Perfection is a word that comes to mind when speaking of meals at Jean-Georges. Heaven is another word and divine yet another. Located in the Trump International Hotel and Tower (see) across from Central Park, Jean-Georges is a shrine to haute cuisine. Drawing influences from around the world, the menu is conceived and impeccably executed by celebrity chef-owner (and author) Jean-Georges Vongerichten. Vongerichten is a man of meticulous discipline, and it shows on the plate. Nothing is present that shouldn't be there. Under Vongerichten's direction, ingredients shine, flavors spark, and the mouth trembles. Suffice it to say that you will be in heaven within minutes of the meal's commencement. The room is sophisticated and stunning, yet remains comfortable. You'll find that it's filled nightly with well-known names, high-powered financial moguls, actors, models, and local New Yorkers who are lucky enough to score reservations. Call well in advance. It is worth the time it may take you to get through. If you can't manage to secure a table, try your luck at Nougatine, the popular café in the outer bar area. It has a simpler menu but will give you a taste of what Vongerichten is capable of. The bar is also a lovely place to meet for an aperitif or a cocktail before dinner or a walk through the park. *Secret Inspector's Notes:* On a lucky evening, Donald Trump may be dining at his favorite table with his guest du jour being catered to hand and foot by the proficient and attentive staff. French menu. Dinner. Bar. Jacket required. Reservations required. Valet parking available. Outdoor seating. **$$$$**

D

★ ★ ★ **PICHOLINE.** *35 W 64th St (10023). Phone 212/724-8585; fax 212/875-8979.* Picholine is a great choice for dinner if you happen to be attending an opera, ballet, or play at Lincoln Center. Don't feel like you need to be heading over to Lincoln Center in order to dine here, though; chef-owner Terrance Brennan's lovely, serene restaurant is easy to enjoy all by itself, which is probably why Picholine is often pleasantly packed with a savvy set of New Yorkers at both lunch and dinner, with no ticket stubs to be found. The menu changes with the seasons, and the chef uses organic and local ingredients as much as possible. Picholine is a safe bet for both adventurous diners and conservative eaters and for vegetarians and meat lovers alike. The menu runs the gamut from the exotic to the familiar, offering a wide selection of dishes from the land and the sea. Folks with a weakness for cheese are in the right place as well. The cheese list (not to mention the great wine list) is one of the best in the city, and room must be saved to indulge in several types. The wine list, though seriously priced, offers a variety of selections to match all courses, and the staff is helpful and eager to be of assistance with any request. *Secret Inspector's Notes:* Picholine has by far the best cheese program in New York. True cheese lovers may want to just visit the bar for a full-bodied glass of wine and a mind-altering plate of cheese. Be forewarned, though; the dining room staff is unabashedly stuffy and snooty and must be ignored at times so as not to detract from the fantastic flavors offered by the talented kitchen. French, Mediterranean menu. Closed holidays. Dinner. Bar. **$$$**

D

★ ★ **RAIN.** *100 W 82nd St (10024). Phone 212/501-0776; fax 212/501-9147.* Thai menu. Closed Dec 25. Dinner. Bar. **$$**

D

★ ★ ★ **ROSA MEXICANO.** *61 Columbus Ave (10023). Phone 212/977-7700. www.rosamexicano.com.* Mexican menu. Dinner. **$$$**

★ ★ **SARABETH'S.** *423 Amsterdam Ave (10024). Phone 212/496-6280; fax 212/787-9655. www.sarabeths.com.* Closed Dec 25. Dinner, Sat, Sun brunch. Totally nonsmoking. **$$**

D

★ ★ **SHUN LEE.** *43 W 65th St (10023). Phone 212/595-8895; fax 212/799-3598.* You won't find typical white-carton options at this urban Chinese outpost with an eclectic menu. The drama is evident in the décor and on the plates—from the white ceramic monkeys hanging off the bar to the specialty sweetbreads with black mushrooms. Chinese menu. Closed Thanksgiving. Lunch, dinner. Bar. Jacket required. **$$$**

D

★ ★ **TAVERN ON THE GREEN.** *Central Park at W 67th St (10023). Phone 212/873-3200; fax 212/580-4265. www.tavernonthegreen.com.* Contemporary American menu. Lunch, dinner, Sat, Sun brunch. Bar. Elaborate décor; in 1874 building within Central Park. Valet parking available. Garden terrace. **$$$**

D

Upper East Side

Long associated with wealth, much of the Upper East Side—stretching from 57th Street north to 106th Street and Fifth Avenue east to the East River—is filled with elegant mansions and brownstones, clubs, and museums. Many of the city's most famous museums—including the Metropolitan Museum of Art—are located here, along with several posh hotels and Gracie Mansion, home to New York City's mayor.

But the neighborhood is about more than just wealth. Remnants of what was once a thriving German community can be found along the 86th Street-Second Avenue nexus, while a Puerto Rican and Latin community begins in the upper 80s, east of Lexington Avenue. At the corner of 96th Street and Third Avenue is a surprising sight—the Islamic Cultural Center, a modern, gold-domed mosque flanked by a skinny minaret.

Many of the Upper East Side's cultural institutions are located on Fifth Avenue, facing Central Park, along what is known as "Museum Mile." The Frick Collection, housing the private art collection of the former 19th-century industrialist Henry Clay Frick, marks the mile's southernmost end, at 70th Street. El Museo del Barrio, dedicated to the art and culture of Latin America, marks the northernmost end, at 104th Street. In between reign the grand Metropolitan Museum of Art (at 82nd Street), huge flags flapping out front, and the circular, Frank Lloyd Wright-designed Guggenheim Museum (at 88th Street)—to name just two.

The Plaza Hotel beckons from the southern end of the Upper East Side (Fifth Avenue, between 58th and 59th streets). This magnificent French Renaissance-style edifice was built in 1907 and is now owned by Donald Trump. Directly across Fifth Avenue from the hotel, FAO Schwarz is an imaginative toy store that's as much fun for adults as it is for kids. Central Park is directly across 59th Street. Horse-drawn hansoms and their drivers congregate along the streets here, waiting hopefully for tourists interested in taking a clip-clopping tour. The small but state-of-the-art Central Park Zoo can be found in the park near Fifth Avenue and 65th Street.

Shoppers will want to take a gander at the many upscale boutiques lining Madison Avenue between 57th and 90th streets, or take a stroll over to Bloomingdale's (Lexington Avenue at 59th Street). Fifty-Seventh Street holds numerous world-famous galleries, including PaceWildenstein (32 East 57th Street) and Andre Emmerich (41 East 57th Street), as well as such popular tourist stops as the Warner Brothers Studio Store (57th Street at Fifth Avenue) and Niketown (6 East 57th Street). The infamous St. Patrick's Day Parade, attracting hordes of rowdy revelers, travels down Fifth Avenue from 86th Street to 44th Street every March 17th.

What to See and Do

The Asia Society Galleries. *725 Park Ave (10021). Phone 212/288-6400. www.asiasociety.org.* Masterpieces of Asian art, donated by founder John Rockefeller, make up most of this museum's permanent collection. Its works include sculptures, ceramics, and paintings from places like China, Korea, Japan, and India. In addition, the museum offers a schedule of films, performances, and lectures. The Asia Society also has a lovely indoor sculpture garden and café, which make for a nice stop on a hectic day of sightseeing. (Tues-Sun; closed Mon) **$$$**

Central Park. (see Midtown West)

Cooper-Hewitt National Design Museum. *2 E 91st St, at Fifth Ave. Phone 212/849-8400. www.si.edu/ndm.* Once home to 19th-century industrialist Andrew Carnegie, this 64-room 1901 Georgian mansion is now a branch of the Smithsonian Institution dedicated to design and the decorative arts. The exhibits are temporary and focus on such subjects as ceramics, furniture, textiles, and metalwork. Out back is a romantic garden, where concerts are sometimes presented. (Tues-Thurs 10 am-5 pm, Fri 10 am-9 pm, Sat 10 am-6 pm, Sun noon-6 pm; closed holidays) **$$**

El Museo del Barrio. *1230 Fifth Ave (10029). Phone 212/831-7272. www.elmuseo.org.* Dedicated to Puerto Rican and other Latin American art, this museum features changing exhibits on both contemporary and historic subjects and houses a superb permanent collection of *santos de palo,* or carved wooden saints. The museum also hosts films, theater, concerts, and educational programs. Inquire about bilingual tours. (Wed-Sun; closed holidays.) **$$**

The Frick Collection. *1 E 70th St (10021). Phone 212/288-0700. www.frick.org.* The mansion of Henry Clay Frick, wealthy tycoon, infamous strikebreaker, and avid collector of art, contains a remarkably diverse assemblage of paintings. The walls of one room are covered with large, frothy Fragonards depicting the "Progress of Love." In other rooms are masterworks by Bellini, Titian, Holbein, Rembrandt, El Greco, Turner, Degas, and many others. A superb collection in a superb setting. See it in one afternoon. (Tues-Sun; closed holidays) No children under 10; under 16 only with adult. **$$$$**

Jewish Museum. *1109 Fifth Ave at 92nd St. Phone 212/423-3200. www.jewishmuseum.org.* Devoted to Jewish art and culture, ancient and modern. Historical exhibits; contemporary painting and sculpture. (Mon-Thurs and Sun, afternoons; closed Jewish holidays) **$$$**

Kitchen Arts. *1435 Lexington Ave (10128). Phone 212/876-5550. www.kitchen artsandletters.com.* Great cooks and novices alike can spend hours in this store, which features more than 10,000 cookbooks from all over the world. You can find the hottest new books by the most popular chefs, as well as those that have been out of print for years. Whether you want to prepare complicated desserts or perfect the art of the grilled cheese sandwich, this store will have the right cookbook for you. (Mon-Sat; closed Sun, major holidays)

Lexington Avenue. *Take the #6 Lexington Ave subway to 28th St.* It may be only a three-block area just south of Murray Hill, but this neighborhood is brimming with the sights and sounds of India. Stores sell Indian and Pakistani spices, pastries, videos, cookware, saris, and fabrics. Restaurants cater to both Muslim and Hindu tastes, suiting both beefeaters and vegetarians. The low prices are a treat as well.

★ **Metropolitan Museum of Art.** *1000 Fifth Ave at 82nd St. Phone 212/535-7710. www.metmuseum.org.* Vast, exhilarating, and a little unsettling to first-time visitors because of the number and diversity of its collections, the Metropolitan Museum of Art contains more than 2 million objects spanning a period of more than 5,000 years. Even with a map and an audio guide (for which you pay extra), getting lost is not difficult—it is also part of the experience. Finding the Rooftop Garden and its population of modern sculptures is easy. Stumbling across Michelangelo's sketch for the Sistine Chapel or the stunning state-of-the-art Costume Gallery may be a rewarding surprise. From the ancient Roman tomb, The Temple of Dendur, to a room designed by Frank Lloyd Wright in 1912, and from Picasso's powerful portrait of Gertrude Stein to the oddly surrealistic wood panel, St. Anthony in the Wilderness by an unknown Italian master, the Met presents both familiar masterpieces and intriguing hidden treasures. You could spend days here. Plan to spend enough time to see what you'll most enjoy! Call ahead or ask at the Information Desk about free tours, concerts, lectures, and films. There are always special exhibits and children's programs, but strollers are not allowed on Sundays or at special exhibits. (Tues-Sun; closed Jan 1, Thanksgiving, Dec 25) **$$$$**

Museum of the City of New York. *1220 Fifth Ave (10029). Phone 212/534-1672. www.mcny.org.* Explore unique aspects of the city in this Upper East Side mansion dating back to 1930. Displays include a toy gallery with dollhouses; collections of decorative arts, prints, and photographs; and an exhibit on Broadway, complete with costumes and set designs. Other exhibits feature slide shows, paintings, memorabilia, and sculptures, all dedicated to the fascinating history of the city up to the present day. (Wed-Sat 10 am-5 pm, Sun noon-5 pm; closed Mon, legal holidays) **$$$**

Solomon R. Guggenheim Museum. *1071 Fifth Ave (10128). Between E 88th and 89th sts. Phone 212/423-3500. www.guggenheim.org.* Some say that the Guggenheim looks like a giant snail or an upside-down wedding cake. Few would deny that Frank Lloyd Wright's brilliant concept of ever-widening concrete circles around a central atrium provided an intriguing new way to display art—especially in 1959 when the museum opened. Take the elevator to the top and walk down the gently sloping spiral to view temporary exhibits that draw a diversity of viewers. Past shows have included "Centre Pompidou" from Paris, "Norman Rockwell: Pictures for the American People," and "Art of the Motorcycle." A smaller adjoining rotunda and tower hold a stunning permanent collection heavy in works by Wassily Kandinsky, Paul Klee, Francois Leger, and Marc Chagall, as well as by the French Impressionists. Pablo Picasso is well represented, especially in his early Blue Period, including "Woman Ironing," the artist's well-known depiction of labor and fatigue. Free docent-led tours are scheduled daily at noon. (Sat-Wed 10 am-5:45 pm, Fri 10 am-8 pm; closed holidays) **$$**

Sotheby's Auctions. *1334 York Ave (10021). Phone 212/606-7000. www.sothebys.com.* Get a taste of high society at a Sotheby's auction. Whether you're just a spectator or you have lots of spare cash with which to purchase something wonderful, attending an auction at this institution is a thrilling, fast-paced experience. Sotheby's has held auctions for items belonging to the Duke and Duchess of Windsor and other celebrities. It has fashion, book and manuscript, and vintage car departments, just to name a few. Sotheby's Arcade features more affordable items. Publications like *New York* magazine and *The New York Times* contain listings of upcoming events. (Closed major holidays)

Temple Emanu-El. *One E 65th St (10021). Phone 212/744-1400. www.emanuelnyc.org.* Largest Jewish house of worship in the world; Reform Congregation founded in 1845. Romanesque temple seats 2,500; Beth-El chapel seats 350. (Daily; no visiting on High Holy Days) Tours (by appointment, upon written request).

Whitney Museum of American Art. *945 Madison Ave, at E 75th St. Phone 212/570-3676. www.whitney.org.* Bauhaus-trained architect Marcel Breuer's museum is menacingly cantilevered toward Madison Avenue. Its bold, sculptural quality makes it a fitting home for modern and contemporary art. The impressive permanent collection takes American art from the early 20th century into the 21st, showing realistic works by Thomas Hart Benton, Edward Hopper, and Georgia O'Keeffe as well as works by later artists such as Alexander Calder, Louise Nevelson, Robert Rauschenberg, and Jasper Johns. The controversial Whitney "Biennial" showcases the latest works of contemporary artists. (Tues-Sun; closed Jan 1, Thanksgiving, Dec 25) **$$$$**

Special Events

Central Park Concerts. *Central Park (see MIDTOWN WEST). Phone 212/360-3456.* Free performances by the New York Philharmonic and the Metropolitan Opera Company on the Great Lawn, mid-park at 81st St. June-Aug.

Hispanic Day Parade. *Fifth Ave between 44th and 86th sts (10036).* Mid-Oct.

Macy's Thanksgiving Day Parade. *34th and 72nd sts (10001). Phone 212/494-5432; 212/494-4495.* If you have a child or you want to feel like a kid again yourself, spend Thanksgiving Day morning enjoying this wonderful and festive New York event. Amazing floats, cheerful clowns (who are all volunteers and are either Macy's employees or friends and families of Macy's employees), and celebrities are all part of the parade, which starts at 9 am and ends at around noon. The atmosphere is always jovial and will put you in the holiday spirit. Since you may spend most of the time standing, wear comfortable shoes, dress in layers, bring snacks, and duck into nearby eateries for hot drinks and bathroom breaks. Keep in mind that standing for several hours may be too tiring for children under 5 (unless they spend most of the time perched atop your shoulders, which may be too tiring for you!). One of the best viewing spots is on Herald Square in front of Macy's.

Hotels

★ ★ ★ ★ **THE CARLYLE.** *35 E 76th St (10021). Phone 212/744-1600; toll-free 800/227-5737; fax 212/717-4682. www.rosewoodhotels.com.* Discreetly tucked away on Manhattan's Upper East Side, The Carlyle has maintained the allure of being one of New York's best-kept secrets for more than 70 years. A favorite of many movie stars, presidents, and royals, The Carlyle feels like an exclusive private club with its white-glove service and impeccable taste. Its art collection is extraordinary, from Audubon prints and Piranesi architectural drawings to English country scenes by Kips. Art factors largely at The Carlyle, where all rooms are equipped with direct lines to Sotheby's. The rooms are completed in an Art Deco décor and are enhanced by striking antiques and bountiful bouquets. Populated by power brokers and socialites, The Carlyle Restaurant defines elegance. Bemelmans Bar proudly shows off its murals by *Madeline* creator Ludwig Bemelmans, while guests have been tapping their toes to the tunes of Bobby Short for more than 30 years in the Café Carlyle. 180 rooms, 35 story. Pets accepted, some restrictions. Check-out noon, check-in 3 pm. TV; cable (premium), VCR available, CD available. In-room modem link. Room service 24 hours.

Restaurant, bar; entertainment. In-house fitness room, massage, sauna, steam room. Valet parking. **$$$$**

D ⚑ 🏃 ⊠

★ ★ ★ **HOTEL PLAZA ATHENEE.** *37 E 64th St (10021). Phone 212/734-9100; toll-free 800/447-8800; fax 212/772-0958. www.plaza-athenee.com.* Hotel Plaza Athéneé is the perfect place to enjoy a little bit of France while visiting New York. Located between Park and Madison avenues in one of the city's most exclusive neighborhoods, this elegant hotel is a perfect hideaway with a decidedly residential feel. Celebrating its place among the boutiques of Madison Avenue, the townhouses and apartment buildings of Park Avenue, and the greenery of Central Park, the Plaza Athéneé indeed feels like a home away from home for its guests. A palette of blues, golds, and reds creates the French contemporary décor of the rooms and suites. Some suites have dining rooms, while others have indoor terraces or outdoor balconies. The exotic flavor of the Bar Seine, with its vibrant colors and striking furnishings, transports guests to a faraway land, while Arabelle Restaurant combines gracious French style with delicious continental cuisine. 150 rooms, 17 story. Pets accepted. Check-out noon, check-in 3 pm. TV; cable (premium), VCR available. In-room modem link. Room service 24 hours. Restaurant, bar. In-house fitness room. Concierge. **$$$$**

D ⚑ 🏃 ⊠

★ ★ **HOTEL WALES.** *1295 Madison Ave (10128). Phone 212/876-6000; toll-free 800/428-5252; fax 212/860-7000. www.boutiquehg.com.* 92 suites, 10 story. Complimentary continental breakfast. Check-out noon. TV; cable (premium), VCR available. Restaurant. Room service. Health club privileges. Valet parking. Restored 1902 hotel; original fireplaces. **$$$**

★ ★ ★ ★ **THE LOWELL.** *28 E 63rd St (10021). Phone 212/838-1400; toll-free 800/221-4444; fax 212/319-4230. www.lhw.com.* Located in a landmark 1920s building in the historic district of the Upper East Side, The Lowell provides a refreshing change of pace. Its rooms and suites capture the essence of an elegant country house with a delightful blend of English prints, floral fabrics, and Chinese porcelains. Many suites boast woodburning fireplaces—a rarity in Manhattan. All rooms are individually decorated, and The Lowell's specialty suites are a unique treat. The Garden Suite takes its inspiration from English country gardens and has two terraces, one complete with a rose garden and fountain. The glamour of the 1930s silver screen is recalled in the Hollywood Suite, while the Gym Suite, originally created for Madonna, is perfect for exercise buffs. The English influences extend to the Pembroke Room, where a proper tea is served, as are breakfast and brunch. Resembling a gentleman's club, the Post House (see), a well-respected New York steakhouse, is a paradise for carnivores. *Secret Inspector's Notes:* The rooms may seem sparse in their modernism for guests who prefer more conventional styles of décor. Those leaning toward modernism will find the rooms serene in their functionality and simplicity. 70 rooms, 17 story. Check-out noon, check-in 3 pm. TV; cable (premium), VCR available. In-room modem link. Fireplaces. Room service 24 hours. Restaurant.

Babysitting services available. In-house fitness room, health club privileges. Valet parking. Concierge. **$$$$**

★ ★ ★ **THE MARK NEW YORK.** *25 E 77th St (10021). Phone 212/ 744-4300; toll-free 800/THEMARK; fax 212/744-2749. www.mandarin oriental.com.* Take a break from the shopping of Madison Avenue and the museums of the Upper East Side and enter the haven of The Mark New York, where style and comfort combine for an exceptional experience. Situated on a quiet tree-lined street, The Mark feels like an elegant private home. The hotel's eclectic décor perfectly blends the clean lines of Italian design with the lively spirit of English florals. Asian decorative objects and Piranesi prints complete the look in the hotel's rooms and suites. Sophisticated cuisine is highlighted at Mark's Restaurant, where the Master Sommelier also offers wine-tasting courses and themed dinners. Afternoon tea at The Mark is especially notable thanks to the Tea Master, who ensures that little bits of America and the Orient are brought to this British tradition. Mark's Bar, a jewel-toned bôite, is particularly popular with local denizens as well as hotel guests. 176 rooms, 16 story. Pets accepted. Check-out noon, check-in 3 pm. TV; cable (premium), VCR available. In-room modem link. Room service 24 hours. Restaurant, bar. In-house fitness room, sauna, steam room. Valet parking. Concierge. **$$$**

★ ★ ★ ★ **THE PIERRE NEW YORK, A FOUR SEASONS HOTEL.** *2 E 61st St (10021). Phone 212/838-8000; toll-free 800/743-7734; fax 212/940-8109. www.fourseasons.com.* Regal and esteemed, The Pierre New York is the definition of a grand old hotel. Relishing its location across from Central Park on Fifth Avenue, The Pierre has been a city landmark since 1930. Owned by Charles Pierre and John Paul Getty, among others, The Pierre is now managed by Four Seasons, which carefully maintains the integrity of this historic building while imparting its signature service levels with mixed success. Guests linger for hours in the impressive lobby, soaking up the ambience of old-world Europe. The rooms and suites are traditional with floral prints and antique reproductions. The Rotunda, where breakfast, light lunch, and afternoon tea are served, is a magical place where the cares of the world disappear under a ceiling of trompe l'oeil murals. Influenced by Renaissance paintings, the murals depict pastoral scenes of mythological figures intertwined with icons of the 1960s, including Jacqueline Kennedy Onassis. *Secret Inspector's Notes:* Don't be disappointed by the small rooms, aging bathrooms, and occasionally brusque service. This is still a hotel in the ultimate location for accessing all the wonders of Manhattan in the surrounding blocks. 201 rooms, 41 story. Pets accepted. Check-out noon, check-in 3 pm. TV; cable (premium), VCR available. In-room modem link. Room service 24 hours. Restaurant, bar; entertainment. Babysitting services available. In-house fitness room, health club privileges, massage. 24-hour valet parking. Business center. Concierge. **$$$$**

★ ★ ★ ★ **THE REGENCY HOTEL.** *540 Park Ave (10021). Phone 212/759-4100; toll-free 800/233-2356; fax 212/826-5674. www.loewshotels.com.* Home of the original power breakfast, where deals are sealed and fortunes are made, The Regency consistently ranks as one of New York's top hotels. Combining the appearance of a library and a private club, The Regency provides attentive service that extends above and beyond the ordinary to create a memorable stay. International design influences create a warm atmosphere throughout the well-appointed rooms, while the fitness and business centers cater to guests with specific goals in mind. Creature comforts abound in the luxurious rooms and suites, from the Frette linens to the "Did You Forget" closet stocked with items often left at home. Pets are even welcomed in grand style with room service designed exclusively for man's best friend, as well as dog-walking services and listings of pet-friendly establishments. Unwind at Feinstein's, where Grammy-nominated Michael Feinstein entertains nightly, or savor a delectable meal at 540 Park (see) or The Library. 351 rooms, 20 story. Pets accepted. Check-out noon, check-in 3 pm. TV; cable (premium), VCR available, CD available. In-room modem link. Room service 24 hours. Restaurant, bar. In-house fitness room, massage, sauna. Valet parking. Business center. Concierge. **$$$**

D 🐾 🏋 🏊 🏃

★ ★ ★ ★ **THE STANHOPE, A PARK HYATT HOTEL.** *995 Fifth Ave at 81st St (10028). Phone 212/774-1234; toll-free 800/233-1234; fax 212/517-0088. www.hyatt.com.* Since 1926, The Stanhope Park Hyatt New York has endured as one of New York's favorite hotels. Directly across from the prestigious Metropolitan Museum of Art on Fifth Avenue, The Stanhope is situated in the middle of famed Museum Mile, with the Guggenheim, Whitney, and Cooper-Hewitt museums enticing visitors just several blocks away. The Stanhope's gracious European style is evident in its public spaces, where antiques and gold-leafing details catch the eye. The rooms and suites are richly decorated with pastel walls, antique reproduction furnishings, and Chinoiserie accents. The dark wood paneling of the Bar makes it an intimate spot for gatherings, while Melrose entertains in grand style with contemporary American cuisine. In perhaps one of the most enviable dining spots in New York, Melrose opens its outdoor terrace for dining with a view of the Met in warmer months. 185 rooms, 17 story. Pets accepted; fee. Check-out noon. TV; cable (premium), VCR available. Restaurant, bar. Room service. Exercise room, massage, sauna. Valet parking. Business center. Concierge. **$$$**

D 🐾 🏋 🏊 SC 🏃

★ ★ ★ **THE SURREY HOTEL.** *20 E 76th St (10021). Phone 212/288-3700; toll-free 800/637-8483; fax 212/628-1549. www.mesuite.com.* Like staying at the home of a rich great-aunt, this hotel has the understated grandeur of a faded residence. You'll see old-world charm upon entering the lobby, with its 18th-century English décor, wood-paneled elevators, and leather sofas. The studio, one-bedroom, and two-bedroom suites have a similar look, with molded ceilings, beveled-glass mirrors, and antique accents. Some have kitchenettes, and others have full kitchens. Suites also offer Web

TV, Nintendo, VCRs, and bathrobes—all the comforts of home. The hotel's best feature is its restaurant—world-renowned chef Daniel Boulud's Café Boulud serves up gourmet French cuisine (at prices to match). 131 rooms, 16 story. Pets accepted. Check-out noon, check-in 3 pm. TV; cable (premium), VCR available. In-room modem link. Restaurant, bar. Room service. Exercise equipment. Concierge. **$$$**

D 🐾 🏋 ⊠

All Suite

★ ★ **LYDEN GARDENS.** *215 E 64th St (10021). Phone 212/355-1230; toll-free 800/637-8483; fax 212/758-7858. www.mesuite.com.* 131 kitchen units, 13 story. Check-out noon, check-in 3 pm. TV; cable (premium). Room service. In-house fitness room. Valet parking. Concierge. **$$$**

D 🏋 ⊠

Restaurants

★ ★ ★ ★ **AUREOLE.** *34 E 61st St (10021). Phone 212/319-1660. www. aureolerestaurant.com.* Hidden away inside a lovely brownstone on Manhattan's Upper East Side, Aureole is inviting and warm and feels like a special place to dine. The waitstaff's gracious hospitality ensures that you continue to feel that way throughout your meal. The luxurious space is bathed in cream tones and warm lighting and is furnished with over-stuffed wine-colored banquettes. (An enclosed courtyard garden opens for warm-weather dining.) Diners at Aureole are generally here to celebrate something, as it is one of New York's most impressive eateries. The crowd is mostly middle-aged and from the upper echelon of New York society, although Aureole is not a stuffy place. It is friendly and cozy and well suited for just about any occasion, from couples looking for romance to colleagues looking to have a delightful business dinner together. Owner and celebrity chef Charlie Palmer offers his guests the delicious opportunity to dine on a wonderfully prepared menu of what he calls Progressive American fare. But it doesn't really matter what label you give it, because it's all great. There are always two tasting menus—one vegetarian and another inspired from the market—in addition to a parade of terrific à la carte selections. The extensive and celebrated wine program includes bold wines from California, Spain, and Italy. *Secret Inspector's Notes:* Aureole has impressed diners for more than ten years and, amazingly enough, continues to improve over time, always getting a little bit better and brighter. Contemporary American menu. Closed Sun; holidays. Lunch, dinner. Bar. Jacket required. Reservations required. **$$$$**

★ **BISTRO DU NORD.** *1312 Madison Ave (10028). Phone 212/289-0997; fax 212/426-5271.* French menu. Sat, Sun brunch. Bar. Totally nonsmoking. **$$**

★ ★ **BOATHOUSE CAFE.** *72nd St in Central Park (10021). Phone 212/517-2233; fax 212/517-8821. www.thecentralparkboathouse.com.* American menu. Lunch, dinner, Sun brunch. Bar. Children's menu. Outdoor seating. **$$$**

D

★ ★ ★ **CAFÉ BOULUD.** *20 E 76th St (10021). Phone 212/772-2600; fax 212/772-7755. www.danielnyc.com.* Daniel Boulud is one very committed chef. So committed, in fact, that he is the chef-king of a little empire of French restaurants in New York City. Café Boulud is his less formal version of his haute temple of French gastronomy, Daniel. But less formal is a relative term. Café Boulud is a majestic space, perfect for quiet conversation and intimate dining. The service is helpful and unobtrusive. The chef is a whiz at pleasing the palate and offers a choice of four à la carte menus: La Tradition (French Classics and Country Cooking), La Saison (The Rhythm of the Seasons), Le Potager (Vegetarian Selections from the Farmer's Market), and Le Voyage (a menu inspired from a changing international destination—Mexico, Morocco, etc.). The wine program is ambitious, and the staff is unintimidating and eager to assist with pairings, making the total dining experience like a little slice of French heaven. French cuisine. Lunch, dinner. Bar. Jacket required. Reservations required. Outdoor seating. **$$$**

D

★ ★ **CAFÉ NOSIDAM.** *768 Madison Ave (10021). Phone 212/717-5633; fax 212/717-4436. www.sidewalk.com.* Italian, American menu. Lunch, dinner, Sun brunch. Bar. Casual attire. Reservations required. Outdoor seating. **$$$**

D

★ ★ **CAFÉ TREVI.** *1570 1st Ave (10028). Phone 212/249-0040.* Northern Italian menu. Closed Sun. Dinner. Bar. Children's menu. **$$**

D

★ ★ **COCO PAZZO.** *23 E 74th St (10021). Phone 212/794-0205; fax 212/794-0208. www.cocopazzo.com.* Italian menu. Closed most major holidays. Lunch, dinner. Bar. Jacket required. Reservations required. **$$**

D

★ ★ ★ ★ **DANIEL.** *60 E 65th St (10021). Phone 212/288-0033; fax 212/933-5250. www.danielnyc.com.* Daniel Boulud is one of those chefs who could make scrambled eggs taste like manna from heaven. He has a magic touch that warms you from the inside out. For this reason, Daniel is a dining experience. It is not dinner. The experience starts when you enter the palatial front room, continues as you sip an old-fashioned cocktail in the romantic, low-lit lounge, and is taken to new heights when you take a seat at your table, your home for the hours you will spend as the fortunate culinary guest of Boulud. French food at other restaurants is good. With Boulud facing the stove, it is sublime. Potato-crusted sea bass is a signature. The crisp, golden coat, fashioned from whisper-thin slices of potatoes, protects the fish while it cooks and seals in its juices so that it melts on the tongue. It is wonderful. Wine service is another perk. Friendly and helpful, the staff wants you to learn and wants to help you choose the right wine for your meal and your wallet. You will have a new favorite wine before leaving. After dessert, you will think that you're free to go, but not so fast. There are petit fours, of course, and then the pièce de resistance: madeleines. Daniel is famous for these delicate, fluffy, lemony little cakes served warm, just seconds out of the oven. When you are finally free to go, you may not want to. *Secret Inspector's Notes:* The atmosphere at Daniel is unlike any other. Lively, active, pulsating, and elegant all at once, it is an experience well worth the cost. But the experience should not be overstated, as the service can be overburdened at times and the food is not as perfect as you might expect. French cuisine. Closed Sun. Dinner. Bar. Jacket required. **$$$$**

D

★ ★ **HARRY CIPRIRANI'S.** *781 Fifth Ave (10022). Phone 212/753-5566; fax 212/308-5653. www.cipriani.com.* This outpost of the famous Venetian Cipriani empire, located in the Sherry Netherland hotel, has a history all its own. Italian menu. Breakfast, lunch, dinner. Understated décor; display of photos, posters and lithographs, reminiscent of Hemingway in Harry's Bar in Venice. Jacket. Reservations accepted. **$$$$**

D

★ **JACKSON HOLE.** *1611 2nd Ave (10028). Phone 212/737-8788.* Hours: 10-1 am; Fri, Sat to 4 am; Sat, Sun brunch 10:30 am-3 pm. Closed Thanksgiving, Dec 25. Breakfast, lunch, dinner. Bar. Outdoor dining. **$**

D

★ ★ ★ **JO JO.** *160 E 64th St (10021). Phone 212/223-5656; fax 212/755-9038.* Located in a charming old townhouse, Jo Jo was one of the first restaurants from acclaimed star-chef and restaurateur Jean-Georges Vongerichten. It was recently renovated and given a turn-of-the-century feel, with deep jewel tones, velvet and silk fabrics, and 17th-century terracotta tiles. While the dining room has been made over, the menu has stayed much the same, with dishes that highlight Vongerichten's French-Asian style, such as goat cheese and potato terrine with chive oil, roast chicken with chickpea fries, and tuna spring rolls with soybean coulis. Jo Jo is a wonderful spot for elegant, restful, special-occasion dining. Contemporary American menu. Closed major holidays. Lunch, dinner. Bar. Casual attire. **$$$**

KAI. (not yet rated) *822 Madison Ave (10021). Phone 212/988-7277.* Specializing in *kaiseki,* artistic meals made up of precious, miniature courses, Kai is a slim, shoebox-size restaurant with clay walls and chocolate-brown plank floors that you will find tucked into a sliver of a space above a Madison Avenue Japanese tea shop. The procession of food is breathtaking, each dish an artistic portrait composed of delicate vegetables, flavorful tea-smoked meats, and glistening seafood. After your harmonic meal, settle in with some tea, steeped and poured with skill from stunning, Asian-deigned iron kettles. To replicate the experience at home, stop by at the tea shop downstairs and purchase one to go. Japanese menu. Closed Sun; most major holidays. Lunch, dinner. Casual attire. **$$$**

★ ★ **KINGS' CARRIAGE HOUSE.** *251 E 82nd St (10028). Phone 212/734-5490.* Irish, English menu. Closed Dec 25. Lunch, dinner. Bar. Turn-of-the-century carriage house; romantic, intimate atmosphere. Reservations required high tea and Fri-Sat dinner. Totally nonsmoking. **$$$**

D

★ ★ **LE BOEUF A LA MODE.** *539 E 81st St (10028). Phone 212/249-1473; fax 212/737-7879.* French menu. Closed major holidays; also Sun (July-Aug). Dinner. Bar. Outdoor seating. **$$$**

D

★ ★ ★ **LENOX ROOM.** *1278 3rd Ave (10021). Phone 212/772-0404; fax 212/772-3229. www.lenoxroom.com.* Restaurateur Tony Fortuna has managed to bring a bit of slick, downtown style to this quiet, residential (some might say culinarily comatose) neighborhood on the Upper East Side. Thanks to Fortuna, the vibrant life inside Lenox Room more than makes up for the lack of a pulse beating at nearby eateries. At Lenox, you will find a sexy bar and lounge with cool cocktails and inventive tiers of cocktail cuisine, and a swanky, intimate dining room offering a smart New American menu. Lenox is a sure thing for a business lunch, a ladies-only cocktail outing, or a spirited dinner with friends. Not only will the food win you over, but Fortuna's gracious hospitality will have you scheduling your next visit before you leave. New American menu. Closed major holidays. Lunch, dinner, Sun brunch. Bar. **$$$**

D

★ ★ ★ **LE REFUGE.** *166 E 82nd St (10021). Phone 212/861-4505; fax 212/736-0384.* Located within walking distance of the Metropolitan Museum of Art and the lush greenery of Central Park, Le Refuge is a classically charming French restaurant that offers a small slice of Paris in New York, without the smoking, of course. Aside from the lack of cigarette smoke, the difference between the two is negligible. The upper crust of society gathers at Le Refuge for its Parisian elegance and its impressive wine list that pairs up perfectly with the selection of simple, bistro-style fare, like farm-raised duck with fresh fruit and filet mignon with peppercorn sauce. French menu. Closed holidays. Lunch, dinner, Sat, Sun brunch. Casual attire. Outdoor seating. **$$$**

★ ★ **LUSARDI'S.** *1494 2nd Ave (10021). Phone 212/249-2020; fax 212/585-2941.* Italian menu. Seasonal menu/dishes. Closed most major holidays. Lunch, dinner. Bar. Casual attire. Reservations required. Totally nonsmoking. **$$$**

★ ★ ★ **MANHATTAN GRILLE.** *1161 1st Ave (10021). Phone 212/888-6556; fax 212/832-2956. www.manhattangrille.com.* This neighborhood steakhouse has a serious loyal following. The dry-aged beef is right at home in the clubby, comfortable environment. American menu. Closed Thanksgiving, Dec 25. Lunch, dinner, Sun brunch. Bar. **$$$**

D

★ ★ ★ **MAYA.** *1191 1st Ave (10021). Phone 212/585-1818; fax 212/734-6579. www.maya.citysearch.com.* Mexican menu. Closed Jan 1, Dec 25. Dinner, Sun brunch. Bar. Casual attire. Reservations required. Totally nonsmoking. Own tortillas. **$$$**

D

★ **MEZZALUNA.** *1295 3rd Ave (10021). Phone 212/535-9600; fax 212/517-8045.* Italian menu. Closed Dec 25. Lunch, dinner. Bar. Outdoor seating. **$$$**

★ **OUR PLACE.** *1444 3rd Ave (10028). Phone 212/288-4888; fax 212/744-3620.* Chinese menu. Closed Thanksgiving. Lunch, dinner. Bar. Interior designed by protégé of I.M. Pei. **$$$**

D

★ ★ ★ **PARK AVENUE CAFE.** *100 E 63rd St (10021). Phone 212/644-1900; fax 212/688-0373. www.parkavenuecafe.com.* Sophisticated and savvy New Yorkers head to Park Avenue Cafe for luxurious lunch meetings, intimate dinners, and large party outings. The warm, blond-wooded room is bright and airy and feels easy and comfortable. The menu of inspired seasonal dishes uses clean, simple flavors that please the palate. Desserts whipped up by famed pastry chef Richard Leach make you feel like a kid again; finger-licking may be necessary. New American menu. Closed Jan 1, Dec 25. Dinner, Sun brunch. Bar. Casual attire. **$$$$**

★ ★ ★ **PAYARD PATISSERIE AND BISTRO.** *1032 Lexington Ave (10021). Phone 212/717-5252; fax 212/717-0986. www.payard.com.* Willpower must be left outside of Payard. Aside from the great selection of sandwiches, salads, and Parisian bistro staples served in this lovely, butter-yellow French pastry shop, the desserts are as tempting as they come. But this should come as no surprise considering that the baker in question is François Payard, a master of sweets and treats. While lunch and dinner are good choices, Payard's afternoon tea is a wonderful way to get acquainted with his talents. French, steak menu. Closed Sun, major holidays. Lunch, dinner. Bar. Totally nonsmoking. **$$$**

★ **PIG HEAVEN.** *1540 2nd Ave (10028). Phone 212/744-4887; fax 212/744-2853.* Chinese menu. Lunch, dinner, Sat, Sun brunch. Bar. Reservations required. **$$**

D

★ ★ ★ **THE POST HOUSE.** *28 E 63rd St (10021). Phone 212/935-2888; fax 212/371-9265. www.theposthouse.com.* New York has many steakhouses, and The Post House is one of the power lunch club's favorites. The comfortable dining room, with a long bar, has an easy feel thanks to polished parquet floors, wooden wainscoting, and leather armchair seating. The menu sports a super selection of salads, signature appetizers like cornmeal-fried oysters, and a shimmering raw bar in addition to entrées like grilled chicken, rack of lamb, and meat-eater delights like prime rib, filet mignon, and the signature

"Stolen Cajun Rib Steak." An extensive wine list emphasizes California wines and some rare gems from Burgundy and Bordeaux. Steak menu. Closed Jan 1, Thanksgiving, Dec 25. Lunch, dinner. Bar. Casual attire. **$$$**

★ ★ ★ ★ **RM.** *33 E 60th St (10022). Phone 212/319-3800; fax 212/319-4955.* After ten years at the helm at Oceana, chef Rick Moonen decided to set off on a ship of his own. At RM, his sparkling new namesake eatery, seafood remains the star attraction. Moonen has a gift with the ocean's bounty, and with the new space, he has found new inspiration and a source of revitalization. The new American menu at RM sets off sparks, focusing on the freshest catches and perfectly blending seasonal ingredients with vibrant global flavors. The sophisticated dining room is dressed in soothing neutral tones, with lots of blond wood and warm, golden lighting, lending the restaurant a Zen vibe. Despite the high-income power crowds that fill the restaurant for business lunches and civilized, exquisite dinners, the dining room remains a serene retreat from Midtown stress. Seafood menu. Closed Sun. Lunch, dinner. Bar. Jacket required. Reservations required. **$$$**
D

★ **SERENDIPITY 3.** *225 E 60th St (10022). Phone 212/838-3531; fax 212/688-4896. www.serendipity3.com.* American menu. Closed Dec 25. Lunch, dinner. Favorite of celebrities. **$$**

★ ★ **SHABU-TATSU.** *1414 York Ave (10021). Phone 212/472-3322.* Japanese menu. Closed holidays. Lunch, dinner, Sat, Sun brunch. Bar. Cook your own meal; each table surrounds a stovetop. Totally nonsmoking. **$$$**
D

★ ★ **SUSHI OF GARI.** *402 E 78th St (10021). Phone 212/517-5340.* Japanese menu. Closed 2nd Sun of month. Dinner. Entertainment. Casual attire. **$$$$**
D

★ ★ **WILLOW.** *1022 Lexington Ave (10021). Phone 212/717-0703; fax 212/717-0725.* French menu. Closed Dec 25. Lunch, dinner, Sun brunch. Bar. Casual attire. Reservations required dinner. Outdoor seating. Totally nonsmoking. **$$$**

Midtown Manhattan

Stretching from 34th Street to 57th Street, the Harlem River to the East River, Midtown is the heart of Manhattan. Most of the city's skyscrapers are here, along with most of its offices, major hotels, famous shops, the Empire State Building, Times Square, the Broadway theaters, the Museum of Modern Art, Rockefeller Center, Grand Central Station, and the New York Public Library.

Fifth Avenue is the center of Midtown, dividing the city into east and west. Although nothing more than a line on a map as late as 1811, the thoroughfare had become New York's most fashionable address by the Civil War. It began to turn commercial in the early 1900s and is now lined with mostly shops and office buildings.

Towering over the southern end of Midtown is the Empire State Building (350 Fifth Avenue, at 34th Street), one of the world's most famous skyscrapers. Built in the early 1930s, the building took just 14 months to erect and remains an Art Deco masterpiece.

Forty-Second Street is lined with one major attraction after another. On the corner of Third Avenue soars the magnificent Chrysler Building, another Art Deco masterpiece; Grand Central Station, whose magnificent concourse was recently restored to the tune of $200 million, is at Lexington Avenue. At Fifth Avenue beckons the New York Public Library, behind which spreads Bryant Park, where many free events are held during the summer months.

West of Seventh Avenue along 42nd Street begins Times Square, which stretches north to 48th Street along the Seventh Avenue-Broadway nexus. The best time to come here is at night, when the huge state-of-the-art neon lights that line the square begin to shine. Much cleaned up in recent years, Times Square is also a good place to catch street performers and, of course, Broadway theater. Many of the city's most famous theaters are located on the side streets around Times Square.

North and a little east of Times Square, Rockefeller Center reigns as an Art Deco complex stretching between 48th and 51st streets, Sixth and Fifth avenues. Built by John D. Rockefeller during the height of the Depression, Rockefeller Center is home to the landmark Radio City Music Hall, the NBC Studios, and a famed skating rink filled with outdoor enthusiasts during the winter months.

Along Fifth Avenue just south and north of Rockefeller Center, find some of the city's most famous shops—Saks Fifth Avenue, Tiffany's, Steuben Glass, and Cartier, along with Trump Tower at 56th Street. Between 50th and 51st streets soars the Gothic Saint Patrick's Cathedral, the largest Roman Catholic cathedral in the United States; the Museum of Modern Art, a must-stop for any art lover, is on 53rd Street just west of Fifth.

Midtown East

What to See and Do

Astro Minerals Gallery of Gems. *185 Madison Ave (10016). Phone 212/889-9000; 212/394-ASTRO. www.astrogallery.com.* Display of minerals, gems, jewelry; primitive and African art. (Daily; closed Jan 1, Thanksgiving, Dec 25) **FREE**

Gramercy Park and Environs

Largely residential, the East Side between 14th and 34th streets is home to two inviting squares—Gramercy Park at Irving Place between 20th and 21st streets, and Union Square at Broadway between 14th and 17th streets. A long line of trendy restaurants and bars beckon along Park Avenue between 17th and 23rd streets, while a bit farther north is Little India, centered on Lexington Avenue between 27th and 29th streets. The neighborhood lacks the vibrancy of some of Manhattan's better-known neighborhoods but has a quiet charm of its own, with residents ranging from young professionals to middle-class families to the upper middle class.

One of the most fashionable squares in the city, Gramercy Park is composed of elegant brownstones and townhouses surrounding an enclosed green to which only residents have the key. At the southern edge of the park stand two especially impressive buildings—the National Arts Club (15 Gramercy Park South) and the Players Club (16 Gramercy Park South). The National Arts Club was once home to New York governor Samuel Tilden, whereas the Players Club once belonged to the great thespian Edwin Booth, the brother of the man who assassinated Abraham Lincoln. Just east of Gramercy Park stands Theodore Roosevelt's Birthplace (28 East 20th Street), a museum filled with the world's largest collection of Roosevelt memorabilia.

Farther south, find Union Square, a booming park surrounded by sleek megastores, upscale restaurants, and fashionable bars. A popular farmers Greenmarket operates in the park on Monday, Wednesday, Friday, and Saturday mornings, and free concerts and other events sometimes take place here during the summer. To the immediate east of the square are several excellent off-Broadway theaters.

Broadway between Union Square and Madison Square (between 23rd and 26th streets, Fifth and Madison avenues) was once known as the "Ladies Mile" because of the many fashionable department stores located here. Many were housed in extravagant cast-iron buildings, which still stand, now holding more modern emporiums.

At the corner of Broadway and 23rd Street is the famous 1902 Flatiron building, built in the shape of a narrow triangle and only 6 feet wide at its northern end. Meanwhile, reigning over Madison Park to the east are the enormous Art Deco Metropolitan Life Insurance Building (Madison Avenue, between 23rd and 25th streets) and the impossibly ornate Appellate Division of the New York State Supreme Court (Madison Avenue at 25th Street).

Still farther north and east lies Little India. Though not as thriving as it once was, it still houses a number of excellent Indian restaurants, sari shops, and spice stores, which attract shoppers from all over the city.

Bloomingdale's. *1000 3rd Ave (10022). Phone 212/705-2000; toll-free 800/ 472-0788. www.bloomingdales.com.* Everyone in New York knows the name Bloomingdale's and the famous Bloomie's shopping bags. This world-renowned department store, loved by locals and tourists alike, sells a mix of merchandise in a sleek, modern setting. You can find designer clothing for men and women, high-quality housewares, jewelry, cosmetics, and just about everything else. Although prices are high, you can find good sales. (Daily; closed Thanksgiving, Dec 25)

Central Park. (see MIDTOWN WEST)

Christie's Auctions. *20 Rockefeller Plaza (10020). Phone 212/636-2000. www.christies.com.* Get a taste of high society at a Christie's auction. Whether you're just a spectator or you have lots of spare cash with which to purchase something wonderful, attending an auction at this institution is a thrilling, fast-paced experience. Items sold at auction at Christie's have included the "Master of Your Domain" script from the television show *Seinfeld,* gowns worn by the late Princess Diana, and a Honus Wagner baseball card (the most expensive card ever sold). Special departments are devoted to areas like wines, cameras, and cars. Publications like *New York* magazine and *The New York Times* contain listings of upcoming events. (Closed major holidays)

Chrysler Building. *405 Lexington Ave, at E 42nd St.* New York's famous Art Deco skyscraper. The graceful pointed spire with triangular windows set in arches is lighted at night. The impressive lobby features beautiful jazz-age detailing.

The Garment District. *6th Ave to 8th Ave and from 34th St to 42nd St.* This crowded area, heart of the clothing industry in New York, has hundreds of small shops, factories, and streets jammed with trucks and hand-pushed delivery carts. Also in this area is Macy's.

Grand Central Station. *450 Lexington Ave (10017). 42nd St, between Vanderbilt and Lexington. Phone 212/935-3960. www.grandcentralterminal .com.* (1913) Built in the Beaux Arts style and recently renovated for $200 million, this is one of New York's most glorious buildings. It has a vast 125-foot-high concourse, glassed-in catwalks, grand staircases, shops, restaurants, and a star-studded, aquamarine ceiling. Tours offered Wed by Municipal Art Society; meet at information booth in center of concourse at 12:30 pm. **$$**

Lexington Avenue. *Take the #6 Lexington Ave subway to 28th St.* It may be only a three-block area just south of Murray Hill, but this neighborhood is brimming with the sights and sounds of India. Stores sell Indian and Pakistani spices, pastries, videos, cookware, saris, and fabrics. Restaurants cater to both Muslim and Hindu tastes, suiting both beefeaters and vegetarians. The low prices are a treat as well.

★ **Madison Avenue.** *Take the 6 subway to the 77th St stop and walk south. Or take the 4, 5, or 6 subway to the 59th St stop or the N or R subway to the Lexington Ave stop and walk north.* If you are well schooled (or even a novice) in the fine art of window-shopping, this stretch of very exclusive brand-name stores along swanky Madison Avenue is calling your name. Top European designers have shops here, including Giorgio Armani (760 Madison Ave, 212/988-9191), Valentino (747 Madison Ave, 212/772-6969), and Prada (841 Madison Ave, 212/327-4200), to name a few. American designers such as Polo/Ralph Lauren (867 Madison Ave, 212/606-2100) and Calvin Klein (654 Madison Ave, 212/292-9000) also have stores along this chic Manhattan strip. Looking to buy something special for someone back home (or for yourself)? The salespeople in these light and airy stores are usually quite helpful, but don't expect to find anything remotely on the cheap side. On a mild, sunny day, window-shopping here makes for a very relaxing stroll.

New York City Post Office. *341 9th Ave, between 29th and 30th sts. Phone 212/330-2300.* Guided 90-minute tours (Tues-Fri, upon written request to Postmaster, or phone 212/330-2300; one-week advance reservations required). No cameras. Children over 7 only.

Pierpont Morgan Library. *29 E 36th St (10016). Phone 212/685-0610; 212/685-0008. www.morganlibrary.org.* In Murray Hill, find the Pierpont Morgan Library, housed in an elegant neoclassical mansion. Unfortunately, the McKim building, which contained the original library, has closed, but compelling traveling exhibits are frequently on display. The library's permanent collections include priceless medieval and Renaissance manuscripts and old-master drawings, a Gutenberg Bible, autograph and musical transcripts, and medieval gold objects. (Tues-Thurs 10:30 am-5 pm, Fri 10:30 am-8 pm, Sat 10:30 am-6 pm, Sun noon-6 pm; closed Mon, holidays) **DONATION**

★ **Rockefeller Center.** *30 Rockefeller Plaza (10112). Fifth Ave to Ave of the Americas and beyond, 47th St to 51st St with some buildings stretching to 52nd St. Phone 212/632-3975. www.rockefellercenter.com.* Conceived of by John D. Rockefeller during the 1930s, Rockefeller Center is the largest privately owned business and entertainment complex in the world. Enter through the Channel Gardens (Fifth Ave between 49th and 50th) and walk toward the central sunken plaza. Here, a golden statue of Prometheus sprawls benevolently beside a pool and an outdoor café that becomes an ice skating rink in winter. (Yes, you can rent skates.) The center is magical at Christmastime, when a 78,000-light tree towers over Prometheus. The backdrop of the scene is the core skyscraper, the GE Building, home to NBC Studios. You can take a studio tour (adults $17.50, seniors and children $15, no children under 6; phone 212/664-7174), or catch *The Today Show* being broadcast live through the street-level picture window at West 49th and Rockefeller Plaza. The 21-acre complex contains 19 buildings, most built of limestone with aluminum streamlining. But the Art Deco gem of the group is Radio City Music Hall, America's largest theater. Tour the theater or see a show—especially if the high-kicking Rockettes are performing (www.radiocity.com; phone 212/247-4777).

St. Patrick's Cathedral. *Fifth Ave between E 50th and 51st sts (10022).* Irish immigrants and their descendents were largely responsible for the construction and dedication of St. Patrick's Cathedral, the largest Catholic cathedral in the United States. A standout on Fifth Avenue since 1859, the white marble and stone structure dominates the surrounding skyscrapers. Twin

Gothic spires reach heavenward, and some of the stained glass windows were made in Chartres. Cool and calm within, the church bestows a palpable peace on visitors as well as those attending services. It is the resting place of New York's deceased archbishops; they are buried in tombs under the high altar, and their hats hang from the ceiling above. The steps of St. Pat's are a popular meeting place for New Yorkers. (Mon-Fri 11 a-8 pm, Sat 10 am-7 pm, Sun noon-6 pm) **FREE**

Terence Conran Shop. *415 E 59th St (10022). Phone 212/755-9079. www.conran.com.* This British-based retailer has come to the Big Apple, with a shop built right into a pavilion at the Queensboro Bridge. With international flair and a sense of style, the store sells fine—and sometimes unusual—home furnishings, kitchenware, and jewelry familiar to those who read *Wallpaper* and *British Elle Décor.* If you don't blow your budget on these irresistible, ultra-modern accessories, stop for a bite next door at Gustavino's, a French-American restaurant that is just as chic as the store. (Mon-Fri 11 am-8 pm, Sat 10 am-7 pm, Sun noon-6 pm)

United Nations. *405 E 42nd St (10017). Phone 212/963-8687. www.un.org.* These four buildings, designed under the direction of Wallace K. Harrison, were completed between 1950-1952. Regular sessions of the General Assembly start on the third Tuesday in September. Tickets are occasionally available to certain official meetings on a first-come basis. Entrance is on 1st Ave at 46th St, at the north end of the General Assembly Building. In the lobby is an information desk and ticket booth; in the basement are the UN book and gift shops and the UN Post Office, where one can mail letters bearing United Nations stamps. On the fourth floor is the UN Delegates Dining Room. The Conference Building is where the various UN Councils meet. The Secretariat Building is a 550-foot-high rectangular glass-and-steel building; here the day-to-day work of the UN staff is performed. The fourth building is the Dag Hammarskjold Library, open only to UN staff

Winter and Summer Restaurant Weeks

Many of the city's finest restaurants offer two- or three-course, fixed-price lunches at the bargain price of $20 a person during these two weeks in winter and summer. (Yes, for New York City, that is a bargain at a Four-Star restaurant.) Actually, the exact price, if you want to get technical, corresponds to the year ($20.03 in 2003, $20.04 in 2004, etc.). This is a wildly popular promotion that natives can't wait to get their hands on. Check local newspapers at the beginning of your trip to see which restaurants are participating and make a reservation ASAP. This is a great way to experience top dining at great prices. Bon appétit! Second week in Jan, third week in June. www.restaurantweek.com

and delegations, or by special permission for serious research. Guided tours (45 minutes) leave the public entrance lobby at frequent intervals (daily; closed Thanksgiving and several days during year-end holiday season; also weekends Jan-Feb); no children under 5. (Buildings, daily) **$$$**

Whitney Museum of American Art at Philip Morris. *120 Park Ave at 42nd St. Phone 917/663-2550.* Gallery and sculpture court. Changing exhibits annually; free lectures, performances. Gallery talks (Mon, Wed, Fri). Gallery (Mon-Fri). Sculpture court (daily). **FREE**

Special Events

Columbus Day Parade. *Fifth Ave between 44th and 79th sts (10036).*

Hispanic Day Parade. *Fifth Ave between 44th and 86th sts (10036).* Mid-Oct.

Macy's Thanksgiving Day Parade. *34th and 72nd sts (10001). Phone 212/494-5432; 212/494-4495.* If you have a child or you want to feel like a kid again yourself, spend Thanksgiving Day morning enjoying this wonderful and festive New York event. Amazing floats, cheerful clowns (who are all volunteers and are either Macy's employees or friends and families of Macy's employees), and celebrities are all part of the parade, which starts at 9 am and ends at around noon. The atmosphere is always jovial and will put you in the holiday spirit. Since you may spend most of the time standing, wear comfortable shoes, dress in layers, bring snacks, and duck into nearby eateries for hot drinks and bathroom breaks. Keep in mind that standing for several hours may be too tiring for children under 5 (unless they spend most of the time perched atop your shoulders, which may be too tiring for you!). One of the best viewing spots is on Herald Square in front of Macy's.

St. Patrick's Day Parade. *Along Fifth Ave.* New York's biggest parade; approximately 100,000 marchers.

Hotels

★ ★ **BEDFORD HOTEL.** *118 E 40th St (10016). Phone 212/697-4800; toll-free 800/221-6881; fax 212/697-1093. www.bedfordhotel.com.* 136 rooms, 58 suites, 17 story. Pets accepted. Complimentary continental breakfast. Check-out 12 pm, check-in 3 pm. TV; cable (premium). In-room modem link. Restaurant, bar. Kitchettes. **$$**

★ ★ ★ **THE BENJAMIN.** *125 E 50th St (10022). Phone 212/715-2500; fax 212/715-2525. www.thebenjamin.com.* Despite the fact that it's set in a classic 1927 building, this hotel has all the high-tech amenities a business traveler could want, including high-speed Internet access and Web TV. It offers comfortable accommodations in a sophisticated setting that features beige, silver, and brown tones throughout the property and in the marble and silver two-story lobby. A particularly nice amenity is the "pillow menu," which offers you a choice of ten different kinds of bed pillows and a guarantee of your money back if you do not wake well rested. The Benjamin's Woodstock Spa and Wellness Center offers many services and treatments with a holistic approach. 209 rooms. Pets accepted. Check-out noon, check-in 3 pm. TV; VCR available. Internet access. Restaurant, bar. Babysitting services available. In-house fitness room, spa. Concierge. **$$$$**

D 🐾 🏃 ⅃

★ ★ **BENTLEY HOTEL.** *500 E 62nd St (10022). Phone 212/644-6000; toll-free 888/664-6295; fax 212/207-4800.* 197 rooms, 21 story. Complimentary continental breakfast. Check-out noon. TV; VCR available. In-room modem link. Restaurant, bar. Health club privileges. Parking. Concierge. **$$**

D ⅃

★ ★ **CLARION HOTEL FIFTH AVENUE.** *3 E 40th St (10016). Phone 212/447-1500; toll-free 800/252-7466; fax 212/213-0972. www.clarionfifthave.com.* 189 rooms, 30 story. Check-out noon, check-in 3 pm. TV; cable (premium). In-room modem link. Restaurant, bar. Room service. Sauna. Garage parking, valet parking available. Business center. Concierge. **$$**

D ⅃ SC 🏃

★ ★ ★ **DYLAN HOTEL.** *52 E 41st St (10017). Phone 212/338-0500. www.dylanhotel.com.* With a grand feeling throughout, the 1903 Beaux Arts-style building, with its ornate facade and spiraling marble staircase, used to be the home of the Chemists Club. The guest rooms are bright and airy, with 11-foot ceilings and elegant marble baths. The rooms' white and blue walls, deep amethyst and steel blue carpeting, and ebony-stained furniture give them a quiet, tailored look without being austere or cold. Situated on a quiet street, the hotel contains the Dylan restaurant, which serves basic fare like burgers and pastas, and a bar for relaxing with a drink. 107 rooms, 20 story. Pets accepted, $45. Check-out noon, check-in 3 pm. TV; cable (premium), VCR available. In-room modem link. Restaurant, bar. Room service. In-house fitness room. Business center. Concierge. **$$$**

D 🐾 🏃 ⅃ SC 🏃

★ ★ ★ ★ ★ **FOUR SEASONS HOTEL NEW YORK.** *57 E 57th St (10022). Phone 212/758-5700; fax 212/758-5711. www.fourseasons.com.* The bustling world of 57th Street's designer boutiques and office towers awaits outside the doors of the Four Seasons Hotel New York, yet this temple of modern elegance provides a serene escape from city life. Designed by legendary architect I. M. Pei, the Four Seasons pays homage to the city's beloved skyscrapers as the tallest hotel in New York. The rooms and suites are testaments to chic simplicity with neutral tones, English sycamore furnishings, and state-of-the-art technology, but it's the service that defines the Four Seasons experience. The staff makes guests feel completely at ease in the monumental building, with ready smiles and generous spirit. The views are terrific, too; floor-to-ceiling windows showcase the dazzling city skyline or the quietude of Central Park. Some rooms offer furnished terraces so that guests can further admire the sights. Fifty Seven Fifty Seven, the restaurant in the hotel, remains the place to see and be seen, while the bar and the Lobby Lounge provide perfect settings for lingering over drinks or casual fare. 368 rooms, 52 story. Pets accepted, some restrictions. Garage, valet parking. Check-out noon, check-in 3 pm. TV; cable (premium), VCR.

In-room modem link. Restaurant, bar. Room service. In-house fitness room, sauna, steam room. Massage. Whirlpool. Business center. Concierge. **$$$$**

D 🐾 🛪 ⊠ 🏃

★ ★ ★ **GRAND HYATT NEW YORK.** *Park Ave at Grand (10017). Phone 212/883-1234; fax 646/213-6659. www.newyork.hyatt.com.* 1,347 rooms, 51 suites, 36 story. Check-out noon, check-in 3 pm. TV; cable (premium). In-room modem link. Room service 24 hours. Restaurant, bar; entertainment. In-house fitness room, health club privileges. Valet parking. Business center. Concierge. Luxury level. Adjacent to Grand Central Station. **$$$**

D 🛪 ⊠ SC 🏃

★ ★ ★ **HOTEL AVALON.** *16 E 32nd St (10016). Phone 212/299-7000; toll-free 888/HI-AVALON; fax 212/299-7001. www.theavalonny.com.* Stately black marble columns and a pretty mosaic floor make an elegant first impression at this Murray Hill boutique hotel located near many area attractions. The elegant lobby is warm and inviting, with the look and feel of a mini European palace. Warm chestnut tones give the place a sense of grandeur, but in a smaller setting that is part of boutique intimacy. The guest rooms feature desk chairs designed for comfort and functionality, as well as Irish cotton linens and velour bathrobes. The Avalon bills itself as a home away from home: each room also comes with a signature body pillow, and afternoon tea is served in the cozy library. 100 rooms, 80 suites, 12 story. Complimentary continental breakfast. Check-out noon. Check-in 3 pm. TV; VCR available. In-room modem link. Restaurant, bar. Valet parking. Concierge. **$$**

D ⊠ SC

★ ★ ★ **HOTEL ELYSEE.** *60 E 54th St (10022). Phone 212/753-1066; toll-free 800/535-9733; fax 212/980-9278. www.elyseehotel.com.* 101 rooms, 14 story. Pets accepted. Complimentary continental breakfast. Check-out 1 pm, check-in 3 pm. TV; VCR available. Restaurant, bar. Room service. Babysitting services available. Health club privileges. **$$$**

D 🐾 ⊠

★ ★ ★ **INTER-CONTINENTAL THE BARCLAY NEW YORK.** *111 E 48th St (10017). Phone 212/755-5900; toll-free 800/327-0200; fax 212/644-0079. www.new-york.interconti.com.* 603 rooms, 84 suites, 14 story. Check-out noon, check-in 3 pm. TV; cable (premium). Internet access. Restaurant, bar. Room service. Health club privileges. Exercise equipment, massage, sauna, steam room. Garage, valet parking. Airport transportation. Business center. Concierge. **$$$**

D 🛪 ⊠ 🏃

★ ★ ★ **THE KIMBERLY HOTEL.** *145 E 50th St (10022). Phone 212/702-1600; toll-free 800/683-0400; fax 212/486-6915. www.kimberlyhotel.com.* If you're looking for an elegant, spacious room designed in bold colors and warm wood furnishings that the whole family will feel comfortable in, the all-suite Kimberly Hotel is for you. The one- and two-bedroom suites feature living rooms, dining areas, and fully equipped separate kitchens. For extra comfort, the suites feature plush robes and goose down or aromatherapy pillows. Many suites also have private terraces with city views. Guests receive free use of the New York Health and Racquet Club. As an extra bonus, guests can take a complimentary cruise on the hotel's 75-foot yacht on weekends from May through October. 186 rooms, 30 story. Pets accepted. Check-out noon, check-in 3 pm. TV; cable (premium), VCR available. Restaurant, bar; entertainment. Room service. Babysitting services available. Sauna. Indoor pool. Concierge. **$$$**

D ◀ ⩯

★ ★ ★ **KITANO HOTEL.** *66 Park Ave (10016). Phone 212/885-7000; fax 212/885-7100. www.kitano.com.* This Japanese import located in Murray Hill features modern guest rooms with soft tones of beige and tan and soundproof windows that ensure peace and quiet. The rooms also feature Web TV, duvets, large desks, and Japanese teacups and green tea. Keeping with the Asian theme are an authentic Japanese tea room, gallery, and elegant shops located off the warm mahogany and marble lobby. Original works of art and sculptures are displayed throughout the hotel. The Nadaman Hakubai restaurant specializes in gourmet Japanese cuisine, and the sun-drenched Garden Café features contemporary continental cuisine. 149 rooms, 18 story. Check-out 11 am, check-in 3 pm. TV; cable (premium), VCR available. In-room modem link. Restaurant, bar; entertainment. Room service. Health club privileges. Valet parking. Concierge. **$$**

D ⩯ SC

★ ★ ★ **LIBRARY HOTEL.** *299 Madison Ave (10017). Phone 212/983-4500. www.library-hotel.com.* As the name suggests, this unique hotel was inspired by a library—the famous New York City Public Library located one block away. Each of the ten floors is dedicated to one of the ten categories of the Dewey Decimal System, which include languages, literature, history, the arts, and religion. Each guest room is furnished in a modern, sleek, yet warm and inviting décor and is stocked with books and art relevant to the floor's particular topic. In keeping with this theme, the hotel features a reading room and a poetry garden with terrace for relaxing and reading. 60 rooms, 10 story. Complimentary continental breakfast. Check-out noon, check-in 3 pm. TV; cable (premium), VCR available. In-room modem link. Restaurant, bar. Business center. Concierge. **$$$**

D 夵 ⏃

★ ★ ★ **LOMBARDY HOTEL.** *111 E 56th St (10022). Phone 212/753-8600; toll-free 800/223-5254; fax 212/754-5683. www.lombardyhotel.com.* An elegant Midtown hotel, the Lombardy was built in the 1920s by William Randolph Hearst. This historic hotel has oversized rooms decorated in a classic, elegant, old-world style with comfortable couches and chairs. The marble baths have oversized showers and an array of upscale toiletries. Flowers, works of art, and crystal chandeliers are featured throughout the property. Above-and-beyond personal services include a seamstress and white-glove attendant service in the elevators. The hotel also has a fully equipped business center and is close to shopping, theaters, and Central Park. 115 rooms, 21 story. Closed Thanksgiving-Dec 25. Check-out 11 am, check-in 3 pm. TV; cable (premium), VCR available. In-room modem link. Restaurant, bar. Room service. Babysitting services available. Business center. In-house fitness room. Concierge. **$$$**

[D] [icons]

★ ★ ★ **METROPOLITAN HOTEL.** *569 Lexington Ave (10022). Phone 212/752-7000; toll-free 800/836-6471; fax 212/758-6311. www.metropolitan hotelnyc.com.* Recently renovated, this East Side business traveler's hotel (formerly the Loews New York) has a casual elegance in its soft tones and king-bed rooms. The Lexington Avenue Grill serves contemporary American cuisine, and the popular Lexy Lounge features a signature cocktail called the Sexy Lexy that is a hit with locals. The business center offers everything from secretarial services to fax capabilities to workstation rentals. The premium business-class program includes a separate check-in and check-out area; private lounge with wine and cheese, continental breakfast, and snacks; and special in-room amenities like fax machines. 667 rooms, 55 suites, 20 story. Pets accepted, some restrictions. Check-out noon. Check-in 3 pm. TV; cable (premium). In-room modem link. Restaurant, bar. Room service. In-house fitness room, sauna. Airport transportation. Business center. Concierge, luxury level. **$$**

[D] [icons]

★ ★ ★ **MILLENNIUM NEW YORK UN PLAZA.** *1 UN Plaza (10017). Phone 212/758-1234; fax 212/702-5051. www.millennium-hotels.com.* Bright lights and big mirrors add glamour to the lobby of this hotel, just steps from the UN. 438 rooms, 40 story. Check-out noon, check-in 3 pm. TV; cable (premium), VCR available. In-room modem link. Restaurant, bar. Room service. Exercise room, massage, sauna. Heated indoor pool. Indoor tennis. Valet parking. Business center. **$$**

[D] [icons]

★ ★ ★ **MORGANS.** *237 Madison Ave (10016). Phone 212/686-0300; fax 212/779-8352.* Another in Ian Schrager's collection of hotels, Morgans is so hip that the front door has no sign, and no address is even posted. The guest rooms are decorated in soft, muted tones; a contrasting black-and-white checkerboard design differentiates the ultra-sleek bathrooms. Added touches to make your stay more pleasant include down comforters and pillows, CD players, and fresh flowers in the rooms. Asia de Cuba restaurant attracts a hip "air-kiss" crowd. (You may see celebrities!) Complimentary breakfast and afternoon tea add to the value. 113 rooms, 19 story. Complimentary continental breakfast. Check-out noon, check-in 3 pm. TV; cable (premium). In-room modem link. Room service 24 hours. Restaurant, bar. Valet parking. Concierge. **$$$**

[D] [icons]

★ ★ ★ ★ **THE NEW YORK PALACE.** *455 Madison Ave (10022). Phone 212/888-7000; toll-free 800/697-2522; fax 212/303-6000. www.newyorkpalace.com.* Return to the Gilded Age at The New York Palace. Marrying the historic 1882 Villard Houses with a 55-story contemporary tower, The Palace brings the best of both worlds together under one roof.

Directly across from St. Patrick's Cathedral, The Palace is convenient for sightseeing or conducting business. First impressions are memorable, and the grand entrance through the gated courtyard of twinkling lights is no exception. The glorious public rooms are masterfully restored and recall their former incarnations as part of the private residences of America's wealthiest citizens at the turn of the century. Set against the backdrop of New York City, The Palace's rooms and suites are a blend of contemporary flair or period décor. The Villard Bar & Lounge captures the imagination of its patrons with its Victorian design. Home to Le Cirque 2000 (see), one of the world's most famous restaurants, The New York Palace is in its own class. 896 rooms, 55 story. Pets accepted. Check-out 3 pm, check-in noon. TV; VCR available. In-room modem link. Room service 24 hours. Restaurant, bar. In-house fitness room, health club privileges, spa, massage, steam room. Parking. Business center. Concierge. **$$$$**

★ ★ ★ **OMNI BERKSHIRE PLACE.** *21 E 52nd St at Madison Ave (10022). Phone 212/753-5800; toll-free 800/843-6664; fax 212/754-5018. www.omnihotels.com.* A soaring atrium, with a wood-burning fireplace, is the focal point of the lobby of this understated hotel. The rooms are designed with an Asian aesthetic, and business travelers will find all they need for a hassle-free stay. 396 rooms, 47 suites, 21 story. Pets accepted. Check-out noon, check-in 3 pm. TV; cable (premium), VCR available. In-room modem link. Room service 24 hours. Restaurant, bar. Babysitting services available. In-house fitness room. Valet parking $32. Business center. Concierge. **$$$**

★ ★ **RADISSON.** *511 Lexington Ave at 48th St (10017). Phone 212/755-4400; toll-free 800/333-3333; fax 212/751-4091.* 705 rooms, 35 suites, 27 story. Check-out noon, check-in 3 pm. TV; cable (premium). Restaurant, bar; entertainment. Room service. In-house fitness room. Business center. Concierge. Near Grand Central Station. **$$**

★ **THE ROGER WILLIAMS.** *131 Madison Ave (10016). Phone 212/448-7000; toll-free 888/448-7788; fax 212/448-7007. www.boutiquehg.com.* 187 rooms, 16 story. Complimentary continental breakfast. Check-out 3 pm, check-out noon. TV; cable (premium), VCR available. In-room modem link. In-house fitness room, health club privileges. Valet parking. Business center. Concierge. **$$**

★ ★ **ROOSEVELT HOTEL.** *45 E 45th St and Madison Ave (10017). Phone 212/661-9600; toll-free 888/833-3969; fax 212/885-6161. www.theroosevelt hotel.com.* 1013 rooms, 30 suites, 19 story. Check-out noon, check-in 3 pm. TV; VCR available. In-room modem link. Restaurant, bar. In-house fitness room. Parking $40. Business center. Concierge. **$$**

★ ★ ★ **SHELBURNE MURRAY HILL HOTEL.** *303 Lexington Ave (10016). Phone 212/689-5200; fax 212/779-7068. www.mesuite.com.* This all-suite hotel has a homey atmosphere and first-rate amenities. You will be treated to comfort and style in the one- and two-bedroom suites with full kitchens, decorated in cherry wood furniture and richly colored draperies and beddings. Grocery shopping service is available for guests as an extra perk. The lobby is intimate, upscale, and inviting. LEX 203 offers bistro cuisine. Additional features include a fully equipped health club with exercise equipment and sauna. 264 rooms, 16 story. Check-out noon, check-in 3 pm. TV; cable (premium), VCR available. In-room modem link. Restaurant, bar. Exercise equipment, sauna. Parking. Concierge. **$$**

D 👤 🏊

★ ★ ★ ★ ★ **THE ST. REGIS.** *2 E 55th St (10022). Phone 212/753-4500; toll-free 800/759-7550; fax 212/787-3447. www.stregis.com.* Located just steps off Fifth Avenue in the heart of Manhattan, The St. Regis reigns as New York's grande dame. Opened in 1904, guests glide past the revolving doors of this Beaux Arts landmark to enter the rarefied world of old New York. The St. Regis defines elegance with its gleaming marble, glittering gold leafing, and sparkling chandeliers. The guest rooms are elegantly decorated in soft pastel colors with Louis XVI-style furnishings, while personal butlers cater to every whim 24 hours a day. Set under a ceiling of magical clouds that casts a dreamlike spell over its patrons, the Astor Court is the perfect place to enjoy traditional afternoon tea. Renowned for its famous Red Snapper cocktail and bewitching Maxfield Parrish mural, the King Cole Bar is a favorite of hotel guests and locals alike. *Secret Inspector's Notes:* "Above and beyond" is clearly the staff's mantra as they strive to fulfill each guest's request with a smile. You'll find yourself grinning from ear to ear as you step into this sanctuary of luxury. Let the staff do their thing, and you won't lift a finger: from the butler on your floor to your server at breakfast, they strive to impress—and most often do! 315 rooms, 20 story. Valet parking. Check-out noon, check-in 3 pm. TV; cable (premium), VCR available. In-room modem link. Room service 24 hours. Restaurant, bar. In-house fitness room, sauna, spa, massage. Business center. Concierge. **$$$$**

D 👤 🏊 👤

★ ★ ★ **SWISSOTEL NEW YORK, THE DRAKE.** *440 Park Ave and 56th St (10022). Phone 212/421-0900; toll-free 800/637-9477; fax 212/371-4190. www.swissotel.com.* 495 rooms, 108 suites, 21 story. Pets accepted. Check-out noon. TV; VCR available. In-room modem link. Room service 24 hours. Restaurant, bar. In-house fitness room, massage, sauna, steam room. Garage, valet parking available. Business center. Concierge. **$$$**

D 🐾 👤 🏊 👤

★ ★ ★ **THE WALDORF=ASTORIA.** *301 Park Ave (10022). Phone 212/355-3000; toll-free 800/925-3673; fax 212/872-7272. www.hilton.com.* Enjoy a taste of old New York at this lodging landmark. The 1931 Art Deco hotel has played host to US presidents and other luminaries and features a grand lobby that is not to be missed. It has murals, mosaics, elaborate design work, and a piano that once belonged to Cole Porter. The rooms are individually decorated, elegant, and traditional in style. The Bull & Bear steakhouse has a 1940s feel and attracts the powerful and wealthy. The ultra-exclusive Waldorf Towers, from floor 28 and above, is even more upscale and private. 1,425 rooms, 42 story. Check-out noon, check-in 3 pm. TV; cable (premium), VCR available. In-room modem link. Restaurant, bar. Room service. Babysitting services available. In-house fitness room, spa, massage, steam room. Business center. Concierge. Luxury level. **$$$**

⬜ 🛆 SC 🏂

★ ★ ★ **W NEW YORK.** *541 Lexington Ave (10022). Phone 212/755-1200; toll-free 888/625-5144; fax 212/319-8344. www.whotels.com.* The chic lobby has the air of an urban ski lodge, with a sunken lobby bar that has tree trunk end tables and colorful rugs. The guest rooms have an organic feel with natural cotton linens and neutral tones. 713 rooms, 18 story. Pets accepted. Check-out noon, check-in 3 pm. TV; cable (premium), VCR available. Internet access. Restaurant, bar. Room service. Exercise room, spa, massage, sauna, steam room. Valet parking. Concierge. **$$$**

⬜ 🐾 🛆 🔄

All Suite

★ ★ **EASTGATE TOWER HOTEL.** *222 E 39th St (10016). Phone 212/687-8000; toll-free 800/637-8483; fax 212/490-2634. www.mesuite.com.* 188 kitchen units, 25 story. Check-out noon. Check-in 3 pm. TV; cable (premium). In-room modem link. Restaurant, bar. Room service. In-house fitness room. Valet parking. Concierge. **$$$**

⬜ 🛆 🔄

Restaurants

★ ★ **BICE.** *7 E 54th St (10022). Phone 212/688-1999; fax 212/752-1329. www.biceny.com.* Italian, Milanese menu. Menu changes daily. Closed Dec 25. Lunch, dinner, late night. Bar. Casual attire. Outdoor seating. Branch of original restaurant in Milan. **$$$**

★ ★ ★ **BRASSERIE.** *100 E 53rd St (10022). Phone 212/751-4840; fax 212/751-8777. www.restaurantassociates.com.* As you enter Brasserie, you may feel all eyes on you, which is probably because they are. The dining room is set down a level, and when you enter, you must walk down a futuristic glass staircase, a dramatic walkway that calls all eyes up. In case the folks at the backlit bar and seated along the long, luxurious banquettes are too busy feasting on the tasty brasserie fare (like duck cassoulet, frisée aux lardons, onion soup, escargots, or goujonettes of sole) to look up and catch your entrance, 15 video screens broadcast images of incoming diners; you'll be captured on film for repeat viewing later. It's best just to get over your stage fright and relax, because it's so easy to enjoy a meal here. French, Asian menu. Breakfast, lunch, dinner, Sun brunch, late night. Entertainment. Casual attire. Reservations required. **$$$**

⬜

★ ★ ★ **BULL AND BEAR STEAKHOUSE.** *301 Park Ave (10022). Phone 212/872-4900; fax 212/486-5107.* Located in the stately Waldorf

Astoria Hotel in Midtown, the Bull and Bear Steakhouse is a testosterone-heavy, meat-eater's haven. The street-level dining room is elegant in a clubby, macho sort of way, and the steaks, all cut from certified aged Black Angus, are fat, juicy, and the way to go, even though the menu does offer a wide variety of other choices, including chicken, lamb, pot pie, and assorted seafood. Classic steakhouse sides like creamed spinach, garlic mashed potatoes, and buttermilk fried onion rings are sinful and match up well with the rich beef on the plate. A terrific selection of red wine will complete your meaty meal nicely. American menu. Lunch, dinner. Bar. Jazz trio Thurs-Fri. **$$$**

D

★ ★ ★ **CIBO.** *767 2nd Ave (10017). Phone 212/681-1616; fax 212/681-9179. www.cibo.citysearch.com.* Contemporary American menu. Closed holidays. Lunch, dinner, Sat, Sun brunch. Bar. **$$$**

★ **COMFORT DINER.** *214 E 45th St (10017). Phone 212/867-4555; fax 212/867-4554.* Closed Dec 25. Breakfast, lunch, dinner. Children's menu. Totally nonsmoking. **$**

★ ★ ★ **DAWAT.** *210 E 58th St (10022). Phone 212/355-7555; fax 212/355-1735. www.restaurant.com/dawat.* Indian menu. Lunch, dinner. Bar. Reservations required. **$$**

D

★ ★ **DELEGATES DINING ROOM.** *UN General Assembly Bldg (10017). Phone 212/963-7625; fax 212/963-2025.* International menu. Specializes in ethnic food festivals, seasonal salads, fresh seafood. Hours: 11:30 am-2:30 pm. Closed Sat, Sun; some major holidays. Reservations required. Service bar. Lunch. Panoramic view of East River. Open to public; identification with photograph required. Jacket. **$$**

D

★ ★ ★ **FELIDIA.** *243 E 58th St (10022). Phone 212/758-1479; fax 212/935-7687. www.lidiasitaly.com.* Celebrated chef and TV personality Lidia Bastianich is the unofficial matriarch of Italian-American cuisine. Her restaurant, Felidia (she and son Joe are partners in Becco, Babbo, and Esca as well), is warm and elegant and draws an elite New York crowd, although it remains free of pretense The lovely dining room is bathed in golden, amber light and is decorated with rich wood-paneled walls, hardwood floors, magnificent flowers, and seasonal vegetable and fruit displays. The menu focuses on a wide array of Italian dishes that you would discover if you journeyed throughout country's varied culinary regions. Diners are expected to eat as they do in Italy, so you'll start with a plate of antipasto or a bowl of *zuppe* (soup), move on to a fragrant bowl of fresh pasta and then to a grilled whole fish, and finally have a bit of dolci for dessert. The Italian wine list is extra-special, so be sure to pair your meal with a few glasses. Italian menu. Menu changes daily. Closed Sun; major holidays. Dinner. Bar. Jacket required. **$$**

D

★ ★ ★ **FIFTY SEVEN FIFTY SEVEN.** *57 E 57th St (10022). Phone 212/758-5757; fax 212/758-5711. www.fshr.com.* A power spot to meet for (at least two) martinis, Fifty Seven Fifty Seven, at the über-civilized Four Seasons Hotel on the magnificent shopping mile of 57th Street, is indeed a hotspot for the city's movers and shakers. This is not to say that mere mortals can't sit down for dinner. Despite the moneyed crowd at the bar, the 22-foot coffered-ceiling dining room remains an oasis of calm, with glossy maple floors and bronzed chandeliers. The gifted crew in the kitchen dresses up classic American fare to suit a demanding urban sensibility. The restaurant also boasts an award-winning international wine list in addition to a fantastic selection of martinis and other perfectly shaken and stirred classic cocktails. Dinner, Sun brunch. Bar. Piano bar. Casual attire. Valet parking available. **$$$$**

D

★ ★ ★ ★ **THE FOUR SEASONS RESTAURANT.** *99 E 52nd St (10022). Phone 212/754-9494; fax 212/754-1077.* The Four Seasons is truly a New York classic. Since 1959, it has been the de facto dining room of media powerhouses, financial movers and shakers, publishing hotshots, legal dealmakers, and the generally fabulous crowd that follows them. Lunch can be an exercise in connect-the-famous-faces, as is the bar, a must for a pre-dinner cocktail or a quick bite. As for what you'll eat when you take a break from gawking at the stars, the food at the Four Seasons is simple but well prepared and takes its cues from around the world. You'll find classically French entrées as well as more contemporary American fare accented with flavors borrowed from Asia, Morocco, and Latin America. Guests at the Four Seasons are often some of the highest rollers, and the room has an energetic buzz that epitomizes the life and breath of the city that never sleeps. It is a scene. Dining here is fun, especially at lunch, if only to be a fly on the wall as deals are made and fortunes are won and lost. *Secret Inspector's Notes:* The pool in The Four Seasons has been the scene of many a scandalous moment when celebrity guests or ladies who lunch kick off their shoes and enjoy Champagne and misbehavior while splashing around. The food and service may disappoint, but the atmosphere and décor never will. Menu changes seasonally. Closed holidays. Breakfast, lunch, dinner. Bar. Children's menu. Jacket required. Reservations required. **$$$$**

D

★ ★ **IL NIDO.** *251 E 53rd St (10022). Phone 212/753-8450; fax 212/486-0705. www.ilnido.citysearch.com.* A bit more rustic than its Il Monello sister, this bistro offers a plethora of antipasti and pastas to begin its northern Italian menu including rigatoni Toscana with tomatoes, white beans and sage. For added entertainment, many entrées are prepared tableside. Northern Italian menu. Closed Sun; holidays. Lunch, dinner. Bar. Casual attire. **$$$**

D

★ ★ **JUBILEE.** *347 E 54th St (10022). Phone 212/888-3569. www.jubileenyc.com.* French bistro menu. Closed Sun in summer; Jan 1, Dec 24-25. Lunch, dinner. Bar. Reservations required dinner. **$$**

★ ★ ★ ★ **KURUMA ZUSHI.** *7 E 47th St, 2nd floor (10017). Phone 212/317-2802; fax 212/317-2803.* Kuruma Zushi is New York's most secreted sushi spot. Located on the second floor of a less-than-impressive Midtown building, with only a tiny sign to alert you to its presence, it is tough to find but well worth the search. Fresh, supple, mouthwatering fish is served with freshly grated wasabi and bright, fiery shavings of ginger. This sushi temple has quite a following, among them Ruth Reichl, the former New York Times restaurant critic and current editor of *Gourmet* magazine, who is vocal about her love of the restaurant's spectacular fish. You will be dreaming about this fish for weeks after your meal has ended. While many consider this the pinnacle of sushi, it does come with quite an insane price tag. Dinner per person can easily hit the $100 mark, which may be why the restaurant, an earth-colored, minimalist room, is most popular with business people on expense accounts and true devotees. Japanese menu. Closed Sun. Dinner. Bar. Totally nonsmoking. **$$$$**

D

★ ★ ★ ★ **LA GRENOUILLE.** *3 E 52nd St (10022). Phone 212/752-1495; fax 212/593-4964. www.la-grenouille.com.* Yes, frog's legs are on the menu at La Grenouille, whose name literally means "The Frog." This stunning Midtown restaurant is the epitome of a classic. If you're craving some sort of fusion hotspot with a loud crowd and a lengthy cocktail list that contains the word Cosmopolitan, you won't be happy here. La Grenouille is elegant and conservative in style and substance. The room is quiet, lovely, and modest; the kitchen serves authentic, sophisticated French cuisine at its finest; and the staff offers service that is refined and seemingly effortless. Now back to those frog's legs, which appropriately are the restaurant's signature. They are served sautéed, Provencal style, and are a must for adventurous diners who have never indulged in them. This is certainly the place to have your first experience with them, although it may spoil you for life. The wine list is mostly French, although some American wines have managed to make the cut as well. Indulging in a cheese course is a nice way to finish your meal, as it is in France. The restaurant is popular at lunch and is frequently crowded with well-preserved businesspeople on lunch hour, being in the heart of Midtown. It is also wonderful spot to take a civilized siesta from hours of shopping along Fifth Avenue and recharge your batteries for the afternoon ahead. *Secret Inspector's Notes:* The flowers at Le Grenouille are a part of the overall atmosphere that pleasantly mimics the French in elegance. They are one of the most charming additions to this transporting dining spot. French menu. Closed Sun, Mon; Aug. Lunch, dinner. Bar. Reservations required. **$$$**

★ ★ **LA MANGEOIRE.** *1008 2nd Ave (10022). Phone 212/759-7086; fax 212/759-6387. www.lamangeoire.com.* Southern French menu. Closed major holidays. Lunch, dinner, Sun brunch. **$$**

D

★ ★ ★ ★ **LE CIRQUE 2000.** *455 Madison Ave (10022). Phone 212/303-7788; fax 212/303-7712. www.lecirque.com.* Located in the stunning New York Palace Hotel (see also NEW YORK PALACE), Le Cirque has set the standard for New York City dining for 20 years. The restaurant, designed

by Adam Tihany, combines old-world charm with modern design. Bright swirls of neon lights and bold, primary-colored banquettes evoke a playful, 21st-century circus theme, while mahogany walls, vintage carpets, and crown moldings maintain the elegance of the original palace-like space. The kitchen does a wonderful job of balancing old and new as well, creating meals (both prix fixe and à la carte) that challenge yet feel safe, and manage to satisfy every taste and appetite. The à la carte menu is divided into several sections: Appetizers, Pasta, Main Courses, Classics, and From the Grill. Desserts are wonderful, showy, artistic creations and should not be turned down. They are worth any added inches on the hips. An extensive wine list and a menu of caviar accent the meal and bring the dining experience into another realm of luxury. Le Cirque is perpetually crowded and with an eclectic mix of socialites, tourists, fashion-forward New Yorkers, influential visitors, and other elite. It is constantly buzzing, yet the energy is not overwhelming. Quite the opposite. The place makes you feel alive and giddy, like a kid in a toy store anticipating many gifts. French cuisine. Lunch, dinner. Bar. Jacket required (dinner). Reservations required. Outdoor seating. **$$$**
D

★ ★ **LE COLONIAL.** *149 E 57th St (10022). Phone 212/752-0808; fax 212/752-7534.* Vietnamese menu. Closed July 4, Thanksgiving, Dec 25. Dinner. Bar. Bamboo furniture, birdcages. **$$**

★ ★ ★ **LE PERIGORD.** *405 E 52nd St (10022). Phone 212/755-6244; fax 212/486-3906. www.leperigord.com.* Le Perigord is one of New York's old-time favorites for sophisticated French dining. The menu of classic dishes, including the restaurant's signature game selection (in season), is geared for diners who define luxury in terms of impeccable, attentive service, elegant furnishings, inspired haute cuisine of the nouvelle French variety, and the quiet of a dining room filled with people enjoying a civilized meal. The food here is delicate and serene, in perfect harmony with the peaceful and majestic dining room. Modern French cuisine. Closed July. Lunch, dinner. Bar. Jacket required. **$$$**

★ ★ ★ ★ **LUTECE.** *249 E 50th St (10022). Phone 212/752-2225; fax 212/223-9050. www.arkrestaurants.com.* With the advent of fusion cuisine and the introduction of a new world of global ingredients to the kitchen, there was perhaps a decline in demand for classic French cuisine. But classics are classics for a reason, and if you crave the grande dame of French cuisine, Lutece is a wonderful choice, even though the kitchen has started to open up its cabinets to flavors of other lands. At Lutece, you'll find classic French cuisine that has been updated nicely, incorporating new life, while adhering to its traditional roots. For example, lemongrass, shiitake mushrooms, ginger, tandoori spices, and Opal basil have found their way onto the menu, flavors that brighten appetizers and entrées prepared with a classic French hand. The restaurant, set in a beautiful townhouse in Midtown Manhattan, is a popular spot for pre-theater dinners and for those out to impress business colleagues or clients at lunch. Though lovely, the elegant room can feel stuffy at times, and for this reason Lutece generally draws an older, more sophisticated crowd. There is a place for civilized fine dining. It is Lutece.

Haute French cuisine. Closed Sun. Lunch, dinner. Bar. Jacket required. Reservations required. **$$$**

★ ★ ★ **MALONEY & PORCELLI.** *37 E 50th St (10022). Phone 212/ 750-2233; fax 212/750-2252. www.maloneyandporcelli.com.* Named for the restaurant owners' attorneys, Maloney & Porcelli is an easy, smart choice for an urban business lunch or a simple dinner out with a group of friends who favor simple, well-executed cuisine served in a classic, clubby environment without fuss or pretense. The New American menu offers straight-ahead choices like a raw bar, thin-crust pizza, and filet mignon from consulting chef David Burke. The wine list contains some real gems as well, making Maloney & Porcelli a favorite for Midtown dining. American menu. Closed Jan 1, Dec 25. Lunch, dinner. Bar. **$$$**

D

★ ★ ★ ★ **MARCH.** *405 E 58th St (10022). Phone 212/754-6272; fax 212/838-5108. www.marchrestaurant.com.* Many people have issues with indulgence. Chef-owner Wayne Nish is not one of them. He believes that his guests should be indulged from the moment they enter his jewel-like, turn-of-the-century-townhouse restaurant to the moment they sadly must part. And a meal at March is just that—pure, blissful indulgence—from start to finish. For this reason (and because it's one of the most romantic spots in New York City), it is truly a special-occasion place, and reservations should be secured well in advance. Nish's menu, of what he calls "New York City Cuisine," is fabulous. Dishes focus on fresh, seasonal products sparked to attention with luxurious ingredients from around the world. Choose from three-, four-, five-, or six-course tasting menus; each is available with or without wine pairings. Go for the wine. Co-owner Joseph Scalice is a gifted wine director, and you're in for a treat. Alfresco dining on the townhouse's rooftop terrace and mezzanine is magical in warm months. *Secret Inspector's Notes:* The service is incredibly accommodating at March, and the kitchen is receptive to guest modifications of tasting menus. The food is inconsistent, though; while some courses are like a taste of heaven, others seem to miss the mark. American menu. Closed most major holidays. Lunch, dinner. Bar. Jacket required. Reservations required. Outdoor seating. **$$$**

D

★ **MED GRILL BISTRO AND CAFE.** *725 Fifth Ave (10022). Phone 212/751-3276; fax 212/421-7554. www.bice.com.* Continental, Italian menu. Closed some major holidays. Lunch. Bar. **$$$**

D

★ ★ ★ **MICHAEL JORDAN'S.** *23 Vanderbilt Ave (10017). Phone 212/ 655-2300; fax 212/271-2324. www.theglaziergroup.com.* Set in a grand 7,000-square-foot space on the northwest balcony of Grand Central Terminal, Michael Jordan's affords bird's-eye views of New Yorkers on the run while providing a bit of tranquility amidst all that rushing. Giant slabs of juicy beef (a porterhouse for two is a signature) are the draw here, but Caesar salads and great big vats of crispy golden fries are also winners. Scores of martini and Manhattan drinkers pile in after work, so for those who can't stomach steak, a liquid refreshment at the three-deep bar may be a nice alternative. Steak menu. Lunch, dinner. Bar. Casual attire. Reservations required. **$$$**

★ ★ **MONKEY BAR.** *60 E 54th St (10022). Phone 212/838-2600; fax 212/838-4595.* American, Continental menu. Closed Dec 25. Lunch, dinner, late night. Bar. Casual attire. **$$$**

D

★ ★ ★ **MORTON'S OF CHICAGO.** *551 Fifth Ave (10017). Phone 585/972-3315; fax 585/972-0018. www.mortons.com.* Steak menu. Closed most major holidays. Lunch, dinner. Bar. Jacket required. Reservations required. **$$$**

D

★ ★ ★ **MR. K'S.** *570 Lexington Ave (10022). Phone 212/583-1668; fax 212/583-1618. www.mrksnyc.com.* Chinese menu. Lunch, dinner. Bar. Casual attire. Reservations required. Totally nonsmoking. **$$$**

D

★ ★ ★ **NADAMAN HAKUBAI.** *66 Park Ave (10016). Phone 212/885-7111. www.kitano.com.* Located in the posh Kitano Hotel (see), Nadaman Hakubai offers authentic Japanese fare in a tranquil, Zenlike space. The menu features a myriad of traditionally prepared seafood dishes like *ika shiokara* (chopped salted squid), *karuge-su* (vinegar-marinated jellyfish), and *karei* (fried, grilled, or simmered flounder). For a special treat, call ahead and reserve a private room for the multicourse chef's choice menu ($120 to $150), or, to savor a simpler meal, choose from the restaurant's swimming selection of sushi, sashimi, and maki rolls, as well as udon and soba noodle dishes. Japanese menu. Lunch, dinner. Casual attire. Totally nonsmoking. **$$$$**

D

★ ★ ★ ★ **OCEANA.** *55 E 54th St (10022). Phone 212/759-5941; fax 212/759-6076. www.oceanarestaurant.com.* Oceana has been one of New York's most lauded seafood spots for more than a decade. Although ten years could have derailed the restaurant, it has stayed a steady course and its mission is as clear as ever: stunning, just-shy-of-swimming seafood tinged with subtle, precise flavors from around the globe. You'll find practically every glorious fish in the sea on the menu, from halibut to tuna, dorade to turbot. Scallops, lobster, and glistening oysters are also on the menu. But there's a nod to the issue of overfishing here as well. Oceana is known for serving only sustainable seafood that is not in danger of becoming extinct. The service is warm and efficient, and the cream-colored, nautical-themed room (portholes dot the walls) is peaceful and comfortable, making Oceana a perennial favorite for power lunchers and pre-theater diners. The wine list is impressive, with a good number of seafood-friendly options at a variety of price points. A signature selection of American caviar from sturgeon, paddlefish, and rainbow trout makes a strong argument for forgoing osetra, beluga, and sevruga. Closed Sun; holidays. Lunch, dinner. Bar. Located in 2-story townhouse; spacious, bilevel dining room. Jacket required. Reservations required. **$$$**

★ ★ **OTABE.** *68 E 56th St (10022). Phone 212/223-7575; fax 212/986-5101.* Japanese menu. Lunch, dinner. Bar. Casual attire. Reservations required. **$$$**

D

★ ★ **OYSTER BAR.** *Grand Central Terminal, Lower Level (10017). Phone 212/490-6650; fax 212/949-5210. www.oysterbarny.com.* Seafood menu. Closed Sun; major holidays. Lunch, dinner. Bar. Casual attire. In landmark railroad station; Gustivino-tiled vaulted ceilings, mahogany paneling. **$$**

D

★ ★ **PARK BISTRO.** *414 Park Ave S (10016). Phone 212/689-1360; fax 212/689-6437.* French menu. Closed major holidays. Lunch, dinner. Bar. Casual attire. **$$$**

D

★ ★ ★ **PATROON.** *160 E 46th St (10017). Phone 212/883-7373; fax 212/883-1118.* Owner Ken Aretsky's popular, clubby, low-lit Patroon is more than a boy's club for juicy steaks. You'll also find women feasting at Patroon, as his American restaurant has that edge that other steakhouses don't—a terrific kitchen with talent for more than just beef (although the beef is fabulous). Of the USDA Prime selections, Steak Diana (named for Aretsky's wife) is a house specialty and is prepared tableside with brown butter, shallots, and wine for an arresting visual presentation. The kitchen also gussies things up with hearty dishes like pork shanks, short ribs, and lighter fare like oysters, shrimp, lump crab, and a slew of stunning seafood. A wide rooftop deck makes summertime fun with great grilled fare and chilly cocktails. American menu. Closed Sun; major holidays; Sat (July-Aug). Dinner. Bar. Casual attire. **$$$**

D

★ ★ ★ **ROSA MEXICANO.** *1063 1st Ave (10022). Phone 212/753-7407; fax 212/753-7433. www.rosamexicano.com.* Mexican menu. Closed Thanksgiving. Dinner. **$$$**

D

★ ★ **SAN MARTIN'S.** *143 E 49th St (10017). Phone 212/832-9270; fax 212/755-1862. www.sanmartinrestibaweb.com.* Continental menu. Lunch, dinner. Bar. Outdoor seating. **$$**

D

★ ★ ★ **SAN PIETRO.** *18 E 54th St (10022). Phone 212/753-9015; fax 212/371-2337. www.sanpietro.net.* San Pietro is one of the restaurants where you walk in a customer and leave a part of the family. Located on a busy Midtown street, San Pietro is owned and run by the three Bruno brothers, who grew up on a family farm along the Amalfi Coast in the southern Italian region of Campagna. At San Pietro, the brothers pay homage their homeland by serving traditional dishes—antipasti, pasta, poultry, fish, veal, and beef—accented with seasonal ingredients and lots of Italian charm. The wine list contains a knockout selection of southern Italian wines to complete the experience. Southern Italian menu. Closed Sun; holidays. Dinner. Bar. Jacket required. Outdoor seating. **$$$**

★ ★ **SCOPA RESTAURANT.** *79 Madison Ave (10016). Phone 212/686-8787; fax 212/686-1214. www.scopanyc.com.* Italian menu. Closed Sun. Lunch, dinner. Bar. Entertainment. Casual attire. Reservations required. **$$**

D

★ ★ ★ **SHUN LEE PALACE.** *155 E 55th St (10022). Phone 212/371-8844; fax 212/752-1936.* The swirling décor of the Adam Tihany-designed dining room should tell you that something special awaits. Restaurateur Michael Tong's haute Chinese offers all your favorites with attentive service. Guest chefs visit frequently from Hong Kong. The special prix fixe lunch is a deal. Chinese menu. Closed Thanksgiving. Lunch, dinner, late night. Bar. Casual attire. Reservations required. **$$$**

D

★ ★ ★ **SMITH & WOLLENSKY.** *797 3rd Ave (10022). Phone 212/753-1530; fax 212/751-5446. www.smithandwollensky.com.* The original, after which the national chain was modeled, this 390-seat, wood-paneled dining room is known for sirloin steaks and filet mignon, but also offers lamb and veal chops. Sides are huge and straightforward, with the likes of creamed spinach and hash browns. Good wines and personable service complete the experience American menu. Closed major holidays. Dinner. Bar. Casual attire. **$$$**

D

★ ★ ★ **SPARKS STEAK HOUSE.** *210 E 46th St (10017). Phone 212/687-4855; fax 212/557-7409.* This temple of beef is one of the standard spots for meat-seekers in New York City. The cavernous dining room has a classic old-world charm to it, with oil paintings, etched glass, and dark wood paneling, and the large bar feels like home as soon as you wrap your fingers around the stem of your martini glass. Sparks is a serious American chophouse, and only serious appetites need apply for entry. There are no dainty portions here, so come ready to feast on thick, juicy steaks, burgers, roasts, racks, and fish (if you must). American, steak menu. Closed Sun; major holidays. Dinner. Bar. Casual attire. Reservations required. **$$$**

D

★ ★ ★ **SUSHI YASUDA.** *204 E 43rd St (10017). Phone 212/972-1001.* Sushi Yasuda is a smartly dressed, minimalist sushi bar and restaurant. Bathed in blond wood, the restaurant looks as a little like an Ikea crew came in and installed all the fixtures. The room maintains a Zen vibe, remaining hushed and serene. Omakase, or chef's choice tasting meals, are offered in addition to a lengthy selection of buttery sushi and glossy sashimi sliced with surgical precision. The fish is fresh and flavorful and begs the question of why we ever cook fish at all. This is some of the most spectacular sushi in the neighborhood in a setting that will leave you relaxed and pleasantly satiated. Closed Sun. Dinner. Casual attire. Totally nonsmoking. **$$$**

★ ★ **TYPHOON BREWERY.** *22 E 54th St (10022). Phone 212/754-9006; fax 212/754-9012.* American, Thai menu. Closed Sun; major holidays. Lunch, dinner. Bar. Casual attire. Reservations required. Totally nonsmoking. **$$**

D

★ ★ ★ **VONG.** *200 E 54th St (10022). Phone 212/486-9592; fax 212/980-3745. www.jeangeorges.com.* When Jean-Georges Vongerichten, Alsatian-born wonder chef, opened a Thai restaurant called Vong, people weren't sure what to make of it. But doubts were soon dispelled as diners began to experience his exciting and exotic French riffs on fiery Thai classics, incorporating spices and flavors of the East with a New York sensibility. The restaurant feels like a wild and mystical night in the Orient, decorated with long, deep banquettes covered with silk pillows in brilliant jewel tones, walls painted crimson red accented with gold leaf, and a long table showcasing a Buddha altar. It's a journey for all of the senses. Thai, French menu. Closed major holidays. Dinner. Bar. Casual attire. **$$$**

D

★ ★ ★ **THE WATER CLUB.** *500 E 30th St (10016). Phone 212/683-3333; fax 212/696-4009. www.thewaterclub.com.* Special occasions were made for The Water Club, a lovely restaurant with romantic, panoramic views of the East River. The shiplike space features soothing, nightly live piano and an intimate, clubby lounge, perfect for relaxing before or after dinner. While poultry and beef are on the menu, The Water Club is known for its seafood. In addition to a gigantic raw bar, you'll find an impressive selection of lobster, scallops, cod, tuna, salmon, and whatever else looks good at the fish markets. On a sunny day, you can't beat brunch out on the deck with a fiery Bloody Mary in hand, watching the ships go by, feeling like you're far away from it all. Seafood menu. Lunch, dinner, Sun brunch. Bar. Piano bar. Located on barge in the East River. Jacket required. Reservations required. Valet parking available. **$$$**

★ ★ **ZARELA.** *953 2nd Ave (10022). Phone 212/644-6740; fax 212/980-1073. www.zarela.com.* Mexican menu. Closed major holidays. Dinner. Bar. Entertainment Tues-Sat. **$$**

Midtown West

What to See and Do

Adventure on a Shoestring. *300 W 53rd St (10019). Phone 212/265-2663.* Year-round walking tours of various neighborhoods, including SoHo, Haunted Greenwich Village, and Chinatown. **$**

American Folk Art Museum. *45 W 53rd St (10019). Phone 212/265-1040. www.folkartmuseum.org.* Folk arts of all types, including paintings, sculptures, quilts, needlework, toys, weather vanes, and handmade furniture. Changing exhibits; lectures and demonstrations. Admission is free on Friday evenings. (Tues-Sun 10 am-6 pm, Fri to 8 pm; closed holidays) **$$**

Eva and Morris Feld Gallery. *2 Lincoln Sq (10023). Phone 212/595-9533. www.folkartmuseum.org.* The original site of the American Folk Art Museum, reopened as a sister gallery, function space, and museum shop after renovations were completed in 2001. (Mon 11 am-6 pm, Tues-Sun 11 am-7:30 pm) **FREE**

Bergdorf Goodman. *754 Fifth Ave (10019). Phone 212/753-7300.* With its designer handbags that can set you back as much as $4,000, $700 swimsuits, and nightgowns that cost $500, Bergdorf Goodman is one of the city's grand-dame department stores. Ladies who lunch, yuppie professionals, and stylish Gen Xers with trust funds are equally at home in this shopping Mecca, located in the heart of the Midtown shopping district, which features a sophisticated selection of clothing, furs, jewelry, tableware, kitchenware, cosmetics, and lingerie. You can find items on sale, but this is not the place for bargain hunters. The selection of merchandise tends to appeal more to those whose taste borders on conservative. The sales staff is attentive and pleasant for those who need assistance in picking out just the right thing. Word to the wise: pack your platinum card. (Daily exc Thanksgiving, Dec 25, Jan 1)

⭐ **Carnegie Hall.** *154 W 57th St (10019). Phone 212/247-7800. www.carnegiehall.org.* Completed in 1891, the celebrated auditorium has been home to the world's great musicians for more than a century. Guided one-hour tours. (Mon-Fri) **$$$$**

⭐ **Central Park.** *59th to 110th sts between Fifth Ave and Central Park West. Phone 212/360-3444 (recorded info); 212/310-6600 (live operator). www.centralpark.org.* Called "the lungs of New York," Central Park was reclaimed in 1858 from 843 acres of swampland that were used as a garbage dump and occupied by squatters. Landscape designer Frederick Law Olmsted's dream was to bring city dwellers the kind of refreshment found only in nature. A century and a half later, the park still does that; today, it's a source of varied outdoor entertainment. Stop at the visitor's center, called The Dairy—midpark at 65th Street—for a map and a calendar of events. If you're looking for active endeavors, you can jog around the Reservoir or rent ice skates at Wollman Rink or at Lasker Rink, which becomes a swimming pool in summer. If you're looking to have a Woody Allen moment on the Lake, rent a rowboat at Loeb Boathouse. Rent a kite from Big City Kites, at Lexington and 82nd Street, and walk over to the park to catch the breeze on the Great Lawn. If you have kids, visit one of the 19 themed playgrounds, the zoo and petting zoo, the Carousel, the raucous storytelling hour at the Hans Christian Andersen statue, and the Model Boat Pond, where serious modelers race their tiny remote-controlled boats on weekends. In summer, something's going on every night, and it's free! See Shakespeare in the Park at the Delacorte Theater. Get comfortable on the Great Lawn to hear the New York Philharmonic or the Metropolitan Opera under the stars. SummerStage brings well-known artists to Rumsey Playfield for jazz, dance, traditional, and contemporary musical performances. The Band Shell is the venue for classical concerts. Take advantage of Central Park. Amble through the forested Ramble. Stroll down the venerable, elm-lined Mall and past the bronze statues of Balto the dog, Alice in Wonderland, and forgotten poets. Bring a picnic!

Chelsea

Primarily middle-class residential and still somewhat industrial, Chelsea—stretching between 14th and 30th streets, from Sixth Avenue to the Hudson River—is not the most tourist-oriented of areas. However, the neighborhood does offer an exciting, avant-garde arts scene, as well as many lovely quiet blocks lined with attractive row houses and rustling trees. A new gay community has moved in recently, bringing with it trendy cafés, shops, and bars, while an enormous, state-of-the-art sports complex, the Chelsea Piers, beckons from the river's edge (between 18th and 22nd streets).

Most of Chelsea was once owned by Captain Thomas Clarke, whose grandson, Clement Charles Clarke, laid out the residential district in the early 1800s. Clement Charles was also a scholar and a poet who wrote the famous poem beginning with the line, "'Twas the night before Christmas…" Another of Clement Charles's legacies is the General Theological Seminary, a peaceful enclave of ivy-covered buildings bounded by the block between Ninth and Tenth avenues and 20th and 21st streets.

Also on the western edge of Chelsea are many of the city's foremost art galleries, which began moving here in the early 1990s as rents in SoHo—their former home—began skyrocketing. An especially large number can be found on West 21st and 22nd streets between Tenth and Eleventh avenues; among them are the Paula Cooper Gallery (534 West 21st Street), the Maximum Protech Gallery (511 West 22nd), and the Dia Center for the Arts (548 West 22nd). One of the pioneers of the area, the Dia Center is really more a museum than an art gallery and usually hosts a variety of eye-popping exhibits, along with an open-air sculpture garden on the roof.

Most of Chelsea's thriving shops, restaurants, and bars—some of which are predominantly gay, some not—stand along Sixth and Eighth avenues between 14th and 23rd streets. Some of the neighborhood's prettiest blocks, lined with elegant row houses, are West 20th, 21st, and 22nd streets between Eighth and Tenth avenues. Also, be sure to take a gander at the Chelsea Hotel (222 West 23rd Street, near Eighth Avenue), a maroon-colored landmark that's all black gables, chimneys, and balconies. Built in 1884, the Chelsea has housed dozens of artists, writers, and musicians over the years, including Arthur Miller, Jackson Pollock, Bob Dylan, and Sid Vicious.

Just north of Chelsea lies the underground Pennsylvania Station (Seventh Avenue at 32nd Street), topped with circular Madison Square Garden, and the General Post Office (Eighth Avenue, between 31st and 33rd streets)—a gorgeous building designed by McKim, Mead & White in 1913. The Garment District, centering on Seventh Avenue in the 30s, also begins here.

The Dairy. *In the Park on 65th St, W of the Central Park Wildlife Conservation Center and the carousel. Phone 212/794-6564.* Exhibition/ Visitor Information Center. Video on history of the park; time-travel video; gift and book shop. (Tues-Sun) **FREE**

Storytelling in the Park. *74th St and Fifth Ave (10021). Phone 212/360-3444.* At Hans Christian Andersen statue in Central Park, near the model boat pond, off 74th St at Fifth Ave (June-Sept, Sat). Recommended for children 5 and older; also in certain playgrounds (July-Aug). **FREE**

Circle Line Cruises. *West 42nd St and 12th Ave (10036). All trains (subway) stop at 42nd St. Then transfer to westbound M42 bus to pier. Phone 212/563-3200. www.circleline.com.* Grab a seat on the port (left) side for a spectacular view of the skyline. Rest your feet and enjoy the sea air as you cruise around Manhattan. Narrated by knowledgeable, personable guides, these tours take you past the Statue of Liberty and under the Brooklyn Bridge; if you opt for the three-hour cruise, you'll also see the New Jersey Palisades, a glorious sight in autumn. Food and drinks are available on board. (Closed Jan 1, Dec 25) **$$$$**

City Center. *131 W 55th St (10019). 55th St between Sixth and Seventh aves. Phone 212/581-1212. www.citycenter.org.* Landmark theater hosts world-renowned dance companies, including the Alvin Ailey American Dance Theater, the Paul Taylor Dance Company, and Merce Cunningham Dance Company. Also presents American music and theater events. Downstairs, City Center Stages I and II host the Manhattan Theatre Club.

Discovery Tour of Brooklyn *49 W 45th St (10036). Phone 212/397-2600.* Six-hour bus tour to many of Brooklyn's sites and neighborhoods. Departs from Gray Line Bus Terminal in Manhattan. (May-Oct, Thurs and Sat) **$$$$**

⭐ **Empire State Building.** *350 Fifth Ave (10018). Phone 212/736-3100. www.esbnyc.com.* A beloved city symbol since it opened in 1931, the Empire State Building is where King Kong battled with airplanes in the movie classic and where visitors go for a panoramic view of Manhattan. Try going at night when the city lights compete with the stars. The slender art deco skyscraper is so popular that visitors are often greeted with a long line for tickets to the observation deck. Ordering them in advance from the Web site will save you time. (Daily) **$$$**

ESPN Zone. *1472 Broadway (10036). Phone 212/921-3776. www.espnzone.com.* Want to have fun in the city on a rainy afternoon? Hang out at the ESPN Zone in the Theatre District. This family-friendly restaurant, filled with huge TV screens, sells sports-related items and gives visitors the chance to view live ESPN broadcasts. The place is loud and boisterous and is a big draw for jocks and jock wannabes; kids get a real kick out of it, too. Have a beer, grab a burger or sandwich, buy a T-shirt or two, and just relax at this sports-lover's paradise. (Daily)

FAO Schwartz. *767 Fifth Ave (10153). Phone 212/644-9400. www.fao.com.* Children will instantly recognize the entrance to FAO Schwartz when they see the tall, brightly colored musical clock that guards the door. Inside, two floors are crowded with live clowns, chemistry sets, train sets, Madame

Alexander dolls, giant stuffed animals, child-sized motorized cars, and all the latest electronic baubles in incredible profusion and magical, mechanical display. At Christmastime, shoppers often have to stand in line just to get in. (Mon-Sat 10 am-9 pm, Sun 11 am-6 pm)

Gray Line. *254 W 54th St (10019). Phone 212/397-2600.* For information on a variety of sightseeing tours, including tours of Manhattan aboard glass-top motor coaches, contact Gray Line of New York. Also day trips and tour packages.

H & M. *435 Seventh Ave (10001). www.hm.com* If the notion of buying affordable versions of everything you couldn't afford on Madison Avenue appeals to your wallet, then H&M is the store for you. This fast-growing international chain, which sells stylish men's, women's, young adult's, and children's clothing, features its own brands at prices that suit most budgets. The shops are bright and airy, and each location has a slightly different mix of inventory. Currently there are five outlets in New York City: 435 Seventh Ave, 125 W 125th St, 1328 Broadway (34th and Herald Square), 640 Fifth Ave, and 558 Broadway (in SoHo). (Daily; closed Thanksgiving, Dec 25)

Henri Bendel. *712 Fifth Ave (10019). Phone 212/247-1100.* The name Henri Bendel was synonymous with chic during the disco era. Today, the store still features hip, trendy women's designer clothes, hats, fragrances, handbags, and jewelry. Whether you're looking for a $1,200 dress or a $500 handbag, this is the shop for you. You may need to break the bank (or two!) to make a purchase, but you just may find yourself decked out in something that the girls back home wished they owned. (Daily; closed Jan 1, Thanksgiving, Dec 25)

International Center of Photography. *1133 Ave of the Americas (10036). Phone 212/857-0000. www.icp.org.* Photography buffs won't want to miss the International Center for Photography, recently relocated from the Upper East Side to Midtown. In these spacious galleries, you'll find changing exhibits featuring everyone from Weegee (Arthur Fellig) to Annie Liebovitz. (Tues-Thurs 10 am-5 pm, Fri 10 am-8 pm, Sat-Sun 10 am-6 pm; closed Mon, holidays) **$$**

***Intrepid* Sea-Air Space Museum.** *12th Ave and 46th St, Pier 86 (10036). Phone 212/245-0072. www.intrepidmuseum.org.* The famous aircraft carrier *Intrepid* has been converted into a museum with gallery space devoted to histories of the ship itself, the modern navy, and space technology. Also on display is a nuclear guided submarine and a Vietnam-era destroyer (available for boarding). Exhibits and film presentations. (Memorial Day-Labor Day, Mon-Fri 10 am-5 pm, Sat-Sun 10 am-6 pm; rest of year, Tues-Sun 10 am-5 pm; closed Thanksgiving, Dec 25) **$$$**

Jacob K. Javits Convention Center. *34th-39th sts along the Hudson River, on 22-acre site SW of Times Square. Phone 212/216-2000. www.javitscenter.com.* One of the world's largest, most technically advanced exposition halls; 900,000 square feet of exhibit space and more than 100 meeting rooms can accommodate six events simultaneously. Designed by I. M. Pei, the center is easily recognized by its thousands of glass cubes that mirror the skyline by day. Café.

Liberty Helicopter Tours. *Heliport at 12th Ave and W 30th St (10001). Take the C/E subways to 34th St and Eighth Ave. Phone toll-free 800/542-9933. www. libertyhelicopters.com* See the grand sights of the city—from the Empire State Building to Yankee Stadium to the Chrysler Building—all from the magnificent view that only a helicopter can offer. Liberty offers six different tours on its six-passenger helicopters, which last from five minutes for those who are a bit nervous to as long as 30 minutes for those who want to see everything. There's even a 30-minute package that enables you to design your own course ($275 per person) and a 15-minute romance package for reserving the entire helicopter ($849), perfect for a special occasion—you even get a bottle of Champagne afterward. Just think, you can pop the question over the beautiful lights of Manhattan! A photo ID is required, and your bags will be screened. No carry-ons are allowed, except for cameras and video equipment. (Daily) **$$$$**

The Lion King. *New Amsterdam Theater, 214 W 42nd St (10036). Phone 212/307-4747. disney.go.com/disneytheatrical/thelionking.* Based on the Disney animated film of the same name, this wildly popular musical is a feast for the eyes, ears, and soul. It has action, adventure, amazing costumes, and inventive characters—with performers singing and dancing their hearts out. Even though it's a kid's story, adults of all ages have flocked to see this musical since it opened in 1998. Because the Tony Award winner is such a spectacle to see, it is worth splurging on expensive tickets to get the best seats available. Justify the price by skimping on dinner or lunch beforehand. Book as early as you can, since this show sells out at just about any time of the year. (Daily) **$$$$**

Macy's Herald Square. *11 Pennsylvania Plz (10001). 34th St at Broadway. Phone 212/695-4400.* "The world's largest store" has everything from international fashion collections for men and women to antique galleries. (Daily; closed Easter, Thanksgiving, Dec 25)

Madison Square Garden. *4 Pennsylvania Plz (10001). On Seventh Ave, between W 31st and W 33rd sts. Phone 212/465-MSG1. www.thegarden.com.* The Garden has been the site of major sporting events, concerts, and other special events for well over a century. The present Garden, the fourth building bearing that name, opened in 1968. (The original Garden was actually on Madison Square.) It is the home of the New York Knicks and Liberty basketball teams, and New York Rangers hockey club. The Garden complex includes the 20,000-seat arena and the Theater at Madison Square Garden, which features performances of the holiday classic *A Christmas Carol* every year.

Movin' Out. *Richard Rodgers Theatre, 226 W 46th St (10036). Phone 212/307-4100. www.movinoutonbroadway.com.* If you love the music of everyone's favorite Piano Man, Billy Joel, and are equally enamored with dance performances, then this very different type of Broadway musical is for you. Based on the songs of Billy Joel, *Movin' Out* tells the saga of several friends' lives and the difficulties they face. The riveting dance numbers were conceived and choreographed by Twyla Tharp. The dancers are fantastic, the numbers are moving and passionate, and the music is brought to life by a wonderful singer with a style that is similar to Billy Joel's but still very much his own. This is not for theatergoers who are looking for the conventional, cookie-cutter musical. *Movin' Out* is its own breed of show that works great and is well worth spending the bucks to get the best seats in the house (if you can). (Tue-Sun) **$$$$**

Museum of Arts & Design. *40 W 53rd St (10019). Phone 212/956-3535. www.americancraftmuseum.org.* Dedicated to the history of American crafts, including textiles, ceramics, and glasswork. Changing exhibits. (Daily 10 am-6 pm, Thurs to 8 pm; closed holidays) **$$**

Museum of Television & Radio. *25 W 52nd St (10019). Phone 212/621-6800. www.mtr.orgwww.mtr.org.* William Paley, the former head of CBS, founded this museum to collect, preserve, and make available to the public the best of broadcasting. View special screenings or, at a private console, hear and see selections of your own choosing from the vast archive of more than 100,000 programs. From the comedy of Burns and Allen to the Beatles in America, and from a teary-eyed Walter Cronkite reporting on President Kennedy's assassination to a tireless Peter Jennings persevering through an endless 9/11, it's there for the asking. (Tues-Sun; closed holidays) **$$$**

New York Public Library. *11 W 40th St (10018). Phone 212/930-0501; 212/661-7220. www.nypl.org.* One of the best research libraries in the world, with more than ten million volumes. Exhibits of rare books, art materials; free programs at branches. One-hour tours of central building (Mon-Sat), library tours at 11 am and 2 pm.

The Producers. *St. James Theater, 246 W 44th St (10036). Phone 212/239-5800. www.producersonbroadway.com.* This show won the most Tony awards ever, and is truly worth all the accolades that it has received. Based on the hysterical Mel Brooks movie, this even funnier musical brings to life the story of two producers who try desperately to put on a Broadway flop. Take that wacky premise, add even wackier characters and very funny song and dance numbers, and you have a delightful night out for lovers of musical theater. You'll laugh from start to finish and even hum some of the catchy, irreverent tunes. This show is destined to be around for a long time. Book very early, since it is always a sell-out with both locals and tourists. (Tue-Sun) **$$$$**

Times Square and the Theater District. *6th to 8th aves and 40th to 53rd sts.* Entertainment center of the city and theatrical headquarters of the country offering plays, musicals, concerts, movies, and exotic entertainments; named for the Times Tower at One Times Square, originally the home of the *New York Times.* (See THEATER in introductory copy.)

TKTS Discount Theater Tickets. *Broadway at 47th St (10036). www.tkts.com* With the price of Broadway shows closing in at $100 for the best seats in the house, TKTS is a godsend to theater lovers. The more popular TKTS booth at Times Square (just look for lots of people standing on two lines) provides up to 50 percent discounted tickets on Broadway, off-Broadway, and some musical and dance events. Tickets are sold for the day of performance for matinees and evening shows. The downtown booth (199 Water St) sells tickets for evening day-of performance and for matinees one day in advance. Generally, you will not be able to get tickets for the hottest shows in town through TKTS, but usually for ones that have been playing for a while or are not doing as well. Lines are long and you are guaranteed nothing by waiting on line. Have a first, second, and third choice in mind. Only cash and traveler's checks are accepted. (Daily)

Trinity Church. *422 W 57th St (10019). Phone 212/602-0800. www.trinitywall street.org.* (1846) The third building to occupy this site; original was built in 1697. Its famous graveyard, favorite lunchtime spot of workers in the financial district, contains the graves of Robert Fulton and Alexander Hamilton. The Gothic Revival brownstone church houses a museum. Parish center with dining room open to the public. Services (daily). **FREE**

Union Square Greenmarket. *14th St and Broadway (10001). The 4, 5, 6, N, R subways stop at Union Square. Phone 212/477-3220. www.cenyc.org.* This bustling year-round farmers market is located at Union Square between 14th and 17th streets and Broadway and Park Avenue. It's a chance to experience a bit of the country in the Big Apple, as farmers and other vendors sell fresh fruits, vegetables, cheeses, homemade pies, herbs, cut flowers, and potted plants. Plan to arrive early for the best selection. (Daily; closed major holidays)

Special Events

Bryant Park Summer Film Festival. *42nd St between Fifth and Sixth aves (10036). Phone 212/512-5700. www.bryantpark.org.* For a relaxing evening taking in the balmy breezes of summer, a picnic with your favorite foods, and an outdoor screening of a classic American film, park yourself on the lawn at Bryant Park for its weekly film showing. Hundreds come each Monday night to see a movie and hang out once the sun goes down. And you can't beat the price! Check the local newspapers to find out what's playing each week. Mon, June-Aug. **FREE**

Fleet Week. *Intrepid Sea-Air-Space Museum, 166 W 46th St (10036). Phone 212/245-0072. www.fleetweek.navy.mil.* In a scene right out of the Gene Kelly, Navy-themed musical, *On the Town,* Navy and Coast Guard ships gather for a parade up the Hudson River that is a true spectacle of springtime in New York. After the ships dock by the museum, they are open to the public for tours. You can find some great photo opportunities here. Other fun sights for all ages include flyovers and 21-gun salutes. Expect to find Navy men all over the city, looking for a good time. Fleet Week is pure Americana that gives the city a real patriotic feeling. Late May.

Ninth Avenue International Food Festival. *Ninth Ave between 37th and 57th sts (10018). Take the A/C/E subway to 34th St and 8th Ave. Phone 212/581-7029. www.9th-ave.com.* This event epitomizes all the gastronomical diversity that is New York City. Taking place during the third weekend in May in the ethnically mixed Hell's Kitchen neighborhood, the two-day festival is a

20-block extravaganza of food booths and entertainment. From burritos to jerk chicken to curried chicken, you can find any kind of food imaginable in this ultimate of block parties. More than 1 million visitors have showed up in the past to this annual that's been going strong for 28 years, so prepare for crowds. Wear comfortable shoes and loose-fitting clothes so that you can pig out in total comfort. Late May.

Ringling Brothers and Barnum and Bailey Circus. *Madison Square Garden, Seventh Ave and 32nd St (10001). Phone 212/465-6741. www.ringling.com.* The kids will have a ball enjoying "the Greatest Show on Earth," which graces the city every spring. Expect the usual circus fare—elephants, trapeze artists, clowns, and the like. For a special treat, view the parade of circus people and animals from 12th Avenue and 34th Street to the Garden on the morning before the show opens. Mar-Apr.

Westminster Kennel Club Dog Show. *Madison Square Garden, Seventh Ave and 32nd St (10001). Phone 212/465-6741; toll-free 800/455-3647. www.west minsterkennelclub.org.* Canine lovers unite! Nearly 3,000 top dogs and their owners take part in this two-day annual extravaganza leading up to the crowning of Best in Show on the second night of competition. Whether you love big or small dogs, you will surely find this event a delight. Here's a real insider's tip: arrive two hours early each night, at about 6 pm, and go to the huge backstage area. Here, you will be able to pet, play with, and nuzzle up to the dogs that vied for Best in Breed in competitions held earlier in the day. (Always ask the owner/handler for permission before petting an animal.) The owners and handlers welcome the public since they love showing off their pooches—they may even convince you to buy a future offspring of their show dogs. This is, by far, the best part of the show. Wear comfortable shoes, since this staging area is massive. Best in Group competitions for the seven groups run from 8-11 pm each night. You can buy tickets for one or both nights. For the best deal, purchase a general-admission, two-day pass. Mid-Feb.

Motels/Motor Lodges

★ **DAYS INN.** *790 8th Ave (10019). Phone 212/581-7000; toll-free 800/544-8313; fax 212/974-0291. www.daysinn.com.* 367 rooms, 15 story. Check-out 1 pm. TV. Restaurant, bar. Room service. Parking $20. **$**

[D] [🐾] [⬛]

★ **HOWARD JOHNSON.** *851 8th Ave (10019). Phone 212/581-4100; fax 212/974-7502. www.hojo.com.* 300 rooms, 11 story. Check-out noon. TV. Restaurant, bar. **$**

[D] [⬛]

Hotels

★ ★ **ALGONQUIN HOTEL.** *59 W 44th St (10036). Phone 212/840-6800; fax 212/944-1419. www.algonquinhotel.com.* 174 rooms, 12 story. Pets accepted. Check-out noon. Check-in 3 pm. TV; cable (premium). Restaurant, bar; entertainment. Babysitting services available. In-house fitness room. Parking. Business center. Visited by numerous literary and theatrical personalities. **$$**

★ **AMERITANIA HOTEL.** *230 W 54th St (10019). Phone 212/247-5000; toll-free 800/922-0330. www.nycityhotels.net.* 219 rooms. Complimentary breakfast. Check-out noon. Check-in 3 pm. TV; cable (premium). In-room modem link. Bar. Concierge. **$$**

★ ★ ★ **BRYANT PARK.** *40 W 40th St (10018). Phone 212/642-2200; fax 212/869-4446. www.thebryantpark.net.* In the shadows of the New York Public Library and Bryant Park, this centrally located hotel offers great views and has a bit of everything for travelers. The modern, sleek, almost minimalist rooms feature hardwood floors and are decorated in white with red accents. Each room offers high-tech amenities like DSL Internet connections, making this hotel a good choice for people traveling on business. Dine at the equally funky Ilo (see), which features dishes like oysters, stuffed duck neck, roasted lamb, and rabbit that vary with the seasons. It's a popular hangout, so you will need reservations. 129 rooms, 20 suites, 25 story. Check-out noon, check-in 3 pm. TV; cable (premium), VCR available. In-room modem link. Restaurant, bar. Babysitting services available. In-house fitness room. Valet parking. Business center. Concierge. **$$$**

★ ★ **COMFORT INN.** *42 W 35th St (10001). Phone 212/947-0200; fax 212/594-3047. www.comfortinnmanhattan.com.* 131 rooms, 12 story. Complimentary continental breakfast. Check-out noon. Check-in 3 pm. TV. In-room modem link. Restaurant, bar. Coffee in lobby. **$**

★ ★ ★ **CROWNE PLAZA.** *1605 Broadway (10019). Phone 212/977-4000; toll-free 800/243NYNY; fax 212/333-7393. www.crowneplaza.com.* Located in the heart of Times Square, near Broadway theaters and Radio City Music Hall. 770 rooms, 17 suites, 46 story. Check-out noon, check-in 3 pm. TV; cable (premium), VCR available (movies). In-room modem link. Restaurant, bar. Room service. Health club privileges. Pool. Business center. Concierge. Luxury level. **$$**

★ ★ ★ **ESSEX HOUSE - A WESTIN HOTEL.** *160 Central Park S (10019). Phone 212/247-0300; toll-free 800/937-8461; fax 212/315-1839. www.essexhouse.com.* An elegant hotel on Central Park South, the Essex House boasts large rooms, spectacular Central Park views, and an elegant ballroom. 501 suites, 19 story. Check-out noon. Check-in 3 pm. TV; cable (premium), VCR. In-room modem link, fax. Room service 24 hours. Restaurant, bar. Babysitting services available. Spa, sauna. Valet parking. Business center. Concierge. **$$$**

★ ★ ★ **THE HELMSLEY PARK LANE.** *36 Central Park S (10019). Phone 212/371-4000; toll-free 800/221-4982; fax 212/521-6666. www.helmsleyhotels.com.* Spectacular, unobstructed views of Central Park distinguish the upper-level rooms of this part-residential hotel. 637 rooms, 46 story. Pets accepted, some restrictions. Check-out noon, check-in 3 pm. TV; VCR available (movies). In-room modem link. Restaurant, bar. Room service. Exercise equipment. Business center. Concierge. **$$$**

D 🏊 🛪 🖂 SC 🏃

★ ★ ★ **HILTON NEW YORK.** *1335 Avenue of the Americas (10019). Phone 212/586-7000; toll-free 212/261-5870; fax 212/315-1374. www.new yorktowers.hilton.com.com.* This large convention hotel has a bustling, urban charm. Several restaurants, shops, and services make it a convenient base from which to explore New York. 2,034 rooms, 44 story. Pets accepted, some restrictions. Check-out noon. TV; cable (premium), VCR available. In-room modem link. Restaurant, bar. Room service. Exercise room, massage, sauna, steam room. Parking. Business center. Concierge. **$$**

D 🏊 🛪 🖂 🏃

★ ★ ★ **HUDSON.** *356 W 58th St (10019). Phone 212/554-6000. www.ianschrager.com.* Part of Ian Schrager's collection of funky, eclectic boutique hotels, this far west side hotel is designed for those who want to bring the great outdoors inside. It features lots of lights and skylights, a combination indoor/outdoor lobby with courtyard garden, a 15th-floor solarium and conservatory, and both al fresco and indoor dining options. American and European artists from a variety of periods and styles created the property's furniture. Penthouse apartments feature private greenhouses and roof gardens. 1,000 rooms, 24 story. Check-out noon. Check-in 3 pm. TV; cable (premium), VCR available. In-room modem link. Restaurant, bar. In-house fitness room. Business center. Concierge. **$$**

🛪 🏃

★ ★ ★ **INTER-CONTINENTAL CENTRAL PARK SOUTH NEW YORK.** *112 Central Park S (10019). Phone 212/757-1900; fax 212/757-9620. www.new-york.interconti.com.* 211 rooms, 25 story. Check-out noon. Check-in 3 pm. TV; cable (premium), VCR available. In-room modem link. Restaurant, bar. Room service. In-house fitness room, health club privileges, massage, sauna. Business center. Concierge. **$$$**

D 🛪 🖂 🏃

★ ★ ★ **THE IROQUOIS.** *49 W 44th St (10036). Phone 212/840-3080; toll-free 800/332-7220; fax 212/719-0006. www.iroquoisny.com.* This hotel underwent a $10 million renovation several years ago, having been restored to its 1923 elegance. It has the feel of a European mansion with French décor. The guest rooms are individually decorated with works of art reflecting New York themes such as Broadway, fashion, and museums. A library provides a sitting area for perusing the hotel's collection of leather-bound editions of the classics. The Triomphe of New York gourmet restaurant features French cuisine, and the Burgundy Room offers breakfast and cocktails. 114 rooms, 12 story. Check-out noon. Check-in 3 pm. TV; cable (premium), VCR available. In-room modem link. Restaurant, bar. Room service 24 hours. In-house fitness room. Concierge. **$$$**

D 太 ⊠

★ ★ ★ **LE PARKER MERIDIEN.** *118 W 57th St (10019). Phone 212/ 245-5000; fax 212/307-1776. www.parkermeridien.com.* 855 rooms, 42 story. Pets accepted. Check-out noon, check-in 3 pm. TV; VCR available. Internet access. Restaurant, bar. Room service. Exercise room, massage, sauna, steam room. Heated indoor pool. Valet parking. Business center. Concierge. **$$$**

D ⬛ ≈ 太 ⟁

★ ★ **THE MANSFIELD.** *12 W 44th St (10036). Phone 212/944-6050; toll-free 800/255-5167; fax 212/764-4477. www.mansfieldhotel.com.* 124 rooms, 27 suites, 13 story. Pets accepted. Check-out noon. Check-in 3 pm. TV; cable (premium), VCR available. Restaurant, bar. Room service 24 hours. Babysitting services available. In-house fitness room, health club privileges. Valet parking. Concierge. **$$**

D ⬛ ⟐ ⊠ SC ⟁

★ ★ ★ **MARRIOTT MARQUIS.** *1535 Broadway (10036). Phone 212/ 398-1900; fax 212/704-8930. www.marriott.com.* 2,007 rooms, 50 story. Check-out noon. TV; cable (premium). Internet access, in-room modem link. Restaurant, bar. Room service. Exercise equipment, sauna. Valet parking. Business center. Concierge. Luxury level. **$$**

D 太 ⊠ ⟁

★ ★ ★ **THE MICHELANGELO HOTEL.** *152 W 51st St (10019). Phone 212/765-1900; toll-free 800/237-0990; fax 212/541-6604. www.michelangelo hotel.com.* If you are a lover of all things Italian, plan to stay at this ornate hotel during your next visit to New York. Special touches include opera music played in public spaces, Buon Di breakfast with cappuccino and Italian pastries, and Baci chocolates at turndown. The extra-large rooms are decorated in Art Deco, country French, or neoclassical style. Cherry wood furnishings have black accents and brass mounts. The rooms also feature woven fabrics from Italy. The hotel's upscale restaurant, Limoncello, serves Italian cuisine, and The Grotto offers more casual dining and a selection of fine cigars. 178 rooms, 52 suites, 7 story. Pets accepted. Complimentary continental breakfast. Check-out 1 pm, check-in 3 pm. TV; cable (premium), VCR available. In-room modem link. Restaurant, bar. Room service. Health club privileges, exercise equipment. Valet parking. Concierge. **$$$$**

D ⬛ 太 ⊠

★ ★ ★ **MILLENNIUM HOTEL NEW YORK BROADWAY.** *145 W 44th St (10036). Phone 212/768-4400; toll-free 800/622-5569; fax 212/768-0847. www.millenniumbroadway.com.* Colorful murals that evoke the 1930s adorn the lobby of this fine midtown hotel. There are several grades of guest room, all of which are tastefully appointed, from "classic" to "premier" providing accomodations to meet the needs of most travelers. 750 rooms, 52 story. Pets accepted. Check-out noon. Check-in 4 pm. TV; cable (premium), VCR available. In-room modem link. Restaurant, bar. Room service. Babysitting services available. In-house fitness room. Valet parking. Business center. Concierge. Postmodern skyscraper with Moderne setbacks, Deco detailing; incorporates landmark Beaux Arts Hudson Theatre (1903), which has been restored. **$$**

★ ★ ★ **THE MUSE.** *130 W 46th St (10036). Phone 212/485-2400; fax 212/485-2900. www.themusehotel.com.* A designers' dream, this hotel has restored its unique, triple-arched, limestone and brick facade to give it a dramatic feel. Adding to the drama is a 15-foot vaulted ceiling with a commissioned mural depicting the nine muses in the lobby. Original artwork celebrating the theater and the performing arts hangs in each room, decorated in a warm color scheme of rust, burgundy, pear green, and muted blue-green and cherry wood furniture. Custom linens and duvet-covered feather beds add to guests' comfort. Guest baths feature green marble with stone vanities. Other distinguishing features include in-room spa services, balconies, and DVD players. 200 rooms, 19 story. Pets accepted. Check-out noon. Check-in 3 pm. TV; cable (premium), VCR available. In-room modem link. Restaurant, bar. Babysitting services available. In-house fitness room. Business center. Concierge. **$$$**

★ ★ ★ **PARAMOUNT.** *235 W 46th St (10036). Phone 212/764-5500; toll-free 800/225-7474; fax 212/575-4892. www.ianschrager.com.* Ian Schrager does it again. One-of-a kind, funky but comfortable furniture (such as a wood chair upholstered with a large silkscreen image of a growling dog) dots the lobby. Guest rooms are decorated in white tones, with ultra-modern furniture and Scottish lambswool throws. The Mezzanine Restaurant features a Latin-inspired tasting and tapas menu. For foodies, the hotel has a Dean & Deluca takeout shop that offers mouthwatering items you can enjoy back in your room. 600 rooms, 13 suites, 19 story. Check-out noon. TV; cable (premium), VCR available. In-room modem link. Restaurant, bar. Room service. Exercise equipment. Parking. Business center. Concierge. Public areas and guest rooms designed in a high-tech, futuristic style. **$$**

★ ★ ★ ★ **THE PENINSULA NEW YORK.** *700 Fifth Ave (10019). Phone 212/956-2888; toll-free 800/262-9467; fax 212/903-3949. www.peninsula.com.* Situated on Fifth Avenue in Midtown, The Peninsula is a perfect location for exploring the sights and sounds of New York City, whether you're heading for the stores, catching a concert at nearby Carnegie Hall or Radio City, or relaxing in Rockefeller Center. The lobby is magnificent with its sweeping staircase carpeted in crimson. Bellhops in crisp white uniforms escort guests to rooms and suites, where lush fabrics and warm tones create a sensual ambience. The Peninsula is known for setting standards in the industry, which is evident in the fact that guests are able to regulate the temperature, lighting, and entertainment systems from their beds with a simple touch. The fitness center, overlooking the city, brings new meaning to "exercise high," while the hotel's lively mood is celebrated in its bars and restaurants. With its staggering views above the city, the Pen-Top Terrace & Bar should not be missed, regardless of the prices of cocktails, which are as high as the tower itself. 239 rooms, 23 story. Complimentary continental breakfast. Check-out noon, check-in 3 pm. TV; cable (premium), VCR available. In-room modem link. Room service 24 hours. Restaurant, bar. In-house fitness room, spa, massage, sauna, steam room. Indoor pool. Valet parking. Business center. Concierge. **$$$$**

D ⩰ 🕴 ⬩ 🚶

★ ★ ★ **THE PLAZA.** *Fifth Ave at Central Park S (10019). Phone 212/ 759-3000; toll-free 800/527-4727; fax 212/759-3167. www.fairmont.com.* Considered by many to be the grande dame of New York City lodgings, this massive, opulent hotel filled with lush furniture, pricey stores, and chandeliers has played host to dignitaries, celebrities, and just about every rich and famous person who has lived throughout its history. The rooms are elegant, too, with crystal chandeliers, formal furnishings, and 14-foot ceilings. The Oak Room is a classic steakhouse with an equally formal feel, and the Palm Court is legendary for its high tea and overflowing Sunday brunch. Bring an extra credit card to dine at either venue. 805 rooms, 60 suites, 18 story. Pets accepted. Check-out noon. TV; cable (premium), VCR available. In-room modem link. Restaurant, bar. Room service. Exercise equipment. Business center. Concierge. **$$$**

D 🐾 🕴 ⬩ 🚶

★ ★ ★ **RENAISSANCE NEW YORK HOTEL TIMES SQUARE.** *714 7th Ave (10036). Phone 212/765-7676; fax 212/765-1962. www.renaissan cehotels.com.* You'll find all of the conveniences at this business hotel located just north of Times Square. The lobby, located three floors above the street, has an appealing Art Deco theme that carries into the comfortable guestrooms. 305 rooms, 26 story. Check-out noon. Check-in 3 pm. TV; cable (premium), VCR available. In-room modem link. Restaurant, bar. Room service. Exercise equipment, massage. Parking. Business center. Concierge. **$$$**

D 🕴 ⬩ SC 🚶

★ ★ ★ ★ ★ **THE RITZ-CARLTON NEW YORK CENTRAL PARK.** *50 Central Park S (10019). Phone 212/308-9100; fax 212/207-8831. www.ritzcarlton.com.* Rising above Central Park and flanked by prestigious Fifth Avenue and fashionable Central Park West, the Ritz-Carlton has one of the most coveted locations in town. This genteel hotel is exquisite down to every last detail, from the priceless antiques and artwork to the bountiful floral displays. The light-filled rooms and suites are a pastel-hued paradise, with sumptuous fabrics and plush furnishings. No detail is overlooked; rooms facing the park include telescopes for closer viewing. The distinguished ambience and white-glove service make this a top choice of wellheeled travelers. Atelier garners praise from top critics for its modern French cuisine. Dedicated to excellence in all areas, the hotel even includes an outpost of the renowned European La Prairie Spa. 277 rooms, 40 suites, 15 story. Pets accepted. Complimentary continental breakfast. Check-out noon. Check-in 3 pm. TV; cable (premium), DVD available. In-room modem link.

Restaurant, bar. Room service 24 hours. In-house fitness room, spa, massage, steam room. Business center. Concierge. Luxury level. **$$$$**

[D] [☎] [✗] [⊠] [🚶]

★ ★ ★ **ROYALTON.** *44 W 44th St (10036). Phone 212/869-4400; toll-free 800/635-9013; fax 212/869-8965. www.ianschragerhotels.com.* Join the in crowd at this Ian Schrager hotel. Designed by Philippe Starck, the Royalton raised the bar on hipness when it opened a decade ago. Every detail is just so, from the stylish vodka bar to the lobby lounge where guests recline on cushioned steps to the small, minimalist guest rooms with modern, custom-made beds. The cream-colored rooms feature fresh flowers, down comforters and pillows, VCRs, CD players, and subtle lighting. The bathrooms are right out of the future, with stainless steel and glass fixtures. Some rooms have fireplaces and round tubs for two. The lobby also has a steely, minimalist look that is clean and sleek. The restaurant 44 is popular with local movers and shakers. 169 rooms, 16 story. Check-out 1 pm, check-in 3 pm. TV; cable (premium), VCR available. In-room modem link. Restaurant, bar. Room service. Babysitting services available. In-house fitness room. Valet parking. Concierge. **$$$**

[D] [✗] [⊠]

★ ★ **SALISBURY HOTEL.** *123 W 57th St (10019). Phone 212/246-1300; toll-free 888/NYC5757; fax 212/977-7752.* 201 rooms, 17 story. Check-out noon. Check-in 3 pm. TV; VCR available. In-room modem link. Parking $23. Concierge. **$$**

[D]

★ ★ ★ **SHERATON NEW YORK HOTEL AND TOWERS.** *811 7th Ave (10019). Phone 212/581-1000; fax 212/262-4410. www.sheraton.com.* This large, comfortable hotel is one of Sheraton's flagships—good for business or pleasure. Close to the theater district, the rooms are large by New York standards and the service is friendly. 1,750 rooms, 50 story. Check-out noon. Check-in 3 pm. TV; cable (premium), VCR available. Pool privileges. In-room modem link. Restaurant, bar. Babysitting services available. In-house fitness room, sauna. Business center. Luxury level. **$$**

[D] [≈] [✗] [⊠] [🚶]

★ ★ **THE SHOREHAM HOTEL.** *33 W 55th St (10019). Phone 212/247-6700; toll-free 800/553-3347; fax 212/765-9741.* 176 rooms, 37 suites, 11 story. Complimentary continental breakfast. Check-out noon. Check-in 3 pm. TV; cable (premium), VCR available. In-room modem link. Restaurant, bar. Valet parking. Concierge. Renovated hotel built 1930. **$$**

[D] [⊠] [SC]

★ ★ ★ **SOFITEL.** *45 W 44th St (10036). Phone 212/354-8844; fax 212/354-2450. www.accor-hotels.com.* 398 rooms, 30 story. Pets accepted, some restrictions. Check-out 1 pm, check-in 12 pm. TV; cable (premium), VCR available. In-room modem link. Restaurant, bar. Room service 24 hours. Babysitting services available. In-house fitness room, massage. Concierge. **$$$**

[D] [☎] [✗]

★ ★ **WARWICK HOTEL.** *65 W 54th St (10019). Phone 212/247-2700; toll-free 800/223-4099; fax 212/247-2725. www.warwickhotels.com.* 426 rooms, 33 story. Check-out 1 pm. TV; cable (premium). Restaurant, bar. Exercise equipment. Business center. **$$$**

D 🕃 🐾 ⊠ 🕺

★ ★ **WYNDHAM HOTEL.** *42 W 58th St (10019). Phone 212/753-3500; toll-free 800/257-1111; fax 212/754-5638.* 212 rooms, 16 story. Pets accepted. Check-out noon, check-in 3 pm. TV; cable (premium). In-room modem link. Restaurant, bar. Valet parking. **$$**

D 🐾 ⊠

All Suite

★ ★ ★ **DOUBLETREE HOTEL.** *1568 Broadway (10036). Phone 212/ 719-1600; toll-free 800/325-9033; fax 212/921-5212. www.doubletree.com.* If you're looking for an all-suite hotel in Times Square, look no further. It is located only steps away from the theater district. 460 suites, 43 story. Pets accepted. Check-out noon, check-in 3 pm. TV; cable (premium), VCR available. Internet access. Restaurant, bar. Room service. Exercise equipment. Parking $35. Concierge. **$**

D 🐾 🕃 ⊠ SC

Restaurants

★ ★ ★ **21 CLUB.** *21 W 52nd St (10019). Phone 212/582-7200; fax 212/ 974-7562. www.21club.com.* This one-time speakeasy is now one of New York City's most celebrated spots for lunch, dinner, and lots of drinks—at least for the well-heeled Wall Street, media, and superstar regulars who frequent its best tables. Chef Erik Blauberg turns out stellar, seasonal American-French fare, with standards that shine and inventive twists that delight. The restaurant has a distinguished air to it, with a clubby, brass-railed bar (often the sight of dealmakers clinking martini glasses), luxurious linen-lined tables, golden lighting, antique oil paintings, and old photos hung on wood-paneled walls. The deep wine list explores the world at large and works well to complement the cuisine. American menu. Closed Sun; holidays; also Sat (July 4-Labor Day). Lunch, dinner. Bar. Jacket required. **$$$**

D

★ ★ ★ ★ ★ **ALAIN DUCASSE.** *155 W 58th St (10019). Phone 212/ 265-7300. www.alain-ducasse.com.* When word came that the famed French wizard of gastronomy, Alain Ducasse, was opening a restaurant in New York, the city's food world began salivating. And while the excess, such as the choice of half a dozen pens to sign the bill, drew some criticism at its opening, people started to embrace the restaurant once they experienced Ducasse firsthand. Ducasse has superhuman culinary powers; food doesn't taste this way anywhere else, and it sure doesn't arrive at a table this way anywhere else. Elegant to the point of being regal, Ducasse is a restaurant designed to please every one of the senses: sight, sound, smell, taste, and touch. The room frequently fills with attractive diners. Hours later, when dinner is over and you attempt to get up and walk to the door, you receive a gift for breakfast the next morning: a gift-wrapped buttery, fruit-laced brioche that will make you swoon. If you manage not to dig into it in the cab on the way back to your hotel, you have a will of steel. But divine excess does not come without its price. Dinner at Ducasse will set you back several pretty pennies, but really, isn't paying your mortgage a dull way to spend your money? *Secret Inspector's Notes:* Food is only one of the amazing aspects of a dinner at Alain Ducasse. The service, décor, presentations, and wine service are only a few of the other details that Ducasse handles in an unparalleled way. French menu. Closed Sun; mid-July-early Aug. Dinner. Entertainment. Jacket required. Reservations required. **$$$$**

D

★ ★ ★ **AQUAVIT.** *13 W 54th St (10019). Phone 212/307-7311; fax 212/265-8584. www.aquavit.org.* Chef-partner (and culinary heartthrob) Marcus Samuelsson introduced New York to his splashy brand of modern Scandinavian cuisine a decade ago at Aquavit, an elegant two-story restaurant housed in a historic Midtown townhouse, just a stone's throw from the Museum of Modern Art and the shops of Fifth Avenue. After ten years and a facelift, the restaurant still has a sleek, sophisticated vibe, and the cuisine is even more spectacular. While ingredients like herring, lamb, salmon, caviar, and dill show up with regularity on this Scandinavian-inspired menu, the food here is more uniquely Samuelsson than anything else. What this means is that every dazzling plate achieves a startlingly delicious harmony as the result of the chef's careful and creative combination of textures, flavors, temperatures, ingredients, and the cooking styles of France, Asia, and Sweden. A shot of smooth, citrus-tinged aquavit complements dinner nicely, as does a selection from the impressive wine list. Scandanavian menu. Closed major holidays. Lunch, dinner. Bar. Casual attire. **$$$**

★ ★ ★ **ATELIER.** *50 Central Park S (10019). Phone 212/521-6125.* Located across from Central Park in the posh Ritz-Carlton hotel, Atelier is a stunning, civilized restaurant that feels like luxury from the moment you are seated in one of its cushy banquettes. To match the surroundings, the kitchen offers beautiful dishes for adventurous and high-minded foodies—this is super-modern French cuisine of the haute variety. The food is often cloaked in foams, gelees, and mousses with lots of contrasting textures and flavors dancing on the plate for a wild and delicious meal. French menu. Breakfast, lunch, dinner. Bar. Jacket required. Reservations required. **$$$$**

D

★ ★ ★ **BARBETTA.** *321 W 46th St (10036). Phone 212/246-9171; fax 212/246-1279. www.barbettarestaurant.com.* Barbetta is the grand old dame of the theater district. This classic Italian restaurant opened its doors in 1906 and is still owned by the same loving family, the Maioglios. Located in a pair of historic early-19th-century townhouses, this restaurant is a classic charmer that's all about super-elegant, old-world dining. The menu doesn't aim anywhere other than where its heart is—Italy—but don't expect just pasta. The kitchen offers a great selection of seafood, poultry, and beef prepared with seasonal ingredients and lively flavors. The tree-lined outdoor garden is an enchanted spot to unwind over dinner or drinks. Italian menu. Closed Sun. Lunch, dinner. Bar. Outdoor seating. **$$$**

D

★ ★ **BECCO.** *355 W 46th St (10036). Phone 212/397-7597; fax 212/977-6738. www.becconyc.com.* Italian menu. Closed Dec 25. Lunch, dinner. Bar. Casual attire. Reservations required. Totally nonsmoking. Three dining rooms on two levels. **$$$**

D

★ ★ ★ **BEN BENSON'S.** *123 W 52nd St (10019). Phone 212/581-8888; fax 212/581-1170. www.benbensons.com.* At this popular Midtown testosterone-infused steakhouse, you'll find yourself elbow to elbow with celebrities, politicians, sports stars, and the city's financial elite. As you might expect from a power steak spot, the menu is as big as the egos in the room and includes solid standards like salads, poultry, and seafood that are simply and impeccably prepared. But the magnetic pull here is the restaurant's signature selection of USDA dry-aged Prime Beef, served the form of about a dozen cuts and portion sizes. The huge steaks are matched in size by lobsters the size of small pets. Don't miss the house's signature crispy hashed browns. When the sun is shining, grab a seat outside in the sidewalk dining room, appointed in the same style as the indoor space with deep armchairs, formal white linens, and green-and-white wainscoted planters—an ideal al fresco setting. Steak menu. Closed most major holidays. Lunch, dinner. Bar. Casual attire. **$$$**

★ ★ ★ **BRASSERIE 8 1/2.** *9 W 57th St (10019). Phone 212/829-0812.* Located in the sleek, Gordon Bunshaft-designed "9" building in the heart of West 57th Street, Brasserie 8 1/2 is the perfect spot for all sort of plans. It's a great pick for a power lunch or for shimmering cocktails after work. The long, backlit bar is a mecca for stylish men and women in search of one another. It's also a wise choice for pre-theater dinner and a terrific selection for those who want to relax in a slick, modern setting and enjoy a leisurely meal of updated brasserie classics tweaked to modern attention. The kitchen incorporates accents from Asia and the Mediterranean into these classic dishes, varying each dish just enough from its original base. Be warned that the spacious banquettes are so soft and comfortable that you may never want to get up. American menu. Lunch, dinner. Bar. Jacket required. Reservations required. **$$$**

D

★ **BROOKLYN DINER USA.** *212 W 57th St (10019). Phone 212/977-1957; fax 212/977-3044. www.brooklyndiner.com.* American menu. Breakfast, lunch, dinner, late night. Bar. Children's menu. Casual attire. **$$**

★ ★ **BRYANT PARK GRILL.** *25 W 40th St (10018). Phone 212/840-6500; fax 212/840-8122. www.arkrestaurants.com.* Contemporary American menu. Lunch, dinner. Bar. Children's menu. Casual attire. Outdoor seating. Totally nonsmoking. **$$$**

★ ★ ★ **CAFÉ ATLAS.** *40 Central Park S (10019). Phone 212/759-9191.* The barely breathing economy has taken its toll on some of New York's most elegant and stately dining experiences, among them Atlas, the former temple of avant garde cuisine under wild British wunderkind chef Paul Liebrandt. Reconceived as Café Atlas in the fall of 2002, the pristine restaurant with its haute couture menu (think eel with chocolate sauce) have been revamped, getting nips and tucks in style and substance. The menu now features approachable, seasonal takes on homey standards like steamed mussels with garlic toast and juicy roasted chicken with chanterelles, while the room takes on a cozy, soothing, earthy glow. Café Atlas is a wonderful oasis to escape to for a delicious, civilized meal, at a fraction of the price of its former self. It makes a great case for the makeover. Contemporary American menu. Dinner, Sun brunch. Bar. Casual attire. Reservations required Sun. **$$$**

D

★ **CARNEGIE DELI.** *854 7th Ave (10019). Phone 212/757-2245; fax 212/ 757-9889. www.carnegiedeli.com.* Deli menu. Breakfast, lunch, dinner, late night. No Credit Cards Accepted **$$**

D

★ ★ **CHURRASCARIA PLATAFORMA.** *316 W 49th St (10019). Phone 212/245-0505; fax 212/974-8250. www.churrascariaplataforma.com.* Brazilian menu. Closed Dec 25. Lunch, dinner. Bar. Casual attire. Reservations required. Totally nonsmoking. **$$$**

D

★ ★ **CITE.** *120 W 51st St (10020). Phone 212/956-7100; fax 212/956-7157. www.citerestaurant.com.* American, French menu. Closed most major holidays. Lunch, dinner. Zinc-covered bar. Casual attire. One-room informal bistro. **$$$**

D

★ ★ ★ **DB BISTRO MODERNE.** *55 W 44th St (10036). Phone 212/ 391-2400.* This cool, sexy, ultra-stylish bistro in Midtown is Daniel Boulud's most casual restaurant. But he succeeds in making it a hotspot for foodies and moguls of all sorts without making it ordinary. For Boulud, making a regular restaurant is simply not possible. It's like asking Frank Sinatra to hum a simple tune. In many dishes, Boulud has a magic touch, transforming simple into spectacular with ease. His signature DB Burger is an excellent example of his creative interpretations. He builds the fattest, juiciest round of beef and stuffs it with short ribs and sinful amounts of foie gras and truffles. He serves it on a homemade parmesan brioche bun, with house-stewed tomato confit (instead of ketchup) and a great big vat of fries. Don't think that this will be too much food for you to eat alone—you'll regret offering to share after the first bite. French menu. Closed some major holidays. Lunch, dinner, late night. Bar. Casual attire. Reservations required. **$$$**

D

★ ★ ★ **ESTIATORIO MILOS.** *125 W 55th St (10019). Phone 212/245-7400; fax 212/245-4828.* Milos, as it's called for short (try saying "Estiatorio" over and over again and you'll understand why), is a luxurious, cavernous, whitewashed eatery decorated with umbrella-topped tables and seafood market-style fish displays. Showcasing simple, rustic Greek cooking, this elegant, airy restaurant takes you from the hustle of Midtown to the shores of the Mediterranean in the whirl of a revolving door. Seafood is priced by the pound and is prepared either perfectly grilled over charcoal or in the Greek style called *spetsiota*—filleted and baked with tomatoes, onions, herbs, and olive oil. Greek, Mediterranean menu. Closed Jan 1, Dec 25. Dinner. Bar. Casual attire. **$$$**

D

★ ★ ★ **FIREBIRD.** *365 W 46th St (10036). Phone 212/586-0244; fax 212/957-2983. www.firebirdrestaurant.com.* Firebird is an ode to the glamour and gluttony of St. Petersburg, sometime around its heyday in 1912. Set in a lavish, double townhouse, this restaurant and cabaret is furnished like a majestic Russian palace, with ornate antique furniture, intricate china and etched glass, old-world oil paintings, and 19th-century photographs. The extravagance extends to the food, with Russian classics like blinis with sour cream and caviar, *zakuska* (the Russian equivalent of tapas), borscht made with pork and dill, and sturgeon baked in puff pastry. Vodka flows like water in a fast-running stream, and the wine list is deep as well. Russian menu. Closed Mon; holidays. Dinner. Bar. Entertainment Wed-Sat. Outdoor seating. **$$$**

★ ★ ★ **GALLAGHER'S.** *228 W 52nd St (10019). Phone 212/245-5336; fax 212/245-5426. www.gallaghersnysteakhouse.com.* The theater district has some great longtime restaurant hotspots to choose from, and Gallagher's is one of its brightest stars. This steakhouse is a New York City landmark and former speakeasy and remains decorated as it was the day it opened in November 1927, with plain-planked floors, red checked tablecloths, and dark wood-paneled walls covered in old photos. Specializing in dry-aged beef, the kitchen stays true to simple American fare rather than straying off course for global flourishes that have no place in such a comfortable, back-to-basics establishment. The tried-and-true formula is winning and explains why, after all these years, Gallagher's is a perennial favorite on theater row. American, steak menu. Dinner. Bar. Casual attire. **$$$**

★ ★ ★ **ILO.** *40 W 40th St (10018). Phone 212/642-2255.* Located in the super fabulous Bryant Park Hotel, Ilo is one of those swanky, white-hot spots that defines New York dining. From the sultry, stunning crowd to the whiplash-worthy waitstaff, the crisp, cool cocktails, and the beautiful modern dining room decked out in white and soothing neutral hues, this is a room filled with eye-candy. And the scenery just gets better when the food arrives. Under the talented command of chef-owner Rick Laakkonen (formerly of River Café), the exquisite menu of New American cuisine is a masterpiece of texture, flavor, and style. The food is delicious. But be warned—the signature roast duck for two will leave you speechless, so do all your talking before digging in. American menu. Breakfast, lunch, dinner. Bar. Casual attire. Reservations required. **$$$**

★ ★ ★ **JUDSON GRILL.** *152 W 52nd St (10019). Phone 212/582-5252; fax 212/265-9616. www.judsongrill.citysearch.com.* Judson Grill, located in the heart of Midtown, has a lively bar crowd, but the large, high-ceilinged dining room, filled with widely spaced tables and deep, plush banquettes and decorated with tall, seasonal branch and floral arrangements, remains a serene and civilized place to dine. Chef Bill Telepan honors the seasons and regional farmers' produce with pride, weaving these pristine ingredients together on the plate with creative New American style. While the menu changes often to reflect the best of the markets, you'll always find a great selection of fish, poultry, beef, and vegetarian options as well as a terrific domestic farmstead cheese plate. A wonderful wine list pulls it all together. Closed Sun; major holidays. Lunch, dinner. Bar. Casual attire. **$$$**

D

★ **LA BONNE SOUPE.** *48 W 55th St (10019). Phone 212/586-7650; fax 212/765-6409. www.labonnesoupe.com.* French menu. Closed some major holidays. Lunch, dinner, Sun brunch. Bar. Children's menu. Casual attire. Outdoor seating. **$$**

★ ★ ★ ★ **LA CARAVELLE.** *33 W 55th St (10019). Phone 212/586-4252; fax 212/956-8269. www.lacaravelle.org.* Rita and Andre Jamet, the charming couple who own La Caravelle, are service professionals. They take hospitality very seriously, and it shows. Dining at La Caravelle is a pleasure whether you are looking for a fancy lunch or a long, leisurely dinner. The room is well lit, comfortable and pretty, and lacks pretension. The Jamets are also very aware that the times, they are a changin'; they have updated the menu so that it includes not only French classics but also dishes that meld flavors from faraway places like Japan, India, and the Mediterranean. The menu presents a challenge only in that everything looks (and indeed is) wonderful. La Caravelle's hors d'oeuvre cart, occasionally offered on special days, is a unique treat. An adorable, wheeled vehicle houses a selection of daily amuse bouche—terrines, canapes, salads, and sushi. These delicious little morsels are fabulous for lunch (a plate of eight is enough for an entrée, and four make a good appetizer) or a fun way to start dinner. It's hard to decide where to start or what to eat. But the waitstaff, while formal, are friendly and very happy to help in the decision-making process. There are no bad choices at La Caravelle. *Secret Inspector's Notes:* The food at La Caravelle is better than it has been in years. The menu, now a combination of French classics and newer fusion dishes, offers something for every diner. French menu. Closed Sun; holidays; also 1 week prior to Labor Day. Lunch, dinner. Bar. Children's menu. Jacket required. Reservations required. **$$$$**

★ ★ ★ ★ **LE BERNARDIN.** *155 W 51st St (10019). Phone 212/489-1515; fax 212/265-1615. www.le-bernardin.com.* If you crave the fruits of the sea, if you dream of lush, shimmering plates of pristine, perfectly prepared seafood, if you are a fan of soft, sinking seats, if your idea of paradise is a long, luxurious meal, you will be very happy at Le Bernardin. The restaurant, born in Paris in 1972, has been impressing foodies and novices alike since it moved across the ocean to Manhattan in 1986. After you experience the food and service, it's easy to see why. Le Bernardin is elegant everything—elegant service, elegant food, elegant crowd. It's all very civilized and sophisticated, and it's not the type of place to go for a quick bite. This is real dining at its finest. The sauces are light, aromatic, and perfectly balanced. The ingredients are seasonal and stunning. The presentations are museum-worthy in their perfection. All these elements combined with flawless service make dinner at Le Bernardin an experience that will stay with you for days, even months. The food is thoughtful and innovative, yet simple and approachable. It is the sort of menu that makes you want to try new things. But those craving beef need not enter. Seafood is the star at this distinguished, elegant New York restaurant, and the menu reflects the kitchen's passion for this food. Mind-altering fish first courses are divided between "Simply Raw" and "Lightly Cooked." Equally stellar entrées are completely from the sea, with a reluctant addition of meat at the end, in a section entitled "Upon Request." This is not the strength of the talented kitchen. Enjoy all courses of that which once swam when you're at Le Bernardin, and you won't regret it. *Secret Inspector's Notes:* The service at Le Bernardin is as spectacular as the food. This is a grown-up destination ideal for serious dining moments. French, seafood menu. Closed Sun; holidays. Dinner. Bar. Jacket required. **$$$$**

D

★ ★ **LE MADELEINE.** *403 W 43rd St (10036). Phone 212/246-2993; fax 212/586-7631. www.newyork.sidewalk.com.* French menu. Closed Dec 25. Lunch, dinner. Bar. Children's menu. Casual attire. Outdoor seating. Totally nonsmoking. **$$**

D

★ ★ ★ **MANHATTAN OCEAN CLUB.** *57 W 58th St (10019). Phone 212/371-7777; fax 212/371-9362. www.manhattanoceanclub.com.* In case you didn't get it from the restaurant's name, Manhattan Ocean Club is all about seafood. Stylishly decorated with hand-painted Picasso ceramics on earth-toned walls, this is a very comfortable place, with wide-spaced tables and flattering lighting. The kitchen offers a long sheet of paper as its menu that contains rows of seafood listed by type with corresponding illustrations so that you have a visual idea of what you're eating. All fish can be simply (and perfectly) grilled with extra-virgin olive oil and lemon, or dressed up in one of the kitchen's myriad of innovative global recipes. The chocolate torte for dessert is a must. Seafood menu. Closed major holidays. Lunch, dinner. Bar. Casual attire. Reservations required. **$$$**

★ ★ **MARLOWE.** *328 W 46th St (10036). Phone 212/765-3815; fax 212/765-3933.* French menu. Closed Dec 25. Lunch, dinner, Sun brunch. Bar. Outdoor seating. Totally nonsmoking. **$$**

★ ★ ★ **MICHAEL'S.** *24 W 55th St (10019). Phone 212/767-0555; fax 212/581-6778.* Michael's is the New York City offshoot of owner Michael McCarty's successful Santa Monica restaurant of the same name. Despite most New Yorkers' suspicion of all things born on the West Coast, Michael's has managed to sway this town and draws a steady crowd for lunch and dinner. But lunch is really the time to hit Michael's, as it is the de facto lunchroom for Manhattan's publishing moguls. While the dining room feels a bit dated in its décor (the 1980s come to mind), the kitchen stays up-to-the-minute, using fresh, seasonal ingredients to turn out a menu of smart contemporary American fare. New American menu. Closed Sun; holidays. Breakfast, lunch, dinner. Bar. Casual attire. **$$$**

★ **MICKEY MANTLE'S.** *42 Central Park S (10019). Phone 212/688-7777; fax 212/751-5797. www.mickeymantles.com.* Seafood, steak menu. Lunch, dinner. Bar. Children's menu. Outdoor seating. **$$**

D

★ **NEW YORK KOM TANG.** *32 W 32nd St (10001). Phone 212/947-8482.* Korean barbecue menu. Closed Sun. 24 hour service. Bar. Casual attire. **$$**

★ ★ **OAK ROOM.** *768 Fifth Ave (10019). Phone 212/759-3000; fax 212/546-5270. www.fairmont.com.* A meal in this oak-lined dining room in the Plaza Hotel tastes like a piece of history. Traditional European, American menu. Seasonal menu. Closed July 4, Dec 25. Dinner. Bar. Jacket required. Valet parking available. **$$$**

D

★ ★ **OSTERIA AL DOGE.** *142 W 44th St (10036). Phone 212/944-3643; fax 212/944-5754. www.osteria-doge.com.* Italian menu. Closed Jan 1, Dec 25. Dinner. Bar. **$$**

D

★ ★ ★ **OSTERIO DEL CIRCO.** *120 W 55th St (10019). Phone 212/265-3636; fax 212/265-9283. www.osteriodelcirco.com.* Owned by Sirio Maccioni of Le Cirque 2000, Osterio del Circo carries on his signature brand of homespun hospitality in a more casual, yet no less spirited, atmosphere. The rustic menu of Italian fare includes delicious homemade pastas made from Maccioni Mama Egi's lick-your-plate-clean recipes, as well as thin Tuscan-style pizzas, classic antipasti, and signature main courses like salt-baked Mediterranean seabass and brick-pressed chicken. Because it's located near Carnegie Hall and City Center, it's a great place to stop by before or after the theater. Italian menu. Closed holidays. Lunch, dinner. Bar. Casual attire. **$$$**

D

★ ★ ★ **PETROSSIAN.** *182 W 58th St (10019). Phone 212/245-2214; fax 212/245-2812.* Caviar, caviar, and caviar are the first three reasons to head to Petrossian, an elegant restaurant in Midtown featuring, you guessed it, caviar, served on perfect blinis and crème fraiche. In addition to the great salty roe, you'll find an ultra-luxurious brand of Franco-Russian cuisine that includes classics like borscht, assorted Russian *zazuska* (tapas) like smoked salmon (served with cold shots of vodka—ask for Zyr, one of the best from Russia), and other glamorous plates, including foie gras prepared several different ways and, of course, beef Stroganoff. But don't miss the caviar. Russian menu. Menu changes six times a year. Dinner, Sat, Sun brunch. Bar. Casual attire. **$$$**

★ ★ **REDEYE GRILL.** *890 7th Ave (10019). Phone 212/541-9000; fax 212/245-6840. www.redeyegrillgroup.com.* Another of famed restaurateur Shelly Fireman's creations with a seafood-heavy menu as big as the soaring dining room. A tempting front-door display of fresh fish welcomes diners.

American, seafood, steak menu. Lunch, dinner, brunch, late night. Bar. Casual attire. Outdoor seating. **$$$**

★ ★ ★ **REMI.** *145 W 53rd St (10019). Phone 212/581-4242; fax 212/581-7182.* The cuisine of Venice is the focus of the menu at Remi, an airy, lofty restaurant decorated with ornate Venetian blown-glass lights and murals of the Italian city's romantic canals. Remi has long been a favorite for local businesspeople to dish over lunch, but also makes a terrific choice for drinks, dinner, or a visit before or after a theater show. The kitchen's specialty is brilliant handmade pastas, but the menu also features contemporary Mediterranean takes on fish, beef, poultry, and game. A *ciccetti* menu of Venetian tapas is also available at the bar for nibbling while working through the restaurant's impressive Italian wine list. Closed major holidays. Dinner. Bar. Casual attire. Reservations required. Outdoor seating. **$$**

D

★ ★ **RENE PUJOL.** *321 W 51st St (10019). Phone 212/246-3023; fax 212/245-5206. www.renepujol.com.* French menu. Closed Mon; major holidays. Lunch. Bar. Jacket required. **$$$**

★ ★ **ROCK CENTER CAFE.** *20 W 50th St (10020). Phone 212/332-7620; fax 212/332-7677. www.restaurantassoc.com.* Regional American menu. Seasonal dishes. Breakfast, lunch, dinner, Sat, Sun brunch. Bar. Outdoor seating. **$$$**

D

★ ★ ★ **RUTH'S CHRIS STEAK HOUSE.** *148 W 51st St (10019). Phone 212/245-9600; fax 212/245-0460. www.ruthschris.com.* Like many diners in Midtown, this New Orleans-based steak palace is an out-of-towner. Steak menu. Closed Jan 1, Dec 25. Dinner. Bar. Casual attire. **$$$**

D

★ ★ ★ **SAN DOMENICO.** *240 Central Park S (10019). Phone 212/265-5959; fax 212/397-0844. www.sandomenicony.com.* Tony May's San Domenico is like an Armani suit—classic, elegant, and perfect for every occasion. Located on Central Park South with views of the horse-drawn carriages lined up along the edge of Central Park just outside, San Domenico is one of city's most well regarded restaurants for sophisticated, contemporary Italian cuisine. Pasta, fish, and meat dishes manage to feel rustic yet updated, as the chef teams new-world ingredients and twists with authentic old-world recipes and style. An impressive wine list from the motherland of Italy enriches every bite. Italian menu. Closed Jan 1, Thanksgiving, Dec 25. Dinner. Bar. Casual attire. **$$$$**

★ ★ **SARDI'S.** *234 W 44th St (10036). Phone 212/221-8440; fax 212/302-0865. www.sardis.com.* Continental, Italian menu. Closed Mon. Lunch, dinner, late night. Bar. Established 1921. Casual attire. Famous gathering place of theatrical personalities, columnists, publishers, agents; popular for before-and after-theater dinner or drinks. **$$$**

D

★ ★ ★ **THE SEA GRILL.** *19 W 49th St (10020). Phone 212/332-7610; fax 212/332-7677. www.restaurantassociates.com.* The Sea Grill is home to some of the most delicious seafood in the city. This lavish, ocean-blue restaurant dressed up in aquamarine and off-white tones sports a slick bar and prime wintertime views of ice skaters twirling (and crashing) on the rink under the twinkling Christmas tree at Rockefeller Plaza. Summertime brings al fresco dining and lots of icy cool cocktails to pair up with veteran chef Ed Brown's fantastic contemporary seafood menu. Crab cakes are his signature, and they deserve to be ordered at least once. Other dishes—salmon, cod, halibut, skate, you name it—are just as special, as Brown infuses his cooking with techniques and flavors from Asia and the world at large. Seafood menu. Menu changes. Closed Sun; major holidays. Dinner. Bar. Casual attire. Outdoor seating. **$$$**

D

★ ★ ★ **SHAAN.** *57 W 48th St (10020). Phone 212/977-8400; fax 212/977-3069.* Shaan offers traditional northern Indian cuisine of the distinctly delicious variety. The restaurant is located just a stone's throw from Rockefeller Center, so it makes a great pit stop during holiday shopping and skating. Shaan offers dishes from the clay tandoor oven, as well as savory vegetarian, lamb, chicken, and fish dishes served with steaming bowls of fragrant rice. A heavenly selection of breads, like naan, poori, and roti, makes mopping up the wonderfully aromatic sauces easy work. On Friday and Saturday nights, the restaurant usually hosts classical Indian musicians for a transporting evening. Indian menu. Closed major holidays. Dinner. Bar. Entertainment Fri-Sat. Casual attire. **$$$**

D

★ **SIAM GRILL.** *586 9th Ave (10036). Phone 212/307-1363.* Thai menu. Closed some major holidays. Lunch, dinner. **$$**

★ **STAGE DELI.** *834 7th Ave (10019). Phone 212/245-7850; fax 212/245-7957. www.stagedeli.com.* Kosher deli menu. Deli counter. Breakfast, lunch, dinner, late night. Bar. Children's menu. Casual attire. Enclosed sidewalk dining. Celebrity photos. **$$**

D

★ ★ ★ ★ **SUGIYAMA.** *251 W 55th St (10019). Phone 212/956-0670; fax 212/956-0671.* If you're searching for an oasis of calm in the center of Midtown Manhattan, head to Sugiyama and your blood pressure will drop upon entry. The dining room is warm and tranquil and has a Zen air to it. The spare, warm room fills up quickly at lunch with strikingly well-appointed businesspeople on expense accounts. But even filled to capacity, it maintains a soothing energy. Sugiyama's specialties are prix fixe kaiseki-style meals. Those who are not well suited to culinary adventures should search for calm somewhere else. It's not worth the visit to order only sushi. Kaiseki are multicourse meals that were originally part of elaborate, traditional Japanese tea ceremonies, but at Sugiyama they have evolved into a procession of precious little plates, holding petite portions that are as tasty as they are appealing to the eye. Lead by head chef and owner Nao Sugiyama, the chefs here have a talent for presentation—every dish is a work of art. Meals are tailored to suit your appetite and preferences and start with sakizuke (an amuse bouche) followed by a seasonal special (zensai), soup, sashimi, sushi, salad, and beef or seafood cooked over a hot stone (ishiyaki), among other sumptuous Japanese delicacies. Soups are Nao's specialty, and warm broths have never been so dynamic and exciting. Dining at Sugiyama is an unexpected adventure. The chef's enthusiasm and energy are contagious, and you can't help departing with a giant grin knowing that you've just had an experience like no other. *Secret Inspector's Notes:* Enjoying kaiseki at Sugiyama is undoubtedly one of the most fun and educational dining experiences to be had. Japanese menu. Closed Sun, Mon. Dinner. Entertainment. **$$$**

D

★ ★ ★ **TOWN.** *15 W 56th St (10019). Phone 212/582-4445.* Located in the swanky Chambers Hotel, Town is an oasis of hipness, featuring a white-hot, low-lit lounge and bar with some of the most inventive and well-made cocktails in the city. Move downstairs to the sexy, oversized-banquetted, David Rockwell-designed dining room, and you'll find it filled edge to edge with high-powered media and fashion folks digging into chef-owner Geoffrey Zakarian's brilliant high-styled, modern American fare. Contemporary American menu. Lunch, dinner. Bar. Casual attire. Reservations required. **$$$**

★ ★ ★ **TRATTORIA DELL'ARTE.** *900 7th Ave (10019). Phone 212/245-9800; fax 212/265-3296. www.trattoriadellarte.com.* Trattoria dell'Arte is the perfect choice if Carnegie Hall or a performance at City Center is on your list. Owned by Shelly Fireman, this lively and popular restaurant offers easy, approachable Italian cuisine in a comfortable, neighborly setting. The scene here is festive, so expect it to be loud with diners who are clearly enjoying the generous plates of homemade pastas, selections from the spectacular antipasti bar, seafood, and meats, all prepared in simple Mediterranean style. Italian menu. Closed Thanksgiving, Dec 25. Lunch, dinner, Sat, Sun brunch. Bar. Casual attire. Opposite Carnegie Hall; frequented by celebrities. **$$$**

D

★ ★ ★ **TUSCAN SQUARE.** *16 W 51st St (10020). Phone 212/977-7777; fax 212/977-3144. www.tuscansquare.com.* Restaurateur Pino Longo is a native Italian whose airy, comfortable Tuscan Square restaurant brings his idyllic homeland to life, warding off all cases of homesickness here in the big, boisterous city. Located in Rockefeller Center, Tuscan Square is a great place to relax and unwind at lunch or dinner. It offers a taste of the Italian countryside with a sunny, frescoed dining room and impressive antipasti and homemade pastas, as well as more robust regional specialties that match up well with the deep selection of Chianti, Barbaresco, Barolo, Montepulciano, Orvieto, and Pinot Grigio. Italian menu. Closed Sun; major holidays. Lunch, dinner. Bar. Casual attire. Totally nonsmoking. **$$$**

D

★ **VIRGIL'S REAL BARBECUE.** *152 W 44th St (10036). Phone 212/921-9494; fax 212/921-9631. www.virgilsbbq.com.* Barbecue menu. Closed Dec 25. Lunch, dinner, late night. Bar. Children's menu. Casual attire. Totally nonsmoking. **$$**

D

Greenwich Village/SoHo

Although New York's fabled bohemian neighborhood has gone seriously upscale and more mainstream in recent decades, evidence of its iconoclastic past can still be found in its many narrow streets, off-Broadway theaters, cozy coffee shops, lively jazz clubs, and tiny bars. Stretching from 14th Street south to Houston Street, and from Broadway west to the Hudson River, **Greenwich Village** remains one of the city's best places for idle wandering, people watching, boutique browsing, and conversing over glasses of cabernet or cups of cappuccino.

Washington Square Park anchors the neighborhood to the east and, though it's nothing special to look at, is still the heart of the Village. On a sunny afternoon, everyone comes here: kids hot-dogging on skateboards, students strumming guitars, old men playing chess, and lovers entwined in each other's arms. Bordering the edges of the park are a mix of elegant townhouses and New York University buildings.

Just south and west of Washington Square, find Bleecker and MacDougal Streets, home to coffee shops and bars once frequented by the likes of James Baldwin, Jack Kerouac, Allen Ginsberg, and James Agee. Le Figaro (corner of Bleecker and MacDougal) and the San Remo (93 MacDougal) were favorites back then and still attract crowds today, albeit mostly made up of tourists.

A bit farther west is Seventh Avenue South, where you'll find the Village Vanguard (178 Seventh Avenue South, at 11th Street)—the oldest and most venerable jazz club in the city. Also nearby are the Blue Note (131 West 3rd Street, near 6th Avenue), New York's premier jazz supper club, and Smalls (183 West 10th Street, near 7th Avenue South), one of the best places to catch up-and-coming talent.

At the corner of Seventh Avenue South and Christopher Street stands Christopher Park, where a George Segal sculpture of two gay couples commemorates the Stonewall Riots, which marked the advent of the gay-rights movement. The Stonewall Inn, where the demonstration began in 1969, once stood directly across from the park at 51 Christopher, and Christopher Street itself is still lined with many gay establishments.

At the corner of Sixth Avenue and West 10th Street reigns the gothic towers and turrets of Jefferson Market Library, a stunning maroon-and-white building that dates to 1876. Across the street from the library is Balducci's (424 Sixth Avenue), a famed gourmet food shop.

Short for South of Houston (HOW-stun), **SoHo** is New York's trendiest neighborhood, filled with an impossible number of upscale eateries, fancy boutiques, of-the-moment bars, and, most recently, a few astronomically expensive hotels. Contained in just 25 blocks bounded by Houston and Canal streets, Lafayette, and West Broadway, SoHo attracts trend followers and tourists by the thousands, especially on weekend afternoons, when the place sometimes feels like one giant open-air bazaar.

From the late 1800s to the mid-1900s, SoHo was primarily a light manufacturing district, but starting in the 1960s, most of the factories moved out and artists—attracted by the area's low rents and loft spaces—began moving in. Soon thereafter, the art galleries arrived, and then the shops and restaurants. Almost overnight, SoHo became too expensive for the artists—and, more recently, the art galleries—who had originally settled the place, and a mecca for big-bucks shoppers from all over the world.

Nonetheless, SoHo still has plenty to offer art lovers. Broadway is lined with one first-rate museum after another, while Mercer and Greene streets, especially, boast a large number of galleries. Some top spots on Broadway include the Museum for African Art (593 Broadway), presenting an excellent array of changing exhibits; the New Museum for Contemporary Art (583 Broadway), one of the oldest, best-known, and most controversial art spaces in SoHo; and the Guggenheim Museum SoHo (575 Broadway), a branch of the uptown institution. To find out who's exhibiting what and where in SoHo, pick up a copy of the *Art Now Gallery Guide,* available at many bookstores and galleries.

SoHo is also home to an extraordinary number of luscious cast-iron buildings. Originally meant to serve as a cheap substitute for stone buildings, the cast-iron facades were an American invention, prefabricated in a variety of styles—from Italian Renaissance to Classical Greek—and bolted onto the front of iron-frame structures. Most of SoHo's best cast-iron gems can be found along Broadway; keep an eye out for the Haughwout Building (488 Broadway), the Singer Building (561 Broadway), and the Guggenheim Museum SoHo.

Top thoroughfares for shopping include Prince and Spring streets, Broadway, and West Broadway. Numerous clothing and accessory boutiques are located along all these streets; West Broadway also offers several interesting bookstores. For antiques and furnishings, check out Lafayette Street; for craft and toy stores, try Greene and Mercer streets.

Restaurants and bars line almost every street in SoHo, but one especially lively nexus is the intersection of Grand Street and West Broadway. West Broadway itself is also home to a large number of eateries, some of which offer outdoor dining in the summer.

What to See and Do

Angelika Film Center. *18 W Houston St (10012). Phone 212/995-2000. www.angelikafilmcenter.com.* Get a taste of genuine SoHo living at this cultural institution that has attracted lovers of artsy movies for years. But the Angelika is even more than that. It is a special place—a world away from today's overcrowded, noisy multiplexes teeming with soccer moms and screaming kids. You'll find a generally urbane crowd at the independent films shown at the theater. And the Angelika Café in the lobby area is a great little place to grab a latté and a scone before the flick or a soda and a sandwich after the movie. On Sunday mornings, you'll find locals relaxing in the café, enjoying their coffee and *The New York Times*. Hang out here for a while and you'll feel more like a real New Yorker than a tourist. **$$**

Blue Note. *131 W 3rd St (10012). Phone 212/475-8592. www.bluenote.net.* For some of the world's best names in jazz, head downtown to Greenwich Village to the Blue Note. This bastion of fine jazz has played host over the years to many well-known jazz performers, as well as rising stars. Although the cover charge is higher here than at many other venues, the acts are worth it. Monday nights can be had for around $10, when the record companies promote new releases by their artists. The club also serves a variety of food and drinks if you want to grab dinner while listening to some cool tunes. (Daily) **$$$$**

Bottom Line. *15 W 4th St (10012). Phone 212/228-6300. www.bottomline cabaret.com.* This club seems to have been here for as long as there has been a music scene in Greenwich Village. Many legendary rockers and R&B artists, including such greats as Bruce Springsteen and Stevie Wonder, played gigs here early in their careers. Today, the mix of performers features some fun, semiregular acts like Buster Poindexter (aka David Johansen) of "Hot Hot Hot" fame. Tickets sell out early for the more popular artists, so check the listings in local newspapers for upcoming headliners. The Bottom Line also serves a variety of food and drinks.

Chelsea Piers Sports and Entertainment Complex. *24th St and West Side Hwy (10011). Piers 59-62 on the Hudson River from 17th to 23rd Sts. The entrance is at 23rd St. Take the C/E subway to 23rd St. Phone 212/336-6666. www.chelseapiers.com.* For the best in recreational activities all in one location, keep heading west until you hit Chelsea Piers. The 1.7-million-square-foot complex features an ice skating rink, a bowling alley, climbing walls, a driving range, basketball, rollerblading, and more. There also are pubs and restaurants to grab a meal after doing all these activities. Stop in for a cold one at the Chelsea Brewing Co., the state's largest microbrewery. Make a point to visit the complex at sundown, to view the beautiful sunset off the river. Both kids and adults can spend a nice few hours at this mega sports center. (Daily)

Church of the Ascension. *12 W 11th St (10011). 10th St and Fifth Ave. Phone 212/254-8620.* (1840) Episcopal. English Gothic; redecorated 1885-1889 under the direction of Stanford White. John La Farge's mural, *The Ascension of Our Lord,* surmounts the altar; the sculptured angels are by Louis Saint-Gaudens. (Daily)

Dean & DeLuca. *560 Broadway (10012). Phone 212/226-6800. www.dean anddeluca.com.* From Portuguese cornbread to 80 percent pure cocoa and dark chocolate bars to a dozen kinds of gourmet mushrooms, Dean & DeLuca is a food lovers' paradise. The pastries and breads rival those of any bakery in Paris; the selection of salads, smoked fish, and meats is astounding; and the produce is so good that it puts the word *fresh* to shame. The personalized

Greenwich Village Walking Tour

Although no longer the "leading edge" of the art world and radical-ism, Greenwich Village remains a uniquely dynamic neighborhood. Start in Washington Square Park, lined by New York University buildings and site of the famous arch. The park normally buzzes with street performers, in-line skaters, and playing families. Leave the park from the south side. Judson Memorial Church stands on the corner of West 4th Street and Thompson Street. Designed by Stanford White, the church is noted for its stained glass windows and front marble work. Thompson Street is lined with chess clubs. At Bleecker Street, turn right. Look for Le Figaro (186 Bleecker Street) and Café Borgia (185 Bleecker Street), a pair of old-time coffee houses.

Turn right onto MacDougal Street. Here stand two landmark cafes: Café Reggio (119 MacDougal Street) and Café Wha? (115 MacDougal Street), as well as Minetta Tavern (113 MacDougal Street), an old standby that serves good Italian food. Make a U-turn, turn right onto Minetta Lane, then right onto Minetta Street, both lined with classic Village townhouses. Cross Sixth Avenue and enter the heart of Bleecker's "neighborhood" shopping-including some of the fin-est Italian bake shops in the city. Continue across Seventh Avenue and turn left onto Barrow Street. This block features a number of classic, redbrick row houses (49 and 51 Barrow Street are Federalist-style) and Chumley's Bar (86 Barrow Street), once a speakeasy and famous writer' hangout. Look for 75 Barrow Street, a strange, nar-row house where Edna St. Vincent Millay once lived, and 77 Barrow Street, which was built in 1799, making it the Village's oldest house. Turn right on Bedford, passing a late 19th-century horse stable (95 Bedford), an early 19th-century home with a pair of Tudor-style tow-ers aptly named Twin Peaks (102 Bedford), and a mid-19th-century home built in the Greek Revival style (113 Bedford).

Turn right onto Christopher Street, a throbbing, busy street that's the heart of the Village gay life. Go right onto Bleecker, then left onto Seventh Avenue. Sweet Basil (414 Seventh Avenue) is famed jazz club, as is Village Vanguard (178 Seventh Avenue South). Turn right on Grove Street and right again on Waverly Place. At 165 Waverly Place stands the Northern Dispensary, built during the 1831 cholera epidemic. Turn left onto Sixth Avenue. The circa-1876, castlelike, Gothic-style Jefferson Market Library is located on 10th Street. Also of note on Sixth Avenue are Balducci's (424 Six Avenue), a legend-ary gourmet food shop, and Bigalow's (414 Sixth Avenue), the city's oldest continuously operating pharmacy. Continue north and turn right onto 11th Street to minuscule Second Cemetery of the Spanish and Portugese Synagogue. Or, return south and turn left onto 8th Street, another major shopping street.

At Fifth Avenue, turn right. Just before Washington Square Park is the picturesque cul-de-sac Washington Square Mews. For more shopping, continue east on 8th Street and then turn south on Broadway. These blocks, not long ago a forsaken neighborhood of old warehouses and sweatshop factory buildings, now thrive with major retailing chains like Tower Records, the Gap, and more.

mini-cakes, available for any occasion, cost a bundle—but they're worth every fattening bite. Come early or late, because it can get very crowded (especially on weekends), and you want to spend your time browsing and stocking up on goodies as well as cookware and kitchen accessories. Forget about your budget and just let your taste buds do the shopping. (Daily)

Forbes Magazine Galleries. *60 Fifth Ave (10011). Phone 212/206-5548.* Housing the collections of the idiosyncratic media tycoon Malcolm Forbes, this museum includes exhibits of more than 500 toy boats, 12,000 toy soldiers, about a dozen Faberge eggs, and numerous historical documents relating to American history. (Tues, Wed, Fri, Sat 10 am-4 pm; closed holidays)

Foods of New York Walking and Tasting Tours. *95 Christopher St (10014). Phone 212/239-1124. www.food.nyc.citysearch.com.* These two all-inclusive tours offer you a chance to sample a variety of food and drink while seeing historical sites and soaking up the city's atmosphere. The tour of the Chelsea Food Market and the Far West Village (also known as the Meatpacking District) includes tastings from Chelsea's nearly one-block-long indoor food market. This complex includes five bakeries and the largest produce shop in New York. Sample fresh milk from Hudson Valley dairies, buffalo mozzarella cheese flown in from Italy, homemade preserves, and seeded country French sourdough bread. The second tour of Greenwich Village's off-the-beaten-track sites includes stops at 15 unique food establishments, a 1920s speakeasy, and the narrowest house in the area. Tastings on this tour include homemade chocolates, Italian rice balls, Turkish falafel, and wine. All tastings are done on the go. Wear comfortable shoes and check the weather forecast before reserving a spot. (Tues-Sun) **$$$$**

Guggenheim SoHo *575 Broadway (10012). Phone 212/423-3500.* This small art museum has 30,000 square feet of exhibition space; also here is the permanent exhibit of at pop artist Andy Warhol's *The Last Supper.* (Thurs-Mon 11 am-6 pm; closed holidays) **FREE**

Hogs and Heifers Saloon. *858 Washington St (10014). Phone 212/929-0655. www.hogsandheifers.com.* A biker bar with celebrities' bras hanging off deer antlers? Only in Manhattan. Located in the Meatpacking District, this bar has hosted celebs like Julia Roberts and Drew Barrymore—who decided to leave their bras behind as eye candy for patrons. Other showbiz biggies like Harrison Ford and Danny DeVito also have been known to frequent this wild place; you never know who you'll run into on any given night. In addition to downing cheap beer, you'll be treated to music and bar-top dancing.

The bar also has a less-famous uptown location at 1843 First Ave, phone 212/722-8635. (Daily)

Joseph Papp Public Theater. *425 Lafayette St, in the former Astor Library. Phone 212/260-2400.* Complex of six theaters where Shakespeare, new American plays, new productions of classics, films, concerts, and poetry readings are presented.

Joyce Gold History Tours. *141 W 17th St (10011). Phone 212/242-5762. www.nyctours.com.* Take a walk through time with a professional who knows endless stories, both serious and frivolous, about Manhattan and its people. Since 1976, Joyce Gold has led all tours personally, rain or shine. No reservations are necessary, and tours last from 2 to 2 1/2 hours. Stops include Grand Central Terminal, Harlem, the East Village, Chinatown, and Fifth Avenue. Check the Web site for specific subjects, dates, meeting places, and departure times. **$$$**

Loehmans. *101 Seventh Ave (10011). Phone 212/352-0856.* Women who are ravenous for famous brands of clothing at discount prices and are willing to do whatever it takes to take home the best items (near-fistfights have been witnessed) will love Loehmans. This department store is well known to generations of New York women and still has a good reputation for bargains. The five-story store sells mostly women's clothing, jewelry, handbags, shoes, and accessories; it offers a smaller selection of men's apparel. (Daily)

Murray's Cheese Shop. *257 Bleecker St (10014). Phone 888/692-4339. www.murrayscheese.com.* For the best gourmet cheese selection in the city, pop into this 63-year-old New York institution in lower Manhattan. The shop will entice any discerning palate with its 250 varieties of domestic and imported cheeses, as well as a selection of breads, olives, antipasti, and personalized gift baskets. Murray's also has a second, newer location in Midtown at 73 Grand Central Terminal. (Daily)

Serena. *222 W 23rd St (10011). Phone 212/255-4646.* If you want to be a part of "the scene" and "be seen," Serena is the bar and lounge for you. It serves food and drinks and is known as an after-hours hangout for the chic and the hip. The place has a plush, dark look to it. But, look carefully, because you may see some celebrities sipping champagne off in a corner somewhere. (Daily)

SOB's. *204 Varick St (10014). Phone 212/243-4940. www.sobs.com.* Lovers of the Brazilian beat, as well as hip-hop, reggae, salsa, African music, and other kinds of international sounds, have flocked since 1982 to this venerable SoHo nightclub. SOB's—Sounds of Brazil—features new performers and well-known stars who always get the crowd up and dancing. Monday nights are famous for Latin dance lessons, with an entrance fee of just $5 before 7 pm. Novices are most welcome to try out their dancing shoes during these classes. Saturday Night Samba features dancers and Brazilian performers. Every evening has a different theme and varied performers. For your dining pleasure, Latin and Brazilian cuisine are on the menu. While other clubs are quiet for the weekdays, SOB's continues to come alive. (Daily) **$$$$**

SoHo Street Vendors. *The N/R subways stop at Canal or Prince St, or you can take the A/C/E subways to Canal St. Then wander around the general area, since street vendors change locations. Phone 212/369-6004.* Shopping from street vendors in this hip section of the city is a fun experience largely due to the haggling, which seems to come naturally to many native New Yorkers. If you're not comfortable doing this, bring along a buddy for moral support. Never accept a first offer, and don't look for authenticity. Just have fun with it. If you see something you like, grab it, because the same vendor may not be back at the same spot the next day. Vendors peddle a multitude of treasures, including trendy clothing, cool jewelry, and paintings, drawings, and other artwork. With so many items to choose from, you're sure to come away with something you haven't seen anywhere else before—or won't see until the trend hits your neck of the woods months later.

Sullivan Street Bakery. *73 Sullivan St (10012). Phone 212/334-9435. www. sullivanstreetbakery.com.* If bread is your passion, then enter these doors and take in the sights and smells of the Sullivan Street Bakery. The bakery sells a variety of mouthwatering thin-crust Italian breads, Roman-style pizzas, biscotti, and tarts, as well as coffee to wash it all down. A second location is in Hell's Kitchen at 533 W 47th St (212/265-5580). (Daily)

Washington Square Park. *W 4th St and Waverly Pl (10012). Many subways stop at nearby W 4th St.* For the ultimate in daytime people-watching, head downtown to the heart and soul of Greenwich Village. The bustling 9-acre park, dating back to 1827, serves up a cacophony of jugglers, street musicians, magicians, and countless students from nearby New York University. The park hosts outdoor art fairs in spring and fall, as well as jazz performances in summer. The north end of the park features the historic Washington Memorial Arch. This marble structure was modeled after Paris' Arc de Triomphe and was erected in 1889. (Daily)

Special Events

Greenwich Village Halloween Parade. *Take almost any subway to W 4th St and keep walking uptown into Chelsea. Phone 212/484-1222. www.halloween-nyc.com.* Straights, gays, men, women, kids, seniors, and everyone in between dresses in the wildest of costumes for this annual Halloween tradition in the West Village. Strangers become instant friends and everyone gets into the fun spirit in what has become the largest Halloween parade in the US. Although the crowd may get a bit wild, the event is usually quite safe due to the large police presence and general good feelings exuded by area residents. If you've ever wanted to let it all hang out and wear a costume that will shock everyone you know, this is the place to do it. Prepare to stay out late and enjoy some late-night partying at a local bar (unless you have the kids with you, of course). Late Oct.

Washington Square Art Show. *LaGuardia Pl, between W 4th St and Houston St (10021).* Outdoor art show. Weekends, late May-June and late Aug-early Sept.

Hotels

★ ★ ★ **60 THOMPSON.** *60 Thompson St (10012). Phone 212/431-0400; fax 212/431-0200. www.60thompson.com.* This SoHo boutique hotel features warm and inviting rooms and suites, accented with dark woods and full-wall leather headboards. The rooms will surely please high-tech aficionados, as they offer high-speed Internet connections, DVD players, and CD stereo systems. Matching this in hipness are decadent marble bathrooms with oversized showers. The hotel's Asian-tinged seafood restaurant, Thom (see), is popular with in-the-know locals. It also offers Thom's Bar, in a clubby, intimate setting, as a place for those who want to relax and enjoy a drink. 100 rooms, 8 story. Check-out noon. Check-in 3 pm. TV; cable (premium), VCR available. In-room modem link. Restaurant. Babysitting services available. Business center. Concierge. **$$$**

⊡ ⬚ ⚹

★ ★ ★ ★ **MERCER HOTEL.** *147 Mercer St (10012). Phone 212/966-6060; toll-free 888/918-6060; fax 212/965-3838. www.mercerhotel.com.* Catering to a fashion-forward clientele in New York's SoHo, Mercer Hotel is a boutique hotel in the midst of one of the city's most exciting neighborhoods. This former artists' community stays true to its roots in its many cutting-edge boutiques and galleries. The loft-style Mercer Hotel epitomizes bohemian chic with its exposed brick, steel beams, and hardwood floors. Christian Liaigre, darling of the minimalist décor movement, has designed a sophisticated look for the hotel with simple furnishings and serene neutral colors. The uncluttered look extends to the bathrooms, with clean white tiles and luxurious two-person bathtubs or spacious showers with assorted spray fixtures. The lobby also serves as a lending library stocked with favorite books and videos, and the nearby trend-setting Crunch Gym is accessible to all guests. Mercer Kitchen (see) and Bar reign as hotspots on the local scene, for both their sensational food under the direction of Jean-Georges Vongerichten and their fabulous people-watching. 75 rooms, 6 story. Pets accepted. Check-out 3 pm, check-in 11 am. In-room modem link. Fireplaces. Room service 24 hours. Restaurant. Babysitting services available. Valet parking. Concierge. **$$$$**

⊡ ➤ ⬚

Restaurants

★ ★ ★ **AMUSE.** *108 W 18th St (10011). Phone 212/929-9755.* Amuse is a unique restaurant, which is quite an accomplishment in the scheme of New York City dining. The kitchen offers a clever menu of different-sized plates—$5, $15, or $20 each, depending on portion size—for tasting, sharing, passing, and, above all, enjoying. The menu spans the globe and features lots of full-flavored snacks, appetizers, and entrée-type plates from comfort food favorites to inventive haute creations. This design-your-own-dinner formula fits seamlessly with the slick cocktail-crazed crowds that come in for the scene as much as the terrific and, as the restaurant's name promises, fun food. American menu. Closed Sun. Lunch, dinner. Bar. Casual attire. Reservations required. **$$$**

D

★ ★ ★ **ANNISA.** *13 Barrow St (10014). Phone 212/741-6699.* At Annisa, a cozy, off-the-beaten-path gem in Greenwich Village, chef-partner Anita Lo and partner Jennifer Scism (who runs the front of the house) bring a bit of Asia and a lot of flavor and savvy style to the contemporary American table. With the restaurant's golden glow and elegant, sheer-white curtains draped along the tall walls, it's easy to feel like you're dining somewhere very close to heaven. The simple, approachable menu helps keep you in the celestial mood. An array of wines by the glass and a strong sommelier make pairing wine with dinner a no-brainer. Contemporary American menu. Closed Sun. Dinner. Bar. Casual attire. Reservations required. **$$$**

★ ★ ★ **AQUAGRILL.** *210 Spring St (10012). Phone 212/274-0505; fax 212/274-0587.* When the sun is out and a warm breeze is in the air, you'll find the city's hip locals lounging outside at Aquagrill, a perennial favorite for swimmingly fresh seafood (and great dry-aged steak). With its tall French doors sprung open to the street, Aquagrill has a European elegance and calm to it that makes it an irresistible spot to settle in, even if only for a glass of sparkling wine and a dozen (or two) shimmering oysters. Although the warmer months are the most fun, when there is a nip in the air, the dining room wraps you up, making you feel cozy in an instant. Seafood menu. Closed Mon; holidays; also first week in July. Dinner, Sat, Sun brunch. Bar. Casual attire. Reservations required (dinner, Sun brunch). Outdoor seating. **$$$$**

D

★ ★ ★ **BABBO.** *110 Waverly Pl (10011). Phone 212/777-0303; fax 212/777-3365. www.babbonyc.com.* Dressed in his signature orange clogs and shorts, Mario Batali is the king of rustic authentic Italian cuisine on television's Food Network. But before he was a star of the small screen, he was a cook—and he is one celebrity chef who still is. Here in New York, you'll find him at Babbo, a charming Greenwich Village carriage house turned stylish duplex hotspot where celebrities, foodies, VIPs, and supermodels fill tables (and every nook of space) for the chance to feast on Batali's unique brand of robust and risky Italian fare. The man is known for serving braised pigs' feet, warm lamb tongue, and testa (head cheese). Cult-status signature pastas like beef cheek ravioli and mint love letters—spicy lamb sausage ragu soothed with mint and wrapped in envelopes of fresh pasta—are lick-lipping delicious and demonstrate that some culinary risks are worth taking. Italian menu. Dinner. Bar. Casual attire. **$$$**

D

★ ★ ★ **BALTHAZAR.** *80 Spring St (10012). Phone 212/965-1414; fax 212/966-2502. www.balthazarny.com.* If you don't know what all the hype surrounding Balthazar is about, you most certainly should. Keith McNally's super-fabulous replica of a Parisian brasserie is one of those rare spots that actually deserves the buzz. From the attractive crowds at the bar to the stunning folks who squeeze into the restaurant's tiny tables (you'll be seated as close to a stranger as is possible without becoming intimate), Balthazar is a dazzling, dizzying, wonderfully chaotic destination that sports a perfect menu of delicious brasserie standards like frisee au lardons, pan bagnat, steak frites, and a glistening raw bar built for royalty, not to mention the fresh-baked bread from the Balthazar bakery next door. To feel like a true New Yorker, pick up a bag of croissants, a couple of baguettes, and a dozen tarts on your way out for breakfast or lunch the next day. Balthazar is fun and loud and, in its own electric way, flawless. French menu. Dinner, Sat, Sun brunch. Bar. Casual attire. Reservations required Sat (dinner). **$$$$**

D

★ ★ **BALUCHI'S.** *193 Spring St (10012). Phone 212/226-2828. www.balucis.com.* Indian menu. Lunch, dinner. Casual attire. Totally non-smoking. **$$$**

★ ★ **BLUE RIBBON.** *97 Sullivan St (10012). Phone 212/274-0404.* American, French menu. Closed major holidays. Dinner, late night. Bar. Children's menu. Casual attire. Totally nonsmoking. **$$$**

D

★ ★ ★ **BOND STREET.** *6 Bond St (10012). Phone 212/777-2500.* High-art sushi and sashimi are the calling cards of Bond Street, a hotspot and hipster hangout disguised as a modern Japanese restaurant. Famous fashionistas, celebrities, and supermodels are the typical guests at the white-washed, airy restaurant, and down in the dark and sexy lower-level bar you'll find more of the same. For all the hype, though, Bond Street serves excellent sushi and sashimi, and the extensive and inventive modern Japanese-influenced menu stands up to the scene with impressive resolve. Japanese, sushi menu. Closed major holidays. Dinner, late-night. Bar. Casual attire. **$$$**

★ ★ **BOOM.** *152 Spring St (10012). Phone 212/431-3663; fax 212/431-3643.* International menu. Lunch, dinner, Sat, Sun brunch. Bar. **$$**

D

★ **CAFÉ DE BRUXELLES.** *118 Greenwich Ave (10011). Phone 212/206-1830; fax 212/229-1436.* Belgian, French menu. Closed most major holidays. Lunch, dinner, Sun brunch. Bar. **$$**

D

★ ★ **CAFÉ LOUP.** *105 W 13th St (10011). Phone 212/255-4746; fax 212/255-2022.* French bistro menu. Lunch, dinner, Sun brunch. Bar. Casual attire. **$$**

★ ★ **CANTEEN.** *142 Mercer St (10012). Phone 212/431-7676. www.canteennyc.com.* American menu. Lunch, dinner. Bar. Casual attire. **$$**

★ ★ **CHELSEA BISTRO AND BAR.** *358 W 23rd St (10011). Phone 212/727-2026; fax 212/727-2180. www.nytoday.com/chelseabistro.* French bistro menu. Dinner. Bar. Glass-enclosed terrace. **$$**

D

★ ★ **CHEZ MICHALLET.** *90 Bedford St (10014). Phone 212/242-8309; fax 212/242-0964.* French menu. Closed Jan 1, Dec 25. Dinner, Sat, Sun brunch. Casual attire. Reservations required. Totally nonsmoking. **$$$**

★ ★ ★ **CUB ROOM.** *131 Sullivan St (10012). Phone 212/677-4100; fax 212/228-3425. www.cubroom.com.* The Cub Room was one of the first hotspots to open in SoHo, and it has stood the test of time thanks to chef-owner Henry Meer, who keeps the seasonal Mediterranean-accented menu fresh and fun, offering the perfect brand of upscale fare for the lively bunch that frequents this popular destination. In the chic, living room-style lounge with vintage fabric-covered sofas and a long, serpentine bar, a gregarious and gorgeous crowd sips chilly cocktails, while inside the rustic, country-style dining room, big groups and whispering couples feast on Meer's solid cooking. New American menu. Closed Dec 25. Dinner, Sat, Sun brunch. Bar. Casual attire. **$$**

★ ★ ★ **DA SILVANO.** *260 6th Ave (10014). Phone 212/982-2343.* If one thing is certain about a meal at Da Silvano, it is that before you finish your Tuscan dinner, you will have spotted at least one actor, model, musician, or other such celebrity. Da Silvano is a scene, and a great one at that. With such a loyal and fabulous following, the food could be mediocre, but the kitchen does not rest on its star-infested laurels. This kitchen offers wonderful, robust, regional Italian fare, like homemade pasta, meat, fish, and salad. The sliver of a wine bar next door, Da Silvano Cantinetta, offers Italian-style tapas paired with a wide selection of wines by the glass. But perhaps the best way to experience Da Silvano is on a warm day, where a seat at the wide, European-style sidewalk café offers prime people watching. Italian menu. Closed Dec 25. Lunch, dinner. Casual attire. Outdoor seating. **$$$**

D

★ ★ **DA UMBERTO.** *107 W 17th St (10011). Phone 212/989-0303.* Northern Italian menu. Closed Sun; Jan 1, Dec 25; also week of July 4. Lunch, dinner. Bar. Casual attire. **$$**

D

★ **ELEPHANT AND CASTLE.** *68 Greenwich Ave (10011). Phone 212/243-1400; fax 212/989-9294.* Daily specials. Breakfast, lunch, dinner. Totally nonsmoking. **$$**

★ ★ **FLORENT.** *69 Gansevoort St (10014). Phone 212/989-5779; fax 212/645-2498. www.restaurantflorent.com.* French, American menu. Closed Dec 25. Breakfast, lunch, dinner, 24 hour service, late night. Bar. Children's menu. Casual attire. Chrome- and aluminum-trimmed diner attached to meat market in warehouse area of the Village. No Credit Cards Accepted **$$**

D

★ ★ **GASCOGNE.** *158 8th Ave (10011). Phone 212/675-6564; fax 212/627-3018. www.gascognenyc.com.* French menu. Closed some major holidays. Lunch, dinner. Bar. Casual attire. Outdoor seating. **$$**

★ ★ **GHENET RESTAURANT.** *284 Mulberry St (10012). Phone 212/343-1888. www.ghenet.com.* Ethiopian menu. Lunch, dinner. Bar. Casual attire. **$$**

★ ★ **HOME.** *20 Cornelia St (10014). Phone 212/243-9579; fax 212/647-9393.* Contemporary American menu. Closed Dec 25. Breakfast, lunch, dinner, Sat, Sun brunch. Casual attire. Outdoor seating. Totally nonsmoking. **$$**

★ ★ ★ **HONMURA AN.** *170 Mercer St (10012). Phone 212/334-5253.* New Yorkers who are over the lines at Nobu and the crowds at Yama flock to Honmura An, a delightful, serene escape in SoHo where spectacular just-made soba and udon noodles are the house specialty. Bring an appetite, because aside from the noodles, the kitchen has an in for some of the most delicious fish in the city—sashimi, sushi, and maki rolls that will force you to order more even if you have reached maximum food capacity. Japanese menu. Closed Mon. Lunch, dinner. Casual attire. **$$**

★ **I TRE MERLI.** *463 W Broadway (10012). Phone 212/254-8699; fax 212/387-8895. www.itremerli.citysearch.com.* Northern Italian menu. Lunch, dinner. Bar. Over 1,000 wine bottles line exposed brick walls in converted warehouse building. Casual attire. Reservations required Fri-Sun dinner. Outdoor seating. **$$**

D

★ ★ **LA METAIRIE.** *189 W 10th St (10014). Phone 212/989-0343; fax 212/989-0810. www.lametairie.com.* French menu. Lunch, dinner, Sat, Sun brunch. Casual attire. **$$$**

D

★ ★ **LA TRAVIATA.** *461 W 23rd St (10011). Phone 212/243-5497; fax 212/243-5561.* Italian menu. Closed Sun (Memorial Day-Labor Day); July 4. Lunch, dinner, Sun brunch. Bar. Entertainment Wed-Sat. **$$**

★ ★ ★ **LE MADRI.** *168 W 18th St (10011). Phone 212/727-8022; fax 212/727-3168.* Le Madri, or "The Mother," is restaurateur Pino Luongo's flagship Italian restaurant, offering modern takes on authentic Tuscan fare. The vast, sweeping dining room features vaulted ceilings, tall columns, natural wood floors, and extravagant floral arrangements. Start with selections from the monster-sized antipasto table, and move onto to pizzettes straight from the rustic wood-burning oven. Of course, pastas are also a big draw here, especially the simple spaghetti with tomatoes. The menu includes a belt-busting selection of seafood and meats as well. This is a great choice for large parties with hearty, yet discerning, appetites. Italian menu. Closed major holidays. Lunch, dinner. Bar. Casual attire. Outdoor seating. **$$$**

★ ★ **LUPA.** *170 Thompson St (10012). Phone 212/982-5089; fax 212/982-5490. www.luparestaurant.com.* Italian menu. Lunch, dinner. Bar. Entertainment. Casual attire. Outdoor seating. **$$**

D

★ **MANHATTAN BISTRO.** *129 Spring St (10012). Phone 212/966-3459; fax 212/925-1668.* French menu. Closed Memorial Day, Dec 25. Breakfast, lunch, dinner, Sat, Sun brunch. Bar. Casual attire. **$$**

★ ★ ★ **MERCER KITCHEN.** *99 Prince St (10012). Phone 212/966-5454; fax 212/965-3855.* Located in the ultra-chic Mercer Hotel in SoHo, this exposed-brick, subterranean hotspot is constantly teeming with celebrities and those who believe that they are celebrities merely because they are dining in their glow. The Asian-influenced American menu, under the talented direction of chef-owner Jean-Georges Vongerichten, is as swanky as the crowd, with signatures like raw tuna and wasabi pizza and yellowtail carpaccio with lime, coriander, and mint. If you haven't the slightest appetite, head over to the sexy bar, where hipsters sip martinis with abandon. Contemporary American menu. Closed holidays. Lunch, dinner, Sat, Sun brunch. Bar. Casual attire. **$$$**

D

★ ★ ★ **MESA GRILL.** *102 Fifth Ave (10011). Phone 212/807-7400; fax 212/989-0034. www.mesagrill.com.* In the ten years since the Southwestern haven known as Mesa Grill opened its tall, blond-wood doors and chef-owner Bobby Flay reached stardom on cable TV's Food Network, he has, impressively, managed to keep his creative eye on this, his first restaurant. The vaulted, lively room remains a popular spot for margarita-soaked happy hours, as well as a top choice for superb Southwestern-inspired American fare. The vibrant menu changes with the seasons, but famous plates include the cotija-crusted quesadilla stuffed with goat cheese, basil, and red chiles, topped with a charred corn salsa; and the 16-spiced chicken with mango garlic sauce and cilantro-pesto mashed potatoes. Flay's food is not shy, so keep a cold margarita handy to soothe the heat. Southwestern menu. Closed Dec 25. Lunch, dinner. Bar. Casual attire. **$$$**

D

★ ★ **MEZZOGIORNO.** *195 Spring St (10012). Phone 212/334-2112; fax 212/941-6294. www.mezzogiorno.com.* Northern Italian menu. Closed Dec 25. Lunch, dinner. Bar. Outdoor seating. **$$**

D

★ ★ **MI COCINA.** *57 Jane St (10014). Phone 212/627-8273; fax 212/627-0174. www.micocinanyc.com.* Mexican menu. Closed Dec 24-25; also 2 weeks Aug. Lunch, dinner, Sat, Sun brunch. Bar. Children's menu. Casual attire. Outdoor seating. **$$**

D

★ ★ ★ **ONE IF BY LAND, TWO IF BY SEA.** *17 Barrow St (10014). Phone 212/228-0822. www.oneifbyland.com.* This classic French restaurant, set in a restored, turn-of-the-century carriage house in Greenwich Village, is one of New York's most cherished spots for romance and other love-related special occasion dining: anniversaries, engagements, and the like. Dark and elegant, the hushed, candlelit, two-story dining room is richly appointed with antique sconces, heavy velvet drapes, oriental carpets, and blazing fireplaces. The menu here is straight-ahead French, with seasonal accompaniments and modern flourishes that add sparkle to the plate. American menu. Closed most major holidays. Dinner. Bar. In restored 18th-century carriage house once owned by Aaron Burr; many framed historical documents;

dining room overlooks courtyard garden. Casual attire. Reservations required. **$$$**

D

★ **PENANG MALAYSIAN.** *109 Spring St (10012). Phone 212/274-8883; fax 212/925-8530. www.penangnyc.com.* Malaysian menu. Lunch, dinner. Bar. Casual attire. **$$**

★ ★ **PERIYALI.** *35 W 20th St (10011). Phone 212/463-7890; fax 212/924-9403. www.periyali.com.* Offering authentic Greek fare in a soothing Mediterranean-accented setting, Periyali is a wonderful place to experience the delicious seaside cuisine of Athens and beyond. Classics on the menu include octopus marinated in red wine, sautéed sweetbreads with white beans, grilled whole fish, and mezze like taramosalata (caviar mousse), melitzanosalata (grilled-eggplant mousse), and spanakopita (spinach and cheese pie). Periyali has been around for a while, but the restaurant's popularity has not waned. You'll find it full of regulars most days at lunch, although at night the pace is calmer, making it a great choice for a leisurely dinner. Greek menu. Closed Sun. Lunch, dinner. Bar. Casual attire. **$$**

★ ★ **PRAVDA.** *281 Lafayette St (10012). Phone 212/226-4944.* Russian menu. Dinner, late night. Bar. Casual attire. **$$**

★ ★ **PROVENCE.** *38 MacDougal St (10012). Phone 212/475-7500; fax 212/674-7876. www.provence.citysearch.com.* French menu. Closed holidays. Lunch, dinner, Sat brunch. Bar. Casual attire. **$$**

D SC

★ ★ **RAOUL'S.** *180 Prince St (10012). Phone 212/966-3518; fax 212/966-0205. www.raoulsrestaurant.com.* French menu. Dinner, late night. Bar. Casual attire. Reservations required. Outdoor seating. **$$$**

★ ★ ★ **THE RED CAT.** *227 Tenth Ave (10011). Phone 212/242-1122. www.theredcat.com.* Jimmy Bradley, the chef and owner of The Red Cat, is one of those restaurateurs who knows exactly what New Yorkers are looking for in a dining experience: a cool, hip scene? Check. An innovative and exciting menu? Check. A solid international wine list with lots by the glass and a tempting selection of sexy house cocktails? Check, check. Indeed, Bradley delivers it all at his West Chelsea haunt for inspired Mediterranean-accented fare set in a New England-chic space trimmed with white and red wainscoting, hurricane lamps, and deep, long banquettes. This is one place you will want to return to, even if it's just to figure out how to replicate his formula in your own town. Contemporary American menu. Closed Jan 1, Dec 24-25. Dinner. Bar. Casual attire. **$$$**

★ ★ ★ **RHONE.** *63 Ganesvoort St (10014). Phone 212/367-8440. www.rhonenyc.com.* Located in the city's hipster haven known as the Meatpacking District, Rhone is an airy, chic restaurant, lounge, and wine bar that features the wines of its namesake region in France. Sitting in Rhone, with its wide, floor-to-ceiling windows thrown open to the street, you'll feel transported. With about 100 bottles and 30 glasses of Rhone varietals on the list, you'll have no problem finding a match for the ambitious French menu, which includes dishes like potato-crusted seabass and braised lamb shank. Those craving lighter fare may pair their vino with a cheese plate or caviar. Contemporary American menu. Closed Sun. Dinner. Casual attire. **$$$**

★ ★ **SAVORE.** *200 Spring St (10012). Phone 212/431-1212; fax 212/ 343-2605.* Italian menu. Closed Dec 25. Lunch, dinner. Bar. Casual attire. Outdoor seating. Totally nonsmoking. **$$$**

D

★ ★ ★ **SAVOY.** *70 Prince St (10012). Phone 212/219-8570; fax 212/334-4868.* Peter Hoffman, the chef and an owner of Savoy, a comfortable, urban dining spot in SoHo, has been a proponent of the greenmarket cooking for more than ten years. You'll find him with his tricycle-pulled wagon at the local farmers markets several times a week, picking produce for his inspired menu of global fare—dishes taken from Spain, Latin America, France, Morocco, and Greece, as well as America's various regions—brought to life with simple, brilliant ingredients. The intimate dining room upstairs features an open fireplace where many of Hoffman's rustic dishes are cooked right before your eyes in the blazing hearth. French, Mediterranean menu. Closed most major holidays. Lunch, dinner. Bar. Casual attire. **$$$**

D

★ ★ **SOHO STEAK.** *90 Thompson St (10012). Phone 212/226-0602.* American, French menu. Closed major holidays. Lunch, dinner, Sat, Sun brunch. Bar. Casual attire. Outdoor seating. **$$**

D

★ ★ ★ **THOM.** *60 Thompson St (10012). Phone 212/925-2971.* Set in the über-hip, ultra-fabulous stomping ground that is the 60 Thompson Street Hotel, the restaurant Thom manages to marry chic style with terrific food, a combination that is rare in such a swanky hotel. The menu features a modern meld of Asian and American influences, with light, bright flavors and sexy presentations on every plate. Since the ambience is so seductive and the hotel and restaurant so jammed with beautiful people, plan to stop in at the lobby lounge for sumptuous cocktails and lots of scene after dinner. American menu. Breakfast, lunch, dinner, late night. Bar. Casual attire. Outdoor seating. **$$**

D

★ ★ ★ **WALLSE.** *344 W 11th St (10014). Phone 212/352-2300. www. wallserestaurant.com.* Enter this charming restaurant, tucked in a sleepy corner of the West Village, and you are instantly transported to Vienna. Decorated with contemporary art and filled with close, square tables, antique furnishings, deep blue banquettes, and a long, romantic stretch of rich mahogany bar (where the cocktails are stellar), chef Kurt Gutenbrunner's Wallse is a personal and delicious ode to the hearty yet delicate cuisine of his homeland, Austria. The thin, golden-crusted Wiener schnitzel should not be missed. A terrific selection of Austrian wines complements the meal, and a nice slice of strudel will send you off on a sweet note. Austrian menu. Dinner. Bar. Casual attire. Reservations required. **$$$**

★ ★ ★ **WASHINGTON PARK.** *24 Fifth Ave (10011). Phone 212/529-4400.* Chef-restaurateur Jonathan Waxman first wowed New Yorkers with his smart brand of California-inspired cuisine at Jams in the 1980s. With Washington Park, he proves that he still has the gift, and then some. This cheery, sunny, comfortable restaurant, just steps from Washington Square Park on Fifth Ave, features a wonderful daily menu of Greenmarket-inspired meals. And in an ode to Jams, he has brought back the signature JW grilled organic chicken and fries and roasted red pepper pancakes with smoked salmon and caviar—both dishes that remain essential eating. American menu. Lunch, dinner. Bar. Children's menu. Casual attire. **$$$**

D

★ ★ ★ **WOO LAE OAK.** *148 Mercer St (10012). Phone 212/925-8200. www.woolaeoaksoho.com.* If you're searching for a lively spot to gather a large group for some very tasty and authentic Korean food, Woo Lae Oak is the place. This sleek, cavernous multiplex-style space offers some of the best Korean barbecue in the city. Guests grill marinated meats and seafood to a savory char on wicked-cool smokeless grill tables. The food is traditional; novices in the arena of Korean fare should seek assistance from one of the restaurant's très chic yet very friendly waiters. Meltingly creamy black cod simmered in a sweet-hot, garlicky soy sauce is a one of the restaurant's most famous plates, but there isn't a bad choice on the menu. Korean menu. Lunch, dinner. Bar. Entertainment. Casual attire. **$$**

D

★ ★ ★ **ZOË.** *90 Prince St (10012). Phone 212/966-6722; fax 212/966-6718. www.zoerest.com.* Thalia and Stephen Loffredo opened Zoë smack in the heart of SoHo more than ten years ago, and they have managed to maintain its chic yet comfortable American bistro vibe and, better yet, to keep the kitchen inspired. The menu is still in sync with the demanding and fickle New York palate, offering creative, sophisticated American standards painted with global accents and seasonal flourishes and an extensive, heavily American wine list. There is also a terrific cocktail list and a tempting menu of bar snacks to match, all of which makes Zoë an ideal restaurant for brunch, lunch, dinner, or just wine and a bite at the inviting bar. Contemporary American menu. Closed Mon; July 4, Dec 25. Lunch, dinner, Sat, Sun brunch. Bar. Casual attire. Totally nonsmoking. **$$$**

D

East Village/Lower East Side

Once considered part of the Lower East Side, the **East Village** is considerably scruffier and more rambunctious than its better-known sister to the West. For years, it was the refuge of immigrants and the working class, but in the 1950s, struggling writers, actors, and artists—forced out of Greenwich Village by rising rents—began moving in. First came such well-known names as Willem de Kooning and W. H. Auden, followed by the beatniks, the hippies, the yippies, the rock groups, the punk musicians, and the fashion designers.

Only in the 1980s did the neighborhood start to gentrify, as young professionals moved in, bringing with them upscale restaurants and smart shops. Ever since, New York's continuously rising rents have forced out many of the younger, poorer, and more creative types that the East Village was known for just two decades ago. Nonetheless, the neighborhood has not completely succumbed and offers an interesting mix between the cutting edge and the mainstream.

The heart of the East Village is St. Mark's Place, an always-thronging thoroughfare where you'll find everything from punked-out musicians to well-heeled business types, leather shops to sleek bistros. Many of the street's noisiest addresses are between Third and Second avenues; many of its most appealing, farther east. At the eastern end of St. Mark's Place stretches Tompkins Square Park, once known for its drug dealers, now for its families and jungle gyms. Some of the best of the many interesting little shops that fill the East Village can be found on Avenue A near the park; others line Seventh and Ninth streets east of Second Avenue.

The neighborhood's second major thoroughfare, Second Avenue, was home to many lively Yiddish theaters early in the 20th century. All are gone now, but the landmark Second Avenue Deli (at 10th Street)—known for its over-stuffed sandwiches—commemorates the street's past with stars in the sidewalk. At Second Avenue and East Tenth Street is St.-Mark's-in-the-Bowery, an historic church where Peter Stuyvesant—the last of the Dutch governors who ruled Manhattan in the 1600s—is buried. The church is also known for its poetry readings, performance art, and leftist politics.

On the western edge of the East Village sprawls Astor Place, home to Cooper Union—the city's first free educational institution, now a design school—and a huge cube sculpture oddly balanced on one corner. On Lafayette Street at the southern end of Astor Place reigns the Joseph Papp Public Theater, housed in an imposing columned building that was once the Astor Library. The theater is renowned for its first-run productions and for Shakespeare in the Park, a free festival that it produces every summer in Central Park.

Formerly a Jewish ghetto in the 19th and early 20th centuries, the **Lower East Side** is an ethnically mixed neighborhood with a mishmash of mom-and-pop stores and trendy boutiques that will attract those looking for good deals on clothing, accessories, and housewares. The farther east you go, the dicier the area becomes. Because some stores are owned by Orthodox Jews, they aren't open Friday evening or on Saturday.

What to See and Do

Bowlmor Lanes. *110 University Pl (10003). Phone 212/255-8188. www.bowlmor.com.* A New York landmark since 1938, this 42-lane, two-level, "more than a bowling alley" features a restored retro bar and lounge with red booths, a yellow ceiling, and a DJ on Monday nights. Richard Nixon, Cameron Diaz, and the Rolling Stones have all bowled at these lanes, where a colorful Village crowd frequents the place until all hours. Munch on anything from nachos and hamburgers to fried calamari and grilled filet mignon in the restaurant, or have your meal brought straight to your lane. It's a funky, fun hangout, even if you don't bowl. Note that no one under 21 is admitted after 6 pm. (Daily) **$$$$**

Brooklyn Bridge. *Park Row near Municipal Building (10002). Take the 4, 5, or 6 subway to the Brooklyn Bridge/City Hall station, or the N or R subway to the nearby City Hall stop.* For an awesome view of lower Manhattan, Brooklyn, and the New York Harbor, take a leisurely 40-minute stroll across downtown's historic Brooklyn Bridge, the first bridge to cross the East River (actually a tidal estuary between Long Island Sound and New York Harbor) to Brooklyn. Opened in 1883, the bridge was, and still is, seen as a monument to American engineering and creativity. Two massive stone pylons, each pierced with two soaring Gothic arches, rise 272 feet to support an intricate web of cables. A particularly good time of day to take in the views is at sunset. Dress appropriately in cooler weather, since it can be very windy. At the Brooklyn end of the bridge is a lovely half-mile promenade with equally grand views. The bridge is also near the South Street Seaport (see), at the foot of Fulton Street and the East River. **FREE**

Cooper Union. *30 Cooper Sq (10003). Third Ave at 7th St. Phone 212/353-4000. www.cooper.edu.* (1859) 1,000 students. All-scholarship college for art, architecture, and engineering. Great Hall, where Lincoln spoke in 1861, is auditorium for readings, films, lectures, and performing arts.

Jivamukti Yoga Center. *404 Lafayette St (10003). Phone 212/353-0214. www.jivamuktiyoga.com.* Relax and discover your inner peace at one of these soothing yoga classes (second location in Upper East Side at 853 Lexington Ave, New York, NY 10021; 212/396-4200). The reasonable rates, by New York standards, make it affordable for almost anyone to take a quick break from the hectic pace of sightseeing. Book evening classes as early as you can, since they can fill up fast. A little tip: be on the lookout for possible celebrity sightings. (Daily) **$$$**

Lower East Side Tenement Museum. *97 Orchard St (10002). Phone 212/431-0233. www.tenement.org.* The highlight at this one-of-a-kind living history museum is the guided tour of an actual tenement inhabited by real Lower East Side immigrants from the late 19th and early 20th centuries. Three apartments have been restored to their original condition. (You will need reservations for any of the guided tours, of which several are offered.) The museum also offers walking tours around the Lower East Side itself, which give you a feel for the area and what its immigrant residents had to endure upon arriving in America in search of their dreams. (Daily) **$$**

Merchant's House Museum. *29 E 4th St (10003). Phone 212/777-1089. www.merchantshouse.com.* This East Village home, dating back to the 1830s, offers a look into family life in the mid-19th century. The house has been totally preserved inside and out. Original furnishings, architectural details, and family memorabilia from retired merchant Seabury Tredwell and his descendants can be viewed here. The home was lived in until 1933, when it became a museum. Tours are available on weekends. (Thurs-Mon) **$**

New York University. *40 E 7th St (10003). Phone 212/998-4524 (tours); 212/998-6780 (Gallery). www.nyu.edu. (1831)* 15,584 students. One of the largest private universities in the country, NYU is known for its undergraduate and graduate business, medical, and law schools, school of performing arts, and fine arts programs. The university has graduated a large number of "Fortune 500" company executives. Most programs, including the Graduate Business Center, are located on the main campus surrounding Washington Square Park; the medical and dental schools are on the East Side. Tours (Mon-Fri except holidays, from Admissions Office at 22 Washington Sq N). In the Main Building at the northeast corner of Washington Square is the Grey Art Gallery and Study Center, with paintings, drawings, sculpture; changing exhibits (Tues-Sat). Renaissance musical instrument collection in Waverly Building (by appointment).

The Slipper Room. *167 Orchard St (10002). Phone 212/253-7246. www.slipperroom.com.* This club features a mix of offbeat shows and music. From quiz show nights to bawdy burlesque performances to up-and-coming bands, the Slipper Room is a fun, inexpensive place to act silly and party with your friends. The club gets a mixed late night crowd and is the kind of place that attracts fun-loving night owls who like to party until dawn. (Tues-Sat; Sun, Mon special events only) **$**

Theodore Roosevelt Birthplace National Historic Site. *28 E 20th St. Phone 212/260-1616. www.nps.gov/thrb/.* The reconstructed birthplace of the 26th president, who lived here from 1858-1872. Tours of five rooms restored to 1865 appearance. Audiovisual presentation and special events. (Mon-Fri) **$$**

Ukrainian Museum. *203 2nd Ave, between 12th and 13th sts. Phone 212/228-0110. www.ukrainianmuseum.org.* Changing exhibits of Ukrainian folk art, fine art, and history; workshops on weekends in folk crafts. (Wed-Sun; closed holidays, Jan 7) **$$**

Motel/Motor Lodge

★ ★ **MARCEL HOTEL.** *201 E 24th St (10010). Phone 212/696-3800; fax 212/696-0077. www.nycityhotels.com.* 43 rooms, 5 story. Complimentary continental breakfast. Check-out noon. TV; cable (premium), VCR available. In-room modem link. Restaurant, bar. Room service. Health club privileges. Concierge. **$$**

Hotel

★ ★ ★ **W NEW YORK - UNION SQUARE.** *201 Park Ave S (10003). Phone 212/253-9119. www.whotels.com.* 270 rooms, 25 story. Pets accepted. Check-out noon. Check-in 3 pm. TV; cable (premium). In-room modem link. Restaurant, bar. In-house fitness room. Business center. Concierge. Game tables. **$$$$**

B&B/Small Inn

★ ★ ★ **INN AT IRVING PLACE.** *56 Irving Pl (10003). Phone 212/ 533-4600; toll-free 800/685-1447; fax 212/533-4611. www.innatirving.com.* Step back in time to 19th-century New York in this intimate, romantic brownstone hideaway located in a row of 1830s townhouses just south of Gramercy Park. The high-ceilinged guest rooms feature antiques, four- poster beds, and cozy couches and chairs without sacrificing modern ame- nities like remote climate control and Internet access. Enjoy breakfast in bed or take it in the elegant guest parlor. Continental breakfast and afternoon high tea are served at a leisurely pace in this elegant country-style inn. The staff can arrange any special services you need, such as an in-room massage or the booking of theater tickets. 12 rooms, 3 story. Children over 12 years only. Check-out noon, check-in 3 pm. TV; cable (premium), VCR available. In-room modem link. Room service. **$$$$**

Restaurants

★ **2ND AVENUE DELI.** *156 2nd Ave (10003). Phone 212/677-0606; fax 212/ 353-1836. www.2ndavedeli.com.* Deli, Kosher menu. Hours: 8 am-midnight; Fri, Sat to 2 am. Closed Jewish holidays. Breakfast, lunch, dinner. **$$**

D

★ ★ **ANGELO AND MAXIE'S STEAKHOUSE.** *233 Park Ave S (10003). Phone 212/220-9200; fax 212/220-9209. www.angelo-maxies.com.* Steak menu. Closed Dec 25. Lunch, dinner. Bar. Casual attire. **$$$**

D

★ ★ **ANJU.** *36 E 20th St (10003). Phone 212/674-1111.* Korean menu. Closed Sun, Mon. Dinner, late-night. Bar. Casual attire. **$$**

D

★ ★ **BOLO.** *23 E 22nd St (10010). Phone 212/228-2200; fax 212/228-2239. www.bolorestaurant.com.* This crayon-colored dining room mirrors the energy of chef, proprietor and TV personality Bobby Flay. Spanish, tapas menu. Closed Dec 25. Lunch, dinner. Bar. Casual attire. **$$**

★ ★ **CAMPAGNA.** *24 E 21st St (10010). Phone 212/460-0900; fax 212/ 420-8136.* Italian menu. Closed major holidays. Lunch, dinner. Bar. Casual attire. **$$$**

★ ★ ★ **CHICAMA.** *35 E 18th St (10003). Phone 212/505-2233.* Located on the ground floor of ABC Carpet & Home, Chicama is a festive tribute to Latin American cuisine, featuring one of the city's only ceviche bars, not to mention a lively cocktail bar, where minty-fresh, rum-toxic mojitos will make your tongue tingle with delight (although your head may hurt the following morning). The restaurant is rich with rustic charm, with planked floors, lots of vintage appointments, and wood-paneled walls giving the room a cozy farmhouse feel. The menu showcases ceviche but also offers poultry, seafood, and meat dishes blended with exotic ingredients of the Southern Hemisphere, like plantains, cilantro, chiles, and tropical fruits. Latin American menu. Lunch, dinner. Bar. Entertainment. Casual attire. **$$$**

D

★ ★ ★ **CRAFT.** *43 E 19th St (10003). Phone 212/780-0880. www.craftrestaurant.com.* Chef-owner Tom Colicchio's Craft (Colicchio is also a partner and the executive chef at Gramercy Tavern) is a restaurant for two types of people: inventive, adventurous sorts who like to build things and gourmets who appreciate perfectly executed portions of meat, fish, fowl, and vegetables. Why these two sorts of folks? Because at Craft, lovers of Legos delight in creating dinner from the listlike menu of meat, fish, vegetables, mushrooms, and condiments. You choose what to delicious morsels should come together on your plate. (Those who prefer to defer to the chef may opt for a preplanned menu.) Dinner at Craft is a unique, interactive, exciting, and delicious adventure that should be experienced at least once, with like-minded builders. American menu. Closed holidays. Lunch, dinner. Bar. Casual attire. **$$$$**

★ ★ **EAST POST.** *92 Second Ave (10003). Phone 212/387-0065.* Italian menu. Lunch, dinner, late night. Bar. Casual attire. Outdoor seating. **$$**

D

★ ★ ★ **ELEVEN MADISON PARK.** *11 Madison Ave (10010). Phone 212/889-0905; fax 212/889-0918.* Located across from the leafy, historic Madison Square Park, Danny Meyer's grand New American restaurant is a wonderful, soothing spot to take respite from the frenetic pace of a day in New York City. The magnificent dining room boasts old-world charm with vaulted ceilings, clubby banquettes, giant floor-to-ceiling windows, and warm, golden lighting. The crowd is equally stunning: a savvy blend of sexy, suited Wall Street types and chic, fashion-forward New Yorkers. The contemporary seasonal menu features updated American classics as well as a smart selection of dishes that borrow accents from Spain, France, and Asia. Meyer, who also owns Gramercy Tavern and Union Square Café, continues to offer his gracious brand of warmth and hospitality at Eleven Madison Park. You will feel at home in an instant. American menu. Closed Labor Day, Dec 24-25,and Jan 1. Lunch, dinner. Bar. Grand setting in historical landmark building. Casual attire. **$$$**

D

★ ★ **ESSEX RESTAURANT.** *120 Essex St (10002). Phone 212/533-9616.* Closed Mon. Dinner. Bar. Casual attire. **$$**

D

★ ★ **EUZKADI.** *108 E 4th St (10003). Phone 212/982-9788.* Basque menu. Dinner. Bar. Casual attire. Outdoor seating. **$$**

D

★ ★ **FIRST.** *87 1st Ave (10003). Phone 212/674-3823; fax 212/674-8010. www.first.citysearch.com.* Closed Dec 25. Dinner, Sun brunch. Bar. **$$**

★ ★ ★ **FLEUR DE SEL.** *5 E 20th St (10003). Phone 212/460-9100.* Located on a sleepy block of East 20th Street, Fleur De Sel sneaks up on you like a ray of sunshine through the clouds. This lovely buttercup-colored cottage-like restaurant is one of the most enchanted hideaways in the city, serving sophisticated French-American fare in a serene dining room decorated with sheer curtains, soothing creamy walls, and precious bouquets of fresh flowers. It is, quite simply, a lovely setting to enjoy a dinner of stunningly presented, delicate, and deliciously prepared food. French menu. Closed Sun. Dinner. Bar. Casual attire. **$$$**

★ ★ **GLOBAL 33.** *99 2nd Ave (10003). Phone 212/477-8427. www.global 33nyc.com.* International menu. Dinner, late-night. Bar. Casual attire. **$$**
D

★ ★ ★ ★ **GOTHAM BAR AND GRILL.** *12 E 12th St (10003). Phone 212/620-4020; fax 212/627-7810.* Alfred Portale, the chef and owner of Gotham Bar & Grill, is an icon in New York's hallowed culinary circles. The leader of the tall-food movement and a passionate advocate of seasonal greenmarket ingredients, he has been a gastronomic force from behind the stoves at his swanky, vaulted-ceilinged Gotham Bar & Grill for more than a decade. The room is loud, energetic, and packed with a very stylish crowd at both lunch and dinner. The lively bar also draws a regular crowd of black-clad after-work revelers. You'll have no problem finding a dish with your name on it at Gotham. The menu offers something for everyone—salad, fish, pasta, poultry, beef, and game—and each dish is prepared with a bold dose of sophistication. Portale is an icon for a reason. Under his care, simple dishes are taken to new heights. And while the food isn't as tall as it used to be, size really doesn't matter. His food is just terrific. American menu. Menu changes seasonally. Lunch, dinner. Bar. Casual attire. **$$$**

★ ★ ★ ★ **GRAMERCY TAVERN.** *42 E 20th St (10003). Phone 212/477-0777; fax 212/477-1160. www.gramercytavern.com.* Dining at Gramercy Tavern is for people who don't have trouble being very well taken care of. Owner Danny Meyer's perpetually bustling New York eatery oozes warmth and charm without a smidgen of pretension. Chef and co-owner Tom Colicchio delivers on the food in much the same way. While his menu is inventive, it is not overfussed. Pristine, seasonal, locally sourced ingredients shine, and every bite allows the flavors to converse quietly yet speak individually as well. Though formal and elegant in tone, Gramercy Tavern is a fun place to dine. Colicchio's food is so good that you can't help but have a great time, and the waitstaff's enthusiasm for the chef's talent shows, adding to the appeal. In the glorious main room, you can choose from a pair of seasonal tasting menus or a wide array of equally tempting à la carte selections. And if you don't have a reservation, don't fret. Meyer is a fan of democracy and accepts walk-ins in the front Tavern Room. Stroll in, put your name on the list, and you'll have the chance to sample Colicchio's spectacular food (the menu is different than in the main dining room but just as wonderful) and rub elbows with the city's sexy locals. There's a terrific house cocktail list as well, so make a nice toast while you're there. *Secret Inspector's Notes:* Gramercy Tavern continues to achieve excellence in both service and food. No restaurant in New York has a staff that conveys such incredible warmth and food that expresses flavor so eloquently. American menu. Lunch, dinner. Bar. Casual attire. Totally nonsmoking. **$$$**

D

★ ★ **JAPONICA.** *100 University Pl (10003). Phone 212/243-7752; fax 212/ 645-5545.* Japanese menu. Lunch, dinner. Casual attire. **$$$**

D

★ ★ ★ **JEWEL BAKO.** *239 E 5th St (10003). Phone 212/979-1012.* This is one restaurant that sounds like its name—it is a shoebox-sized jewel of a place, serving precious, glorious sushi and sashimi as well as more traditional Japanese meals. The tiny, intimate, and chic East Village sliver of a space is owned by a husband and wife team who make it their mission to ensure that your experience is marked by warm service and gracious hospitality. The restaurant's small size and popular following make reserving a table ahead of time a good plan. Japanese menu. Closed Sun; one week in Aug. Dinner. Casual attire. **$$$**

★ **KHYBER PASS.** *34 Saint Marks Pl (10003). Phone 212/473-0989.* Persian/Afghan menu. Lunch, dinner, late night. Casual attire. Outdoor seating. **$$**

★ ★ **LA BELLE EPOQUE.** *827 Broadway (10003). Phone 212/254-6436. www.belleepoquency.com.* French/Creole menu. Closed Mon, Tues. Dinner, late-night. Bar. Casual attire. Reservations required. **$$**

D

★ ★ **LEMON.** *230 Park Ave S (10003). Phone 212/614-1200; fax 212/674-7782.* American menu. Closed Sun; Jan 1, Thanksgiving, Dec 25. Lunch, dinner, late-night. Bar. Casual attire. **$$**

D

★ ★ **LOLA.** *30 W 22nd St (10010). Phone 212/675-6700; fax 212/675-6760. www.lolany.com.* Contemporary Southern menu. Closed Mon; major holidays. Dinner, brunch, late-night. Bar. Entertainment. Casual attire. Outdoor seating. **$$$**

D

★ ★ ★ **NOVITA.** *102 E 22nd St (10010). Phone 212/677-2222; fax 212/677-2218.* This intimate Gramercy Park gem is the sort of restaurant that wraps you up like a luxurious cashmere shawl. Lovely, elegant, and comfortable, Novita is swathed in buttery, ochre walls, long, deep banquettes, and soothing lighting, making serene dining inevitable. The menu exemplifies refined simplicity, offering well-executed Italian dishes like homemade pappardelle with ragu and porcini mushrooms. The crowd tends to be of the well-heeled and fashionable variety—a stunning mix of moneyed folks from the neighborhood and sexy types from the Elite modeling agency across the street. Italian menu. Closed major holidays. Dinner. Bar. Casual attire. **$$**

★ ★ ★ **OLIVES.** *201 Park Ave S (10003). Phone 212/353-8345. www.whotels.com.* Celebrity chef-restaurateur Todd English's New York debut is a branch of his mega-successful Boston-based bistro. Located in the swanky W Union Square Hotel, the inviting and bustling restaurant has an open kitchen, with buttery walls, an open hearth fireplace, and deep, oval banquettes for luxurious relaxation all night long. The menu stars English's standard (but delicious) Mediterranean formula: boldly flavored, luxurious dishes that are impeccably prepared and artfully presented on the plate. His signature tart filled with olives, goat cheese, and sweet caramelized onions is a winner, but the menu offers a dish for every taste, including lamb, fish, homemade pastas, and pizzas from the wood oven. Mediterranean menu. Breakfast, lunch, dinner. Bar. Casual attire. Outdoor seating. **$$$**

D

★ ★ ★ **PATRIA.** *250 Park Ave S (10003). Phone 212/777-6211; fax 212/ 777-0786. www.patrianyc.com.* Located on the hot restaurant row of Park Avenue South, Patria is a lively and boisterous yet decidedly civilized spot for splashy Nuevo Latino fare. With its long, raised bar and vaulted ceilings, it is a sexy place to meet friends for fresh (and strong) rum-soaked cocktails or linger over a three-course meal. (Both lunch and dinner draw impressive mix of power crowds and fashionistas.) The menu is wild and inspired—dishes include ceviche, empanadas, and spicy plates of steak, pork, and seafood flavored with ingredients drawn from Peru, Cuba, Latin America, and Mexico. The wine list offers some rare bottles from the Southern Hemisphere, although, after a few of the minty-fresh house mojitos, you may decide to skip the wine altogether. Latin American menu. Closed Thanksgiving, Dec 25. Dinner. Bar. Casual attire. **$$$**

★ **REPUBLIC.** *37 Union Sq W (10003). Phone 212/627-7172; fax 212/ 627-7010. www.thinknoodles.com.* Pan-Asian menu. Closed Memorial Day, Dec 25. Lunch, dinner. Bar. Former warehouse converted to noodle shop. Casual attire. Outdoor seating. Totally nonsmoking. **$**

D

★ **SOBA-YA.** *229 E 9th St (10003). Phone 212/533-6966.* Japanese menu. Closed major holidays. Lunch, dinner. Casual attire. Totally nonsmoking. **$$**

★ ★ **STEAK FRITES.** *9 E 16th St (10003). Phone 212/463-7101; fax 212/ 627-2760. www.steakfritesnyc.com.* French bistro menu. Closed Jan 1, Dec 25. Lunch, dinner, Sun brunch. Bar. Casual attire. Outdoor seating. **$$**

D

★ ★ ★ **STRIP HOUSE.** *13 E 12th St (10003). Phone 212/328-0000.* *www.theglaziergroup.com.* If you can get over the fact that you're eating in a restaurant called Strip House (no dollar bills needed here other than to tip the folks in coat check), you will be in for some of the best beef in the city. The low-lit restaurant, swathed in deep red fabric and decorated with old black-and-white photos of burlesque stars, has a great vibe in a bordello-chic sort of way. It is sexy; tawdry it is not. The kitchen does a great job with its selection of steakhouse favorites (a half-dozen steak and chops cooked to chin-wiping perfection) and adds some inspired sides, like truffle-scented creamed spinach, goosefat potatoes, and mixed heirloom tomatoes in season. Steak menu. Dinner. Bar. Casual attire. **$$$$**

D

★ ★ ★ **TABLA.** *11 Madison Ave (10010). Phone 212/889-0667; fax 212/ 889-0914.* Tabla is the Indian-inspired culinary star from restaurant tour de force Danny Meyer (Gramercy Tavern, Union Square Cafe). Chef-partner Floyd Cardoz cleverly peppers his menu with the intoxicating flavors of India—sweet and savory spices, chutneys, meats from a tandoor oven, and soft rounds of pillowy, handmade breads. The result is a delicious introduction to the sumptuous flavors of India, not a crash course that hits you over the head. The stunning, bilevel dining room has an almost mystical quality to it, with its muted jewel-toned accents, rich redwood floors, and soaring windows that face Madison Square Park. Indian menu. Dinner. Bar. Reservations required. **$$$**

D

★ ★ ★ **TOCQUEVILLE.** *15 E 15th St (10003). Phone 212/647-1515. www. tocquevillerestaurant.com.* Owned by husband Marco Moreira (chef) and wife Jo-Ann Makovitsky (front-of-house manager), Tocqueville is a little slice of paradise in the form of a restaurant. This is the sort of place that will calm you from the moment you walk through the tall blond doors into the petite, elegant room warmed with golden light, butter-yellow walls, and stunningly appointed tabletops. The cuisine is as magical as the space. Chef Moreira offers impeccably prepared, inventive New American fare crafted with care from pristine seasonal ingredients hand-picked from local farmers and the nearby greenmarket. Intimate and soothing, Tocqueville is a perfect spot for those seeking quiet conversation and luxurious food. American, French menu. Lunch, dinner. Bar. Casual attire. **$$$$**

★ ★ ★ **UNION PACIFIC.** *111 E 22nd St (10010). Phone 212/995-8500; fax 212/460-5881. www.unionpacificrestaurant.com.* Rocco DiSpirito is one of New York City's hottest young chefs. A Food Network star (*The Melting Pot*), he looks as though he just walked off the pages of GQ. And he isn't just easy on the eyes. This man can cook—and really well. His culinary domain, Union Pacific, is an elegant oasis for sophisticated New American fare, with an emphasis on the fruits of the sea. The modern dining room, furnished with deep, plush banquettes, is warmed by ultra-flattering lighting. (It takes at least ten years off.) An extensive and carefully chosen wine list, the restaurant's serene waterfall, and operatic food ensure a blissful experience. Dispirito's talent is balance, contrasting textures, temperatures, and flavors to make the palate sing and swoon. Succulent Taylor Bay scallops, for example, are topped with uni (sea urchin) and set in a bright pool of tomato water dotted with mustard oil. The dish is one of DiSpirito's signatures. After one bite, you'll wonder how you've done without it for this long. *Secret Inspector's Notes:* Service at Union Pacific is inconsistent, and while the food is phenomenal, the service is sometimes not in keeping with the lofty price tags at this lively spot. Contemporary American menu with Asian accents. Closed Sun. Lunch, dinner. Bar. Casual attire. Totally nonsmoking. **$$$**

D

★ ★ ★ **UNION SQUARE CAFE.** *21 E 16th St (10003). Phone 212/243-4020; fax 212/627-2673.* Union Square Cafe is the first restaurant from the man who brought New York Gramercy Tavern, Eleven Madison, Tabla, and Blue Smoke: Danny Meyer. This bright, warm, cheery, bilevel restaurant and bar is still packing in locals and wooing tourists with Meyer's signature hospitality, chef Michael Romano's divine New American fare, and an award-wining wine list. While the menu changes with the seasons and often features produce from the Greenmarket across the way, the chef's succulent signature grilled tuna burger should not be considered optional. If a table doesn't seem possible (reservations are tough to score), a seat at the bar is a fabulous—and more authentic New Yorker—alternative. Contemporary American bistro. Closed major holidays. Dinner. Bar. Casual attire. **$$$**

SC

★ ★ ★ **VERITAS.** *43 E 20th St (10003). Phone 212/353-3700; fax 212/353-1632. www.veritas-nyc.com.* If a passion for wine runs through your veins, then a visit to Veritas should be considered mandatory. At this stylish Gramercy Park gem, you'll find a magnificent wine list that, at last count, was 2,700 bottles long. Despite its intimidating length, wine neophytes should not be deterred. There is no fear factor here. The staff is friendly and knowledgeable and all too happy to help you find a suitable wine to match your meal and budget. Bottles range from $20 to $1,300. While wine is the primary draw for Veritas, the food gives the wine a run for its money. It is specifically created with wine in mind and perfectly complements the beverage of focus. The full menu is available at the sleek bar, which is a nice option if you want a quick bite and some (or lots of) wine. Whether you're seated at the bar or tucked into a snug and intimate booth, the restaurant's contemporary American menu is easy to love. Robust flavors, seasonal ingredients, and a light hand in the kitchen make for magical meals. Veritas is a perfect place to explore wine and food alike. *Secret Inspector's Notes:* Veritas is an intimate restaurant with warm service. The food is outstanding, and with proper wine assistance, the complete experience is ideal for a special occasion or a romantic meal. New American cuisine. Dinner. Bar. **$$$**

D

Lower Manhattan

What to See and Do

Bowling Green. *25 Broadway (10004).* Originally a Dutch market, this is the city's oldest park, said to be the place where Peter Minuit purchased Manhattan for $24 worth of trinkets. The park fence dates from 1771.

Castle Clinton National Monument. *Contact the Superintendent, Manhattan Sites, 26 Wall St, 10005. Phone 212/344-7220. www.nps.gov/cacl/.* (1811) Built as a fort, this later was a place of public entertainment called Castle Garden where Jenny Lind sang in 1850 under P. T. Barnum's management. In 1855, it was taken over by the State of New York for use as an immigrant receiving station. More than 8 million people entered the US here between 1855-1890; Ellis Island was opened in 1892. The castle became the New York City Aquarium in 1896, which closed in 1941 and reopened at Coney Island in Brooklyn (see). The site has undergone modifications to serve as the visitor orientation/ferry departure center for the Statue of Liberty and Ellis Island. Ferry ticket booth; exhibits on Castle Clinton, Statue of Liberty, and Ellis Island; visitor center. **FREE**

Century 21. *22 Cortland St (10007). Phone 212/227-9092. www.c21stores.com.* This is a can't-miss store if you want designer merchandise at rock-bottom prices and have time to look through aisles of items. The three-story department store, which was closed for months after the September 11, 2001, terrorist attack on the nearby World Trade Center, is back in business and going stronger than ever. Century 21 sells men's, women's, and children's clothing; cosmetics; housewares; and electronics. The store's extended morning hours are a benefit for both New Yorkers who want to make purchases before work and for tourists who are early-birds. You won't be disappointed, and neither will your wallet or your wardrobe. But you may need to take a cab back to your hotel since you'll be so loaded down with shopping bags. (Daily; closed major holidays)

Chinatown. *6-8 Doyers St (10013). Take the J, M, N, R, 6, or Z subway to Canal St. You'll be in the heart of Chinatown. Phone 212/267-3510. www.chinatown-online.com.* How does the thought of 200 restaurants grab you? Or dozens of jewelry stores and gift shops? Or maybe you're into shops selling Asian antiques, feng shui items, and herbal remedies. Whatever you want to buy, from cheap and kitschy to pricey and unique, you'll find it in this noisy, crowded, and invigorating enclave of lower Manhattan. And if you crave authentic Chinese food, you can visit this area over and over again to sample the flavorful mix of Cantonese, Szechwan, and Hunan dishes served up by mom-and-pop restaurateurs. Most of these eateries entice diners with massive meals that will suit even the most budget-conscious travelers. Tip: While many establishments close on Christmas Day, Chinatown's restaurants remain open and are usually filled with holiday diners.

Federal Hall National Memorial. *26 Wall St (10005). Phone 212/825-6874.* (1842) Greek Revival building on the site of the original Federal Hall, where the Stamp Act Congress met (1765), George Washington was inaugurated

(Apr 30, 1789) and the first Congress met (1789-1790). Originally a custom house, the building was for many years the sub-treasury of the US. The JQA Ward statue of Washington is on the Wall St steps. (Mon-Fri) **FREE**

City Hall Park. *Broadway and Chambers St (10007).* Architecturally, City Hall is a combination of American Federalist and English Georgian, with Louis XIV detailing. It is built of marble and brownstone.

Ellis Island Immigration Museum. *Ellis Island and Battery Park (10004). Boat from Castle Clinton on Battery to Statue of Liberty includes a stop at Ellis Island. Ellis Island has been incorporated into the monument. Phone 212/363-3200 or 212/883-1986. www.nps.gov/elis.* The most famous port of immigration in the country. From 1892 to 1954, more than 12 million immigrants began their American dream here. The principle structure is the Main Building with its Great Hall, where the immigrants were processed; exhibits; 28-minute film; self-service restaurant. Same hours as Statue of Liberty. **$**

   Staten Island Ferry. *South Ferry Plaza and Battery Park (10301). Departs from the ferry terminal at the intersection of Whitehall, State, and South sts, just E of Battery Park. Phone 718/815-BOAT.* This famous ferry to St. George, Staten Island, offers passengers a close look at both the Statue of Liberty and Ellis Island, as well as extraordinary views of the lower Manhattan skyline. **FREE**

Federal Reserve Bank of New York. *33 Liberty St. Phone 212/720-6130. www.ny.frb.org.* Approximately 1/3 of the world's supply of gold bullion is stored here in a vault 80 feet below ground level; cash handling operation and historical exhibit of bank notes and coins. Tours (Mon-Fri; closed holidays). Sixteen years and older only; no cameras. Tour reservations required at least one week in advance. **FREE**

Fraunces Tavern Museum. *54 Pearl St. Phone 212/425-1778.* (1907) Museum housed in the historic Fraunces Tavern (1719) and four adjacent 19th-century buildings. The museum interprets history and culture of early America through permanent collection of prints, paintings, decorative arts, and artifacts, changing exhibitions, and period rooms, one of which, the Long Room, is the site of George Washington's farewell to his officers at the end of the Revolutionary War (1783). The museum offers a variety of programs and activities including tours, lectures, and films. (Tues-Sat) Dining room. (Daily) **$$**

George Gustav Heye Center of the National Museum of the American Indian. *One Bowling Green St (10004). Phone 212/514-3700.* World's largest collection of materials of the native peoples of North, Central, and South America. (Daily) **FREE**

Museum of Chinese in the Americas. *70 Mulberry St, 2nd Floor (10013). Phone 212/619-4785. www.moca-nyc.org.* This cultural and historical museum in Chinatown, also known as MoCA, is a small but fascinating place, filled with photographs, mementos, and poetry culled from nearly two decades of research in the community. Women's roles, religion, and Chinese laundries are among the subjects covered in the exhibits. (Tues-Sun noon-5 pm) **DONATION**

Chinatown

The only truly ethnic neighborhood still thriving in Manhattan, Chinatown is filled with teeming streets, jostling crowds, bustling restaurants, exotic markets, and prosperous shops. Once limited to a small enclave contained in the six blocks between the Bowery and Mulberry, Canal, and Worth streets (now known as "traditional Chinatown"), it has burst these boundaries in recent years to spread north of Canal Street into Little Italy and east into the Lower East Side.

Chinatown is the perfect neighborhood for haphazard wandering. In traditional Chinatown, especially, every twist or turn of the small, winding streets brings mounds of shiny fish—live carp, eels, and crabs—piles of fresh produce—cabbage, ginger root, Chinese broccoli—or displays of pretty, colorful objects—toys, handbags, knickknacks. Bakeries selling everything from moon cakes and almond cookies to "cow ears" (chips of fried dough) and pork buns are everywhere, along with the justifiably famous Chinatown Ice Cream Factory (65 Bayard Street, near Mott), selling every flavor of ice cream from ginger to mango.

Chinese men, accompanied by only a handful of women, began arriving in New York in the late 1870s. Many were former transcontinental railroad workers, who came to escape the persecution they were experiencing on the West Coast. But they weren't especially welcomed on the East Coast either, and soon thereafter, the violent "tong wars" between criminal Chinese gangs helped lead to the Exclusion Acts of 1882, 1888, 1902, and 1924, forbidding further Chinese immigration. Chinatown became a "bachelor society," almost devoid of women and children—a situation that continued until the lifting of immigration quotas in 1965.

Today, Chinatown's estimated population of 100,000 is made up of two especially large groups—the well-established Cantonese community, who have been in New York for over a century, and the Fujianese community, a much newer and poorer immigration group who come from Fujian Province on the southern coast of mainland China. The Cantonese own many of the prosperous shops and restaurants in traditional Chinatown, whereas the Fujianese have set up rice-noodle shops, herbal medicine shops, and outdoor markets along Broadway and neighboring streets between Canal Street and the Manhattan Bridge.

To learn more about the history of Chinatown, visit the Museum of the Chinese in the Americas (70 Mulberry Street, at Bayard). To get a good meal, explore almost any street, with Mott Street—the neighborhood's main thoroughfare—holding an especially large number. Pell Street is especially known for its barber and beauty shops and for its Buddhist Temple (4 Pell Street). The neighborhood's biggest festival is the Chinese New Year, celebrated between mid-January and early February; then, the streets come even more alive than usual with dragon dances, lion dances, and fireworks.

Museum of Jewish Heritage. *18 First Pl (10004). In Battery Park City. Phone 212/509-6130. www.mjhnyc.org.* Opened in 1997, this museum features thousands of moving photographs, cultural artifacts, and archival films documenting the Holocaust and the resilience of the Jewish community. It's housed in a building the shape of a hexagon, symolic of the Star of David. The newly constructed East Wing houses a theater, special-exhibit galleries, a memorial garden, and a café. (Sun-Wed 10 am-5:45 pm, Thurs 10 am-8 pm, Fri and the eve of Jewish holidays 10 am-3 pm; closed Sat, Jewish holidays, and Thanksgiving) **$$**

[D]

New York City Fire Museum. *278 Spring St (10013). Phone 212/691-1303. www.nycfiremuseum.org.* Although it isn't, strictly speaking, a children's museum, the New York City Fire Museum has great appeal for kids. Housed in an actual firehouse that was used until 1959, the museum is filled with fire engines new and old, helmets and uniforms, hoses and lifesaving nets. Retired firefighters take visitors through the museum, reciting fascinating tidbits of firefighting history along the way. (Tues-Sat 10 am-5 pm, Sun 10 am-4 pm) **DONATION**

New York Stock Exchange. *20 Broad St, 3rd Fl (10005). Phone 212/656-5165. www.nyse.com.* The world's largest securities market, where on an average day 1.43 billion shares (approximately $36.6 billion) are traded. The Visitors' Gallery is closed indefinitely for security reasons. Call for updated information.

Police Museum. *25 Broadway. Phone 212/301-4440. www.nycpolicemuseum. org.* Exhibits of police uniforms, badges, and equipment. (Daily; closed holidays; schedule may vary) **FREE**

South Street Seaport. *Fulton and Water sts, at the East River. Phone 212/732-7678. www.southstreetseaport.com.* Festival marketplace with more than 100 shops and 40 restaurants in Seaport Plaza, Schermerhorn Row, and Museum Block, and the multifloored Pier 17, which extends into the East River.

South Street Seaport Museum. *207 Front St (10038). South and Fulton sts, at the East River. Phone 212/748-8600. www.southstseaport.org.* Eleven-block area restored to display the city's maritime history, with emphasis on South Street in the days of sailing vessels. Museum piers now moor the *Ambrose,* a lightship (1908); the *Lettie G. Howard,* a Gloucester fishing schooner (1893); the fully-rigged *Wavertree* (1885); the *Peking,* a German four-masted barque (1911); and the *Pioneer,* a schooner (1885).

Permanent and changing maritime exhibits incl models, prints, photos, and artifacts. Tours. Harbor excursions. Children admitted only when accompanied by adult. (Apr-Sept, daily; rest of year, Mon, Wed-Sun; closed Jan 1, Thanksgiving, Dec 25)

St. Paul's Chapel. *211 Broadway (10007). Phone 212/602-0874.* A chapel of Trinity Church, this example of Georgian architecture, finished in 1766, is the oldest public building in continuous use on Manhattan Island. George Washington's pew is in the north aisle; chancel ornamentation by L'Enfant; Waterford chandeliers. Concerts (Mon and Thurs at noon). (Daily) **FREE**

Statue of Liberty Exhibit. *52 Vanderbilt Ave, 4th Fl (10017).* Photographs, artifacts, and history dioramas with light and sound effects depict the construction of the Statue of Liberty.

⭐ **Statue of Liberty National Monument.** *Liberty Island (10004). Ferry tickets and departures from Castle Clinton National Monument in Battery Park. Phone 212/363-3200; 212/269-5755. www.nps.gov/stli/.* This worldwide symbol of freedom is the first thing passengers see as their ships sail into New York Harbor. A gift from France in 1886 (her iron skeleton was designed by Gustave Eiffel, creator of Paris's Eiffel Tower), she stands 152 feet high on an 89-foot pedestal, indomitable and welcoming. Currently, the statue itself is closed for security reasons, but the grounds are open so you can meet Lady Liberty up close. Ellis Island, the most famous port of immigration in the US, became part of the national monument in 1965. Between 1892 and 1954, 12 million immigrants first stepped on American soil at Ellis Island. When it closed in 1954, it had processed 40 percent of living American families. You can look for your ancestors' names on the Wall of Honor or visit the dramatic Immigrants' Living Theater and the cavernous Great Hall, where nervous immigrants awaited processing. Passing the Statue of Liberty on the return trip may prove to be a heart-stirring, thought-provoking experience. (Daily; closed Dec 25) **$$**

Wall Street. *1155 Avenue of the Americas, fifth floor (10036). Walk one block E to the corner of Broad St (which goes S) and Nassau St (which goes N).*

Woolworth Building. *233 Broadway (10279).* This neo-Gothic skyscraper by Cass Gilbert was the tallest building in the world (792 feet, 58 stories) when it was built. Frank W. Woolworth, the dime-store king, paid $13.5 million cash for his "cathedral of commerce" when it was completed in 1913.

World Financial Center. *West St between Liberty and Vesey sts. Phone 212/ 945-0505. www.worldfinancialcenter.com.* The center includes more than 40 shops and restaurants on and around the Winter Garden, a 120-foot-high, vaulted glass and steel atrium.

Special Events

Chinese New Year. *Mott and Pell sts (10013).* Parade with lions, dragons, costumes, firecrackers. Early-mid-Feb.

TriBeCa

Short for *Triangle Below Canal*, TriBeCa is a former industrial district encompassing about 40 blocks between Canal, Chambers, and West streets, and Broadway. Like SoHo, its more fashionable cousin to the north, the neighborhood discarded its working-class roots years ago and now has its share of expensive restaurants and boutiques. Upper-middle-class residents have replaced factory workers, and avant-garde establishments have replaced sweatshops.

Nonetheless, TriBeCa is much quieter than SoHo—and many other sections of Manhattan—and, in parts, still retains its 19th-century feel, complete with cobblestone streets and dusty facades. After dark, especially, much of the area seems close to deserted.

TriBeCa's main thoroughfares are Broadway, West Broadway, and Church Street, three wide roads comfortable for strolling. West Broadway was originally built to relieve the congestion of Broadway and is home to a few art galleries, including the SoHo Photo Gallery (15 White Street, at West Broadway), a cooperative gallery featuring the work of 100-plus members. At Church and Walker streets reigns the sleek new TriBeCa Grand, the neighborhood's first upscale hotel.

Also well known is the TriBeCa Film Center, housed in the landmark Martinson Coffee Company warehouse (375 Greenwich Street, at Franklin Street). The center was started in 1989 by actor Robert DeNiro, who wanted to create a site where filmmakers could talk business, screen films, and socialize. Today, the center houses the offices of several major producers and the TriBeCa Grill, a chic eatery usually filled with more celebrity watchers than celebrities. At Greenwich and Harrison streets stand the Harrison Houses, a group of nine restored Federal-style homes. Several were designed by John McComb, Jr., New York's first architect. East of the houses, at the northwest corner of Harrison and Hudson streets, find the former New York Mercantile Exchange. In this five-story building, complete with gables and a tower, $15,000 worth of eggs would change hands in an hour around the turn of the century. Today, TriBeCa is still the city's distribution center for eggs, cheese, and butter; a few remaining wholesales cluster around Duane Park, one block south of the former exchange, between Hudson and Greenwich streets.

At the southern end of TriBeCa is Chambers Street, where you'll find the Borough of Manhattan Community College (199 Chambers Street, near West Street). At the western end of Chambers, cross over West Street via the TriBeCa Bridge to reach a public recreation center called Pier 25.

JVC Jazz Festival. *Park Row between Beekman and Ann sts (10038). Phone 212/501-1390. www.festivalproductions.net/jvcjazz/newyork.htm.* World-famous musicians perform in Avery Fisher Hall, Carnegie Hall, Town Hall, and other sites throughout the city. Last two weeks in June.

San Gennaro Festival. *Little Italy. Mulberry St between Canal and Houston sts (10013). Phone 212/768-9320.* Mid- or late Sept.

South Street Seaport Events. *207 Front St (10038).* Throughout the year, concerts, festivals, and special events are staged in the seaport area; weather permitting, passengers are taken for a sail around the harbor aboard the *Pioneer;* the museum's Children's Center hosts a variety of special programs, workshops, and exhibits. In the fall, a fleet of classic sailing vessels is assembled to compete in a race for the Mayor's Cup.

Motels/Motor Lodges

★ ★ **BEST WESTERN SEAPORT INN.** *33 Peck Slip (10038). Phone 212/766-6600; toll-free 800/HOTEL-NY; fax 212/766-6615. www.bestwestern.com/seaportinn.* 72 rooms, 7 story. Complimentary continental breakfast. Check-out 11 am, check-in 3 pm. TV; VCR available (movies $6.95). In-room modem link. In-house fitness room, health club privileges. Business center. Located in historic district in restored 19th-century building. **$$**

[D] [≊] [SC]

★ ★ **HOLIDAY INN DOWNTOWN.** *138 Lafayette St (10013). Phone 212/966-8898; fax 214/363-3978. www.holiday-inn.com.* 227 rooms, 14 story. Check-out noon, check-in. TV. In-room modem link. Restaurant, bar. Valet parking. Concierge. Renovated landmark building. **$**

[D] [≊] [SC]

Hotels

★ ★ ★ **CHAMBERS.** *15 W 56th St (10013). Phone 212/974-5656; fax 212/974-5657. www.chambershotel.com.* Located just steps from some of New York's finest retail shops, the trendy hotel has a modern, open-air feel to it. The public spaces—including the soaring lobby with a double-sided fireplace—and the loftlike guest rooms feature modern, funky works of art of all kinds. The spacious, high-tech rooms with hand-troweled cement walls offer amenities like slippers you can actually keep, umbrellas, robes, cordless phones, and flat-screen TVs. Just off the lobby, Town restaurant (see) serves fine American cuisine accented with French and Asian influences. It is popular with locals, so reservations are suggested for dinner. 77 rooms, 30 story. Pets accepted. Check-out noon. Check-in 3 pm. TV; cable (premium), VCR available. In-room modem link. Restaurant, bar. Babysitting services available. Valet parking. Business center. Concierge. **$$$**

[D] [🐾] [🛅]

★ ★ ★ **MARRIOTT NEW YORK FINANCIAL CENTER.** *85 West St (10006). Phone 212/385-4900; toll-free 800/228-9290; fax 212/227-8136. www.marriott.com.* 498 rooms, 38 story. Check-out noon. TV; cable (premium). In-room modem link. Restaurant, bar. Room service. Exercise room, sauna, steam room. Indoor pool. Valet parking. Business center. Concierge, luxury level. Walking distance to Wall St, ferry to Statue of Liberty. **$$**

D ⇌ ⇌ SC 🚶

★ ★ ★ **MILLENIUM HILTON.** *55 Church St (10007). Phone 212/693-2001; toll-free 800/HILTONS; fax 212/571-2316. www.hilton.com.* This tall, sleek Financial District hotel was built to match the skyscrapers around it. 561 rooms, 55 story. Check-out noon, check-in 3 pm. TV; cable (premium). In-room modem link. Room service 24 hours. Restaurant, bar. Babysitting services available. In-house fitness room, exercise room, massage, sauna. Indoor pool. Garage; valet parking fee. Business center. Concierge. **$$$**

⇌ 🚶 🚶

★ ★ ★ ★ **THE REGENT WALL STREET.** *55 Wall St (10005). Phone 212/845-8600; fax 212/845-8601. www.regenthotels.com.* The Regent Wall Street is the premier address in the heart of one of the world's most influential financial capitals. Just a short walk from the New York Stock Exchange, The Regent welcomes tired guests after a long day of trading or touring nearby SoHo, Chinatown, and South Street Seaport. The Regent's landmark Greek Revival building dates from 1842 and in former incarnations served as the Merchants Exchange and the Customs House, where writer Herman Melville toiled for many years. Rooms and suites are a beautiful blend of Italian contemporary décor with a masculine feel, and the fabulous bathrooms offer deep-soaking bathtubs. Fitness-minded guests will appreciate the terrific Health Club & Spa, with state-of-the-art equipment and relaxing treatments. Casual American dining is available at 55 Wall or 55 Wall Terrace, where the many ethnic neighborhoods of New York influence the inventive menu. *Secret Inspector's Notes:* The Regent's lounge plays host to many of New York's financial players seeking a place to unwind and enjoy a cigar, martini, or exceptional glass of wine at the conclusion of a fast-paced day. 144 rooms, 15 story. Pets accepted, some restrictions. Check-out noon. TV; cable (premium), VCR available. In-room modem link. Restaurant, bar. Exercise equipment, sauna. Business center. Concierge. **$$$**

D 🍴 🚶 ⇌ 🚶

★ ★ ★ ★ **THE RITZ-CARLTON NEW YORK BATTERY PARK.** *2 West St (10004). Phone 212/344-0800; fax 212/344-3801. www.ritzcarlton.com.* Watch the world from The Ritz-Carlton New York, Battery Park. While only a five-minute walk from Wall Street and the Financial District, The Ritz-Carlton feels light years away with its staggering views of the Hudson River, the Statue of Liberty, and Ellis Island from its location on the southern tip of Manhattan. This 38-story glass and brick tower is a departure from the traditional Ritz-Carlton European style, from the contemporary glass artwork bestowed upon the public and private spaces to the modern furnishings in rooms and suites. The service is distinctly Ritz-Carlton, however, with exceptional concierge service and Bath Butlers who create special concoctions for bath time. The view is omnipresent throughout the hotel, whether you're gazing through a telescope in a harbor view room, enjoying a cocktail while viewing Lady Liberty at Rise, the 14th-floor bar, or savoring a delicious meal at 2 West. 298 rooms, 39 story. Pets accepted. Check-out noon, check-in 3 pm. TV; cable, VCR available, CD player. In-room modem link. Room service 24 hours. Restaurant, bar. Babysitting services available. In-house fitness room, spa, massage, sauna. Parking. Business center. Concierge. Luxury level. **$$$$**

D ❧ ⍐ ⇲ ⍐

★ ★ ★ **SOHO GRAND HOTEL.** *310 W Broadway (10013). Phone 212/965-3000; fax 212/965-3200. www.sohogrand.com.* Calculated cool is the best way to describe this trendy downtown hotel. The second-floor lobby doubles as a popular lounge. The guest rooms are simple in design, with tones of black and white and clean, uncluttered baths. All rooms have stereos, and some have rocking chairs. The lobby provided a comfortable gathering place, with high ceilings, couches, and exotic plants. Each floor also features a pantry with complimentary coffee, tea, and espresso. The Grand Bar & Lounge serves a mix of dishes, from macaroni and cheese to lobster tea sandwiches to chickpea-fried rock shrimp. The lounge also features music and DJs—a good place to hang out after a day of sightseeing. 364 rooms, 17 story. Pets accepted. Check-out noon. TV; cable (premium), VCR available. In-room modem link. Restaurant, bar. Room service. Exercise equipment, massage. Garage parking. Concierge. **$$$**

D ❧ ⍐ ⇲

Restaurants

★ ★ ★ **AMERICAN PARK AT THE BATTERY.** *State St (10004). Phone 212/809-5508; fax 212/809-6064. www.americanpark.com.* With Lady Liberty and her torch in full view, American Park at the Battery offers sweeping views of the Hudson River and a simple, well-executed menu that includes a giant, glistening raw bar and an extensive selection of seafood, steaks, and chops from the grill and the wood-burning oven. The summer months are perfect for alfresco dining and after-work cocktails as the sun goes down. The restaurant also offers brunch and is a magical spot to take a rest from inline skating around Battery Park and the newly refurbished Hudson River waterfront. Seafood menu. Closed Dec 25. Lunch, dinner, Sat, Sun brunch. Bar. Casual attire. Outdoor seating. **$$$**

D

★ ★ ★ **ARQUA.** *281 Church St (10013). Phone 212/334-1888; fax 212/966-2432.* Arqua is one of those restaurants that beckon sidewalk travelers to come inside. The long, rectangular room is warmed with an almost magical light and feels like spring, with its butter yellow-washed walls, tall windows, and vaulted ceilings. It is a soothing, dreamy room. Once inside, you'll find the menu is as charming as the décor. The Italian menu of delicately presented plates includes a traditional selection of antipasti, insalate, pasta fresca, pesce, and carni that is supplemented by a wonderful list of daily specials. Italian menu. Closed major holidays; also last two weeks in Aug. Lunch, dinner. Casual attire. **$$$**

★ ★ ★ **BAYARD'S.** *1 Hanover Sq (10004). Phone 212/514-9454. www.bayards.com.* French menu. Closed Sun. Lunch, dinner. **$$$**

★ ★ ★ ★ **BOULEY.** *120 W Broadway (10013). Phone 212/964-2525. www.bouley.net.* After a hiatus following 9/11, acclaimed chef David Bouley is back behind the stoves at his temple of haute French gastronomy. Housed in the newly renovated and impeccably decorated space that was once his more casual bistro, Bouley Bakery, the new Bouley is taking a stab at winning back Manhattan's most discerning and divine diners—and succeeding. The elegant and oh-so-civilized place is packed with well-heeled foodies, fashionistas, political pundits, and celebs who understand that a night in Mr. Bouley's care is nothing short of miraculous. Bouley delivers on every front: the service is charming, the seasonal ingredients are stunning, the French technique is impeccable, and his kitchen magic is nothing short of brilliant. French menu. Lunch, dinner. Bar. Casual attire. Reservations required. **$$$**

[D]

★ ★ **CAPSOUTO FRERES.** *451 Washington St (10013). Phone 212/966-4900; fax 212/925-5296. www.capsoutofreres.com.* Contemporary French menu. Lunch, dinner, Sat, Sun brunch. Bar. In converted neo-Flemish, landmark warehouse (1891). Outdoor seating. **$$$**

★ ★ ★ **CHANTERELLE FRENCH RESTAURANT.** *2 Harrison St (10013). Phone 212/966-6960. www.chanterellenyc.com.* Long hailed as one of the most romantic restaurants in New York City, Chanterelle has been the scene of many a bent-knee, velvet-box-in-hand proposal. Indeed, this restaurant is a New York dining icon. But Chanterelle, located on a sleepy corner in Tribeca, offers much more than romance. Husband-and-wife owners David and Karen Waltuck (he is the chef, she works the room) have been serving brilliant, unfussy, modern French fare for more than 20 years. The menu, handwritten each week, reflects the best products available from local greenmarkets and regional farmers, and the award-winning wine list makes meals here even more memorable. French menu. Closed Sun; major holidays; also first week of July. Lunch, dinner. Bar. Jacket required. Reservations required. **$$$$**

[D]

★ ★ ★ ★ **DANUBE.** *30 Hudson St (10013). Phone 212/791-3771; fax 212/267-1526. www.bouley.net.* Danube is the creation of David Bouley, the inspired and famed chef who has created many notable New York establishments. It is a stunning place to spend an evening. It has the feel of an old Austrian castle, with dark wood; deep, plush banquettes; and soft, warm lighting. It repeatedly draws a glamorous crowd that craves Bouley's masterful technique and creativity. Bouley's regal, majestic restaurant celebrates the cuisine of Austria within the framework of a New York restaurant. On the menu, you'll find a couple of Austrian-inspired dishes interspersed with lighter, modern, and truly exciting seasonal New American dishes. Bouley has a rare talent, and his food is spectacular, though not for those who are fearful of taking some risks at dinner. This is not a creamed-corn-and-roast-chicken place. The staff offers refined service, and the wine list is eclectic and extensive. As you would expect, it includes some gems from Austria. The cocktail lounge at Danube is a perfect spot to relax and get cozy before or after dinner. It is low-lit and romantic, and the bartenders serve delicious, perfectly balanced cocktails. American, Austrian menu. Dinner. Bar. Entertainment. Casual attire. Reservations required. **$$$$**

D

★ ★ ★ **DUANE PARK CAFE.** *157 Duane St (10013). Phone 212/732-5555; fax 212/732-3864. www.duaneparkcafe.com.* If you are searching for a cozy yet hip neighborhood bistro for dinner, consider the search over. Duane Park Café, located on a tiny little street in Tribeca, has been filling this niche for more than a decade, offering easy, candlelit dining and a smart, New American menu with French, Italian, and Asian influences. There is a good crowd at the bar as well, so if a cold beer or a glass of wine (the list is American, Italian, and French) is on your agenda, Duane Park Café will fit the bill. New American menu. Closed most major holidays; also first week July. Lunch, dinner. Bar. Casual attire. **$$$**

★ ★ **EL TEDDY'S.** *219 W Broadway (10013). Phone 212/941-7070; fax 212/941-7074.* Contemporary Mexican menu. Closed Jan 1, Dec 25. Lunch, dinner. Bar. Located in white building with replica of Statue of Liberty's spiked crown on roof. Casual attire. Outdoor seating. **$$**

D

★ ★ **GIGINO TRATTORIA.** *323 Greenwich St (10013). Phone 212/431-1112; fax 212/226-3855. www.giginony.com.* Southern Italian menu. Closed Jan 1, Memorial Day, Dec 25. Lunch, dinner. Bar. Outdoor seating. **$$$**

D

★ ★ **IL CORTILE.** *125 Mulberry St (10013). Phone 212/226-6060; fax 212/431-7283. www.ilcortile.com.* Italian, American menu. Closed Thanksgiving, Dec 24, 25. Lunch, dinner. Bar. Casual attire. Reservations required. **$$$**

D

★ **KIRAN.** *94 Chambers (10007). Phone 212/732-5011.* Indian menu. Buffet, lunch, dinner. Bar. Casual attire. **$$**

D

★ ★ ★ **LAYLA.** *211 W Broadway (10013). Phone 212/431-0700; fax 212/431-0920. www.myriadrestaurantgroup.com.* The foods of the Mediterranean and Middle East are the focus at Layla, Drew Nieporent's sultry, *Arabian Nights*-style restaurant that offers belly dancing nightly, with wickedly good cocktails to inspire diners to join in. (You might discover a new talent.) In between swilling and dancing, you can feast on soft, puffy, tandoor-oven-baked breads to dip into the restaurant's delicious signature mezze like hummus, muhammara, and tzatziki. The menu keeps the taste buds' interest piqued with a wide selection of robust, aromatic-spiced dishes like tagine of duck and harissa-marinated baby chicken kebobs with sweet, jeweled rice and toasted almonds. Mediterranean, Middle Eastern menu. Closed Sun; most major holidays. Lunch, dinner. Bar. Outdoor seating. Totally nonsmoking. **$$**

★ ★ ★ **MONTRACHET.** *239 W Broadway (10013). Phone 212/219-2777; fax 212/274-9508. www.myriadrestaurantgroup.com.* Montrachet is the first restaurant from restaurateur Drew Nieporent. (He also owns Nobu and Tribeca Grill, among others.) While the restaurant is pushing 20, it is still one of the most prized and romantic dining experiences to be had in New York City. The seasonal, modern French-American menu and the warm, attentive service remain as fresh and inspired as they were on day one. Montrachet's wine list has been met with critical acclaim and marries well with the sophisticated fare, making for delightful dining. French menu. Closed Sun; major holidays. Lunch, dinner. Bar. Casual attire. Reservations required. **$$$**

★ ★ ★ **NOBU.** *105 Hudson St (10013). Phone 212/219-0500; fax 212/219-1441.* There is a place in New York where folks have been known to cry when they eat because the food is so good. That place is Nobu. The lively room is decorated with seaweed-like wall coverings and bamboo poles and has a serene vibe despite the high-energy, high-fashion crowd that packs in nightly for some of famed chef Nobu Matsuhisa's simply spectacular sushi and unique brand of Asian-Latin—inspired seafood. Lime, soy, chiles, miso, cilantro, and ginger are flavors frequently employed to accent many of the chef's succulent creations. A signature dish is black cod with miso, and it's a signature for good reason. The fish is coated in a sweet miso glaze, and once it enters your mouth, it slowly vaporizes, melting away like ice over a flame. The omakase ("chef's choice") menu is an option for those with an adventurous palate. If you can't get a reservation (call well in advance and be prepared for many busy signals), you can always try to sneak in at the sushi bar. Be warned, though; once you eat sushi here, it's hard to eat it anywhere else. *Secret Inspector's Notes:* Due to Nobu's popularity, a simpler version that does not take reservations was opened nearby. Next Door Nobu is a perfect way to sample the fantastic cuisine minus the impossible reservation hassle. Be prepared for difficult service at Nobu; food this good is shared only after you prove your worthiness. Japanese menu. Closed holidays. Lunch, dinner. Casual attire. Reservations required. **$$$**

D

★ ★ **ODEON.** *145 W Broadway (10013). Phone 212/233-0507; fax 212/406-1962.* American, French menu. Lunch, dinner, Sun brunch. Late night. Bar. Children's menu. Brasserie in 1930s, cafeteria-style Art Deco. Casual attire. Outdoor seating. **$$**

D

★ ★ ★ **PICO.** *349 Greenwich St (10013). Phone 212/343-0700.* If Portugal broke away from its European anchor and floated over to North America, say perhaps to the island of Manhattan, what might result is the brilliant cuisine featured at chef-owner John Villa's Pico, an airy, elegant Tribeca restaurant. But don't think traditional Portuguese cuisine. While the seasonal ingredients tend to be drawn from that land, the menu is Portuguese through the eyes of a modern New York City chef. The signature suckling pig with crispy potatoes and wildflower honey should be considered necessary eating. The wine list features many gems from Portugal that pair seamlessly with the cuisine, but attention should also be paid to the brilliant cocktail list that is as wild and wonderful as the cuisine. American, Portuguese menu. Closed Sun. Lunch, dinner. Bar. Casual attire. Outdoor seating. **$$$**

D

★ ★ **SCREENING ROOM.** *54 Varick St (10013). Phone 212/334-2100; fax 212/334-8209. www.thescreeningroom.com.* American menu. Closed Mon. Lunch, dinner, Sun brunch. Bar. Children's menu. Casual attire. Casual décor with movie theater. Outdoor seating. **$$$**

D

★ **SWEET AND TART.** *20 Mott St (10013). Phone 212/964-0380; fax 212/571-7696. www.sweetandtart.com.* Chinese menu. Lunch, dinner, late-night. Casual attire. Reservations required. **$$**

★ ★ **TAORMINA.** *147 Mulberry St (10013). Phone 212/219-1007; fax 212/219-1009.* Italian menu. Closed Thanksgiving, Dec 25, 31. Lunch, dinner. Bar. Reservations required. Valet parking available. **$$**

D

★ ★ ★ **TRIBECA GRILL.** *375 Greenwich St (10013). Phone 212/941-3900; fax 212/941-3915.* This New York icon from super-restaurateur Drew Nieporent (Nobu, Montrachet) and partner Robert DeNiro is a shining example of what a restaurant should offer. First, hospitality—the service is warm, attentive, and knowledgeable without an ounce of pretension. Second, atmosphere—the Grill is a comfortable, urban dining room with exposed brick walls, oil paintings by Robert DeNiro, Sr., and a magnificent cherry wood, wraparound bar that looks like it fell of the set of *Cheers.* Third, food—the kitchen features an approachable, contemporary, seasonal American menu with dishes for every type of diner, from wild foodies to simple roast chicken eaters. Finally, wine—Tribeca Grill offers an impressive and diverse wine program led by David Gordon, who has earned the restaurant much praise and admiration near and far. Tribeca Grill, which is more than 10 years old, remains a winner on all counts. American menu. Dinner, Sun brunch. Bar. Casual attire. **$$$**

D

★ ★ **YANKEE CLIPPER.** *170 John St (10038). Phone 212/344-5959; fax 212/344-5316.* Closed Thanksgiving, Dec 25. Lunch, dinner. Bar. Three dining areas; main dining room resembles dining salon on a luxury liner; display of ship models and prints of ships. **$$**

Bronx

Area code 718

Information Chamber of Commerce, 2885 Schley Ave, 10465; 718/829-4111

Jonas Bronck, a Swedish settler, bought 500 acres of land from the Dutch in 1639, lending his name to the future borough. Locally it is always referred to as "the Bronx," never simply "Bronx." It is the only borough in New York City on the North American continent (the others are all on islands).

What to See and Do

Arthur Avenue. *Take the D or 4 subway to Fordham Rd and transfer to the BX12 bus to the East Fordham Rd/Arthur Ave stop.* Old-world charm abounds in this charming section of the Bronx, which has been the home for generations of Italian families for more than a century. The crowded storefronts of mom-and-pop shops sell everything from fine Italian wines and homemade pastas to imported cheeses and meats to gifts and cookware. And then there's the mouthwatering restaurants, pizza parlors, and pastry shops—some dating back to the 1920s—to entice your palate. Every calorie is worth it, and you won't break the bank in these reasonably priced eateries and shops. There's even a small repertory theater, the **Belmont Playhouse,** dedicated to works by Italian writers. Tip: Many shops offer discounts on Columbus Day. (Closed major holidays)

The Bartow-Pell Mansion Museum. *895 Shore Rd (10464). In Pelham Bay Park. Phone 718/885-1461. www.bartowpellmansionmuseum.org.* Greek Revival stone mansion (circa 1840) furnished in the Empire period; gardens (seasonal); carriage house. (Wed, Sat, and Sun noon-4 pm; closed holidays) Guided tours and luncheon tours (by appointment). **$**

Bronx Museum of the Arts. *1040 Grand Concourse. At 165th St. Phone 718/681-6000. www.bxma.org.* Changing exhibits focus on contemporary art and current cultural subjects pertaining to the Bronx. Concerts, family workshops, and special events. (Wed noon-9 pm, Thurs-Sun noon-6 pm) Free admission Wed. **DONATION**

Bronx Zoo. *Fordham Rd and Bronx River Pkwy (10460). Liberty Lines runs an express bus to the zoo gates. Catch the BXM11 Bus at designated stops on Madison Ave. Call 718/652-8400 for the stop nearest you. Phone 718/367-1010. www.bronxzoo.com.* See the endangered snow leopards, come nose to nose with a gorilla, and encourage your kids to ride a camel at the imaginative, exciting Children's Zoo. And don't miss the Bengali Express, a 25-minute monorail ride over forests and plains that are populated by elephants, lions, tigers, and other prowling, playing wildlife. This is the largest urban zoo in the United States, the heart of the Wildlife Conservation Society's efforts to save animals and wild places. The superb and cutting-edge exhibits re-create naturalistic habitats for many of the zoo's more than 4,000 animals. Be sure to see the Congo Gorilla Forest and the new habitat, Tiger Mountain. (Daily) **$$$**

City Island. *Island off the SE coast of the Bronx mainland (10464). E of Hutchinson River Pkwy, through Pelham Bay Park, via City Island Bridge. Phone 718/829-4111. www.cityisland.com.* Referred to as "a bit of New England in the city," City Island is devoted to shipping and shipbuilding. Seafood restaurants; City Island Historical Nautical Museum (Sun).

North Wind Undersea Museum. *610 City Island Ave (10464). Phone 718/885-0701.* (Daily)

Edgar Allan Poe Cottage. *E Kingsbridge Rd and Grand Concourse (10458). Phone 718/881-8900.* (1812) Poe wrote *Annabel Lee, The Bells,* and *Ulalume* while living here (1846-1849). Period furniture; exhibits about the poet and his wife. Films, tours (Sat and Sun). **$$**

Fordham University. *441 E Fordham Rd (10458). In North Bronx. Phone 718/817-4000. www.fordham.edu.* (1841) 15,000 students. All four original Gothic structures of the Rose Hill campus are designated landmarks: University Chapel (St. John's Church), St. John's Residence Hall, Administration Building, and Alumni House. A second campus is at 60th and Columbus Ave, across from the Lincoln Center for the Performing Arts.

The Hall of Fame for Great Americans. *University Ave and W 181st St (10453). Hall of Fame Terrace, on the campus of Bronx Community College. Phone 718/289-5161.* A 630-foot, open-air colonnade provides the framework for bronze busts of great Americans; exhibits. **FREE**

Museum of Bronx History. *3266 Bainbridge Ave, at E 208th St. Phone 718/881-8900.* Valentine-Varian House (1758), site of Revolutionary War activities; exhibits on Bronx history. (Sat and Sun) **$$**

The New York Botanical Garden. *200th St and Kazimiroff Blvd (10458). Bronx Park, entrance on Southern Blvd, S of Moshulu Pkwy. Phone 718/817-8700. www.nybg.org.* One of the largest and oldest in the country, this botanical garden consists of 250 acres of natural terrain and 48 gardens. The garden also has the last 40 acres of the forest that once covered New York City. The Enid A. Haupt Conservatory has 11 distinct plant environments with changing exhibits and permanent displays, including the Fern Forest, Palm Court, and Desert Houses. Tours. Education courses. (Tues-Sun) **$$**

Pelham Bay Park. *E of the Hutchinson River (10475). Hutchinson River and Hutchinson River Pkwy (W); the city's northern limits; Pelham Pkwy, Burr Ave, Bruckner Expy, and Watt Ave (S); and Eastchester Bay and Long Island Sound (E) at NE corner of the Bronx. Phone 718/430-1832.* The city's largest park (2,764 acres) has Orchard Beach, 13 miles of shoreline, fishing, two golf courses (18-hole), a wildlife refuge, an environmental center, a nature trail, a visitor center, tennis courts, ball fields, a running track, riding stables and bridle paths, and picnicking.

Van Cortlandt House Museum. *Broadway and 246th St (10025). In Van Cortlandt Park. Phone 718/543-3344. www.vancortlandthouse.org.* (1748) Georgian house is furnished in the 18th-century Dutch-English manner. (Tues-Fri 10 am-3 pm, Sat-Sun 11 am-4 pm; closed holidays) **$**

Wave Hill. *675 W 252nd St (10471). 249th St and Independence Ave. Phone 718/549-3200. www.wavehill.org.* This Hudson River estate was, at various times, home to such notables as Mark Twain and Arturo Toscanini; it's now a public garden and cultural center featuring Wave Hill House (1843), gardens, four greenhouses, nature trails, woods, and meadows. The grounds consist of 28 acres overlooking the Hudson. Special events include concerts, dance programs, art exhibits, and education and nature workshops. (Spring-summer Tues-Sun 9 am-5:30 pm, Wed until 9 pm; fall-winter Tues-Sun 9 am-4:30 pm; closed holidays) Free admission Tues, also Sat mornings. **$**

Yankee Stadium. *161st St and River Ave. Phone 718/293-4300. www.yankees.com.* Home of the New York Yankees.

B&B/Small Inn

★ **LE REFUGE INN.** *620 City Island Ave (10464). Phone 718/885-2478; fax 718/885-1519.* 7 rooms, 3 story. Check-out 11 am, check-in 1:30 pm. TV. Restaurant, bar. Victorian house (1880) with individually decorated rooms featuring many antiques. On Long Island Sound with views of Manhattan. Totally nonsmoking. **$**

Restaurants

★ **ANN & TONY'S.** *2407 Arthur Ave (10458). Phone 718/364-8250.* Italian menu. Closed Mon. Lunch, dinner. Bar. Children's menu. Casual attire. **$$**
D

★ **BLACK WHALE.** *279 City Island Ave (10464). Phone 718/885-3657. www.dineatblackwhale.com.* American menu. Lunch, dinner, Sun brunch. Bar. Children's menu. Casual attire. **$$**

★ ★ **EMILIA'S.** *2331 Arthur Ave (10458). Phone 718/367-5915; fax 718/367-1483. arthuravenuebronx.com/emilia's.htm.* Italian menu. Closed Mon; Dec 25. Lunch, dinner. Bar. Reservations accepted. Family-style restaurant. **$$**
D

★ **JOE & JOE RESTAURANT.** *1001 Castle Hill Ave (10472). Phone 718/597-4150.* Italian, American menu. Lunch, dinner. Bar. Children's menu. Casual attire. **$$**
D

★ ★ **LOBSTER BOX.** *34 City Island Ave (10464). Phone 718/885-1952; fax 718/885-3232. www.lobsterbox.com.* Seafood menu. Lunch, dinner. Bar. Casual attire. Valet parking available. **$$**
D

★ **NORWOOD CAFE RESTAURANT.** *291 E 204 St (10467). Phone 718/882-5485.* American menu. Breakfast, lunch, dinner. Children's menu. Casual attire. **$**

Ⓓ

★ **SKYVIEW GLATT-KOSHER DELI.** *5665 Riverdale Ave (10471). Phone 718/796-8596.* Kosher deli menu. Breakfast, lunch, dinner. Casual attire. **$$**

Brooklyn

Area code 718

Information Brooklyn Historical Society, 128 Pierrepont St, 11201, phone 718/254-9830; or the NYC Convention & Visitors Bureau

Many of the novels, plays, films, and television shows about New York City—ranging from *Death of a Salesman* to *The Honeymooners*—are set in Brooklyn rather than Manhattan, perhaps because of widely differing characters of these two boroughs. While Manhattan is world-class in sophistication and influence, Brooklyn, famous for such things as the hot dogs on Coney Island, is and always has been quintessentially American.

Yet there is much more to Brooklyn than the popular stereotype. Manhattanites flock to performances at the renowned Brooklyn Academy of Music, and the Egyptology collection at the Brooklyn Museum compares with those in London and Cairo. Brooklyn's beautiful Prospect Park was designed by Olmsted and Vaux, who considered it more beautiful than another park they designed—Central Park in Manhattan.

The most heavily populated borough, Brooklyn handles about 40 percent of New York City's vast shipping. Brooklyn was pieced together from 25 independent villages and fought valiantly before allowing itself to be taken into New York City in 1898.

What to See and Do

Atlantic Avenue. *Take the M/N/R subway to Court St; the 2/3/4/5 subway to Borough Hall; or the A/C/F subway to Jay St/Borough Hall.* Imagine a colorful shopping bazaar in downtown Cairo, and you've just pictured Atlantic Avenue. This area has a mix of more than 30 antique and gifts shops, ethnic food and bread stores, and savory Middle Eastern restaurants. If you crave real falafel, kebabs, and hummus at value prices, this is the neighborhood to visit. You also can enjoy a mild day by wandering around nearby Brooklyn Heights, with its quaint brownstone apartments and quiet streets.

Brooklyn's History Museum. *128 Pierrepont St (11201). Phone 718/624-0890. www.brooklynhistory.org.* Headquarters of the Brooklyn Historical Society since 1881. Permanent and changing exhibits deal with Brooklyn history.

Displays cover Coney Island, the Brooklyn Dodgers, the Brooklyn Bridge, and the Brooklyn Navy Yard; original set of *The Honeymooners* TV show; baseball cards; wax figures. Two-tiered library. (Tues-Sat; closed holidays) **$$**

Brooklyn Academy of Music. *30 Lafayette Ave, Fort Greene/Clinton Hill. Phone 718/636-4100. www.bam.org.* (1907) Founded in 1859, BAM is the oldest performing arts center in America, presenting original productions in contemporary performing arts in the Next Wave Festival each fall, noted national and international theater, dance, and opera companies, and classical and contemporary music programs.

Brooklyn Children's Museum. *145 Brooklyn Ave (11213). At St. Mark's Ave. Phone 718/735-4400. www.bchildmus.org.* Founded in 1899, this is the world's oldest children's museum. Interactive exhibits, workshops, and special events. "The Mystery of Things" teaches children about cultural and scientific objects. "Music Mix" welcomes young virtuosos. Many other hands-on exhibits. (Wed-Fri 2-5 pm, Sat-Sun 10 am-5 pm; also school holidays) **$$**

Brooklyn Heights Promenade. *The R subway goes to the nearby City Hall stop. Phone 718/965-8900.* For a peaceful stroll and a great view of Manhattan, visit this 1/3-mile-long waterfront area, stretching from Orange Street on the north to Remsen Street on the south. Pack a lunch, claim a bench, and enjoy the sights of the city skyline, Ellis Island, and Statue of Liberty. The promenade is lined with lovely homes and is a popular outdoor hangout for Brooklyn Heights yuppies during the summer. If you're in town over Independence Day weekend, this is usually a great place to view the Fourth of July fireworks. (Daily)

Coney Island. *1208 Surf Ave (11224). Phone 718/372-5159. www.coney island.com.* Although it's become a bit frayed, you can still experience a bit of old New York along Coney Island's beachfront boardwalk. Take a ride on the legendary Cyclone roller coaster at **Astroland Amusement Park** (1000 Surf Ave, 718/372-0275, www.astroland.com; open on weekends in Apr, seven days a week June-Labor Day). Afterward, grab the perfect hot dog, waffle fries, and a lemonade at Nathan's Famous. For some really cheesy thrills, experience the nearby circus sideshow shown on weekends in summer. **FREE** Also in the area are

New York Aquarium. *W 8th St and Surf Ave (11224). Phone 718/265-FISH. www.nyaquarium.org.* A varied collection of marine life that includes sharks, beluga whales, seals, seahorses, jellyfish, penguins, sea otters, and walruses. Dolphin feedings (Apr-Oct, outdoors); sea lion shows. Restaurant. (Opens daily at 10 am; closing times vary by season) **$$$**

Sheepshead Bay. *2575 Coney Island Ave (11223). Just E and slightly N of Coney Island via Ocean Pkwy or Shore Pkwy. Phone 718/627-6611.* This area has all the requisites of an ocean fishing community: seafood restaurants, clam bars, tackle shops, fishing boats, and some lovely views.

Gateway National Recreation Area. *Kings Hwy and Flatbush Ave (11234). 718/338-3338.* One of the nation's first two urban national parks. A barrier peninsula across Rockaway Inlet from Coney Island via Flatbush Ave and the Marine Pkwy Bridge. This sprawling, urban recreation area consists of approximately 26,000 acres of land and water in two states—New York and New Jersey: Floyd Bennett Field in Brooklyn (Jamaica Bay in Brooklyn and Queens), Breezy Point on the Rockaway Peninsula in Queens, Miller Field, and Great Kills Park on southeastern Staten Island and the Sandy Hook Unit in New Jersey. Jamaica Bay Wildlife Refuge in Broad Channel, Queens (9,000 acres) offers wildlife observation and hiking trails. Floyd Bennett Field has nature observation opportunities. Jacob Riis Park in Queens, with a mile-long boardwalk, offers beach and waterfront activities. Fort Tilden in Queens offers exhibits, nature walks, guided and self-guided tours of old defense batteries, sporting events, and fishing. Canarsie Pier in Brooklyn offers free weekend summer concerts and restaurants. The Staten Island Unit offers hiking trails, organized athletic programs, and recreational activities. Concession services at some units.

New York Transit Museum. *Boerum Pl at Schermerhorn St (11201). Phone 718/243-8601. www.mta.nyc.ny.us/museum.* Exhibits on the history of the New York City transit system displayed within a 1930s subway station. Subway cars on display, including a 1903 "El" car. Photographs, maps, antique turnstiles. (Tues-Sun; closed holidays) **$$**

Prospect Park. *211 9th Ave (11215). Bounded by Parkside Ave, Ocean Ave, Flatbush Ave, and Prospect Park W and SW. Phone 718/438-0100; 718/965-8951. www.prospectpark.org.* Planned by Olmsted and Vaux, designers of Central Park, its 526 acres include the impressive Grand Army Plaza with Memorial Arch (N end of park), the 90-acre Long Meadow, and a 60-acre lake. Boathouse Visitor Center has information on park history and design; art shows (Apr-Nov). Ball fields, boating, ice rink, bridle paths, tennis courts, bandshell, historic carousel, and the Lefferts Homestead, a 1783 Dutch colonial farmhouse. Directly across Flatbush Ave is

Brooklyn Botanic Garden. *1000 Washington Ave (11225). Phone 718/623-7200. www.bbg.org.* For a peaceful respite away from Manhattan, hop the 1 or 2 subway to Eastern Parkway in Brooklyn and enjoy a natural wonder: the 52-acre Brooklyn Botanic Garden. It features a gorgeous Japanese garden; the Steinhardt Conservatory, which has several greenhouses filled with a variety of plants; and the Fragrance Garden, designed specifically for the blind. There are rose gardens, the annual cheery blossom festival, and many other beautiful sights to behold as well. (Tues-Fri, Apr-Sept; Tues-Sun, Oct-Mar) **$** Nearby is

Brooklyn Museum of Art. *200 Eastern Pkwy (11238). Phone 718/638-5000. www.brooklynart.org.* Although it's often overlooked by tourists, the Brooklyn Museum of Art is one of the city's foremost art institutions. Similar to the Metropolitan in some ways, it is housed in a lovely Beaux Arts building, with collections spanning virtually the entire history of art. Highlights include a large Egyptian wing, a superb Native American collection, and a major permanent assemblage of contemporary art. In addition to staging some of the more unusual and controversial exhibits in town, the museum also hosts a "First Saturday" series (the first Saturday of every month, 5-11 pm) featuring free concerts, performances, films, dances, and dance lessons. The sculpture garden with architectural ornaments from buildings demolished in the New York City area is a lovely spot. (Wed-Fri 10 am-5 pm, Sat-Sun 11 am-6 pm; closed Jan 1, Thanksgiving, Dec 25) **$$$**

Hotel

★ ★ ★ **MARRIOTT BROOKLYN BRIDGE NEW YORK.** *333 Adams St (11201). Phone 718/246-7000; toll-free 800/228-9290; fax 718/246-0563. www.brooklynmarriott.com.* 376 rooms, 7 story. Check-out 11 am, check-in 4 pm. TV; cable (premium), VCR available. Restaurant, bar. Babysitting services available. Indoor pool. Sauna. Business center. In-room modem link. Concierge. **$$$**

D ⚐ 👫 ⤢ 🏃

Restaurants

★ ★ ★ **CUCINA.** *256 5th Ave (11215). Phone 718/230-0711; fax 718/230-0124. www.cucinarestaurant.com.* Over the past five years, Park Slope has slowly become a destination neighborhood in Brooklyn, packed with up-and-coming movers and shakers in the art, finance, and media worlds. But Cucina was a staple in Park Slope years before the trendsetters moved in and has stayed true to its winning formula all along—terrific rustic Italian food served with genuine charm and hospitality in an elegant, warm, inviting dining room that is the perfect place for large gatherings or intimate tables for two. Italian menu. Closed Mon, Thanksgiving, Dec 25. Dinner. Bar. Children's menu. **$$**

D

★ ★ **GIANDO ON THE WATER.** *400 Kent Ave (11211). Phone 718/387-7000; fax 718/387-7138. www.giandoonthewater.com.* Italian menu. Lunch, dinner. Bar. Casual attire. Valet parking available. **$$$**

D

★ ★ ★ **PETER LUGER STEAK HOUSE.** *178 Broadway (11211). Phone 718/387-7400; fax 718/387-3523. www.peterluger.com.* Peter Luger's is to steak what Martin Scorsese is to directing movies. This place is king of cow. While you will have to make your way through hordes of self-important suits and smug regulars to get to the noisy, brass-accented dining room, the mind-altering dry-aged steaks make the journey worthwhile. The beef here is fork-tender, with a smoky char and wanton amounts of rich, meaty flavor. The porterhouse can be split among two, three, or four, and you'll have enough to take home for Fido. But with meat like this, you may want to keep the leftovers for yourself. New Yorkers in the know head to Luger's for lunch, when the kitchen serves a killer lunch-only burger for a bargain price of $5.95. Steak menu. Lunch, dinner. Bar. Casual attire. Reservations required. No Credit Cards Accepted **$$$**

D

★ ★ ★ **RIVER CAFE.** *1 Water St (11201). Phone 718/522-5200; fax 718/875-0037. www.rivercafe.com.* Sweeping views of the twinkling New York City skyline lure tourists and romance seekers to The River Café, but truth be told, this is one of the city's few tourist destination restaurants that really delivers on the cuisine as well as the eye-candy views. The sophisticated American menu is prepared with seasonal ingredients and smart, simple accents that do not overwhelm the senses. The menu offers fish lovers plates like lobster ravioli, seared yellowfin tuna, and potato-crusted fried oysters, while dishes like seared duck breast, rabbit risotto, lamb shank, and rack of veal give carnivores a good selection to choose from. American menu. Lunch, dinner. Bar. Jacket required. Reservations required. Valet parking available. Outdoor seating. **$$$$**

D

★ ★ **TOMMASO.** *1464 86th St (11228). Phone 718/236-9883; fax 718/236-9883. www.tommaso-brooklyn.com.* Italian menu. Closed Dec 25. Lunch, dinner. Bar. Casual attire. Opera Thurs-Sun evenings. **$$**

D

★ **ZAYTOONS RESTAURANT.** *472 Myrtle Ave (11205). Phone 718/623-5522. www.zaytoons.com.* Middle Eastern menu. Lunch, dinner. Casual attire. **$**

D

Queens

Area code 718

By far the largest borough geographically, Queens occupies 121 square miles of Long Island. Like Brooklyn, it was assembled from a number of small towns, and each of these neighborhoods has retained a strong sense of identity. Parts of the borough are less densely settled than Brooklyn, and the majority of Queens's population are homeowners. Many manufacturing plants, warehouses, and shipping facilities are in the portion called Long Island City, near the East River. Forest Hills, with its West Side Tennis Club, at Tennis Place and Burns Street, is a world-famous center for tennis. Flushing Meadows Corona Park has been the site of two world's fairs; many facilities still stand.

Transportation

AIRPORTS
At LaGuardia: information 718/476-5000; lost and found 718/533-3988; cash machines, upper level Main Terminal, Finger 4, Delta Terminal. *At Kennedy:* information 718/656-4444; lost and found 718/244-4225.

CAR RENTAL AGENCIES
See IMPORTANT TOLL-FREE NUMBERS.

PUBLIC TRANSPORTATION

Subway and elevated trains, buses (New York Transit Authority), phone 718/330-3322 or 718/330-1234.

RAIL PASSENGER SERVICE

Amtrak 800/872-7245.

What to See and Do

American Museum of the Moving Image. *35th Ave and 36th St, in Astoria (11106). Phone 718/784-0077. www.ammi.org.* On site of historic Astoria Studios, where many classic early movies were filmed. Museum devoted to art and history of film, television, and video and their effects on American culture. Permanent and changing exhibitions; two theaters with film and video series (screenings weekends). (Tues-Sun; closed holidays) **$$$**

Astoria. *Phone 718/286-2667. www.queens.nyc.us.* Experience your own "Big Fat Greek Wedding" in this Hellenic community, just 15 minutes from Midtown Manhattan, which offers the best Greek food this side of Athens. Astoria has an estimated Greek population of 70,000—the largest community outside of Greece—which means that the area is alive with music, culture, and melt-in-your mouth saganaki and baklava. Food markets, gift shops, bakeries, restaurants, and intimate cafés await your shopping and dining pleasure. Finish your excursion by relaxing on a nice, sunny day with a cup of Greek coffee in nearby Astoria Park and take in a great view of upper Manhattan. If you want to combine this Greek experience with other area attractions, the American Museum of the Moving Image (718/784-0077) and the historic Kaufman Astoria Motion Picture Studios (718/392-5600) are located in Astoria. This fun neighborhood proves that there *is* life in the outer boroughs of New York City.

Bowne House. *37-01 Bowne St. Phone 718/359-0528.* (1661) One of the oldest houses in New York City was built by John Bowne, a Quaker who led a historic struggle for religious freedom under Dutch rule; 17th-19th-century furnishings. (Tues, Sat, and Sun afternoons; closed Easter and mid-Dec-mid-Jan) Under 12 admitted only with adult. **$**

Flushing Meadows-Corona Park. *Flushing and Metropolitan aves (11368). Grand Central Pkwy to Van Wyck Expy and Union Tpke to Northern Blvd. Phone 718/217-6034.* Originally a marsh, this 1,255-acre area became the site of two world's fairs (1939-1940 and 1964-1965). It is now the home of the United States Tennis Association National Tennis Center, where the US Open is held annually (phone 718/760-6200). The park is also the site of some of the largest cultural and ethnic festivals in the city. Facilities include an indoor ice rink, carousel, 87-acre Meadow Lake, and the Playground for All Children, designed for disabled and able-bodied children. Park rangers conduct occasional weekend tours.

> **New York Hall of Science.** *47-01 111th St (11368). 111th St and 48th Ave. Phone 718/699-0005. www.nyhallsci.org.* Exhibition hall with hands-on science and technology exhibits. (Daily) Free admission Thurs and Fri afternoons. **$$$**

The Queens Museum of Art. *25th Ave and 76th St (11368). New York City Building. Phone 718/592-9700. www.queensmuse.org.* Interdisciplinary fine arts presentations, major traveling exhibitions; permanent collection includes 9,000-square-foot panorama of New York City, the world's largest three-dimensional architectural model. (Tues-Fri, also Sat and Sun afternoons; closed Jan 1, Thanksgiving, Dec 25) **$$**

Shea Stadium. *123-01 Roosevelt Ave (11368). 126th St and Roosevelt Ave. Phone 718/507-6387. www.mets.com.* Home of the New York Mets. **$$$$**

Isamu Noguchi Garden Museum. *36-01 43rd Ave (11101). Phone 718/204-7088. www.noguchi.org.* Sculpture fans will want to visit the Isamu Noguchi Museum, just a short trip from Manhattan. Housed in the sculptor's former studio, complete with an outdoor sculpture garden, the museum is filled with Noguchi stone, metal, and woodwork. (Apr-Nov; Mon, Thurs, Fri 10 am-5 pm; Sat-Sun 10 am-6 pm; closed Tues, Wed) **DONATION**

John F. Kennedy International Airport. *Belt Pkwy and Van Wyck Expy (11430).* The airport's 4,930 acres cover an area roughly one-third the size of Manhattan. Much of the air traffic going overseas is handled through here. (See AIRPORT INFORMATION)

LaGuardia Airport. *Located at Grand Central Pkwy and 94th St (See AIRPORT INFORMATION) Phone 718/565-5100.*

The Museum of Modern Art (MoMA). *33rd St at Queens Blvd. Phone 212/708-9400. www.moma.org.* The Museum of Modern Art (MoMA) possesses a marvelously comprehensive collection—roughly 100,000 pieces—from post-impressionist to abstract expressionist to pop, including masterpieces of photography and objects of modern design. But the main museum is closed until early 2005 for renovations and rebuilding. Meanwhile, the most popular works in the permanent collection, including Van Gogh's "Starry Night" and Picasso's "Les Demoiselles d'Avignon," are available for viewing at MoMa Queens. While here, however, only about 50 to 75 of these works can be displayed at a time. Some museum-goers find the $12 admission fee to be on the high side for such a small museum, especially since both the Guggenheim and the Whitney, in Manhattan proper, offer a greater selection. However, contemporary art lovers will probably find that it's still worth the trip out to Queens, only 20 minutes by subway from Midtown Manhattan, to see some stunning modern masterworks and perhaps a MoMA special exhibit. Take the 7 local train to 33rd St in Queens; the museum is across the street. (Thurs-Mon; closed Thanksgiving, Dec 25) **$$$**

Queens Botanical Garden. *43-50 Main St. Phone 718/886-3800. www.quensbotanical.org.* Collections include large rose, herb, Victorian wedding, bee, woodland, and bird gardens; arboretum. (Tues-Sun) **DONATION**

Special Events

Aqueduct. *110-00 Rockaway Blvd (11420). Take the A train to the Aqueduct stop. Phone 718/641-4700. www.nyra.com/aqueduct.* Yes, people actually do take the A train! Hop on the subway for a short ride out to Queens for an afternoon of thoroughbred races, held from late October through early May. Races take place Wednesday through Sunday and begin at 1 pm. The track also has pretty lawns and gardens that come alive in spring. You can't beat the cheap admission price, so splurge a little and place some bets. **$**

Belmont Park. *2150 Hempstead Tpke (11003). Just outside of Queens in Nassau County, on Cross Island Pkwy via Hempstead Tpke and Plainfield Ave, in Elmont, L.I. Phone 516/488-6000. www.nyra.com/belmont.* This 430-acre racetrack is the home of the third jewel in horse racing's Triple Crown, the Belmont Stakes. This major spectacle is held in June and attracts gamblers, horse lovers, and spectators from all walks of life. It's one of the oldest annual sporting events in the nation, so make your plans in advance and reserve seats early. Hopefully, you will get a good-weather day on which to enjoy this event. The regular season racing at Belmont Park is from May through July and from September through October. Sundays are Family Fun Days; kids can play in the playground in the Backyard area. (Wed-Sun, May-July and Sept-Oct) **$**

US Open Tennis. *USTA National Tennis Center, Flushing Meadows-Corona Park (11351). Take the #7 subway to the Willets Point-Shea Stadium stop. Phone 718/760-6200. www.usopen.org.* Tennis fans from near and far flock to the US Open tennis tournament each September. You can see your favorite players, the stars of tomorrow, and a host of celebrities in the audience at this upper-crust sporting event. Tickets go on sale in late May or by the beginning of June, and those matches held closer to the finals sell out first. Purchase tickets as early as possible. Buying a ticket to the Arthur Ashe Stadium, the main court, gives you admission to all the other courts on the grounds. However, these seats tend to be more in the back, since the better seats go to corporate sponsors. Bring a pad to keep your own score, binoculars, sunscreen, and sunglasses for day games. Late Aug-early Sept.

Motels/Motor Lodges

★ ★ ★ **CROWNE PLAZA.** *104-04 Ditmars Blvd (11369). Phone 718/457-6300; toll-free 800/692-5429; fax 718/899-9768. www.crowneplaza.com.* 358 rooms, 200 with shower only, 7 story. Crib free. Garage parking. TV; cable (premium), VCR (movies available). Indoor pool; whirlpool, poolside service. Complimentary coffee in rooms. Restaurant 6 am-midnight. Bar 4 pm-2 am. Check-out noon. Coin laundry. Convention facilities. Business center. In-room modem link. Concierge. Gift shop. Free airport transportation. Tennis privileges. Exercise room; sauna. Many refrigerators. Luxury level. Located adjacent to LaGuardia. **$$**

D 🖍 🛏 🏋 ✈ 🏊 SC 🏋

★ ★ **HOLIDAY INN.** *14402 135th Ave (11436). Phone toll-free 800/692-5359; fax 718/322-2533. www.holiday-inn.com.* 360 rooms, 12 story. Check-out noon. TV; cable (premium), VCR available (movies). Restaurant, bar. Exercise equipment, sauna. Indoor pool, whirlpool. Free airport transportation. **$$**

D 🛏 🏋 ✈ 🏊

Hotel

★ ★ ★ **CROWNE PLAZA JFK AIRPORT.** *151-20 Baisley Blvd (11434). Phone 718/489-1000. www.crowneplaza.com.* 184 rooms, 12 story. Check-out noon. TV; cable (premium), VCR available. In-room modem link. Restaurant, bar. Exercise equipment. Business center. Concierge. **$**

🕴 ✈ 🚶

Restaurants

★ ★ ★ **CHRISTOS HASAPO-TAVERNA.** *41-08 23rd Ave, Astoria (11105). Phone 718/726-5195. www.christossteakhouse.com.* Greek, steak menu. Lunch, dinner. Bar. Casual attire. Outdoor seating. No Credit Cards Accepted **$$$**

★ ★ **IL TOSCANO.** *42-05 235th St, Douglaston (11363). Phone 718/631-0300; fax 718/225-5223.* Italian menu. Hours: 5-10 pm. Closed Mon. Dinner. Bar. Casual, trattoria atmosphere. Reservations required. **$$**

D

★ ★ **MANDUCATIS.** *13-27 Jackson Ave (11101). Phone 718/729-4602; fax 718/361-0411.* Italian menu. Closed Sun (July-Aug); last 2 weeks in Aug; also most major holidays. Lunch, dinner. Bar. Attractive, comfortable neighborhood restaurant. **$$**

D

★ ★ **PARK SIDE.** *107-01 Corona Ave (11368). Phone 718/271-9274; fax 718/271-2454.* Italian menu. Hours: noon-11:30 pm. Lunch, dinner. Bar. Valet parking available. Outdoor seating. **$$$**

D

★ ★ ★ **PICCOLA VENEZIA.** *42-01 28th Ave (11103). Phone 718/721-8470; fax 718/721-2110. www.piccola-venezia.com.* Northern Italian menu. Closed Tues; Jan 1, Dec 25, also July 24-Aug 24. Lunch, dinner. Valet parking available. Attractive restaurant with exposed brick walls and etched mirrors. **$$$**

D

★ ★ **PING'S SEAFOOD.** *8302 Queens Blvd (11373). Phone 718/396-1238.* Chinese menu. Closed Sun. Lunch, dinner. **$$**

★ **TAVERNA KYKLADES.** *33-07 Ditmars Blvd, Astoria (11105). Phone 718/545-8666.* Greek, seafood menu. Lunch, dinner. Casual attire. Outdoor seating. **$$**

★ ★ **WATER'S EDGE.** *44th Dr at the East River (11101). Phone 718/482-0033; fax 718/937-8817. www.watersedgenyc.com.* On the riverfront opposite the United Nations complex; views of the New York City skyline. Specializes in seafood, lobster. Hours: noon-3 pm, 5-11 pm; Fri, Sat 5:30-11:30 pm. Closed Sun. Lunch, dinner. Bar. Reservations required. Valet parking. Outdoor dining. Complimentary riverboat transportation to and from Manhattan. **$$**

D

Staten Island

Area code 718

Information Staten Island Chamber of Commerce, 130 Bay St, 10301; 718/727-1900; or the NYC Convention & Visitors Bureau

Staten Island, twice the size of Manhattan with only one twenty-fourth the population, is the most removed, in distance and character, from the other boroughs. At one time, sightseers on the famous Staten Island Ferry rarely disembarked to explore the almost rural character of the island. The completion of the Verrazano Bridge to Brooklyn, however, brought growth and the beginning of a struggle between developers and those who would preserve the island's uncrowded appeal.

What to See and Do

Conference House. *7455 Hylan Blvd. Phone 718/984-6046.* Built in the mid-1680s by an English sea captain, this was the site of an unproductive meeting on Sept 11, 1776, between British Admiral Lord Howe, Benjamin Franklin, John Adams, and Edward Rutledge to discuss terms of peace to end the Revolutionary War. The meeting helped to produce the phrase the "United States of America." Rose, herb gardens; open-hearth cooking; spinning and weaving demonstrations. (Apr-Nov, Fri-Sun) **$**

The Greenbelt/High Rock. *Victory Blvd and Arthur Kill Rd. 200 Nevada Ave in Egbertville, 7 miles from Verrazano Bridge via Richmond Rd. Phone 718/667-2165.* An 85-acre nature preserve in a 2,500-acre park. Visitor center, trails. Environmental programs, workshops. Self-guided tours. Urban park ranger-guided tours (by appointment). (Daily) No picnicking or camping. **FREE**

Historic Richmond Town. *441 Clarke Ave, Richmond and Arthur Kill rds. Phone 718/351-1611. www.historicrichmondtown.org.* Outdoor museum complex depicts three centuries of history and culture of Staten Island and surrounding region. Daily life and work of a rural community shown in trade demonstrations and tours of shops and buildings. Among the restoration's 27 historic structures are the Historic Museum; Voorlezer's House (circa 1695), the oldest surviving elementary school in the US; general store; trademen's shops. Special events and demonstrations. (Wed-Sun afternoons; extended hours July-Aug; closed Jan 1, Thanksgiving, Dec 25) **$$**

Jacques Marchais Museum of Tibetan Art. *338 Lighthouse Ave, between New Dorp and Richmondtown. Phone 718/987-3500. www.tibetanmuseum.com.* Perched on a steep hill with views of the Atlantic Ocean, this museum houses the collection of Jacqueline Norman Klauber, who became fascinated with Tibet as a child. Highlights of the exhibits include a series of bright-colored masks and a large collection of golden *thangkas,* or religious images, plus terraced sculpture gardens and a koi pond. (Wed-Sun 1-5 pm) **$**

Snug Harbor Cultural Center. *1000 Richmond Terrace. Phone 718/448-2500. www.snug-harbor.org.* Founded in 1833 as a seamen's retirement home, Snug Harbor is now a performing and visual arts center with 28 historic buildings featuring Greek Revival and Victorian architecture; art galleries (Wed-Sun, fee); children's museum (Tues-Sun afternoons); botanical garden, sculpture, 83 acres of parkland. (Daily; closed Thanksgiving, Dec 25)

Staten Island Zoo. *Barrett Park, between Broadway and Clove Rd in W New Brighton. Phone 718/442-3100. www.statenislandzoo.org.* Maintained by the Staten Island Zoological Society. Large collection of native and exotic reptiles, varied species of rattlesnakes, amphibians, marine reef fishes, mammals, birds. Children's center includes a miniature farm. (Daily; closed Jan 1, Thanksgiving, Dec 25) Free admission on Wed afternoon, inquire for hours. **$$**

Side Trips — Day Trips

If you need a little break from the bright lights and hustle and bustle of the Big Apple, there are a plethora of peaceful day trips you can take. You may enjoy the quiet beauty of the Catskills and the Hamptons or sitting seaside in Mystic, Connecticut or perhaps learning a little bit of U.S. history in Philadelphia, Pennsylvania is more your style. You can recharge your batteries during the day and be back in NYC in plenty of time for a magnificent night out.

Atlantic City, NJ

2 hours 12 minutes; 127 miles from New York City

Settled 1854 **Pop** 40,517 **Elev** 8 ft **Area code** 609

Information Atlantic City Convention & Visitors Authority, 2314 Pacific Ave, 08401; 609/449-7147, 888/ACVISIT, or 800/ BOARDWALK

Web www.atlanticcitynj.com

Honeymooners, conventioneers, Miss America, and some 37 million annual visitors have made Atlantic City the best-known New Jersey beach resort. Built on Absecon Island, the curve of the coast shields it from battering northeastern storms while the nearby Gulf Stream warms its waters, helping to make it a year-round resort. A 60-foot-wide boardwalk extends along 5 miles of beaches. Hand-pushed wicker rolling chairs take visitors up and down the Boardwalk.

Absecon Lighthouse ("Old Ab"), a well-known landmark, was first lit in 1857 and now stands in an uptown city park. The game of Monopoly uses Atlantic City street names.

What to See and Do

Absecon Lighthouse. *Pacific and Vermont aves. Phone 609/449-1360. www.absconlighthouse.org.* Climb the 228 steps to the top of this 1857 lighthouse, designed by Civil War general George Gordon Meade. Tallest lighthouse in New Jersey, third-tallest in US. (July-Aug, daily; Sept-June, Thurs-Mon; closed holidays) **$$**

Atlantic City Boardwalk Hall. *1 Ocean Way (08401). Phone 609/348-7000.* Seats 13,800; special events, concerts, boxing, ice shows, sports events; site of the annual Miss America Pageant.

Edwin B. Forsythe National Wildlife Refuge, Brigantine Division. *9 miles N on US 9. Contact PO Box 72, Great Creek Rd, Oceanville 08231. Phone 609/652-1665.* Wildlife drive; interpretive nature trails (daily). Over the years, more than 200 species of birds have been observed at this 45,000-acre refuge. Public-use area has an 8-mile wildlife drive through diversified wetlands and uplands habitat; most popular in the spring and fall, during the course of the waterbird migration, and at sunset, when the birds roost for the evening. Refuge headquarters (Mon-Fri). **$$**

Fishing. Surf and deep-sea fishing. License may be required, check locally. Charter boats (Mar-Nov). Many tournaments are scheduled. Contact Atlantic City Party and Charter Boat Association.

Garden Pier. *Boardwalk and New Jersey Ave. Phone 609/347-5837.* Atlantic City Art Center and Atlantic City Historical Museum are located here. (Daily) **FREE**

Historic Gardner's Basin. *800 New Hampshire Ave, at N end of city. Phone 609/348-2880.* An 8-acre, sea-oriented park featuring the working lobstermen; Ocean Life Center, eight tanks totalling 29,800 gallons of aquariums, exhibiting more than 100 varieties of fish and marine animals, 10 exhibits featuring themes on the marine and maritime environment. Picnicking. (Daily; closed Jan 1, Thanksgiving, Dec 25)

Historic Town of Smithville and the Village Greene at Smithville. *1 N New York Rd, Smithville (08201). Special events throughout the year. 7 miles W on US 30 to Absecon, then 6 miles N on US 9, at Moss Mill Rd. Phone 609/652-7777 or -0440.* (1787) Restored 18th-century village with specialty shops and restaurants. Also carousel, train ride, and paddle boats. Village (daily).

Lucy, the Margate Elephant. *Decateur and Atlantic Ave (08402). S via Atlantic Ave in Margate. Phone 609/823-6473.* Only elephant in the world you can walk through and come out alive. Guided tour and exhibit inside this six-story elephant-shaped building. Built 1881; spiral stairs in Lucy's legs lead to main hall and observation area on her back. Gift shop. (Mid-June-Labor Day, daily; Apr-mid-June and Sept-Oct, Sat and Sun only) **$$**

Marine Mammal Stranding Center & Museum. *Over bridge and 2 miles N, at 3625 Atlantic-Brigantine Blvd. Phone 609/266-0538.* One of few marine mammal rescue and rehabilitation centers in US. Injured dolphins, turtles, and other marine animals are brought to center for treatment. Museum offers exhibits on mammal species; recuperating animals can be viewed at center. Dolphin and whale-watch trips available (fee; reservations required). (Mid-June-Labor Day, Tues-Sun, Labor Day-Dec 25, weekends; Dec 25-May, call for schedule) **DONATION**

Noyes Museum. *12 miles NW via US 9, on Lily Lake Rd in Oceanville. Phone 609/652-8848.* Rotating and permanent exhibits of American art; collection of working bird decoys. (Tues-Sun; closed holidays). **$$**

Recreation areas. Beach (Memorial Day-mid-Sept; free), surfing at special areas (daily), boating; bicycling and rolling chairs on Boardwalk (daily), golf, tennis.

Renault Winery. *72 N Bremen Ave (08215). 16 miles W on US 30 in Egg Harbor City. Phone 609/965-2111.* Guided tour (approximately 45 minutes) includes wine-aging cellars; press room; antique wine-making equipment; free wine tasting (daily). Restaurants. **$**

The Shops on Ocean One. *1 Atlantic Ocean (08401). Boardwalk at Arkansas Ave. Phone 609/347-8082.* A 900-foot, three-deck shopping pier houses shops, food court, and restaurants. (Daily) **FREE**

Storybook Land. *6415 Black Horse Pike (08234). 10 miles W via US 40, 322. Phone 609/641-7847.* More than 50 storybook buildings and displays depicting children's stories; live animals; rides; picnic area, concession (May-mid-Sept, daily; Mar-Apr and mid-Sept-Thanksgiving, Sat and Sun only). Christmas Fantasy with Lights and visiting with Mr. and Mrs. Santa (Thanksgiving-Dec 30, nightly). Admission includes attractions and unlimited rides. **$$$**

Special Events

Atlantic City Marathon. *Phone 609/601-1RUN.* Mid-Oct.

LPGA Atlantic City Classic. *401 S New York Rd (08201). Phone 609/927-7888.* Late June.

Miss America Pageant. *2301 Boardwalk (08401). Atlantic City Boardwalk Hall.* Usually first or second weekend after Labor Day.

Motels/Motor Lodges

★ ★ **CLARION HOTEL.** *8029 Black Horse Pike, West Atlantic City (08232). Phone 609/641-3546; toll-free 800/999-9466; fax 609/641-9740. www.clarionhotel.com.* 110 rooms, 2 story. Check-out 11 am. TV; cable (premium), VCR available. Coin laundry. Restaurant 7 am-10 pm. Service bar. Supervised children's activities (June-Aug) ages 8-15. Exercise room, sauna. Pool, wading pool. Indoor and outdoor tennis, pro. Airport transportation. Meeting rooms, business services. On bay. **$**

D 🐾 🏊 🏋 🛥

★ **COMFORT INN.** *539 E Absecon Blvd, Absecon (08201). Phone 609/641-7272; toll-free 800/233-4656; fax 609/646-3286. www.comfortinn.com.* 205

rooms, 7 story. Complimentary continental breakfast. Check-out noon. TV; cable (premium). **$**

[D] [icon]

★ **DAYS INN.** *6708 Tilton Rd, Egg Harbor City (08234). Phone 609/641-4500; fax 609/645-8295. www.daysinn.com.* 117 rooms, 5 story. Family rates; package plans; holidays (2-day minimum); higher rates special events; lower rates rest of year. Crib free. TV; cable (premium), VCR available. Complimentary continental breakfast. Restaurant adjacent 7 am-midnight. Check-out 11 am. Meeting rooms. Business services available. In-room modem link. Coin laundry. Exercise equipment. Pool; lifeguard. Playground. Game room. Some refrigerators, microwaves. Picnic tables. **$**

[D] [icon] [icon] [icon]

★ **FAIRFIELD INN.** *405 E Absecon Blvd, Absecon (08201). Phone 609/646-5000; toll-free 800/228-2800; fax 609/383-8744. www.fairfieldinn.com.* 200 rooms, 6 story. Complimentary continental breakfast. Check-out 11 am. TV; cable (premium). In-room modem link. Pool. **$**

[D] [icon] [icon]

★ **HAMPTON INN.** *240 E White Horse Pike, Absecon (08201). Phone 609/652-2500; toll-free 800/426-7866; fax 609/652-2212. www.hamptoninn.com.* 129 rooms, 4 story. Complimentary continental breakfast. Check-out 11 am. TV; cable (premium), VCR available. In-room modem link. Laundry services. Pool, whirlpool. Free airport transportation. **$**

[D] [icon] [icon] [icon]

★ **HAMPTON INN.** *7079 Black Horse Pike, West Atlantic City (08232). Phone 609/484-1900; fax 609/383-0731. www.hamptoninn.com.* 143 rooms, 6 story. Family rates; higher rates: holidays (2-day minimum). Crib free. Complimentary continental breakfast. Check-out 11 am. TV; cable (premium). Coffee in rooms. Meeting room, business services. **$**

[D] [icon] [icon] [SC]

★ ★ **HOLIDAY INN.** *111 S Chelsea Ave (08401). Phone 609/348-2200; toll-free 800/548-3030; fax 609/345-5110. www.holiday-inn.com.* 220 rooms, 21 story. Check-out 11 am. TV; cable (premium). In-room modem link. Restaurant, bar. Health club privileges. Pool, poolside service. **$**

[icon] [icon] [icon] [icon]

★ **SUPER 8.** *229 E US 30; 633 White Horse Pike, Absecon (08201). Phone 609/652-2477; fax 609/748-0666. www.super8.com.* 58 rooms, 2 story. Check-out noon. TV; cable (premium). **$**

[D] [icon]

Hotel

★ ★ ★ **SHERATON ATLANTIC CITY CONVENTION CENTER HOTEL.** *2 Miss America Way (08401). Phone 609/344-3535. www.sheraton.com.* 502 rooms, 12 story. Check-out noon. TV; cable (premium), VCR available. In-room modem link. Laundry services. Restaurant, bar. In-house fitness room. Indoor pool, whirlpool. Business center. Concierge. Casino. **$$**

Resorts

★ ★ ★ **MARRIOTT SEAVIEW RESORT AND SPA.** *401 S New York Rd, Absecon (08201). Phone 609/652-1800; toll-free 800/932-8000; fax 609/652-2307. www.marriott.com.* A golfers dream, this hotel is located on 650 acres near Reeds Bay and offers two 18-hole championship golf courses. Other amenities include an indoor and an outdoor pool, a full spa nearby, health club, tennis courts and attraction nearby. 297 rooms, 3 story. Check-out 12:30 pm, check-in 4 pm. TV; cable (premium), VCR available (free movies). In-room modem link. Laundry services. Dining room, bar. Room service. In-house fitness room, sauna. Game room. Indoor pool, outdoor pool, whirlpool, poolside service. 36-hole golf, pro, 9-hole putting green; golf school. 8 tennis courts, 4 lighted, pro. Business center. Located on 670-acre estate. **$$**

★ ★ ★ **RESORTS CASINO HOTEL.** *1133 Boardwalk, Absecon (08401). Phone 609/344-6000; toll-free 800/336-6378; fax 609/340-7684. www.resortsac.com.* The rooms in this oceanfront casino property have a summery decor with bright plaid comforters and white wood furniture. Fine dining options are numerous highlighting Asian, Italian, and French cuisines and the Le Palais' Sunday champagne brunch is worth a visit. 662 rooms, 15 story. Check-out noon. TV. In-room modem link. Restaurant, bar open 24 hours. In-house fitness room, sauna, steam room. Game room. Indoor pool, outdoor pool, whirlpool. Valet parking. Airport transportation. Concierge. First casino in Atlantic City. **$**

Casinos

★ ★ ★ **BALLY'S PARK PLACE CASINO RESORT.** *Park Place and Boardwalk (08401). Phone 609/340-2000; fax 609/340-4713. www.ballysac.com.* A geometric glass chandelier twinkles overhead at the entrance to this large, classic casino. There are several dining options to choose from, including several that fit into the Wild West theme of the hotel's annex casino. A cut above many of the others in Atlantic City. 1,268 rooms, 49 story. Check-out noon. TV; cable (premium). In-room modem link. Restaurant open 24 hours. Bar. In-house fitness room, massage, sauna, steam room. On beach. Indoor pool, outdoor pool, whirlpool, poolside service. Valet parking; self-park garage. **$**

★ ★ ★ **CAESARS ATLANTIC CITY HOTEL CASINO.** *2100 Pacific and Arkansas aves (08401). Phone 609/348-4411; toll-free 800/524-2867; fax 609/343-2405. www.caesars.com.* Touted as "Rome on the Jersey shore" this opulent oceanfront hotel and 120,231-square-foot casino houses 26,000 square feet of meeting space. There are Chinese, Japanese, American steakhouse and Roman-themed eateries plus nine additional casual restaurants and lounges. 1,138 rooms, 20 story. Check-out noon. TV; cable (premium), VCR available (movies). Bar open 24 hours. Restaurant. In-house fitness room, massage, sauna, steam room. Pool, whirlpool. Outdoor tennis. Airport transportation. **$**

★ ★ **CLARIDGE CASINO & HOTEL.** *Boardwalk and Park Places (08401). Phone 609/340-3400; toll-free 800/257-8585; fax 609/340-3875. www.claridge.com.* 504 rooms, 24 story. Check-out noon. TV; cable (premium). Bar open 24 hours. Room service 24 hours. Restaurant. In-house fitness room, sauna, steam room. Indoor pool, whirlpool. Concierge. **$**

★ ★ ★ **HILTON CASINO RESORT.** *Boston and the Boardwalk (08401). Phone 609/347-7111; toll-free 877/432-7139; fax 609/340-4858. www.hiltonac.com.* 803 rooms, 22 story. Check-out noon. TV; cable (premium), VCR available. Restaurant, bar; entertainment. Free supervised children's activities (June-Aug). In-house fitness room, sauna. Game room. Indoor pool, whirlpool, poolside service. Valet parking. Concierge. On beach. **$$**

★ ★ **SANDS CASINO HOTEL.** *Indiana and Brighton Park (08401). Phone 609/441-4000; toll-free 800/227-2637; fax 609/441-4630. www.acsands.com.* 534 rooms, 21 story. Check-out noon. TV; cable (premium), VCR available. Restaurant (see also BRIGHTON STEAKHOUSE), bar; entertainment. In-house fitness room, sauna. Valet, garage parking. Airport transportation. Concierge. **$**

★ ★ **SHOWBOAT CASINO & HOTEL.** *801 Boardwalk (08401). Phone 609/343-4000; toll-free 800/621-0200; fax 609/343-4057. www.harrahs.com.* 755 rooms, 25 story. Check-out noon. TV; cable (premium), VCR available. Restaurant, bar open 24 hours; entertainment. Supervised children's activities. In-house fitness room, sauna. Game room. Pool, whirlpool. Airport transportation. **$**

★ ★ ★ **TROPICANA CASINO AND RESORT.** *Brighton Ave and the Boardwalk (08401). Phone 609/340-4000; toll-free 800/843-8767; fax 609/ 343-5211. www.tropicana.net.* This resort and casino offers over 1,600 rooms and suites, spectacular entertainment, fine dining, and nonstop action. 1,624 rooms, 23 story. Check-out noon. TV; cable (premium), VCR available. In-room modem link. Restaurant, bar open 24 hours. In-house fitness room, sauna. Indoor pool, outdoor pool, whirlpool, poolside service. Lighted tennis. Valet, garage parking. Business center. **$**

★ ★ ★ **TRUMP MARINA HOTEL & CASINO.** *Huron Ave and Brigantine Blvd (08401). Phone 609/441-2000; toll-free 800/777-1177; fax 609/345-7604. www.trumpmarina.com.* 728 rooms, 27 story. Check-out noon. TV; cable (premium), VCR available. In-room modem link. Restaurant open 24 hours, bar; entertainment. In-house fitness room, massage, sauna, steam room. Health club privileges. Game room. Pool, children's pool, whirlpool, poolside service. Outdoor tennis, lighted courts. Lawn games. Garage parking. **$$**

D ⚐ ⌀ ⛩ ⛷ ⊠

★ ★ ★ **TRUMP PLAZA HOTEL & CASINO.** *The Boardwalk and Mississippi Ave (08401). Phone 609/441-6000; toll-free 800/677-7378; fax 609/441-7881. www.trumpplaza.com.* 904 rooms, 38 story. Check-out noon. TV; cable (premium), VCR available. In-room modem link. Restaurant open 24 hours, bar; entertainment. In-house fitness room, massage, sauna, steam room. Game room. Indoor pool, whirlpool. Outdoor tennis. Concierge. **$$**

D ⚐ ⌀ ⛩ ⊠

★ ★ ★ **TRUMP TAJ MAHAL CASINO RESORT.** *1000 Boardwalk (08401). Phone 609/449-1000; toll-free 800/825-8888; fax 609/449-6818. www.trumptaj.com.* 1,250 rooms, 52 story. Check-out noon. TV; cable (premium). Restaurant open 24 hours. Bar; entertainment. In-house fitness room, spa, massage, sauna, steam room. Game room. Indoor pool, whirlpool, poolside service. Bicycles available. Valet parking. Business center. Concierge. Casino. **$$**

D ⌀ ⛩ ⊠ ⛷

Restaurants

★ ★ ★ **BRIGHTON STEAKHOUSE.** *Indiana Ave at Brighton Park (08401). Phone 609/441-4300. www.acsands.com.* In addition to thick cuts of steak, veal and lamb as well as the usual seafood, this surf 'n turf spot in the Sands casino also serves up live piano music. American menu. Closed Tues, Wed. Dinner. Bar. Reservations required. **$$$**

D

★ **CAPTAIN YOUNG'S SEAFOOD EMPORIUM.** *2801 Atlantic Ave (08401). Phone 609/344-2001.* Closed Thanksgiving, Dec 25. Lunch, dinner. Bar. **$$**

D

★ ★ **CHEF VOLA'S.** *111 S Albion Place (08401). Phone 609/345-5022; fax 609/266-2649.* Italian menu. Closed Mon; Thanksgiving, Dec 24-25. Dinner. Reservations required. Photographs of celebrities. No Credit Cards Accepted. **$$$**

★ ★ **DOCK'S OYSTER HOUSE.** *2405 Atlantic Ave (08401). Phone 609/345-0092; fax 609/345-7893. www.shorecast.com.* Dinner. Bar. Children's menu. Casual atmosphere in family-owned restaurant since 1897. Reservations accepted. **$$**

D

★ **GRABELS RESTAURANT LOUNGE.** *3901 Atlantic Ave (08401). Phone 609/344-9263; fax 609/344-6433. www.grabels.com.* Continental menu. Closed Dec 24. Dinner. Bar. Piano Wed-Sun. Children's menu. Casual attire. **$$**

D

★ **IRISH PUB AND INN.** *St James Pl and Boardwalk (08401). Phone 609/344-9063; fax 606/344-7225. www.theirishpub.com.* American, Irish menu. Irish balladeer Thurs-Sun (summer). Informal, Irish pub atmosphere. Hours: Open 24 hours. Lunch, dinner. Bar. Patio dining. No Credit Cards Accepted. **$**

D

★ ★ **OLD WATERWAY INN.** *1660 W Riverside Dr (08401). Phone 609/347-1793; fax 609/347-0075. www.oldwaterwayinn.com.* Cajun/Creole, seafood menu. Closed Mon, Tues (Oct-Apr). Dinner. Bar. Children's menu. Outdoor seating. **$$**

D

★ ★ **SCANNICCHIO'S.** *119 S California Ave (08401). Phone 609/348-6378; fax 609/345-5711.* Italian menu. Closed most major holidays. Dinner. Bar. Reservations required. **$$**

D SC

★ ★ **STEVE AND COOKIE'S BY THE BAY.** *9700 Amherst Ave (08402). Phone 609/823-1163; fax 609/823-9571. www.steveandcookies.com.* Contemporary American menu. Closed Dec 24, Dec 25. Dinner. Bar. Live music. Children's menu. Casual attire. **$$**

D

The Catskills

2 hours 30 minutes; 137 miles from New York City

Settled 1662 **Pop** 11,849 **Elev** 47 ft **Area code** 518 **Zip** 12414

Information Greene County Promotion Dept, NY Thrwy exit 21, PO Box 527; 518/943-3223 or 800/355-CATS

Web www.greene-ny.com

This is the eastern entrance to the Catskill Mountains resort area. The town is at the west end of the Rip Van Winkle Bridge, over the Hudson River across from the manufacturing town of Hudson (see). The legendary Rip is said to have slept for 20 years near here.

What to See and Do

Catskill Game Farm. *400 Game Farm Rd (12414). 8 miles W on NY 23, 5 miles S on NY 32. Phone 518/678-9595.* Children may feed tame deer, donkeys, llamas, other animals. Rides; picnic grounds; cafeteria. (May-Oct, daily) **$$$$**

Zoom Flume Waterpark. *East Durham and Rte 145. 13 miles from Exit 21 off NY state thrwy. Phone 518/239-4559 or 800/888-3586.* Catskill's largest water park. Gift shop. Restaurant. (Mid-June-Labor Day daily) **$$$$**

Motels/Motor Lodges

★ **CARL'S RIP VAN WINKLE.** *810 Rte 23B (12451). Phone 518/943-3303; fax 518/943-2309. www.ripvanwinklemotorlogde.com.* 6 kitchen units, 27 cabins. Check-out 11 am. TV; cable (premium). Fireplace in some cabins. Pool, children's pool. Lawn games, hiking trails. Many room phones. On 160 wooded acres. **$**

★ ★ **CATSKILL MOUNTAIN LODGE.** *334 Rte 32A (12463). Phone 518/678-3101; toll-free 800/686-5634; fax 518/678-3103. www.thecatskills.com/catmtldg.htm.* 42 units, 2 kitchen units. Check-out 11 am. TV; cable. Bar. Game room. Pool, children's pool. Lawn games. **$**

★ **RED RANCH.** *4555 NY 32 (12414). Phone 518/678-3380; toll-free 800/962-4560. www.redranchmotel.com.* 39 rooms, 2 story. Check-out 11 am. TV; cable (premium). Game room. Pool, children's pool. Downhill, cross-country ski 10 miles. Lawn games. **$**

Resorts

★ ★ ★ **FRIAR TUCK RESORT AND CONVENTION CENTER.** *4858 State Rte 32 (12414). Phone 518/678-2271; toll-free 800/832-7600. www.friartuck.com.* 525 rooms, 5 story. Check-out noon, check-in 3 pm. TV; cable (premium). Laundry services. Dining room, bar; entertainment. Supervised children's activities (summer, winter). Exercise room, sauna, steam room. Game room. Three pools, one indoor, whirlpool. Lighted tennis. Downhill/cross-country ski 12 miles. Business center. Theater. **$**

★ ★ **WOLFFIS MAPLE BREEZE RESORT.** *360 Cauterskill Rd (12414). Phone 518/943-3648; toll-free 800/777-9653; fax 518/943-9335. www.wolffsresort.com.* 42 rooms, 2 story. Check-out 11 am, check-in 1 pm. TV; cable (premium). Dining room, bar; entertainment. Supervised children's activities. Game room. Pool. Outdoor tennis. Lawn games, Boats, rowboats. **$**

Restaurant

★ ★ **FERNWOOD.** *341 Malden Ave (12463). Phone 518/678-9332.* Continental menu. Specializes in shrimp scampi, linguini bucaniera. Hours: 5-10 pm. Closed Mon, Tues; Dec 25. Reservations accepted. Bar. Dinner. Children's menu. Outdoor dining. Family-owned since 1966. **$$**

Amagansett (The Hamptons)

2 hours 30 minutes; 107 miles from New York City
See also East Hampton, Montauk, Sag Harbor

Pop 1,067 **Elev** 40 ft **Area code** 631 **Zip** 11930

Information East Hampton Chamber of Commerce, 79A Main St, East Hampton 11937; 516/324-0362

Web www.easthamptonchamber.com

What to See and Do

Miss Amelia's Cottage Museum. *Rte 27A and Windmill Ln. Phone 631/ 267-3020 or 631/267-8989.* This original home is part of the history of Amagansett, a quaint village on the South Fork. Mary Amelia Schellinger, who was the last of her family to live in this 1725 house, was a descendant of Jacob Schellinger, the founder of Amagansett. She lived in the home without electricity or water for years. The cottage features its original colonial furnishings, so you get a true sense of what a home looked like so many centuries ago. (June-Sept 10-am-4 pm) **DONATION**

Town Marine Museum. *Bluff Rd, 1/2 mile S of NY 27, on ocean. Phone 631/267-6544 or 631/324-6850.* Exhibits on commercial and sport fishing, offshore whaling from colonial times to present; underwater archaeology, sailing, aquaculture, commercial fishing techniques; garden; picnicking. Programs administered by the East Hampton Historical Society. (July-Aug, daily; June and Sept, weekends only) **$**

Motel/Motor Lodge

★ **SEA CREST ON THE OCEAN.** *2166 Montauk Hwy (11930). Phone 631/267-3159; toll-free 800/SEADAYS; fax 631/267-6840.* 74 kitchen units, 2 story. Check-out 11 am. TV; cable (premium). Laundry services. Heated pool. **$**

B&B/Small Inn

★ ★ **MILL GARTH COUNTRY INN.** *23 Windmill Ln (11930). Phone 631/267-3757; fax 631/267-3675.* 12 kitchen units, 2 story, 4 suites, 5 cabins.

Complimentary continental breakfast. Check-out 11 am, check-in 3 pm. TV in sitting room. Health club privileges. Lawn games. Built 1840, became an inn in the late 1800s; stone originally from ancient windmill. **$$$**

D SC

Restaurants

★ **CAFÉ ON MAIN.** *195 Main St (11930). Phone 631/267-2200.* American menu. Breakfast, lunch. Casual attire. **$$**

★ ★ **ESTIA.** *177 Main St (11930). Phone 631/267-6320.* New American menu. Breakfast, lunch, dinner. Bar. Casual attire. **$$**

★ ★ **GORDON'S.** *231 Main St (11930). Phone 631/267-3010; fax 631/267-3027.* Continental menu. Specializes in seafood, veal. Hours: 6-10 pm; July-Aug from 6 pm. Closed Mon; Thanksgiving, Dec 25; Feb. Dinner. **$$**

D

★ **LOBSTER ROLL.** *1980 Montauk Hwy (11930). Phone 631/267-3740. www.lobsterroll.com.* Seafood menu. Closed Nov-Apr; also weekdays May and Oct. Lunch, dinner. Children's menu. Outdoor seating. **$$**

D

East Hampton (The Hamptons)

2 hours 10 minutes; 105 miles from New York City
See also Sag Harbor, Southampton

Settled 1648 **Pop** 19,719 **Elev** 36 ft **Area code** 516 **Zip** 11937

Information East Hampton Chamber of Commerce, 79A Main St; 631/324-0362

Web www.easthamptonchamber.com

East Hampton is an old Long Island village, founded in 1648 by a group of farmers. Farming was the main livelihood until the mid-1800s, when the town began to develop into a fashionable resort.

What to See and Do

Guild Hall Museum. *158 Main St (11937). Phone 631/324-0806.* Regional art exhibits; changing shows. Art and poetry lectures, classes. Library covering art and artists of the region. (June-Sept, daily; rest of year, Wed-Sun; closed Thanksgiving, Dec 25) Also here is

John Drew Theater at Guild Hall. *Phone 631/324-0806. www.guildhall.org/theater.ihtml.* A 382-seat theater for films, plays, concerts, lectures, and children's performances. **DONATION**

Historic Mulford Farm. *10 James Ln. Phone 631/324-6850.* (1680) Living history farm museum; 18th-century New England architecture; colonial history; period rooms; costumed interpretation. (Afternoons: July and Aug, daily; June and Sept, weekends only; rest of year, by appointment) **$** Nearby is

> **Historic Clinton Academy.** *151 Main St. Phone 631/324-6850.* (1784) First preparatory school in New York. Now museum housing collection of artifacts of Eastern Long Island. (Afternoons: July and Aug, daily; June and Sept, weekends only) **$**

Home Sweet Home House. *14 James Ln (11937). Phone 631/324-0713.* Named after the popular 19th-century song, "Home Sweet Home," written by John Howard Payne, this house was originally owned by Payne's grandfather, Aaron Isaacs (the first Jewish person to settle in the area). The historic home in this historic village features beautiful antiques and china, and is dedicated to Payne, who was also an actor, playwright, and diplomat. History buffs visiting East Hampton will enjoy this attraction. (Mon-Sat 10 am-4 pm, Sun 2-4 pm) **$**

Hook Mill. *36 N Main St, on Montauk Hwy.* Completely equipped 1806 windmill. Guided tours. (Memorial Day-Labor Day, Wed-Mon) **$**

Pollock-Krasner House and Study Center. *830 Fireplace Rd. Phone 631/324-4929.* Jackson Pollock's studio and house plus a reference library on 20th-century American art. (May-Oct, Thurs-Sat, by appointment only) **$$**

Motel/Motor Lodge

★ **EAST HAMPTON HOUSE.** *226 Pantigo Rd (11937). Phone 631/324-4300; fax 631/329-3743. www.theeasthamptonhouse.com.* 52 rooms, 2 story. Check-out 11 am, check-in 3 pm. TV; cable (premium). In-house fitness room. Outdoor pool. Outdoor tennis. **$$**

B&B/Small Inns

★ ★ **THE 1770 HOUSE.** *143 Main St (11937). Phone 631/324-1770; fax 631/324-3504. www.1770house.com.* 7 rooms, 2 story. Children over 12 years only. Check-out 11:30 am, check-in 2 pm. Restaurant, bar. Restored 18th-century house; antique furnishings. **$$$**

★ ★ ★ **CENTENNIAL HOUSE.** *13 Woods Ln (11937). Phone 631/324-9414; fax 631/324-0493. www.centhouse.com.* Situated at the eastern tip of Long Island, this bed and breakfast was built in 1876 and restored with English country decor in 1987. A charming guest cottage is a nice alternative to the main house, and hearty breakfasts accompany all rooms. 6 rooms, 2 story. Pets accepted. Children over 12 years only. Complimentary continental breakfast. Check-out 11 am, check-in 2 pm. TV. Some fireplaces. Outdoor pool. Totally nonsmoking. **$$$**

★ ★ **HEDGES INN.** *74 James Ln (11937). Phone 631/324-7100; fax 631/ 324-5816.* 11 rooms, 3 story. No room phones. Check-out noon, check-in 2 pm. TV; cable (premium). Restaurant. Victorian house built (circa 1870) with wraparound porch. **$$**

★ ★ ★ **J. HARPER POOR COTTAGE.** *181 Main St (11937). Phone 631/324-4081; fax 631/329-5931. www.jharperpoor.com.* This stuccoed English Tudor house in the Hamptons has been refurbished into a quaint inn. Enjoy a relaxing afternoon in the living room in the cottage—a perfect spot to sit and read a book. 5 rooms, 2 story. Check-out noon, check-in 2 pm. TV. Indoor pool. Original house built 1650. **$$$**

★ ★ **MAIDSTONE ARMS.** *207 Main St (11937). Phone 631/324-5006; fax 631/324-5037. www.maidstonearms.com.* The Osborne family originally built this as a private residence in the 1750s. It has been operating as an inn since the 1870s. Guests can enjoy the bustle of the Hamptons during the summer months, or settle in by the fireplaces during winter stays. 19 rooms, 3 story, 4 suites. Check-out noon, check-in 2 pm. Restaurant, bar. Room service. Sitting area. **$$$**

Restaurants

★ ★ ★ **DELLA FEMINA.** *99 N Main St (11937). Phone 631/329-6666.* American menu. Closed Wed in off-season. Dinner. Bar. Casual attire. Outdoor seating. **$$$**

★ ★ ★ **EAST HAMPTON POINT.** *295 Three Mile Harbor (11937). Phone 631/329-2800; fax 631/329-2876. www.easthamptonpoint.com.* American menu. Closed Sept-Mar. Lunch, dinner. Bar. Children's menu. Casual attire. Reservations required. Valet parking available. Outdoor seating. **$$**

★ ★ **FARMHOUSE RESTAURANT.** *341 Pantigo Rd (11937). Phone 631/324-8585. www.hamptonsfarmhouse.com.* American menu. Dinner. Bar. Casual attire. Outdoor seating. **$$$**

★ ★ **JAMES LANE CAFE AT THE HEDGES.** *74 James Ln (11937). Phone 631/324-7100. www.jameslancecafe.com.* Italian, American menu. Mediterranean menu. Closed Tues and Wed (Oct-May). Lunch, dinner. In 1870s Victorian home. Casual attire. Valet parking. Outdoor seating. **$$$**

★ ★ **LAUNDRY.** *31 Race Ln (11937). Phone 631/324-3199; fax 631/324-9327. www.thelaundry.com.* American menu. Closed Wed after Labor Day; Thanksgiving, Dec 25, 31. Dinner. Bar. Casual attire. Outdoor seating. Once operated as a commercial laundry; courtyard, garden. **$$**

★ ★ ★ **MAIDSTONE ARMS.** *207 Main St (11937). Phone 631/324-5006; fax 631/324-5037. www.maidstonearms.com.* A charming white clapboard house with striped awnings, this inn is as inviting inside as it is outside. It consistently sets the standard for fine dining in the Hamptons, with a range of hearty and light-fare contemporary dishes. Enjoy a cigar and a game of backgammon in the Water Room Lounge after dinner. Contemporary American menu. Breakfast, lunch, dinner, Sun brunch. Bar. **$$$$**

★ ★ **MARYJANE'S IL MONASTERO.** *128 N Main St (11937). Phone 631/324-8008; fax 631/324-3523.* American, Italian menu. Closed Jan; Thanksgiving, Dec 25. Lunch, dinner. Bar. Children's menu. Casual attire. 3 dining rooms. **$$**

D

★ ★ **MICHAEL'S.** *28 Maidstone Park Rd (11937). Phone 631/324-0725; fax 631/324-8602.* Seafood, American menu. Closed Dec 25; Wed off-season. Dinner. Bar. Casual attire. **$$**

D

★ ★ **NICK & TONI'S.** *136 N Main St (11937). Phone 631/324-3550; fax 631/324-7001.* Mediterranean menu. Closed Dec 25. Dinner, Sun brunch. Bar. Casual attire. Reservations required. **$$$**

D

★ ★ **PALM.** *94 Main St (11937). Phone 631/324-0411; fax 631/324-6122. www.thepalm.com.* Continental, steak menu. Closed Mon in winter. Dinner. Bar. Turn-of-the-century décor. Casual attire. **$$$**

D

Greenport (The Hamptons)

2 hours; 100 miles from New York City
See also Riverhead, Shelter Island, Southold

Pop 4,180 **Elev** 10 ft **Area code** 516 **Zip** 11944

Greenport is a bit of New England on Long Island. There are clean, uncrowded beaches to enjoy, as well as several wineries. This nautical, artsy, harborside village exudes charm, offering a mix of craft shops, art galleries, antique stores, restaurants, ice cream parlors, and candy shops. Stroll by the water and stop for some clams, or buy some one-of-a-kind nautical knick-knacks. Take your time and take in the old-world atmosphere, especially on a warm, sunny day. Walk a little bit off Main Street and you can admire some of the old Victorian houses that are still lived in today. This area has particular appeal and ease since you can park your car and walk everywhere. Keep in mind that summer weekends can be crowded with locals.

What to See and Do

East End Seaport & Maritime Museum. *North Ferry Dock, Third St (11944).* *Phone 631/477-2100. www.eastendseaport.org.* The maritime history of Long Island's East End is depicted through exhibits that include actual yachts used during World War II, a small aquarium, and submarine mock-ups. Lectures on nautical history are offered, and there are special exhibits in summer—when the area really comes to life. There also is a maritime festival held in late September that offers a parade and various other events—this and the museum together make for a nice afternoon. (June-Oct, daily 11 am-5 pm; closed Tues) **FREE**

Orient Point, NY-New London, CT, Ferry. *41720 NY 25, Orient (11957). 8 miles NE at end of NY 25 in Orient Point. Phone 631/323-2525 or 860/443-5281.* Ninety-minute crossing. (Daily; closed Dec 25) One-day round trips. Reservations required for vehicle. **$$$$**

Special Event

Greenport Maritime Festival. *Main St and Rte 48. Phone 516/477-0004.* Wooden boat regatta, fishing tournament, whale boat race; clam chowder tasting contest. Late Sept.

Motels/Motor Lodges

★ **SILVER SANDS MOTEL.** *1 Silvermere Rd (11944). Phone 631/477-0011; fax 631/477-0922. www.silversands-motel.com.* 35 rooms, 1 story. Complimentary continental breakfast. Check-out 11 am. TV. Game room. Heated pool. On bay. **$**

D 🛋 ⛱ 🏊

★ ★ **SOUND VIEW INN.** *57185 N Rd (11944). Phone 631/477-1910; fax 631/477-9436.* 49 rooms, 2 story. Check-out noon. TV; VCR available. Restaurant, bar. Sauna. Pool. Tennis. On beach. **$**

D 🛋 🎾 ⛱ 🏊

★ **SUNSET MOTEL.** *62005 Rte 48 (11944). Phone 631/477-1776. www.sunsetgreenport.com.* 11 rooms, 2 story. Closed Nov-mid-Apr. Check-out 11 am. TV. Lawn games. **$$**

D 🛋 🏋 🎾 🏊

Restaurants

★ **CHOWDER POT PUB.** *104 3rd St (11944). Phone 631/477-1345.* Hours: noon-2:30 pm, 5-9 pm; Fri, Sat to 10 pm. Closed Mon; also winter weekdays. Lunch, dinner. Bar. Outdoor seating. **$$**

★ ★ **CLAUDIO'S.** *111 Main St (11944). Phone 631/477-0627; fax 631/477-0894. www.claudios.com.* Specializes in seafood, steak. Reservations accepted.

Bar. Lunch, dinner. Entertainment. Parking. Outdoor dining. Clam bar on dock. Souvenirs of America's Cup defenders decorate walls. View of fishing harbor. Family-owned for more than 100 years. **$$**

D

Montauk (The Hamptons)

2 hours 40 minutes; 120 miles from New York City

Pop 3,851 **Elev** 18 ft **Area code** 631 **Zip** 11954

Information Chamber of Commerce, PO Box 5029; 631/668-2428

This is a lively fishing town on Long Island, with a big business in deep-sea fishing (tuna, shark, marlin, striped bass, and other varieties). Boats can be rented, and there are miles of uncrowded sandy beaches to enjoy.

What to See and Do

Hither Hills State Park. *3 miles W on NY 27. Phone 631/668-2554.* Swimming beach, bathhouse, lifeguards, fishing; nature and hiking trails, picnicking, playground, concession, tent and trailer sites (mid-Apr-Nov; reservations required). Standard fees.

Montauk Point State Park. *6 miles E on NY 27; easternmost tip of Long Island. Phone 631/668-2554.* Barren moor with sea view. Montauk Lighthouse, built 1795; museum, tours (summer weekends; fee). Fishing; hiking, biking, picnicking, concession. Standard fees.

Montauk Seal Watching. *Phone 631/668-3781.* This is one of the few attractions on the South Fork that takes place only in winter. Put on your warmest coat, hat, and boots and take part in a two- to three-hour guided beach walk with an expert to watch the seals in action. Check ahead to see what times the tours are being given on any specific day, which is also weather-dependent. If you are a nature or animal lover, this is a wonderful, different kind of experience unlike anything else on Long Island. Adults and children alike will enjoy this—something for the whole family. Don't forget to bring the camera and binoculars. (Jan-Mar, weekends) **$**

Motels/Motor Lodges

★ **BURCLIFFE BY THE SEA.** *397 Old Montauk Hwy (11954). Phone 631/668-2880; fax 631/668-3129.* 7 kitchen units. Check-out 10 am. TV; cable (premium). **$$**

★ **DRIFTWOOD MOTEL & COTTAGES.** *2718 Montauk Hwy (11954). Phone 631/668-5744; toll-free 800/643-7438; fax 631/267-3081. www.duneresorts.com.* 57 rooms, 2 story. Check-out 11 am. TV; cable (premium), VCR available. Pool. Outdoor tennis. **$$**

⊡ ♨ ⚡ 🏃 ⚞ ⚍ ⛵

★ ★ **ROYAL ATLANTIC BEACH RESORT.** *S Edgemere St (11954). Phone 631/668-5103; fax 631/668-4172.* 152 kitchen units, 2 story. Check-out 11 am. TV; cable (premium). Restaurant, bar. Heated pool, poolside service. **$$**

⊡ ⚍

★ **SANDS MOTEL.** *S Emerson Ave and S Emery St (11954). Phone 631/668-5100.* 42 rooms, 22 kitchen units, 2 story. Check-out 11 am. TV; cable (premium), VCR available. Pool. Lawn games. **$**

♨ ⚡ ⚍

★ **WAVE CREST RESORT.** *170 Old Montauk Hwy (11954). Phone 631/668-2141; fax 631/668-2337.* 65 kitchen units, 2 story. No elevator. Closed Nov-Apr. Check-out 11 am. TV; cable (premium), VCR available. Indoor pool. Hither Hills State Park adjacent. **$**

♨ ⚍

Hotel

★ ★ **PANORAMIC VIEW.** *272 Old Montauk Hwy (11954). Phone 631/668-3000; fax 631/668-7870.* 118 kitchen units, 3 story. Closed Dec-Mar. Children over 10 years only. Check-out 11 am, check-in 2 pm. TV; cable (premium), VCR available. In-room modem link. Laundry services. Game room. Pool. No credit cards accepted. **$$**

⊡ ♨ ⚍

Resorts

★ **BEACHCOMBER RESORT.** *727 Old Montauk Hwy (11954). Phone 631/668-2894; fax 631/668-3154.* 88 kitchen units, 2 story. Check-out 11 am. TV; cable (premium), VCR available. Heated pool. Sauna. **$$**

⊡ ♨ ⚡ ⚍ ⛵

★ ★ **GURNEY'S INN RESORT AND SPA.** *290 Old Montauk Hwy (11954). Phone 631/668-2345; toll-free 800/445-8062; fax 631/668-3576. www.gurneys-inn.com.* 109 rooms, 4 story. No elevator. Check-out 11:30 am, check-in 3:30 pm. TV; cable (premium), VCR available. Dining room, bar; entertainment. Exercise room, sauna, steam room. Indoor pool, whirlpool. Airport transportation. **$$$**

♨ ⚍ 🏃 ⚞

★ ★ ★ **MONTAUK YACHT CLUB.** *32 Star Island Rd (11954). Phone 631/668-3100; toll-free 800/692-8668; fax 631/668-3303. www.montaukyacht*

club.com. This property is tucked along Long Island's South Fork East End. The 60-foot lighthouse replica, built in 1928, is still a focal point, and there are abundant recreational facilities. 84 rooms, 2 story. Check-out 11 am, check-in 3 pm. TV; cable (premium). Dining room, bar. Exercise equipment, sauna. Three pools, one indoor. Outdoor tennis. Marina, sailing, waterskiing. **$$**

D ⚓ 🏄 🏊 🏃 ↘ SC

Restaurants

★ ★ **CROW'S NEST.** *4 Old West Lake Dr (11954). Phone 631/668-2077.* American menu. Lunch, dinner. Bar. Children's menu. Casual attire. **$$**

★ ★ **DAVE'S GRILL.** *468 W Lake Dr (11954). Phone 631/668-9190. www.davesgrill.com.* Specializes in seafood, pasta. Own pastries. Hours: 5:30-10:30 pm. Closed Wed; also Nov-Apr. Bar. Dinner. Parking. Outdoor dining. Casual; located on fishing docks. **$$**

D

★ ★ **GOSMAN'S.** *500 W Lake Dr (11954). Phone 631/668-5330.* Specializes in fresh seafood. Hours: noon-10 pm. Closed Nov-Mar. Lunch, dinner. Noon-2 am. Children's menu. Outdoor dining. **$$**

D

★ ★ **HARVEST.** *11 S Emory St (11954). Phone 631/668-5574. www.harvest2000.com.* Closed Thanksgiving, Dec 25. Dinner. Bar. Outdoor seating in herb garden. Bacci courts. **$$$**

D

★ **MONTAUKET.** *88 Firestone Rd (11954). Phone 631/668-5992.* American menu. Lunch, dinner. Bar. Children's menu. Casual attire. Outdoor seating. **$$**

★ ★ **OYSTER POND.** *4 South Elmwood Ave (11954). Phone 631/668-4200.* American menu. Lunch, dinner. Bar. **$$**

D

★ ★ **RUSCHMEYER'S.** *161 Second House Rd (11954). Phone 631/668-2877; toll-free 800/637-7708. www.ruschmeyers.com.* Menu changes. Hours: 5-10 pm; May-Memorial Day, mid-Sept-Columbus Day Fri-Sun 5-9 pm; early-bird dinner 5-6 pm. Closed rest of year. Dinner. Bar. Children's menu. Outdoor seating. **$$**

D

★ **SHAGWONG RESTAURANT.** *774 Montauk Hwy (11954). Phone 631/668-3050. www.shagwong.com.* Specializes in fresh seafood. Menu changes daily. Lunch, dinner, Sun brunch. Hours: noon-midnight; early-bird dinner 4:30-6 pm; Sun 11am-2 pm (brunch), 6-10 pm. Bar. Covered patio dining. Photographs of Old Montauk and celebrity guests. Original tin ceiling (1927). **$**

D

Riverhead (The Hamptons)

1 hour 20 minutes; 77 miles from New York City

Pop 27,680 **Elev** 19 ft **Area code** 631 **Zip** 11901

Information Chamber of Commerce, 542 E Main St, PO Box 291; 631/727-7600

Web www.riverheadchamber.com

Suffolk County's thousands of acres of rich farmland, first cultivated in 1690, have made it one of the leading agricultural counties in the United States. Potatoes, corn, and cauliflower are abundant here.

What to See and Do

Atlantis Marine World. *431 E Main St (11901). Phone 631/208-9200. www.atlantismarineworld.com.* This aquarium offers children and adults alike the chance to observe marine life up close and personal—and safely. You'll see sharks swimming in a 120,000-gallon tank, playful sea lions, and a live coral reef display. Marine World also houses the Riverhead Foundation for Marine Research and Preservation (phone 631/369-9840), where you can witness marine animals nursed back to health. (Daily 10 am-5 pm; closed Dec 25) **$$$**

Briermere Farms. *4414 Sound Ave (11901). Phone 631/722-3931.* Forget the calorie count when you walk into this small roadside farmstand and bakery. The many varieties of homemade fruit and cream pies are worth every delectable bite—in fact, they are the closest thing to grandma's recipe that you will find. From traditional flavors like cherry and peach to more exotic tastes such as blackberry apple and blueberry cream, the pies are so chock full of fresh fruit that they are actually heavy to carry. But don't stop there: also indulge in Briermere's home-baked breads, muffins, and cookies. For healthier interests, they also sell fresh fruits and vegetables. Insider's tip: go early in the day for the best selection, and be ready to wait in line on just about any day in the summer. (Daily 9 am-5 pm)

Brookhaven National Laboratory. *14 miles W of Riverhead via NY 24 and NY 495, in Upton. Phone 631/344-2345.* The Exhibit Center Science Museum is housed in the world's first nuclear reactor built to carry out research on the peaceful aspects of nuclear science. Participatory exhibits, audiovisual presentations, and historic collections. Tours (Mid-July-Aug, Sun; closed holiday weekends). **FREE**

Palmer Vineyards. *108 Sound Ave (11901). Phone 631/722-WINE. www.palmervineyards.com.* Opened in 1986, this 55-acre winery is one of the most award-winning wineries on the North Fork, with an interesting, eclectic variety of wines. Palmer offers everything from Cabernet Franc to Chardonnay to special Reserve wines that have a unique, rich flavor. Pack a picnic, enjoy a tasting and a tour, and buy some wine to enjoy with lunch and to bring home to friends and family. Save some money for the gift shop, too. (June-Oct, daily 11 am-6 pm; Nov-May, daily 11 am-5 pm)

Pindar Vineyards. *Rte 25, in Peconic. (11958). Phone 631/734-6200. www.pindar.net.* Even though Long Island's wine country does not have the reputation of Napa Valley, this well-known winery and its smaller counterparts in this lovely agricultural area are making a name for themselves. No trip to Long Island's wine country is complete without a stop at Pindar. On 550 lush acres, it is the North Fork's largest winery and one of the most established. Founded in 1979, it offers free tastings of the 16 varieties of wine it produces. They include more common types such as merlot, chardonnay, and cabernet sauvignon and lesser-known varieties such as syrah and viognier. The winery is airy and comfortable and provides daily guided tours. Don't forget to visit the gift shop and pick up some goodies to bring home. **FREE**

Splish Splash. *2549 Splish Splash Dr (11901). Phone 631/727-3600. www.splishsplashlongisland.com.* Considered one of the top five water parks in the US, this 64-acre delight for children (and adults as well) has everything wet, from tubing on a river to a mammoth speed slide to a wild roller coaster water ride. For the very young, there are kiddie rides and baby pools. Plan to buy lunch or snacks, since no outside food is allowed in the park. Also, arrive before the park opens to beat some of the crowds, and try going on an overcast day when more people will stay away and you'll have your pick of rides. (Mid-June-Labor Day, daily 9:30 am-7 pm) **$$$$**

Suffolk County Historical Society. *300 W Main St. Phone 631/727-2881. www.riverheadli.com.* Dating back to 1886, this museum chronicles Suffolk County's colorful history and rich traditions in farming, whaling, and Native American culture. Displays include furniture, tools, antique bicycles and carriages, and a pottery collection, and features a library containing newspapers, books, and photographs relating to Suffolk and its people. (Tues-Sat 12:30 pm-4:30 pm) **FREE**

Tanger Outlet Center. *1770 W Main St (11901). Phone 631/369-2732. www.tangeroutlet.com.* Welcome, all bargain hunters. This outdoor outlet mall is a great place to pick up almost any kind of merchandise you can think of—clothes, china, jewely—at below retail prices. The mall has nearly 200 stores, most of them name brands such as Banana Republic and Gap. Sometimes you'll have to do some digging to find the best possible prices, but it's worth it if you want well-known brands. Keep in mind that weekends tend to be more crowded, so consider a weekday jaunt to this East End destination. (Mon-Sat 9 am-9 pm, Sun 10 am-7 pm)

Vintage Tours. *Phone 631/765-4689. www.northfork.com/tours.* If you and your traveling companion(s) would like to imbibe, relax and leave the driving to someone else. For a reasonable price, Vintage Tours will pick you up at your hotel in a comfortable 15-passenger van and take you to at least three wineries in a four- to five-hour jaunt. Also included are wine tastings, behind-the-scene winery tours, a gourmet picnic lunch suited to your tastes, and stops at the North Fork's wonderful farm stands for the best in fresh vegetables and fruit. The company operates Friday-Sunday, but weekday trips can be arranged. **$$$$**

Special Event

Riverhead Country Fair. *200 Howell Ave (11901). Phone 631/727-1215. Downtown.* Agricultural, needlecraft exhibits and competitions; farm animal exhibit; entertainment, midway, music. Mid-Oct.

Motel/Motor Lodge

★ ★ **BEST WESTERN EAST END.** *1830 Rte 25 (11901). Phone 631/369-2200; toll-free 800/272-6232; fax 631/369-1202. www.bestwestern.com.* 100 rooms, 2 story. Check-out 11 am. TV; cable (premium). Restaurant, bar. Pool. **$$**

D ⊠ SC

Sag Harbor (The Hamptons)

2 hours; 105 miles miles from New York City
See also Shelter Island, Southampton

Settled 1660 **Pop** 2,313 **Elev** 14 ft **Area code** 631 **Zip** 11963

Information Chamber of Commerce, PO Box 2810; 631/725-0011

Web www.sagharborchamber.com

This great whaling town of the 19th century provided prototypes from which James Fenimore Cooper created characters for his sea stories. Sheltered in a cove of Gardiners Bay, the economy of Sag Harbor is still centered around the sea.

What to See and Do

Custom House. *161 Main St. Phone 631/692-4664.* Served as custom house and post office during the late 18th and early 19th centuries; antique furnishings. (July-Aug, Tues-Sun; May-June and Sept-Oct, Sat and Sun) **$$**

Morton National Wildlife Refuge. *4 miles W on Noyack Rd. Phone 631/286-0485.* A 187-acre sanctuary with sandy and rocky beaches and wooded bluffs. Nature trails; ponds and lagoon for wildlife observation, nature study, photography, and environmental education. (Daily; beach closed Apr-Aug)

Sag Harbor Whaling and Historical Museum. *200 Main St (11963). Phone 631/725-0770. www.sagharborwhalingmuseum.org.* Listed on the National Register of Historic Places, this museum, housed in a mansion, celebrates Sag Harbor's long history of whaling. It features items such as the tools used to capture whales, a replica of a whaleboat, whale teeth and bones, and other materials associated with whaling. Captain Ahab would have been proud of such a fine testament to the sea and its mammoth mammals! (May-Oct, daily 10 am-5 pm, Sun 1-5 pm) **$**

Restaurants

★ ★ ★ **AMERICAN HOTEL.** *Main St (11963). Phone 631/725-3535; fax 631/725-3573. www.theamericanhotel.com.* Located at the rear of the hotel lobby, this restaurant boasts a romantic, atrium dining room filled with ivy, antiques, whaling memorabilia and framed maps and paintings. The daily-changing, new-French menu reflects the fresh catch and seasonal ingredients. French menu. Hours: 5-10 pm; Sat, Sun also noon-4 pm. Closed Jan 1, Dec 24, 25. Reservations accepted. Bar. Lunch, dinner. Inn built in 1846. Atrium room. **$$**

★ ★ **ESTIA'S LITTLE KITCHEN.** *1615 Sag Harbor (11930). Phone 631/725-1045.* New American menu. Closed Tues. Breakfast, lunch, dinner. Casual attire. Reservations required (dinner). **$$**

★ ★ **IL CAPPUCINO.** *30 Madison St (11963). Phone 631/725-2747; fax 631/725-5783.* Northern Italian menu. Hours: 5:30-10:30 pm; Fri, Sat to 11 pm; Sun 5-10 pm. Closed Thanksgiving, Dec 25. Service bar. Dinner. Children's menu. **$**

D

★ ★ **SPINNAKER'S.** *63 Main St (11963). Phone 631/725-9353; fax 631/725-7340.* Specializes in lobster, homemade desserts. Hours: 11:30 am-10 pm; Fri, Sat to 11 pm. Closed Thanksgiving. Reservations accepted. Bar. Lunch, dinner. Sun brunch. Children's menu. Piano bar Sat evenings. Dining room has dark wood and brass accents. **$**

D

Shelter Island (The Hamptons)

2 hours 10 minutes; 102 miles from New York City
See also East Hampton

Settled 1652 **Pop** 1,234 **Elev** 50 ft **Area code** 631 **Zip** 11964

Information Chamber of Commerce, PO Box 598; 631/749-0399

Quakers, persecuted by the Puritans in New England, settled Shelter Island in Gardiners Bay off the east end of Long Island. The island is reached by car or pedestrian ferry from Greenport, on the north fork of Long Island, or from North Haven (Sag Harbor), on the south. There is a monument to the Quakers and a graveyard with 17th-century stones plus two historical museums; the 18th-century Havens House and the 19th-century Manhanset Chapel. Also here is the 2,200-acre Nature Conservancy's Mashomack Preserve, with miles of trails for hiking and educational programs. The island offers swimming, boating off miles of sandy shoreline, biking, hiking, tennis, and golfing.

Motels/Motor Lodges

★ ★ **DERING HARBOR INN.** *13 Winthrop Rd (11965). Phone 631/749-0900; fax 631/749-2045.* 22 rooms, 2 story. Closed Nov-Apr. Check-out noon. TV. Restaurant. Pool. Outdoor tennis. Lawn games. **$$**

★ **PRIDWIN HOTEL AND COTTAGES SHELTER ISLAND.** *81 Shore Rd (11964). Phone 631/749-0476; toll-free 800/273-2497; fax 631/749-2071.* 40 rooms, 8 kitchen units, 3 story. No elevator. Complimentary full breakfast. Check-out noon. TV. Restaurant, bar; entertainment. Game room. Pool. Outdoor tennis. **$$**

★ ★ **SUNSET BEACH.** *35 Shore Rd (11965). Phone 631/749-2001; fax 631/749-1843. www.sunsetbeachli.com.* 20 rooms, 10 kitchen units, 2 story. Complimentary continental breakfast. Check-out 11 am. TV. Restaurant, bar. **$$**

B&B/Small Inn

★ ★ ★ **RAM'S HEAD INN.** *108 Ram Island Dr (11965). Phone 631/749-0811; fax 631/749-0059. www.shelterislandinns.com.* A summer island getaway with 17 rooms, all air-conditioned, some with shared bath. Play on the beach and tennis courts and enjoy free use of sailboats and kayaks. Bicycles are for rent on the island. Book in-season weekend stays early. 17. rooms, 2 story. No A/C. Complimentary continental breakfast. Check-out noon, check-in 3 pm. Restaurant, bar. Sauna. Outdoor tennis. Colonial-style inn (1929); extensive grounds; on beach. Totally nonsmoking. **$$**

Restaurants

★ ★ ★ **CHEQUIT INN.** *23 Grand Ave (11964). Phone 631/749-0018; fax 631/749-0183. www.shelterislandinns.com.* This casual Victorian inn dishes up seafood delights and classic American cuisine for guests and visitors to the Shelter Islands. The homestyle Atlantic cod fish & chips with fresh tartar sauce is a proprietary specialty. Seafood menu. Closed Nov-mid-May. Lunch, dinner. Bar. Entertainment weekends. Inn was originally built (circa 1870) around a maple tree that, now enormous, still shades the terrace that overlooks Dering Harbor. Outdoor seating. **$$$**

★ ★ ★ **RAM'S HEAD INN.** *108 Ram Island Dr (11965). Phone 631/ 749-0811; fax 631/749-0059. www.shelterislandinns.com.* Specializes in duck,seafood. Own baking. Hours: 5-9 pm; closed Mon-Wed after Labor Day until Apr. Reservations accepted. No A/C. Bar. Wine list. Dinner. Outdoor dining. Dining room with fireplace, opens to veranda overlooking Coecles Harbor. **$$**

D

Southampton (The Hamptons)

1 hour 40 minutes; 94 miles from New York City
See also Riverhead

Settled 1640 **Pop** 54,712 **Elev** 25 ft **Area code** 631 **Zip** 11968

Information Chamber of Commerce, 76 Main St; 631/283-0402

Web www.southamptonchamber.com/

Southampton has many colonial houses. The surrounding dunes and beaches are dotted with luxury estates.

What to See and Do

Conscience Point National Wildlife Refuge. *North Sea Rd (11968). Phone 631/286-0485.* With 60 acres, this refuge is known for its maritime grass- lands. A host of birds and fowl call this area home in the colder months, and a different variety migrate here in the warmer season. The refuge opened in 1971, and over the years has played host to many guests, both feathered and non-feathered. Conscience Point, itself overlooks the North Sea Harbor and is a quiet area. This refuge is for those who want such peace and quiet while they are touring. (Hours vary)

Old Halsey House. *249 S Main St (11968). Phone 631/283-2494.* (1648) Oldest English frame house in state. Furnished with period furniture; colo- nial herb garden. (Mid-July-mid-Sept, Tues-Sun) **$$**

Parrish Art Museum. *25 Jobs Ln, town center. Phone 631/283-2118.* Includes 19th and 20th-century American paintings and prints; repository for William Merritt Chase and Fairfield Porter; Japanese woodblock prints; collection of Renaissance works; changing exhibits; arboretum; perform- ing arts and concert series; lectures; research library. (Mid-June-mid-Sept, Mon-Tues and Thurs-Sat, also Sun afternoons; rest of year, Mon and Thurs- Sun; closed holidays) **$**

Shinnecock Indian Outpost. *Old Montauk Hwy (11968). Phone 631/283- 8047. www.shinnecocktradingpost.com.* This funky shop sells tax-free cigarettes, American Indian crafts, clothes, and glassware. The prices are reasonable, and you can do your browsing and shopping quite early in the morning, should you wish to avoid too many crowds. There also is a deli, where you can get your morning coffee and bagel. The Outpost makes for an quick and easy stop before you begin your day of sightseeing. (Summer, Mon-Sun 6:30 am-7 pm, to 6 pm rest of year)

Southampton College of Long Island University. *Montauk Hwy (NY 27A). Phone 631/283-4000.* (1963) 1,200 students. Liberal arts, marine science research. Tour of campus.

Southampton Historical Museum. *17 Meeting House Ln. Phone 631/283-2494.* This mansion, built in 1843, depicts Southampton's colorful history. It has some original furnishings, American Indian items, photos, and quilts. In addition to the house, the museum's grounds include a one-room schoolhouse, drugstore, paint shop, blacksmith shop, and carpentry store. There also are special exhibits at different times of the year. (Tues-Sat 11 am-5 pm, Sun 1-5 pm) **$$**

Water Mill Museum. *41 Old Mill Rd, in Water Mill. Phone 631/726-4625.* Restored gristmill, 18th century, houses old tools, other exhibits; craft demonstrations. (Memorial Day-mid-Sept, Mon, Wed, also Sat-Sun afternoons) **$$**

Special Events

Hampton Classic Horse Show. *240 Snake Hollow Rd, N of NY 27, in Bridgehampton. Phone 631/537-3177.* Horse show jumping event. Celebrities, food, shopping, family activities. Last week Aug.

Powwow. *Shinnecock Indian Reservation, just off NY 27A. Phone 631/283-6143.* Dances, ceremonies, displays. Labor Day weekend.

Motel/Motor Lodge

★ ★ **SOUTHAMPTON INN.** *91 Hill St (11968). Phone 631/283-6500; toll-free 800/732-6500; fax 631/283-6559.* 90 rooms, 2 story. Pets accepted, some restrictions; fee. Check-out 11 am, check-in 4 pm. TV; cable (premium). In-room modem link. Restaurant, bar; entertainment; dancing Fri, Sat. Children's activity center. Outdoor pool, poolside service. Outdoor tennis. Lawn games. Concierge. **$$**

⬛ ⬛ ⬛ SC

B&B/Small Inn

★ ★ **THE VILLAGE LATCH INN.** *101 Hill St (11968). Phone 631/283-2160; fax 631/283-3236.* 67 rooms, 2 story. Pets accepted; fee. Complimentary breakfast. Check-out 11 am, check-in 4 pm. TV; cable (premium), VCR available. Pool. Outdoor pool. Outdoor tennis. **$$$**

⬛ ⬛ ⬛ ⬛

Restaurants

★ ★ **BASILICO.** *10 Windmill Ln (11968). Phone 631/283-7987.* Eclectic, northern Italian menu. Full vegetarian menu. Closed some major holidays. Lunch, dinner. Bar. Casual attire. **$$**

D

★ ★ **COAST GRILL.** *1109 Noyack Rd (11968). Phone 631/283-2277; fax 631/287-4493.* American, seafood menu. Lunch, dinner. Bar. Casual attire. **$$**
[D]

★ **GOLDEN PEAR.** *99 Main St (11968). Phone 631/283-8900; fax 631/283-7719.* American menu. Menu changes daily. Breakfast, lunch. Casual attire. **$$**

★ ★ **JOHN DUCK JR.** *15 Prospect St (11968). Phone 631/283-0311; fax 631/283-0282.* American, German menu. Closed Mon; Dec 24, 25. Lunch, dinner. Bar. Children's menu. Established 1900; 4th generation of owner-ship. Casual attire. Valet parking available. **$$**
[D]

★ ★ **LE CHEF.** *75 Jobs Ln (11968). Phone 631/283-8581; fax 631/283-0601. www.lechefbistro.com.* Continental, French menu. Lunch, dinner. Bar. Casual attire. **$$**
[D]

★ ★ **LOBSTER INN.** *162 Inlet Rd (11968). Phone 631/283-1525; fax 631/283-8159.* American, seafood menu. Closed Thanksgiving, Dec 24, 25. Lunch, dinner. Bar. Children's menu. Casual attire. Outdoor seating. **$$**
[D]

★ ★ **MIRKO'S.** *Water Mill Sq (11976). Phone 631/726-4444; fax 631/726-4472. www.mirkosrestaurant.com.* Continental menu. Specializes in pasta, seafood, veal chops. Hours: 6-11 pm; winter to 10 pm. Closed Tues; Mon-Wed in winter; also Jan. Reservations required. Bar. Dinner. Outdoor dining. Fireplace. **$$**
[D]

Southold (The Hamptons)

1 hour 48 minutes; 95 miles from New York City
See also Riverhead

Settled 1640 **Pop** 20,599 **Elev** 32 ft **Area code** 631 **Zip** 11971

Information Greenport-Southold Chamber of Commerce, 1205 Tuthill Rd Extension, 11971; 631/765-3161

What to See and Do

Greenport Pottery. *64725 Main Rd (11971). Phone 631/477-1687.* For a great selection of homemade pottery, this is the place to go on the North Fork. The owner creates beautiful, softly-colored lamps, vases, mugs, dishes, decorative plates, and other items in his shop. You can custom order items, and he will ship just about anywhere. In addition to the fine craftsmanship, the pottery is extremely reasonably priced—just a fraction of what comparable shops in the tonier Hamptons would charge. For these prices, you can buy a few items for yourself and bring some gifts for your favorite family members and friends back home. Tip: Drive slowly, because the place is small and you just might breeze past it. (Daily 10 am-5 pm; closed Tues)

Horton Point Lighthouse & Nautical Museum. *Lighthouse Park, 54325 Main Rd. Phone 631/765-5500 or 631/765-3262.* (Memorial Day-Columbus Day, Sat and Sun limited hours) **DONATION**

The Old House. *On NY 25, on the Village Green in Cutchogue. Phone 631/734-7122.* (1649) Example of early English architecture; 17th and 18th-century furnishings. Also on Village Green are the **Wickham Farmhouse** (early 1700s) and the **Old Schoolhouse Museum** (1840). (July-Labor Day, Sat-Mon; Sept-Oct, by appointment) **DONATION**

Southold Indian Museum. *Bayview Rd (11971). Phone 631/765-5577.* This museum celebrates Long Island's Native American history, and features displays of artifacts like weapons, tools, and pottery, as well as other items used by the Long Island Algonquins. Special exhibits change regularly, with some featuring Indian music and dance. Also on display are artifacts from South, Central, and Western American Indians. **$**

Motel/Motor Lodge

★ **SANTORINI BEACHCOMBER RESORT MOTEL.** *3800 Duck Pond Rd (11935). Phone 631/734-6370; fax 631/734-5579. www.santorinibeach.com.* 50 rooms, 2 story. 11 room phones. TV. Pool; wading pool. Complimentary coffee in rooms. Check-out 11 am. Game room. Refrigerators. Balconies. Swimming beach. **$**

D 🛴 ⚓

Restaurant

★ ★ **SEAFOOD BARGE.** *62980 Main Rd (11971). Phone 631/765-3010; fax 631/765-3510. www.seafoodbarge.com.* Seafood menu. Lunch, dinner. Bar. **$$**

D

Westhampton Beach (The Hamptons)

1 hours 30 minutes; 80 miles from New York City
See also Riverhead

Pop 1,902 **Elev** 10 ft **Area code** 631 **Zip** 11978

Information Greater Westhampton Chamber of Commerce, 173 Montauk Hwy, PO Box 1228; 631/288-3337

Surrounded by water, this resort area offers fishing and water sports. Nearby are hiking and nature trails.

What to See and Do

Main Street in Westhampton Beach. This is a very pleasant "in" shopping jaunt during the summer months. You can buy funky, stylish beachwear (and lots of it); children's clothing; homemade ice cream; ceramics; and books— just to name a few things. Park the car and let your feet do the rest. Tip: Try to make it out here on a weekday in summer; weekends are quite crowded.

Wertheim National Wildlife Refuge. *Approximately 10 miles W on NY 80 to Smith Rd S, in Shirley. Phone 631/286-0485.* A 2,600-acre refuge for wildlife including deer, fox, raccoon, herons, hawks, ospreys, and waterfowl. Fishing, boating, canoeing; walking trail, photography. Environmental education. (Daily) **FREE**

Restaurants

★ ★ **DORA'S.** *105 Montauk Hwy (11977). Phone 631/288-9723; fax 631/288-0607.* American menu. Closed Thanksgiving, Dec 24-25; also Mon-Wed Sept-Memorial Day. Lunch, dinner. Bar. Casual attire. **$$**

SC

★ ★ ★ **PATAGONIA WEST.** *379 Dune Rd (11978). Phone 631/288-5250; fax 631/288-5050. www.patagonia-west.com.* Argentinian menu. Closed Nov-Feb. Lunch, dinner. Bar. Casual attire. Outdoor seating. **$$$**

Hartford, CT
2 hours; 118 miles from New York City

Settled 1633 **Pop** 139,739 **Elev** 50 ft **Area code** 860

Information Greater Hartford Convention & Visitors Bureau, One Civic Center Plaza, Suite 300, 06103; 860/728-6789 or 800/446-7811 (outside CT)

Web www.enjoyhartford.com

The capital of Connecticut and a major industrial and cultural center on the Connecticut River, Hartford is headquarters for many of the nation's insurance companies.

Roots of American democracy are deep in Hartford's history. The city was made virtually independent in 1662 by Charles II, but an attempt was made by Sir Edmund Andros, governor of New England, to seize its charter. The document was hidden by Joseph Wadsworth in a hollow tree, since known as the Charter Oak. The tree was blown down in 1856; a plaque on Charter Oak Avenue marks the spot.

Hartford has what is said to be the oldest continuously published newspaper in the United States, the *Courant.* Founded in 1764, it became a daily in 1837. Trinity College (1823), the American School for the Deaf, the

Connecticut Institute for the Blind, and the Institute of Living (for mental illness) are located in the city.

Transportation

AIRPORT
Hartford Bradley International Airport. Information 860/627-3000; lost and found 860/627-3340; cash machines, Terminal B, Concourse A.

CAR RENTAL AGENCIES
See IMPORTANT TOLL-FREE NUMBERS.

PUBLIC TRANSPORTATION
Buses (Connecticut Transit), phone 860/525-9181.

RAIL PASSENGER SERVICE
Amtrak 800/872-7245.

What to See and Do

Bushnell Park. *Downtown, between Jewell, Elm, and Trinity sts. Phone 860/ 246-7739.* The 41-acre park contains 150 varieties of trees and a restored 1914 carousel (schedule varies; fee); concerts and special events (spring-fall). **FREE**

Butler-McCook Homestead and Main Street History Center. *396 Main St. Phone 860/522-1806; 860/247-8996.* (1782) Preserved house, occupied by four generations of one family (1782-1971), has possessions dating back 200 years; collection of Victorian toys; Japanese armor; Victorian garden. (Wed-Sun; closed holidays) **$$**

Center Church and Ancient Burying Ground. *60 Gold St. Phone 860/247-4080.* Church (1807) is patterned after London's St. Martin-in-the-Fields, with Tiffany stained-glass windows. Cemetery contains markers dating back to 1640.

Connecticut Audubon Society Holland Brook Nature Center. *1361 Main St. Phone 860/633-8402.* On 48 acres adjacent to Connecticut River, the center features a variety of natural history exhibits includes discovery room. Many activities. (Tues-Sun; closed holidays) **$**

Connecticut Historical Society. *1 Elizabeth St. Phone 860/236-5621.* Library contains more than 3 million books and manuscripts. (Tues-Sat; closed holidays). Museum has nine galleries featuring permanent and changing exhibits on state history (Tues-Sun). **$$$**

Connecticut River Cruise. *152 River St, Deep River. Departs from Charter Oak Landing. Phone 860/526-4954.* The *Silver Star,* a reproduction of an 1850s steam yacht, makes one- to 2 1/2-hour trips on the Connecticut River. (Memorial Day-Labor Day, daily; after Labor Day-Oct, Sat-Sun) **$$$**

Elizabeth Park. *Prospect and Asylum aves. Phone 860/242-0017.* Public gardens feature 900 varieties of roses and more than 14,000 other plants; first municipal rose garden in country; greenhouses (all year). Outdoor concerts in summer; ice-skating in winter. (Daily) **FREE**

Harriet Beecher Stowe House. *77 Forest St. Phone 860/522-9258. www. harrietbeecherstowe.org.* (1871) The restored Victorian cottage of the author of *Uncle Tom's Cabin* contains original furniture, memorabilia. Tours. (Tues-Sat, also Sun afternoons; also Mon June-Columbus Day and Dec) **$$$**

Heritage Trails Sightseeing. *Departs from Hartford hotels. Phone 860/677-8867.* Guided and narrated tours of Hartford and Farmington. (Daily) **$$$$**

Mark Twain House. *351 Farmington Ave. Phone 860/247-0998.* (1874) *Tom Sawyer, Huckleberry Finn,* and other books were published while Samuel Clemens (Mark Twain) lived in this three-story Victorian mansion featuring the decorative work of Charles Comfort Tiffany and the Associated Artists; Tiffany-glass light fixtures, windows, and Tiffany-designed stencilwork in gold and silver leaf. Tours. (May-Oct and Dec, daily; rest of year, Mon, Wed-Sun; closed holidays) **$$$**

Museum of American Political Life. *200 Bloomfield Ave, West Hartford. In the Harry Jack Gray Center. Phone 860/768-4090.* Exhibits include life-size mannequins re-creating political marches from 1830s-1960s; 70-foot wall of historical pictures and images; political television commercials since 1952. (Tues-Sun afternoons; closed holidays) **FREE**

Noah Webster Foundation and Historical Society. *227 S Main St in West Hartford. Phone 860/521-5362.* This 18th-century homestead was birthplace of America's first lexicographer, writer of the *Blue-Backed Speller* (1783) and the *American Dictionary* (1828). Period furnishings, memorabilia; costumed guides; period gardens. (Open Mon, Thurs-Sun; closed holidays) **$$**

Old State House. *800 Main St. Phone 860/522-6766.* (1796) Oldest state house in nation, designed by Charles Bulfinch; restored Senate chamber with Gilbert Stuart portrait of Washington; displays and rotating exhibitions. Tourist information center; museum shop. Guided tours by appointment. (Mon-Sat; closed holidays) **FREE**

Raymond E. Baldwin Museum of Connecticut History. *Connecticut State Library, 231 Capitol Ave, opposite Capitol. Phone 860/737-6535.* Exhibits include Colt Collection of Firearms; Connecticut artifacts, including original 1662 Royal Charter; portraits of Connecticut's governors. Library features law, social sciences, history, genealogy collections, and official state archives. (Daily; closed holidays) **FREE**

Science Center of Connecticut. *950 Trout Brook Dr in West Hartford. Phone 860/231-2824.* Computer lab; UTC Wildlife Sanctuary; physical sciences discovery room; walk-in replica of sperm whale; "KaleidoSight," a giant walk-in kaleidoscope; planetarium shows; changing exhibits. (Tues-Sat, also Sun afternoons, also Mon during summer; closed holidays) **$$$**

State Capitol. *210 Capitol Ave, at Trinity St. Phone 860/240-0222.* (1879) Guided tours (1 hour) of the restored, gold-domed capitol building and the contemporary legislative office building (Mon-Fri; closed holidays, also Dec 25-Jan 1); includes historical displays. **FREE**

Talcott Mountain State Park. *8 miles NW via US 44, off CT 185, near Simsbury. Phone 860/677-0662.* The 557-acre park features the 165-foot Heublein Tower, on mountaintop 1,000 feet above Farmington River;

considered best view in state. (Late May-late Aug Thurs-Sun 10 am-5 pm; Labor Day weekend-Oct 31 daily 10 am-5 pm) Picnicking, shelters.

University of Hartford. *4 miles W, at 200 Bloomfield Ave in West Hartford. Phone 860/768-4100.* (1877) 6,844 students. Independent institution on 320-acre campus. Many free concerts, operas, lectures, and art exhibits.

⭐ **Wadsworth Atheneum Museum of Art.** *600 Main St. Phone 860/278-2670.* One of nation's oldest continuously operating public art museums with more than 40,000 works of art, spanning 5,000 years; 15th- to 20th-century paintings, American furniture, sculpture, porcelains, English and American silver, the Amistad Collection of African-American art; changing contemporary exhibits. (Tues-Sun; closed holidays) Free admission Thurs and Sat morning.

Special Events

Christmas Crafts Expo I & II. *Hartford Civic Center. 1 Civic Center Plz (06103). Phone 860/249-6333.* Exhibits and demonstrations of traditional and contemporary craft media. First and second weekends in Dec.

Mark Twain Days. *351 Farmington Ave (06105). Phone 860/247-0998.* Celebration of Twain's legacy and Hartford's cultural heritage with more than 100 events. Concerts, riverboat rides, medieval jousting, tours of Twain House, entertainment. Aug.

Riverfest. *Charter Oak Landing and Constitution Plz. Phone 860/713-3131.* Celebration of America's independence and the Connecticut River. Family entertainment, concerts, food, fireworks display over river. Early July.

Taste of Hartford. *250 Constitution Plz, 3rd Fl. Phone 860/920-5337.* Main Street, downtown. Four-day event features specialties of more than 50 area restaurants; continuous entertainment. June.

Motels/Motor Lodges

★ ★ **HOLIDAY INN.** *363 Roberts St, East Hartford (06108). Phone 860/528-9611; toll-free 800/465-4329; fax 860/289-0270. www.holiday-inn.com.* 130 rooms, 5 story. Crib free. Pets accepted. TV; cable (premium). Indoor pool. Complimentary coffee in rooms. Restaurant 6 am-10 pm. Room service. Bar 4 pm-midnight. Check-out noon. Coin laundry. Meeting rooms. Business services available. In-room modem link. Valet service. Exercise equipment. Some refrigerators. **$**

🔁 ⛱ 🏃

★ **PARKSIDE HOTEL.** *440 Asylum St (06103). Phone 860/246-9900; fax 860/728-1382.* 96 rooms, 9 story. Pets accepted, some restrictions. Check-out noon. TV; cable (premium). Free valet parking. **$**

D 🔁 🐾 ➕ ➕

Hotels

★ ★ **CROWNE PLAZA.** *50 Morgan St (06120). Phone 860/549-2400; toll-free 800/227-6963; fax 860/549-7844. www.crowneplaza.com.* 350 rooms,

18 story. Pets accepted. Check-out noon, check-in 3 pm. TV; cable (premium), VCR available. In-room modem link. Restaurant, bar. In-house fitness room. Outdoor pool, poolside service. Free airport transportation. Business center. **$**

D 🏊 🎾 🐕 🏃 SC 🚶

★ ★ ★ **GOODWIN HOTEL.** *1 Haynes St (06013). Phone 860/246-7500; toll-free 800/922-5006; fax 860/247-4576. www.goodwinhotel.com.* If travelers are looking for luxurious comfort with impeccable service, this beautiful hotel is the place to stay. Guest suites include mahogany sleigh beds and marble baths. 124 rooms, 6 story. Check-out noon. TV; cable (premium), VCR available. In-room modem link. Fireplaces. Restaurant, bar. Room service. In-house fitness room. Valet parking. Concierge. Small, European-style luxury hotel in red-brick, Queen Anne-style building (1881) built for J. P. Morgan. **$$**

D 🐕 🏃 🏊 🚶

★ ★ ★ **HILTON HARTFORD.** *315 Trumbull St (06103). Phone 860/728-5151; fax 860/240-7246. www.hartford.hilton.com.* This hotel is conveniently located in downtown Hartford and connected to Hartford Civic Center and Civic Center Mall. 388 rooms, 22 story. Check-out noon. TV; cable (premium), VCR available. In-room modem link. Restaurant, bar. In-house fitness room, sauna. Indoor pool, whirlpool. Civic Center Plaza adjacent; shops. **$$**

D 🏊 🐕 🏃 🚶

★ ★ ★ **MARRIOTT HARTFORD ROCKY HILL AT CORPORATE RIDGE.** *100 Capital Blvd, Rocky Hill (06067). Phone 860/257-6000; toll-free 800/228-9290. www.marriott.com.* 247 rooms, 4 story. Crib free. Check-out 1 pm. TV; cable (premium). In-room modem link. Refrigerators, minibars. Restaurant 6:30 am-10 pm. Bar to midnight. Exercise equipment. Indoor pool, whirlpool. Meeting rooms, business center. Concierge. **$**

🏊 🐕 🏃

★ ★ ★ **SHERATON HARTFORD HOTEL.** *100 E River Dr, East Hartford (06108). Phone 860/528-9703; toll-free 888/530-9703; fax 860/ 289-4728. www.sheraton.com.* 199 rooms, 8 story. Crib free. Pets accepted. Check-out 11 am. TV; cable (premium). In-room modem link. Valet services, laundry. Restaurant 6:30 am-2 pm, 5-10 pm. Bar. Room service. Playgrounds. Health club privileges. Indoor pool. Meeting rooms, business services. **$**

D 🐾 🏊 🏃 🚶

Restaurants

★ ★ **APP'S.** *451 Franklin Ave (06114). Phone 860/296-2777. www.appshartford.com.* International menu. Closed Mon. Lunch, dinner. Bar. **$$$**

★ ★ **BUTTERFLY.** *831 Farmington Ave, West Hartford (06119). Phone 860/236-2816; fax 860/231-7911.* Chinese menu. Closed Thanksgiving. Lunch, dinner, Sun brunch. Bar. **$$**

D

★ ★ ★ **CARBONE'S.** *588 Franklin Ave (06114). Phone 860/296-9646; fax 860/296-2785.* Italian menu. Closed Sun; major holidays. Lunch, dinner. Bar. **$$**

D

★ **HOT TOMATOES.** *1 Union Pl (06103). Phone 860/249-5100; fax 860/524-8120.* Eclectic menu. Lunch, dinner, late night. Bar. Casual attire. Outdoor seating. **$$**

D

★ ★ **MAX DOWNTOWN.** *185 Asylum St (06103). Phone 860/522-2530; fax 860/246-5279. www.maxrestaurantgroup.com.* Closed most major holidays. Lunch, dinner. Bar. Children's menu. **$$**

D

★ ★ ★ **PASTIS.** *201 Ann St (06103). Phone 860/278-8852; fax 860/278-8854. www.pastisbrasserie.com.* Guests can enjoy an intimate dining experience at this authentic French-style bistro. Steak menu. Closed Sun. Lunch, dinner. **$$**

D

★ ★ **PEPPERCORN'S GRILL.** *357 Main St (06106). Phone 860/547-1714; fax 860/724-7612. www.peppercornsrestaurant.com.* Italian menu. Closed Sun; major holidays. Lunch, dinner. Bar. Children's menu. **$$**

D

★ **RESTAURANT BRICCO.** *78 LaSalle Rd, West Hartford (06903). Phone 860/233-0220; fax 860/233-7503.* Hours: 11:30 am-3 pm, 5-10 pm: Fri, Sat to 11pm: Sun to 9pm. Lunch, dinner. Children's menu. Patio outdoor dining. **$$**

Long Island

30-60 minutes from New York City

Long Island stretches 118 miles east by northeast from the edge of Manhattan to the lonely dunes of Montauk. Much of the island is ideal resort country, with vast white beaches, quiet bays, coves, and woods.

At the eastern tip, Montauk Light stands on its headland; on the southwestern shore is Coney Island. New York City sprawls over the whole of Long Island's two westernmost counties—Queens and Kings (the boroughs of Queens and Brooklyn).

Nassau County, adjoining the city, is made up of suburbs filled with residential communities. Eastward in Suffolk County, city influence eases, and there are firms that have attracted substantial local populations. Potatoes and the famous Long Island duckling are still raised here alongside farms for horse breeding and the vineyards producing Long Island wines.

Long Island has many miles of sandy barrier beaches along the south shore, with fine swimming and surf casting. The bays behind these make natural small-boat harbors. On the more tranquil waters of the north shore is a series of deeper harbors along Long Island Sound, many of them with beaches and offering good sailing opportunities. The island has played a major role in US history from the early 17th century; the record of this role is carefully preserved in many buildings, some 300 years old. Few regions offer such varied interests in so small an area. The Long Island Railroad conducts tours to points of interest on the island (late May to early November). For information about these escorted day excursions, write to the Long Island Railroad, Sales and Promotion Department, #1723, Jamaica 11435; phone 718/217-LIRR. For further information and special events, contact the Long Island Convention & Visitors Bureau, 350 Vanderbilt Motor Pkwy, Suite 103, Hauppage 11788; phone 800/441-4601.

Long Island towns listed in this section are Bethpage, Garden City, Huntington, Oyster Bay, Stony Brook, and Westbury.

What to See and Do

American Airpower Museum. *1300 New Hwy, Farmingdale (11735). Phone 631/293-6398. www.americanpowermuseum.com.* This museum, located in a former hangar of the Republic Aviation Company, is a must for aviation and history buffs. Original warplanes from various battles and eras of the 20th century are on display, along with equipment, vintage flying gear, and maps. The museum also hosts special events. (Thurs-Sun 10:30 am-4 pm) **$$**

Big Duck. *Rte 24, in Flanders. Phone 631/852-8292.* Long Islanders love their ducks! In honor of the quacking animal, this goofy South Fork gift shop and museum is visible from the road as a 20-foot-high white concrete duck (seriously!). The attraction is actually listed on the National Register of Historic Places. The museum portion has various duck items and photos on display. For sale in the shop are specialties like duck-embossed T-shirts, caps, boxer shorts, and ties—knickknacks at their silliest. Both adults and kids will get a kick out of this place. (May-Sept 10 am-5 pm; weekends only through Nov)

Duck Walk Vineyards. *231 Montauk Hwy, in Water Mill. (11976). Phone 631/726-7555. www.duckwalk.com.* This light and airy winery on the South Fork produces some very interesting wines, including a delicately sweet blueberry port that goes great with chocolate, and a boysenberry dessert wine. Duck Walk produces other, more traditional varieties as well, such as merlot and chardonnay. The winery's tasting room sells wines, preserves, books, and other souvenirs. There are verandas overlooking the vineyards to sit, have a leisurely picnic, and enjoy music on weekends in summer. Tours are given Sat-Sun at noon, 2 pm, and 4 pm in the off-season and every day in the warmer months. (Daily 11 am-6 pm) **FREE**

Elizabeth A. Morton National Wildlife Refuge. *Noyac Rd, in Shirley. (11967). Phone 631/286-0485.* At one time, Native American tribes inhabited this area. Today, a variety of birds—some endangered—call this 187-acre refuge home at different times of the year. Both adults and children alike will enjoy observing our feathered friends in the peaceful surroundings, or walking on the nature trail that stretches onto part of a beach. **$**

Holocaust Memorial. *100 Crescent Beach Rd, in Glen Cove (11542). Phone 516/571-8040. www.holocaust-nassau.org.* Exhibits in this small center depicting one of the most devastating events in modern history include sculptures, photographs, and paintings. You also can read accounts of survivors, attend lectures, and view portraits of children who perished during the Nazis' reign of terror in Europe. This is not for the faint-hearted. The center is located on a 204-acre preserve and offers various nature trails. **FREE**

Jones Beach State Park. *Ocean Dr, in Wantash. Phone 516/785-1600. www.nyparks.com.* Many native New Yorkers flock to this 6-mile beachfront when the mercury starts to climb. But this state park has more than a great beach. It offers two Olympic-sized pools, 14 cafeterias and snack stands, playgrounds, basketball courts, a boat basin, paddle tennis courts, a boardwalk for strolling, and softball fields. Pool admission is cheap ($1 to $3), and parking is also inexpensive and plentiful. You can even take a bus from the city if you don't have a car. Bring plenty of sunscreen and plan to spend the whole day. **$**

Quogue Wildlife Refuge and Nature Center. *3 Old Country Rd, in Quogue. (11959). Phone 631/653-4771. www.dec.state.ny.us.* If you enjoy the beauty of nature and the pleasure of animals, this is a place that will be very special to you. The refuge's 305 acres are filled with birds, ducks, geese, and flora and fauna, and include the Distressed Wildlife Complex, which takes care of hurt animals and provides care for them; its keepers have aided a number of species, including hawks and eagles. Special classes and programs are offered here, such as nature walks, field trips, and a summer day camp for children. (Nature Center: Feb-Nov, Tues-Thurs 1-4 pm; Refuge: year-round dawn-dusk) **FREE**

Science Museum of Long Island. *1526 N Plandome Rd, in Plandome. (11030). Phone 516/627-9400.* This is not a traditional museum, but rather a hands-on education center for the study of natural sciences. Children over 3 years may participate in the special workshops and programs, but pre-registration is required. The museum is located in a peaceful setting—36 acres of streams and beachfront. A fun family experience will be had by all, especially the little ones. (Daily from 9 am)

Tilles Center for the Performing Arts. *Rte 25A, CW Post Campus of Long Island University, in Brookville. (11545). Phone 516/299-3100. www.tillescenter.org.* From Michael Feinstein to the New York Philharmonic to the Alvin Ailey American Dance Theater, this center features a variety of music, dance, and theater performers from all walks of life. Well-known performers and lesser-known chamber music concerts and cabaret stars have all appeared at Tilles. The center also hosts local cultural organizations. In addition, it offers a jazz series and folk music festival. It tends to have something for just about every taste year after year. Both young and old will find an event to enjoy at this eclectic concert venue. Prices also vary, and can suit most budgets.

Special Events

Jones Beach Coca-Cola Concert Series. *Tommy Hilfiger at Jones Beach Theater, Ocean Dr, in Wantagh (11793). Phone 516/221-1000. www.jonesbeach.com.* Combine an outdoor amphitheater right off the Atlantic Ocean in a beautiful state park, good friends or that special someone, a balmy summer night, and some of the top names in rock 'n roll, blues, and R&B, and you have one great evening at a Jones Beach concert. Performers vary from summer to summer and have included such legends as Rod Stewart, George Benson, the Moody Blues, Tina Turner, and James Taylor. The crowd is usually mellow and easy-going and varies in age, depending upon the performers. Bring a light jacket or sweater, since ocean breezes can create a slight chill—even on the warmest nights. Word of caution: performances are usually rain or shine with no refunds, so if the skies start to open up you may get drenched. But, this is the chance you take at an outdoor venue. It's worth it. June-Sept.

P. S. 1 Contemporary Arts Center–Warm Up Music Series. *22-25 Jackson Ave in Long Island City (11101). Phone 718/784-2084. www.ps1.org.* This new-wave community arts center in Queens attracts the hippest of DJs and crowds to its Saturday afternoon/evening outdoor dance parties in its courtyard. You won't see dance parties like these anywhere else. All ages are welcome. You'll see a variety of social butterflies and some pretty good dancers here. The center is a short subway or cab ride from Manhattan, and you can't beat the price—so join in the fun. July-Aug; Sat evenings. **$$**

Bethpage (Long Island)

37 minutes; 35 miles from New York City

Pop 16,543 **Elev** 106 ft **Area code** 516 **Zip** 11714

What to See and Do

Bethpage State Park. *Bethpage State Pkwy (11735). Phone 516/249-0700.* 1,475 acres. Hiking, biking, golf (five 18-hole courses), tennis, bridle paths, game fields, picnicking, cross-country skiing. Standard fees. **FREE**

Old Bethpage Village Restoration. *Round Swamp Rd and exit 48. Phone 516/572-8401.* More than 25 pre-Civil War buildings including carpentry, and hat shops, general store, tavern, schoolhouse, church, homes; working farm and craftsmen depict life of mid-1800s; film. Picnic area. (Mar-Dec, Wed-Sun; closed winter holidays) **$$$**

Restaurant

★ **56TH FIGHTER GROUP.** *Rte 110 Republic Airport, Farmington (11735). Phone 631/694-8280; fax 631/694-6011. www.specialtyrestaurant.com.*

Continental menu. Specializes in seafood. Hours: 11 am-3 pm, 4-10 pm; Fri, Sat to midnight; Sun from 4 pm. Lunch, dinner, Sun brunch. Bar 11 am-midnight; weekends to 3:30 am. Children's menu. Reservations required. Outdoor dining. **$$**

D

Garden City (Long Island)

33 minutes; 28 miles from New York City
See also Westbury

Pop 21,672 **Elev** 90 ft **Area code** 516 **Zip** 11530

Information Chamber of Commerce, 230 Seventh St; 516/746-7724

What to See and Do

Cradle of Aviation Museum. *Charles Lindbergh Blvd (11530). Phone 516/572-4111. www.cradleofaviation.org.* This new addition to the area celebrates aviation and space travel, and has been a big hit with both adults and children. With an emphasis on Long Island's important and colorful history in the field of aviation, the museum offers exhibits on World War I, World War II, the Jet Age, and Space Travel, to name a few. There also is an IMAX Theater, which features different films with a feel-like-you-are-there sensation. The Red Planet Café is a respite and place for a snack, and the Museum Store is a must-stop for souvenir hunters. If you or your children have any kind of interest in aviation, you will not want to miss this attraction. (Mon-Sun 10 am-5 pm) **$$$**

Long Island Children's Museum. *11 David Blvd (11530). Phone 516/222-0207. www.licm.org.* This new, very popular museum that is located in a former military base offers many hands-on, interactive exhibits to amuse and educate the little ones. Some of these include a bubble machine that allows children to create bubbles (always a favorite for kids!), climbing ramps, and a beach exhibit that lets kids shape their own sand dune. There also are performances on weekends and programs held during the week. This is a great way to spend an afternoon and the kids are sure to enjoy it. Don't forget to stop by the gift shop for a cute trinket before you leave. The Cradle of Aviation Museum is housed here and additional museums are being planned for the future. (Wed-Sun 10 am-5 pm) **$$**

Roosevelt Field. *Old Country Rd (11530). Phone 516/742-8000. www.shopsimn.com.* Think of just about any item you want to buy, from big to small, inexpensive to pricey, and you can find it here at the nation's fifth-largest mall. Roosevelt Field has 2.3 million square feet of space and 260 stores in a massive space that takes a road map and a tour guide to navigate. Department stores include Nordstrom, Macy's, Sears, and JC Penney. There are also dozens of smaller specialty shops that sell everything from clothing and toys to jewelry and furniture to books and candy. A huge food court offers just about any kind of cheap, quick meal and snack you can imagine. Big shopping holidays (e.g. Memorial Day, and the day after Christmas) and weekends tend to get very crowded, so plan to arrive in the morning. The place is so big that valet parking is even available. (Mon-Sat 10 am-9:30 pm, Sun 11 am-7 pm) **FREE**

Special Event

Antique Car Parade. *Franklin Ave.* More than 300 antique and vintage cars. Easter Sun. Contact the Chamber of Commerce.

Restaurants

★ ★ **AKBAR.** *1 Ring Rd (11530). Phone 516/248-5700; fax 516/248-1835.* Northern Indian menu. Hours: noon-3 pm, 5:30-10 pm; Fri, Sat to 11 pm; Sun noon-3 pm, 5-10 pm; Sun brunch to 3 pm. Reservations required. Service bar. Indian décor. **$**

D

★ ★ **ORCHID.** *730 Franklin Ave (11530). Phone 516/742-1116.* Chinese menu. Specializes in Hunan and Szechwan dishes. Hours: 11:30 am-10 pm; Fri to 11 pm; Sat noon-11 pm; Sun 1-10 pm. Closed Thanksgiving. Reservations required. Bar. Elaborate décor; etched glass and murals. **$**

D

Huntington (Long Island)

48 minutes; 38 miles from New York City
See also Oyster Bay

Settled 1653 **Pop** 195,289 **Elev** 60 ft **Area code** 516 **Zip** 11743

Information Huntington Township Chamber of Commerce, 288 Main St; 516/423-6100

Web www.huntingtonchamber.com

Although the expanding suburban population of New York City has reached Huntington, 37 miles east on Long Island, it still retains its rural character. Huntington is a township including 17 communities, in which there are more than 100 industrial plants. The area has five navigable harbors and 51 miles of shorefront.

What to See and Do

Cold Spring Harbor Whaling Museum. *Main St, 2 miles W on NY 25A, in Cold Spring Harbor. Phone 631/367-3418.* Fully equipped 19th-century whale boat from the brig *Daisy* is on display. Marine paintings, scrimshaw, ship models, changing exhibit gallery. "Mark Well the Whale" permanent exhibit documents Long Island's whaling industry. Permanent exhibit "The Wonder of Whales" includes a hands-on whale bones display, a killer whale skull, and whale conservation information. (Memorial Day-Labor Day, daily; rest of year, Tues-Sun) **$$**

David Conklin Farmhouse. *2 High St at New York Ave. Phone 631/427-7045.* (circa 1750) Four generations of Conklin family lived here. Period rooms (Colonial, Federal, Victorian). (Tues-Fri and Sun; closed holidays) **$$** Other historic buildings include

> **Huntington Trade School.** *209 Main St. Phone 631/427-7045.* (1905) School building houses the offices of the Huntington Historical Society and a history research library. (Tues-Fri) **$$**

> **Kissam House.** *434 Park Ave* (1795) Federal house, barn, sheepshed, and outbuildings; home of early Huntington physicians. Period rooms (1800-1850). (Sun afternoons; closed holidays) **$$**

Heckscher Museum of Art. *2 Prime Ave (11743). Heckscher Park, Prime Ave and NY 25A (Main St). Phone 631/351-3250.* Permanent collection of European and American art dating from 16th century; changing exhibits. (Tues-Sun; closed Thanksgiving, Dec 25) **DONATION**

Joseph Lloyd Manor House. *Lloyd Ln and Lloyd Harbor Rd (11743). Phone 631/271-7760.* (1767) Large colonial manor house, elegantly furnished; 18th-century garden. (Memorial Day-mid-Oct, Sat and Sun afternoons) **$**

Sunken Meadow State Park. *Sunken Meadow Pkwy N and NY 25A (11754). Approximately 9 miles E of town on NY 25A. Phone 631/269-4333.* Swimming beach, bathhouse, fishing (all year); nature, hiking, and biking trails; three 9-hole golf courses (fee). Picnicking, playground, concession. Cross-country skiing. Recreation programs. Standard fees. **$$$**

Target Rock National Wildlife Refuge. *8 miles N via West Neck Rd, follow onto Lloyd Harbor Rd. Phone 631/286-0485.* An 80-acre refuge with hardwood forest, pond, and beach. Fishing; photography, nature trail, wildlife nature study, and environmental education. (Daily) **$$**

Walt Whitman Birthplace State Historic Site. *246 Old Walt Whitman Rd, Huntington Station. Phone 631/427-5240. www.nysparks.com.* The writer is well known on Long Island, where streets and malls are named for him. This simple home, which features 19th-century furnishings (including Whitman's schoolmaster's desk), offers a tour with a video, as well as an exhibit that tells the story of Whitman's life. There is also a tape available of the author himself reading one of his poems. (Mon-Fri 11 am-4 pm, Sat-Sun noon-5 pm; closed holidays) **$**

Special Events

Huntington Summer Arts Festival. *Heckscher Park Amphitheater. 213 Main St (11743). Phone 631/271-8442.* Local, national, and international artists perform dance, folk, classical, jazz, theater, and family productions. Late June-mid-Aug, Tues-Sun.

Long Island Fall Festival at Huntington. *Hickscher Park (11743). Phone 631/423-6100.* Entertainment, carnival, sailboat regatta, food, wine tasting, family activities. Mid-Oct.

Hotels

★ ★ ★ **HILTON HUNTINGTON.** *598 Broad Hollow Rd (11747). Phone 631/845-1000; toll-free 800/445-8667; fax 631/845-1223. www.hilton.com.* This hotel has a great location for travelers visiting the Hamptons, Jones Beach and New York City. Guests enter to find an atrium lobby with running waterfalls and a tropical setting. 302 rooms, 5 story. Crib free. TV; cable (premium), VCR available (movies). Two pools, one indoor; whirlpool, poolside service, lifeguard. Restaurant 6:30 am-11 pm. Bar 11-2 am; entertainment. Check-out noon. Convention facilities. Business services available. In-room modem link. Concierge. Gift shop. Lighted tennis. Exercise equipment. Bathroom phones, minibars; wet bar in suites. **$$**

D ⧖ ⌕ ⅄ ⬎

★ **HUNTINGTON COUNTRY INN.** *270 W Jericho Tpke (11746). Phone 631/421-3900; toll-free 800/739-5777; fax 631/421-5287. www.huntington countryinn.com.* 64 rooms, 2 story. Pets accepted. Complimentary continental breakfast. Check-out noon. TV; cable (premium). Health club privileges. Pool. **$**

D ⧖ ⅊ ⌕ ⅄ ⬎ SC

Oyster Bay (Long Island)

40 minutes; 34 miles from New York City

Settled 1653 **Pop** 6,826 **Elev** 20 ft **Area code** 516 **Zip** 11771

Information Chamber of Commerce, 120 South St, PO Box 21; 516/922-6464

What to See and Do

Coe Hall. *Lexington Ave and Mill River Rd. Phone 516/922-0479.* (1918) Tudor-revival mansion (65 rooms) was a country estate for Coe and his family. Various 16th- and 17th-century furnishings imported from Europe contribute to its atmosphere of a historic English country house. Guided tours. (Daily) **$$**

Planting Fields Arboretum. *Planting Fields Rd, 1-1/2 miles W, off NY 25A. Phone 516/922-9201 or 516/922-9200.* A 400-acre estate of the late William Robertson Coe. Landscaped plantings (150 acres); large collections of azaleas and rhododendrons; self-guided tour; guided tours available; nature trails; greenhouses. (May-Labor Day, daily; rest of year, weekends) **$$**

Raynham Hall Museum. *20 W Main St. Phone 516/922-6808.* Historic colonial house museum with Victorian wing. Home of Samuel Townsend, a prosperous merchant; headquarters for the Queens Rangers during the Revolutionary War. Victorian garden. (Tues-Sun) **$**

★ **Sagamore Hill National Historic Site.** *20 Sagamore Hill Rd (11771). Phone 516/922-4447. www.nps.gov/sahi.* For a price that you simply can't beat, take a 45-55-minute tour of the historic home of former President Theodore Roosevelt. The 23-room mansion has been painstakingly preserved, and shows off the many animal trophies that Roosevelt caught in his legendary hunting trips. The home also features exotic gifts that Roosevelt received from his overseas trips, and well as original furnishings and paintings. Nearby is the Theodore Roosevelt Sanctuary, which cares for injured birds and offers nature walks. The whole experience is a must for history buffs and fans of this colorful, larger-than-life president. (Daily 9:30 am-4 pm; closed Mon and Tues, Oct-May) **$**

Theodore Roosevelt Sanctuary & Audubon Center. *134 Cove Rd (11771). Phone 516/922-3200.* Owned by the National Audubon Society, the memorial contains 12 acres of forest and nature trails. The sanctuary serves as a memorial to Theodore Roosevelt's pioneering conservation achievements. Museum contains displays on Roosevelt and the conservation movement; bird exhibits. Adjacent in Young's Cemetery is **Theodore Roosevelt's grave.** Trails, bird-watching, library. (Daily) **FREE**

Special Events

Friends of the Arts Long Island Summer Festival. *Planting Fiedls Arboretum. Phone 516/922-0061. www.friendsofthearts.com.* For the ultimate evening in great music and relaxation at prices at prices as low as $20 for lawn seats, venture out to this beautiful 409-acre Gold Coast estate. The annual festival specializes in blues, jazz, and easy listening concerts, and has offered up such artists as Michael Feinstein, David Sanborn, David Benoit, and Natalie Cole. Forget the more expensive pavilion seats and buy lawn seats. This way you can bring a picnic with your favorite wines and cheeses. And don't forget your blanket, chairs, plenty of bug repellent, a light jacket, and, of course, that special someone. The crowd tends to be a bit more mature, but very mellow and polite. Arrive at least 1 1/2 hours before the concert starts to scope out your spot on the lawn and to spend some time admiring the flower gardens. One negative: The concerts go on rain or shine. Evenings in June-Sept.

Oyster Festival. *120 South St. Phone 516/922-6464 or 516/624-8082.* Street festival, arts and crafts. Usually weekend after Columbus Day.

Motel/Motor Lodge

★ ★ **EAST NORWICH INN.** *6321 Northern Blvd (11732). Phone 516/922-1500; toll-free 800/334-4798; fax 516/922-1089. www.eastnorwichinn.com.* Located on Long Island's north shore, this quaint property is ideal for a weekend away from the city. 65 rooms, 5 suites, 2 story. Complimentary continental breakfast. Check-out noon. TV; cable (premium). In-room modem link. Exercise equipment, sauna. Heated pool. **$**

D ⇌ 𝅚 ⛷

Restaurants

★ **CANTERBURY ALES OYSTER BAR & GRILL.** *46 Audrey Ave (11771). Phone 516/922-3614; fax 516/922-3730.* Specializes in mesquite-grilled seafood. Hours: 11:30 am-11 pm; Fri, Sat to 1 am; Sun brunch to 3 pm. Closed Thanksgiving, Dec 25. Reservations accepted. Bar. Lunch, dinner. Sun brunch. Children's menu. Parking. New England fish house atmosphere with bistro flair. Historic Teddy Roosevelt library in rear, includes photos. **$$**

D

★ ★ ★ **MILL RIVER INN.** *160 Mill River Rd (11771). Phone 516/922-7768; fax 516/922-4978.* The menu at this creative American restaurant changes weekly. Though the experience is upscale, the dress is business casual. Menu changes daily. Hours: 6-10 pm; Sun 5-10 pm. Closed Dec 25. Dinner. Bar. Reservations required. **$$$**

Stony Brook (Long Island)

1 hour; 60 miles from New York City

Settled 1655 **Pop** 13,727 **Elev** 123 ft **Area code** 631 **Zip** 11790

Originally part of the Three Village area first settled by Boston colonists in the 17th century, Stony Brook became an important center for the shipbuilding industry on Long Island Sound in the 1800s.

What to See and Do

The Museums at Stony Brook. *On NY 25A. Phone 631/751-0066.* Complex of three museums. The Melville Carriage House exhibits 90 vehicles from a collection of horse-drawn carriages. The Art Museum features changing exhibits of American art. The Blackwell History Museum has changing exhibits on a variety of historical themes as well as exhibits of period rooms and antique decoys. Blacksmith shop, schoolhouse, other period buildings. Museum store. (Wed-Sun and Mon holidays; closed other holidays) **$$**

State University of New York at Stony Brook. *Phone 631/689-6000.* (1957) 17,500 students. Academic units include College of Arts and Sciences, College of Engineering and Applied Sciences, and Health Sciences Center. Museum of Long Island Natural Sciences has permanent displays on Long Island natural history. Art galleries in the Melville Library, Staller Center, and the Student Union.

Staller Center for the Arts. *Nicholas Rd and Rte 347 (11794). Phone 631/632-7235, box office phone 631/632-7230.* Houses 1,049-seat main theater, three experimental theaters, art gallery, 400-seat recital hall, and electronic music studio. Summer International Theater Festival. Events all year.

B&B/Small Inn

★ ★ ★ **THREE VILLAGE INN.** *150 Main St (11790). Phone 631/751-0555; toll-free 888/384-4438; fax 631/751-0593. www.threevillageinn.com.* Step back in time with elegance at this harborside inn. Taste buds will dance with delectable meals and homemade breads! Enjoy village shopping and museums; nearby Stonybrook University and Hospital. 26 rooms, 2 story. Crib $10. Check-out noon. Check-in 3 pm. TV; cable. Restaurant (see THREE VILLAGE INN). Bar. Picnic tables. Meeting rooms. Business services available. Some fireplaces. Built in the late 1700s. **$$**

Restaurants

★ ★ ★ **COUNTRY HOUSE.** *NY 25A (11790). Phone 631/751-3332. www.countryhouse.com.* A top choice for American cuisine on the island. The romantic and elegant setting is perfect for special-occasion dining. Specializes in creative American cuisine. Lunch, dinner. Hours: noon-3 pm, 5-10 pm. Closed Jan 1, July 4, Dec 25. Reservations accepted; required dinner. Bar. House built in 1710. **$$**

D

★ ★ **THREE VILLAGE INN.** *150 Main St (11790). Phone 631/751-0555; fax 631/751-0593. www.threevillageinn.com.* Closed Dec 25. Breakfast, lunch, dinner, Sun brunch. Bar. Children's menu. Near harbor. Colonial homestead built in 1751. Attractive grounds; country dining. **$$$**

D

Westbury (Long Island)

30 minutes; 28 miles from New York City

Pop 14,263 **Elev** 100 ft **Area code** 516 **Zip** 11590

What to See and Do

Clark Botanic Garden. *193 I. U. Willets Rd, in Albertson. Phone 516/484-8600.* The 12-acre former estate of Grenville Clark. Includes Hunnewell Rose Garden; ponds, streams; bulbs, perennials, annuals; wildflower, herb, rock, rhododendron, azalea, and daylily gardens; children's garden; groves of white pine, dogwood, and hemlock. (Daily)

Old Westbury Gardens. *71 Old Westbury Rd (11030). Phone 516/333-0048. www.oldwestburygardens.org.* Step back in time to this grand estate, with a historic mansion that dates back to 1906. The 66-room house features grand paintings, magnificent furniture, and wonderful trinkets of all kinds. The gardens, which are delightful to stroll through, are a main attraction. They have a variety of flora and fauna that change with the seasons. Save this attraction for a pleasant sunny day in any season except winter. (Daily 10 am-5 pm; winter hours vary; closed Tues) **$$$**

Westbury Music Fair. *960 Brush Holow Rd (11590). Phone 516/334-0800. www.musicfair.com.* This concert series offers a unique chance to see performances in the theater-in-the-round style. Most of the stars are a bit from yesteryear, and have included Paul Anka, Ringo Starr, Aaron Neville, and Tony Bennett. But, you're sure to have an enjoyable evening. The crowd is usually a bit older and pretty sedate.

Restaurants

★ ★ **BENNY'S.** *199 Post Ave (11590). Phone 516/997-8111.* Northern Italian menu. Closed Sun; major holidays; also last 2 weeks Aug. Lunch, dinner. Reservations required. **$$**

D

★ ★ **CAFÉ BACI.** *1636 Old Country Rd (11590). Phone 516/832-8888; fax 516/222-0769.* Italian, American menu. Specializes in pasta, salad, pizza. Lunch, dinner. Bar. Casual dining. **$**

D

★ ★ **GIULIO CESARE.** *18 Ellison Ave (11590). Phone 516/334-2982.* Italian menu. Closed Sun; major holidays. Lunch, dinner. Bar. **$$$**

D

Mystic, CT

2 hours 30 minutes; 137 miles from New York City

Settled 1654 **Pop** 2,618 **Elev** 16 ft **Area code** 860 **Zip** 06355

Information Tourist Information Center, Building 1D, Olde Mistick Village; 860/536-1641; or Connecticut's Mystic & More!, 470 Bank St, PO Box 89, New London 06320; 860/444-2206 or 800/TO-ENJOY (outside CT)

Web www.mysticmore.com

The community of Mystic, divided by the Mystic River, was a shipbuilding and whaling center from the 17th to the 19th centuries. It derives its name from the Pequot, "Mistuket."

What to See and Do

Denison Homestead. *120 Pequotsepos Rd (06359). 2 miles E of I-95 exit 90, on Pequotsepos Rd. Phone 860/536-9248.* (1717) Restored in the style of five eras (18th to mid-20th centuries); furnished with heirlooms of 11 generations of a single family. Guided tour (Mid-May–mid-Oct, Wed-Mon afternoons; rest of year, by appointment). **$$**

Denison Pequotsepos Nature Center. *109 Pequotsepos Rd. 2 miles NE of I-95 exit 90, on Pequotsepos Rd. Phone 860/536-1216.* An environmental education center and natural history museum active in wildlife rehabilitation. The 125-acre sanctuary has more than 7 miles of trails; family nature walks, films, lectures. (Daily; closed holidays) **$$**

Mystic Aquarium. *55 Coogan Blvd. Phone 860/536-3323.* The exhibits here feature more than 6,000 live specimens from all the world's waters. Demonstrations with dolphins, sea lions, and the only whales in New England delight young and old alike, as do Seal Island, an outdoor exhibit of seals and sea lions in natural settings, and the penguin pavilion. The facility also includes Dr. Robert Ballard's Institute for Exploration, which is dedicated to searching the deep seas for lost ships. The museum's Challenge of the Deep exhibit allows patrons to use state-of-the-art technology to re-create the search for the *Titanic* or explore the biology of undersea ocean vents.(Daily; hours vary by season; closed Jan 1, Thanksgiving, Dec 25) **$$$$**

★ **Mystic Seaport.** *75 Greenmanville Ave (CT 27), 1 mile S of I-95 exit 90. Phone 860/572-5315. www.visitmysticseaport.com.* This 17-acre complex is the nation's largest maritime museum, dedicated to preservation of 19th-century maritime history. Visitors may board the 1841 wooden whaleship *Charles W. Morgan*, square-rigged ship *Joseph Conrad*, or fishing schooner *L. A. Dunton*. Collection also includes some 400 smaller vessels; representative seaport community with historic homes and waterfront industries, some staff in 19th-century costume; exhibits, demonstrations, working shipyard; children's museum, planetarium (fee), 1908 steamboat cruises (May-Oct, daily; fee); restaurants; shopping; special events throughout the year. (Daily; closed Dec 25) **$$$$**

Olde Mistick Village. *Coogan Blvd and CT 27. Phone 860/536-4941.* More than 60 shops and restaurants in 1720s-style New England village, on 22 acres; duck pond, millwheel, waterfalls; entertainment, carillon (May-Oct, Sat and Sun). Village (daily). **FREE**

Special Event

Lobsterfest. *Mystic Seaport. Phone 860/572-5315.* Outdoor food festival. Late May.

Motels/Motor Lodges

★ ★ **DAYS INN.** *55 Whitehall Ave (06355). Phone 860/572-0574; toll-free 800/572-3993; fax 860/572-1164. www.whghotels.com.* 122 rooms, 2 story. Check-out 11 am. TV. In-room modem link. Restaurant 6 am-9 pm; Fri, Sat to 10 pm. Room service. Health club privileges. Pool. Airport transportation. **$**

D ⚹ 🏊 🎿 ⛷ SC

★ ★ ★ **TWO TREES INN.** *240 Indian Tower Rd (06339). Phone 860/312-3000; toll-free 800/369-9663; fax 860/312-4050. www.pequotcasino.com.* For the adventurous traveler, this cozy inn is adjacent to the Foxwoods Resort Casino and has a 24-hour courtesy shuttle to get visitors there. 280 rooms, 3 story, 60 suites. Crib $10. TV; cable (premium), VCR available. Indoor pool; whirlpool. Complimentary continental breakfast. Restaurant 11:30 am-10 pm. Check-out noon. Business services available. Bellstaff. Health club privileges. Refrigerators. Foxwoods Casino adjacent. **$**

D 🏊 ⛷ SC

Hotels

★ **COMFORT INN.** *48 Whitehall Ave (06355). Phone 860/572-8531; toll-free 800/572-9339; fax 860/572-9358. www.whghotels.com.* 120 rooms, 2 story. Complimentary continental breakfast. Check-out 11 am, check-in 3 pm. TV. Babysitting services available. In-house fitness room. **$**

D 🐕 ⛷ ⛷ SC

★ ★ ★ **HILTON MYSTIC.** *20 Coogan Blvd (06355). Phone 860/572-0731; toll-free 800/445-8667; fax 860/572-0328. www.hilton.com.* Conveniently located in the heart of Mystic, the hotel is just minutes from popular attractions including museums, outlets, and the aquarium. 182 rooms, 4 story. Check-out 11 am, check-in 3 pm. TV; cable (premium). In-room modem link. Laundry services. Restaurant, bar. Room service. Children's activity center. In-house fitness room. Indoor pool. Free valet parking. **$**

D ⚹ 🏊 🐕 ⛷

B&B/Small Inns

★ **APPLEWOOD FARMS INN.** *528 Colonel Ledyard Hwy (06339). Phone 860/536-2022; toll-free 800/717-4262; fax 860/536-6015. www.visitmystic.com/applewoodfarmsinn.* 5 rooms, 1 suite, 2 story. No room phones. Pets accepted, some restrictions. Children over 8 years only. Complimentary breakfast. Check-out 11 am, check-in 3 pm. Putting green. Picnic tables. House built 1826, once used as town hall; many fireplaces. Colonial atmosphere. **$**

🐾 ⛷

★ ★ ★ **INN AT MYSTIC.** *Jct US 1 and CT 27 (06355). Phone 860/536-9604; toll-free 800/237-2415; fax 860/572-1635. www.innatmystic.com.* Built hillside, overlooking the harbor and sound, this remarkable inn offers simple elegance during any season. With complimentary tours of the gardens, afternoon tea and pastries, and luxurious guestrooms, this inn is a special treat. 67 rooms, 2 story. Pets accepted. Check-out 11 am, check-in 3 pm. TV;

cable (premium), VCR available. Fireplaces. Restaurant, bar. Room service. Outdoor pool. Outdoor tennis. Long Island Sound 1/4 mile. **$**

★ ★ **THE OLD MYSTIC INN.** *52 Main St, Old Mystic (06372). Phone 860/572-9422; fax 860/572-9954. www.oldmysticinn.com.* 8 rooms, 2 story. No room phones. Check-out 11 am, check-in 2 pm. TV in sitting room; cable. In-room modem link. Lawn games. Built in 1794; early American décor. **$$**

★ ★ **WHALER'S INN.** *20 E Main St (06355). Phone 860/536-1506; toll-free 800/243-2588; fax 860/572-1250.* 49 rooms, 2 story. Complimentary continental breakfast. Check-out 11, check-in 2 pm. TV. In-room modem link. Restaurant. Babysitting services available. Built 1865; colonial décor. **$**

Casino

★ ★ ★ **FOXWOODS RESORT CASINO.** *39 Norwich-Westerly Rd, Ledyard (06339). Phone 860/312-3000. www.foxwoods.com.* The largest casino in the Western Hemishphere, this property features live entertainment, countless restaurants, and nearby golf. 1,417 rooms in 3 buildings, 247 suites, 3 presidential suites, 12 villas. Crib $10. Check-out noon. TV; cable (premium), VCR available. In-room modem link. Some refrigerators. Restaurant open 24 hours. Bar; entertainment. Exercise room. Indoor pool, whirlpool, lifeguard. Barber, beauty shop. Free garage, valet parking. Meeting rooms. Business services. Concierge. Connected to casino. **$$**

Restaurants

★ ★ ★ **BRAVO BRAVO.** *20 E Main St (06355). Phone 860/536-3228.* Creative gourmet dining located in the Whaler's Inn. Lunch is served outdoors and dinner is served inside the beautifully decorated dining room at this local favorite. Italian menu. Closed Mon. Lunch, dinner. Bar. Entertainment. Casual attire. Reservations required. **$$$**

★ ★ ★ **FLOOD TIDE.** *Jct US 1 and CT 27 (06355). Phone 860/536-8140; fax 860/572-1635. www.innatmystic.com.* Complimentary hors d'oeuvres are served in the piano lounge. Gourmet dishes are impressive, and Sunday brunch is spectacular. Continental, French menu. Closed 10 days in Jan. Breakfast, dinner, brunch. Bar. Piano. Children's menu. Casual attire. Reservations required. Outdoor seating. **$$$**

★ ★ **GO FISH.** *Olde Mistick Village (06355). Phone 860/536-2662; fax 860/536-4619.* Seafood menu. Lunch, dinner. Bar. Entertainment. Children's menu. Casual attire. Reservations required. In Olde Mistick Village. **$$**

D

★ **MYSTIC PIZZA.** *56 W Main St (06355). Phone 860/536-3700. www.mystic-pizza.com.* Pizza. Closed Easter, Thanksgiving, Dec 25. Lunch, dinner. Bar. Casual attire. Popular pizza parlor immortalized in the Julia Roberts film of the same name. **$**

D

★ ★ **SEAMEN'S INNE.** *105 Greenmanville Ave (06355). Phone 860/536-9649; fax 860/572-5304. www.seamensinne.com.* Seafood menu. Closed Dec 25. Breakfast, lunch, dinner. Bar. Family entertainment Wed-Sun. Children's menu. 19th-century sea captain's house décor; overlooks river. Casual attire. Outdoor seating. Totally nonsmoking. **$$**

D

Washington, CT

2 hours; 91 miles from New York City

Area code 860

B&B/Small Inn

★ ★ ★ ★ ★ **THE MAYFLOWER INN.** *118 Woodbury Rd (06793). Phone 860/868-9466; fax 860/868-1497. www.mayflowerinn.com.* Just under two hours from New York City in Connecticut's verdant countryside, The Mayflower Inn is a pastoral paradise. Dating from the early 1900s, The Mayflower revives the great tradition of splendid country house hotels. The hotel is set within 28 acres of rolling hills, gurgling streams, stone walls, and lush gardens. Spread among three buildings, the guest rooms and suites bring to mind the English countryside. Four-poster, canopied beds and fireplaces enhance the romantic feel of The Mayflower Inn, perfect for a romantic getaway or a restorative retreat. The hotel's lovely grounds inspire poetry and instill serenity in its visitors. The fitness center, pool, and tennis court provide diversions for active-minded guests, while others head straight for the area's well-known main streets lined with antique shops. Completing the heavenly experience is the restaurant, where fresh, local ingredients inspire the creative menu. *Secret Inspector's Notes:* Breakfast at the Mayflower Inn is worth getting out of your sumptuous bed for; the creations served are fit for a queen. Additionally, the staff throughout the hotel is incredibly warm, professional, and accommodating, greeting guests by name and going beyond general expectations to make your stay delightful. 25 rooms, 2-3 story. Children over 12 years only. Check-out 1 pm, check-in

3 pm. TV; cable (premium), VCR available (movies). In-room modem link. Room service 24 hours. Dining room. In-house fitness room, massage, sauna, steam room. Game room. Heated pool. Outdoor tennis. Valet parking. Totally nonsmoking. **$$$$**

D 🛄 🛌 🏃 🏊 🎿 🎿 🚭

The Adirondack Mountains and Cape Cod are about a 4-hour drive from New York City, but seem to be a world away. You can hike in the pristine beauty of the Adirondacks or stroll along the seashore in Cape Cod. If you are looking to get back to nature after being in NYC for a few days, these are definitely two places worth visiting.

Blue Mountain Lake (Adirondack Mountains)

5 hours; 269 miles from New York City

Pop 250 **Elev** 1,829 ft **Area code** 518 **Zip** 12812

This central Adirondack resort village has mountain trails, splendid views, interesting shops, water sports, good fishing, and hunting.

What to See and Do

Adirondack Lakes Center for the Arts. *Rte 28 (12812). In the village, next to the post office. Phone 518/352-7715. www.telenet.com/~alca.* Concerts, films, exhibitions, theater, and community center.

Adirondack Museum. *NY 30. Phone 518/352-7311. www. adkmuseum.org.* On slope of Blue Mountain overlooking lakes, mountains, and village. Noted for landscaping; indoor and outdoor displays. Exhibits explore logging, transportation, boating, mining, schooling, outdoor recreation, and rustic furniture. Gift shop. (Memorial Day-mid-Oct, daily) **$$$**

Blue Mountain. *1 1/2 miles N.* Three-mile trail to 3,800-foot summit; 35-foot observation tower overlooks Adirondack Park. Blue Mountain Lake Association has map of trails.

Motel/Motor Lodge

★ ★ **HEMLOCK HALL HOTEL.** *Maple Lodge Rd (12812). Phone 518/ 352-7706.* 22 rooms, 1 story. No A/C, room phones. Closed rest of year. Check-out 11 am. Dining room. Game room. Lawn games. Secluded resort inn near woods on lakeshore. No Credit Cards Accepted **$**

🐾

North Creek (Adirondack Mountains)

4 hours 15 minutes; 240 miles from New York City

Pop 950 **Elev** 1,028 ft **Area code** 518 **Zip** 12853

Information Gore Mountain Region Chamber of Commerce Accommodation and Visitors Bureau, 295 Main St, PO Box 84; 518/251-2612 or 800/880-GORE

Web www.goremtnregion.org

What to See and Do

Garnet Hill Lodge , Cross-Country Ski Center, and Mountain Bike Center. *5 miles NW via NY 28, at the top of 13th Lake Rd. Phone 518/251-2444; 518/251-2821. www.garnet-hill.com.* Approximately 35 miles of groomed cross-country trails adjacent state wilderness trails; tennis courts, mountain biking (rentals), hiking trails, fishing, beach and boat rentals on 13th Lake, site of abandoned garnet mine. Restaurant. (Daily) **$$$$**

Gore Mountain. *Approximately 2 miles NW off NY 28. Phone 518/251-2411; 800/342-1234 (snow conditions). www.goremountain.com.* Gondola; two quad, triple, three double chairlifts; two surface lifts; cross-country trails; patrol, school, rentals; cafeteria, restaurant, bar; nursery; lodges; snowmaking. Longest run three miles; vertical drop 2,100 feet. (Nov-Apr, daily; also fall weekends for gondola) **$$$$**

Gore Mountain Mineral Shop. *Barton Mine Rd. Phone 518/251-2706.* Tours of open-pit garnet mine; opportunity to collect loose gem garnets. (Mid-June-Labor Day, daily)

Rafting. Sixteen-mile whitewater rafting trips from Indian Lake to North River. (Apr-Nov) Contact Gore Mountain Region Chamber of Commerce.

Special Events

Adirondack Artisans Festival. *Gore Mountain Ski Center and Main St. Phone 518/251-2612.* First weekend in Aug.

Teddy Roosevelt Celebration. *Phone 518/582-4451.* Town-wide. Sept.

White Water Derby. *421 Old Military Rd (12946). Phone 518/523-1855.* Hudson River. Canoe and kayak competition. First weekend in May.

Motel/Motor Lodge

★ ★ **BLACK MOUNTAIN SKI LODGE & MOTEL.** *2999 NY 8 (12853). Phone 518/251-2800; toll-free 888/846-4858; fax 518/251-5326. blackmountainskilodge.com.* 25 rooms. Pets accepted. Check-out 11 am. TV. Restaurant. Pool. Downhill/cross-country ski 5 miles. **$**

B&B/Small Inn

★ **GARNET HILL LODGE.** *13 Lake Rd, North River (12856). Phone 518/251-2444; toll-free 800/497-4207; fax 518/251-3089. www.garnet-hill.com.* 23 rooms, 2 story. Check-out 11 am, check-in 4 pm. Dining room. Sauna. Tennis. Cross-country ski on site, instructor, rentals. Mountain bicycles. Fishing guides. Nature trails. Airport transportation. Rustic setting. **$$**

Old Forge
(Adirondack Mountains)

5 hours 20 minutes; 294 miles from New York City

Pop 1,060 **Elev** 1,712 ft **Area code** 315 **Zip** 13420

Information Visitor Information Center, NY 28, PO Box 68; 315/369-6983

In almost any season there is fun in this Adirondack resort town, located in the Fulton Chain of Lakes region—everything from hunting, fishing, snowmobiling, and skiing to basking on a sunny beach.

What to See and Do

Canoeing. *Phone 518/457-7433.* An 86-mile canoe trip to the hamlet of Paul Smiths (north of the Saranac Lakes). For information on Adirondack canoe trips contact Department of Environmental Conservation, Albany 12233-4255.

Enchanted Forest/Water Safari. *3183 State Rte 28 (13420). 1/2 mile N on NY 28. Phone 315/369-6145. www.watersafari.com.* This 60-acre water theme park complex features water attractions and traditional amusement rides; circus performances twice daily. (June-Labor Day) **$$$$**

Fern Park. *South Shore Rd, 15 miles NW in Inlet (13420). Phone 315/357-5501.* Hiking, cross-country skiing, snowshoeing, biking, ice skating, baseball, volleyball, basketball; special events. **FREE**

Forest Industries Exhibit Hall. *3311 State Rte 28. 1 mile N on NY 28. Phone 315/369-3078.* Samples of products of forest industries; dioramas; film on managed forests. (Late May-Labor Day, Mon, Wed-Sun; after Labor Day-Columbus Day, weekends only) **FREE**

McCauley Mountain. *2 miles S off NY 28. Phone 315/369-3225.* Double chairlift, two T-bars, two rope tows, pony lift; patrol, school, rentals; snowmaking; cafeteria. Longest run 3/4 miles; vertical drop 633 feet. (Thanksgiving-Apr, Mon and Wed-Sun) Half-day rates. Chairlift to top of McCauley Mountain also operates June-Oct (daily). Picnic area. **$$$$**

Old Forge Lake Cruise. *Main St. Phone 315/369-6473.* Cruises on Fulton Chain of Lakes (28 miles). (Memorial Day-Columbus Day) Also showboat and dinner cruises. **$$$**

Public beach. *On NY 28.* Swimming; lifeguards, bathhouse. (Early June-Labor Day, daily) Tourist Information Center is located here (daily). **$**

Motels/Motor Lodges

★ **BEST WESTERN SUNSET INN.** *NY 28 (13420). Phone 315/369-6836; toll-free 800/780-7234; fax 315/369-2607. www.bestwestern.com.* 52 rooms, 2 story. Pets accepted. Complimentary continental breakfast. Check-out 11 am. TV; cable (premium). Laundry services. Sauna. Indoor pool, whirlpool. Tennis. Downhill ski 3 miles; cross-country ski opposite. **$**

D 🐾 ⚡ 🎿 ➰ 🏊 SC

★ **COUNTRY CLUB MOTEL.** *NY 28 (13420). Phone 315/369-6340.* 27 rooms. Check-out 11 am. TV; cable (premium). Heated pool. Downhill ski 2 miles; cross-country ski adjacent. Lawn games. **$**

D ➰ 🏊 🎿

Hotel

★ **19TH GREEN.** *NY 28 (13420). Phone 315/369-3575.* 13 rooms. Check-out 10 am. TV. Game room. Pool. Downhill ski 3 miles, cross-country ski adjacent. Lawn games. **$**

D ⚡ 🎿 ➰ 🏊 🎿

Restaurant

★ ★ **OLD MILL.** *NY 28 (13420). Phone 315/369-3662.* American menu. Closed 2nd weekend Mar; also Nov-Dec. Dinner. Bar. Children's menu. Converted gristmill. **$$**

D

Plattsburgh (Adirondack Mountains)
5 hours 15 minutes; 316 miles from New York City

Pop 18,816 **Elev** 135 ft **Area code** 518 **Zip** 12901

Information Plattsburgh-North Country Chamber of Commerce, 7601 Rte 9, PO Box 310; 518/563-1000

Web northcountrychamber.com

The Cumberland Bay area of Lake Champlain has been a military base since colonial days. Plattsburgh, at the mouth of the Saranac River, has a dramatic history in the struggle for US independence. The British won the Battle of Lake Champlain off these shores in 1776. Here, in 1814, Commodore Thomas Macdonough defeated a British fleet from Canada by an arrangement of anchors and winches that enabled him to swivel his vessels completely around, thus giving the enemy both broadsides. While this was going on, US General Alexander Macomb polished off the Redcoats on shore with the help of school boys and the local militia. Today, Plattsburgh accommodates both industry and resort trade.

What to See and Do

Alice T. Miner Colonial Collection. *12 miles N on NY 9 in Chazy. Phone 518/846-7336.* Antiques, colonial household items and appliances in 1824 house; sandwich glass collection; gardens. (Tues-Sat; closed Jan, Dec 25) **$$**

Boat excursion. M/V *Juniper*. *Contact Heritage Adventures Inc, 69 Miller St. Phone 800/388-8970.* Leaves from foot of Dock St and cruises Lake Champlain, circling Valcour Island. (May-Sept, two daily departures; also sunset and dinner cruises nightly).

Champlain Monument. *Cumberland Ave and Lorraine (12901).* Statue of the explorer.

Kent-Delord House Museum. *17 Cumberland Ave. Phone 518/561-1035.* (1797) Historic house; British officers' quarters during the Battle of Plattsburgh (War of 1812); period furnishings. Tours (Mar-Dec, Tues-Sat afternoons; rest of year, by appointment only; closed Jan 1, Thanksgiving, Dec 25). **$$**

Macdonough Monument. *41 City Hall Pl (12901). Phone 518/563-7701.* Obelisk commemorates the naval encounter.

State University of New York College at Plattsburgh. *Phone 518/564-2813 or 518/564-2000.* (1889) 6,400 students. On campus is SUNY Plattsburgh Art Museum, comprised of Meyers Fine Arts Gallery and Winkel Sculpture Court; also Rockwell Kent Gallery, with extensive collection of paintings, drawings, prints, and book engravings by American artist Rockwell Kent, famous for his illustrated Shakespeare and *Moby Dick* (Mon-Thurs, Sat, Sun).

Swimming. Municipal Beach. 1 1/4 miles N on US 9, 1 mile E on NY 314. Phone 518/563-4431. **AuSable Point State Park.** 12 miles S on US 9. Beach; fishing; boating; camping. Phone 518/561-7080. **Cumberland Bay State Park.** Adjacent to Municipal Beach. Phone 518/563-5240. All areas (Memorial Day-Oct). Admission fee. Bathhouse, lifeguard; picnicking, concession.

Motels/Motor Lodges

★ ★ **BEST WESTERN THE INN AT SMITHFIELD.** *446 Cornelia St (12901). Phone 518/561-7750; toll-free 800/780-7234; fax 518/561-9431. www.bestwestern.com.* 120 rooms, 2 story. Pets accepted. Check-out noon. TV; cable (premium), VCR available. In-room modem link. Laundry services. Restaurant, bar. Exercise equipment. Indoor pool, poolside service. **$**

[D] [🏊] [🏋] [📠] [SC]

★ **DAYS INN.** *8 Everleth Dr (12901). Phone 518/561-0403; fax 518/561-4192. www.daysinn-plattsburgh.com.* 112 rooms, 3 story. Check-out noon. TV; cable (premium). Exercise equipment. Indoor pool, whirlpool. **$**

[D] [🏊] [🏋] [📠] [SC]

★ **STONEHELM LODGE.** *72 Spellman Rd (12901). Phone 518/563-4800; toll-free 800/443-4344; fax 518/562-1380.* 40 rooms. Check-out 11 am. TV. Restaurant. **$**

[D] [📠]

Restaurant

★ ★ **ANTHONY'S.** *538 Rte 3 (12901). Phone 518/561-6420; fax 518/561-6421.* Continental menu. Closed some major holidays. Lunch, dinner. Bar. Children's menu. **$$**

Wilmington (Adirondack Mountains)

5 hours; 291 miles from New York City
See also Saranac Lake

Pop 1,131 **Elev** 1,020 ft **Area code** 518 **Zip** 12997

Information Whiteface Mtn Regional Visitors Bureau, NY 86, PO Box 277; 518/946-2255 or 888/WHITEFACE

Web www.whitefaceregion.com

Gateway to Whiteface Mountain Memorial Highway, Wilmington is made-to-order for skiers and lovers of scenic splendor.

What to See and Do

High Falls Gorge. *Rte 86. 5 miles S on NY 86. Phone 518/946-2278.* Deep ravine cut into the base of Whiteface Mountain by the Ausable River. Variety of strata, rapids, falls, and potholes can be viewed from a network of modern bridges and paths. Photography and mineral displays in main building. (Memorial Day-mid-Oct, daily) **$$$**

Santa's Home Workshop. *Rte 431 and Whiteface Mtn. (12946). 1 1/2 miles W on NY 431, in North Pole. Phone 518/946-2211.* "Santa's home and workshop," Santa Claus, reindeer, children's rides and shows. (Late-June-mid-Oct, Mon-Wed; Sat, Sun) Reduced rates weekdays spring and fall. **$$$$**

Whiteface Mountain Memorial Highway. *3 miles W on NY 431. Phone 800/462-6236.* A 5-mile toll road to top of mountain (4,867 feet). (Late May-mid-Oct, daily, weather permitting) Trail or elevator from parking area. Views of St. Lawrence River, Lake Placid, and Vermont. Elevator (begins late May).

Whiteface Mountain Ski Center. *3 miles SW on NY 86. Phone 800/462-6236; 518/946-7171 (ski conditions). www.whiteface.com.* Gondola; two triple, seven double chairlifts; snowmaking; patrol, school, rentals; cafeteria, bar, nursery. Longest run 2 1/2 miles; vertical drop 3,350 feet. Chairlift (mid-June-mid-Oct; fee). Lift-serviced mountain biking center; rental, repair shop, guided tours (late June-mid-Oct). (Mid-Nov-mid-Apr, daily) **$$$$**

Motel/Motor Lodge

★ **LEDGE ROCK AT WHITEFACE.** *Rte 86 (12997). Phone 518/946-2302; toll-free 800/336-4754; fax 518/946-7594.* 18 rooms, 2 story. Pets accepted; fee. Check-out 11 am. TV. Game room. Children's pool. Pond with paddleboats. **$**

D 🐾 🛠 🏋 🏊 ⚓

Hotel

★ ★ **HUNGRY TROUT MOTOR INN.** *Rte 86 (12997). Phone 518/946-2217; toll-free 800/766-9137; fax 518/946-7418.* 20 rooms. Closed Apr, Nov. Pets accepted; fee. Check-out 11 am. TV. Bar. Pool, children's pool. Downhill ski 1/2 mile; cross-country ski 12 miles. On Ausable River. **$**

D 🐾 🛠 🏊 🏊 ⚓

B&B/Small Inn

★ ★ **WHITEFACE CHALET.** *Springfield Rd (12997). Phone 518/946-2207; toll-free 800/932-0859. www.whitefacechalet.com.* 16 rooms. Pets accepted. Check-out 11 am, check-in 1 pm. TV. Fireplace in lounge, living room. Dining room, bar. Pool. Tennis. Lawn games. Airport transportation. **$**

🐾 🏋 🏊 SC

Restaurant

★ **WILDERNESS INN #2.** *Rte 86 (12997). Phone 518/946-2391; fax 518/ 946-7290. www.lakeplacid.net/wildernessinn.* Closed Wed in winter; also first 3 weeks Nov. Dinner. Bar. Children's menu. Outdoor seating. Guest cottages available. **$$**

SC

Barnstable (Cape Cod), MA

4 hours 22 minutes; 254 miles from New York City
See also Hyannis, South Yarmouth

Settled 1637 **Pop** 47,821 **Elev** 37 ft **Area code** 508 **Zip** 02630

Information Cape Cod Chamber of Commerce, US 6 and MA 132, PO Box 790, Hyannis 02601-0790; 508/362-3225 or 888/33-CAPECOD

Web www.capecodchamber.org

Farmers first settled Barnstable because the marshes provided salt hay for cattle. Later the town prospered as a whaling and trading center, and when these industries declined, land development made it the political hub of the Cape. It is the seat of Barnstable County, which includes the entire Cape. Like other Cape communities, it does a thriving resort business.

What to See and Do

Cape Cod Art Association Gallery. *3480 Rte 6A. Phone 508/362-2909.* Changing exhibits, exhibitions by New England artists; demonstrations, lectures, classes. (Apr-Nov, daily, limited hours; rest of year, inquire for schedule) **FREE**

Cape Cod Pathways. *3225 Rte 6A (02630). Phone 508/362-3828. www.cape codcommission.org/pathways.* This network of walking and hiking trails is composed of a perfect mix of dirt, sand, and gravel, and when completed will link all the towns in Cape Cod. The Cape Cod Commission oversees the trails and produces a detailed map, yours for the asking by calling or writing. Don't miss the Cape Walk in early June, in which hearty souls hike from one end of the cape to another, or the Walking Weekend in late October, when trail guides lead walks and hikes of varying lengths.(Daily) **FREE**

Donald G. Trayser Memorial Museum. *In Old Custom House and Post Office, Main St on Cobb's Hill, MA 6A. Phone 508/362-2092.* Marine exhibits, scrimshaw, Barnstable silver, historic documents. (July-mid-Oct, Tues-Sat afternoons)

Hyannis Whale Watcher Cruises. *269 Mill Way (02630). Barnstable Harbor. Phone 508/362-6088.* View whales aboard the *Whale Watcher,* a 297-passenger super-cruiser, custom designed and built specifically for whale watching. Naturalist on board will narrate. Café on board. (Apr-Oct, daily) Reservations necessary. **$$$$**

Mill Way Fish and Lobster Market. *276 Mill Way (2630). Phone 508/362-2760. www.millwayfish.com.* Mill Way is both a restaurant that specializes in seafood and vegetarian dishes, and a take-out market, offering fried and grilled dishes, pastas, cod cakes, salads, and other on-the-go meals. Try the unique shellfish sausage that's stuffed with shrimp, lobster, and scallops. (Tues-Sun 10 am-8 pm; closed Mon)

Sturgis Library. *3090 Main St (02630). Phone 508/362-6636.* Oldest library building (1644) in US has material on the Cape, including maritime history; genealogical records of Cape Cod families. Research fee for nonresidents. (Mon-Sat; closed holidays; limited hours) **$$**

West Parish Meetinghouse. *2049 Meetinghouse Way (02668). Jct US 6, MA 149 in West Barnstable. Phone 508/362-4385.* (1717) Said to be the oldest Congregational church in country; restored. Congregation established in London, 1616. Regular Sunday services are held here all year. **FREE**

B&B/Small Inns

★ ★ ★ **ACWORTH INN.** *4352 Old King's Hwy, Rte 6A (02637). Phone 508/362-3330; toll-free 800/362-6363; fax 508/375-0304. www.acworthinn.com.* Whether guests come here to relax and unwind or for a romantic getaway, this bed-and-breakfast has everything one needs for both. Guests can enjoy a day of sightseeing, mountain biking or golf and then return to enjoy a nice cozy evening in the gathering room. 5 rooms, some A/C, 2 story. No room phones, Children over 12 years only. Complimentary full breakfast. Check-out 11 am, check-in 3-7 pm. TV in common room. Concierge. Farmhouse built in 1860. Totally nonsmoking. **$**

🖼

★ ★ ★ **ASHLEY MANOR.** *3660 Main St (02630). Phone 508/362-8044; toll-free 888/535-2246; fax 508/362-9927. www.ashleymanor.net.* A lovely garden and gazebo adorn this beautiful inn. Guests can relax with a book in the library or with afternoon tea in front of the fire. Some activities available to guests include whale watching, biking, and even off-Cape excursions. 6 rooms, 2 story. Phone available. Children over 14 years only. Complimentary full breakfast. Check-out 11 am, check-in 2 pm. Many fireplaces. Tennis. Lawn games. Restored early 18th-century inn on 2-acre estate. **$**

🎾 🖼

★ ★ ★ **BEECHWOOD INN.** *2839 Main St (02630). Phone 508/362-6618; toll-free 800/609-6618; fax 508/362-0298. www.beechwoodinn.com.* Conveniently located close to Barnstable Village, guests can enjoy biking, whale watching and golf. The guest who prefers a relaxing vacation may sit on the porch and enjoy an iced tea or lemonade while rocking on the gliders.

6 rooms, 3 story. No room phones. Complimentary full breakfast. Check-out 11 am, check-in 2 pm. Lawn games. Restored Victorian house (1853); veranda with rocking chairs, glider. Totally nonsmoking. **$**

★ ★ **HONEYSUCKLE HILL B&B.** *591 Old King's Hwy, Rte 6A (02668). Phone 508/362-8418; toll-free 800/444-5522; fax 508/362-8386. www.honeysucklehill.com.* 5 rooms, 2 story. Children over 12 years only. Complimentary full breakfast. Check-out 11 am, check-in 3 pm. Built in 1810, restored Victorian décor. **$**

Restaurants

★ ★ **BARNSTABLE TAVERN AND GRILLE.** *3176 Main St (02630). Phone 508/362-2355; fax 508/362-9012.* Seafood menu. Closed Dec 24-25. Lunch, dinner. Bar. Entertainment. Children's menu. Outdoor seating. Inn and tavern since 1799. **$$**

D

★ ★ **HARBOR POINT.** *Harbor Point Rd (02630). Phone 508/362-2231.* Specializes in fresh seafood, steak. Hours: 11:30 am-10:30 pm; weekends to midnight; Sun brunch 11 am-3 pm. Closed Feb-Mar. Reservations accepted. Bar. Lunch, dinner, Sun brunch. Children's menu. Entertainment. Overlooking bay, marsh abundant with wildlife. Fountain. **$$**

D

★ ★ **MATTAKEESE WHARF.** *271 Mill Way (02630). Phone 508/362-4511; fax 508/362-8826.* Seafood menu. Closed late Oct-early May. Lunch, dinner, brunch. Bar. Entertainment weekends. Children's menu. Valet parking available. **$$**

Bourne (Cape Cod), MA

3 hours 50 minutes; 235 miles from New York City
See also Buzzards Bay, Sandwich

Settled 1627 **Pop** 18,721 **Elev** 19 ft **Area code** 508 **Zip** 02532

Information Cape Cod Chamber of Commerce, US 6 and MA 132, PO Box 790, Hyannis 02601-0790; 508/362-3225 or 888/33-CAPECOD

Web www.capecodchamber.org

Named for Jonathan Bourne, a successful whaling merchant, this town has had a variety of industries since its founding. Originally a center for herring fishing, the town turned to manufacturing stoves, kettles, and later, freight cars. Bourne's current prosperity is derived from cranberries and tourism.

What to See and Do

Aptucxet Trading Post. *24 Aptucxet Rd, off Shore Rd, 1/2 mile W of Bourne Bridge. Phone 508/759-9487.* A replica of a 1627 trading post that may have been the first of its kind in America. Native American artifacts; rune stone believed to be proof of visits to the area by the Phoenicians in 400 B.C.; artifacts in two rooms. On grounds are herb garden, site of original spring, saltworks; railroad station built for President Grover Cleveland for use at his Gray Gables home, his summer White House; Dutch-style windmill; picnic area adjacent to Cape Cod Canal. (July-Aug, daily; last two weekends May and June and Sept-mid-Oct, Tues-Sun) **$**

Bourne Scenic Park. *375 Scenic Hwy (02532). North bank of Cape Cod Canal. Phone 508/759-7873.* Playground, picnicking; bike trails; swimming pool, bathhouse; recreation building; camping (fee); store. (Apr-May, weekends; June-Oct, daily) **$$**

Pairpoint Crystal Company. *851 Sandwich Rd (MA 6A), in Sagamore. Phone 508/888-2344.* (est 1837) Handmade lead crystal ware, glassblowing demonstrations. Viewing (Mon-Fri). Store (Daily). **FREE**

Brewster (Cape Cod), MA

4 hours 35 minutes; 269 miles from New York City

Settled 1656 **Pop** 10,094 **Elev** 39 ft **Area code** 508 **Zip** 02631

Information Cape Cod Chamber of Commerce, US 6 and MA 132, PO Box 790, Hyannis 02601-0790; 508/362-3225 or 888/33-CAPECOD

Web www.capecodchamber.org

What to See and Do

Cape Cod Museum of Natural History. *869 Rte 6A. Phone 508/896-3867; toll-free 800/479-3867.* Exhibits on wildlife and ecology of the area; art exhibits; library; lectures; nature trails; field walks; trips to Monomoy Island. Gift shop. (Daily; closed holidays) **$$**

Cape Cod Repertory Theater Company. *3379 Rte 6A (02631). Phone 508/896-1888. www.caperep.org.* Boasting both an indoor and outdoor theater, the Cape Cod Repertory Theater offers a children's theater two mornings per week (Tues and Fri) in July and August. In addition, you'll find productions for the whole family in the outdoor theater, which sits back in the beautiful woods near Nickerson State Park and is open in fair weather. The indoor theater offers plays and musicals year-round. **$$$**

⭐ **New England Fire & History Museum.** *1/2 mile W of MA 137 on MA 6A. Phone 508/896-5711.* This six-building complex houses an extensive collection of fire-fighting equipment and includes the Arthur Fiedler Memorial Fire Collection; diorama of Chicago fire of 1871; engines dating from the Revolution to the 1930s; world's only 1929 Mercedes Benz fire engine; life-size reproduction of Ben Franklin's firehouse; 19th-century blacksmith shop; largest apothecary shop in the country contains 664 gold-leaf bottles of medicine; medicinal herb gardens; library; films; theater performances. Guided tours. Picnic area. (Memorial Day weekend-mid-Sept, daily; mid-Sept-Columbus Day, weekends) **$$$**

Nickerson State Park. *3488 Rte 6A (02631). Phone 508/896-3491. www.state.ma.us/dem/parks/nick.htm.* Nickerson State Park offers an unusual experience on Cape Cod: densely wooded areas that show no signs of the marshy areas that abound on the Cape. Nickerson offers camping, challenging hiking trails, an 8-mile bike path that connects to the Cape Cod Rail Trail (a 25-mile paved bike trail), fishing, swimming, canoeing, and birdwatching. Also consider areas on the Cape that offer similar activities: Green Briar Nature Center in Sandwich, Lowell Holly Reservation in Mashpee, Ashumet Holly and Wildlife Sanctuary in East Falmouth, Great Island Trail in Wellfleet, Coatue-Coksata-Great Point on Nantucket. (Daily) **FREE**

Ocean Edge Golf Course. *2660 Rte 6A (02631). Phone 508/896-9000. www.oceanedge.com.* This beautiful golf course, just a stone's throw from the ocean, offers 6,665 yards of manicured green, plus five ponds for challenging play. Play during the week in the off-season, and you'll pay extremely reasonable greens fees. Lessons from PGA pros are available. The course is part of a resort that offers accommodations, tennis courts and lessons, a private beach, and 26 miles of paved bike trails (bike rentals are available). (Daily; closed for snow and inclement weather) **$$$$**

Stoney Brook Mill. *Old Grist Mill in West Brewster, on site of one of first gristmills in America.* Museum upstairs includes historical exhibits, weaving. Corn grinding (July and Aug, Thurs-Sat afternoons). **FREE**

Resort

★ ★ ★ **OCEAN EDGE RESORT.** *2907 Main St (02631). Phone 508/896-9000; toll-free 800/343-6074; fax 508/896-9123. www.oceanedge.com.* Ideally situated on the charming Cape Cod Bay and surrounded by lush gardens, this charming English country manor offers guests an oasis of comfort and privacy, while being surrounded by understated elegance and superb service. Discover the charm and character of this 19th century mansion and carriage house. From the quiet elegance of their luxurious guestrooms to the championship 18-hole golf course, 11 tennis courts and premiere health and fitness center, this resort offers timeless tranquility and complete relaxation for a romantic weekend or a quiet business retreat. 32 kitchen units, 2 story. Checkout 11 am, check-in 3 pm. TV; VCR available (movies). In-room modem link. Fireplaces. Dining room, bar; entertainment. Room service. Supervised children's activities (June-Sept); ages 4-12. In-house fitness room, sauna. Six pools, two indoor; whirlpool, poolside service. 18-hole golf, pro, putting green, driving range. Greens fee $68. Outdoor tennis. Lawn games. Bicycle rentals. Hiking. Airport transportation. Business center. Concierge. **$$**

D 🏋️ 🛏️ 🛳️ 🎾 ✈️ 🏊 🚶

B&B/Small Inns

★ ★ **BRAMBLE INN.** *2019 Main St (02631). Phone 508/896-7644; fax 508/896-9332. www.brambleinn.com.* Family owned and operated, this attractive inn with its pine floors, lovely antiques, and charmingly appointed guestrooms offer guests a truly delightful stay. 8 rooms, 2 story. No room phones. Closed Jan-Apr. Children over 8 years only. Complimentary full breakfast. Check-out 11 am, check-in 2 pm. TV in some rooms; cable (premium). Restaurant. Intimate, country atmosphere. **$**

★ ★ ★ **BREWSTER FARMHOUSE INN.** *716 Main St (02631). Phone 508/896-3910; toll-free 800/892-3910; fax 508/896-4232. www.brewsterfarmhouseinn.com.* Get away from it all, rejuvenate, and relax at this charming and elegant inn. Built in 1846 and set amidst a country-like setting, this inn has been charmingly restored and offers guests a delightful stay. 8 rooms, 2 story. Some rooms with shower only, some share bath. No room phones. Children over 16 years only. Complimentary full breakfast. Check-out 11 am, check-in 3 pm. TV; cable (premium). Pool, whirlpool. Lawn games. Built 1850; antiques and reproductions. Totally nonsmoking. **$**

★ ★ **CAPTAIN FREEMAN INN.** *15 Breakwater Rd (02631). Phone 508/896-7481; toll-free 800/843-4664; fax 508/896-5618. www.captainfreemaninn.com.* 12 rooms, 3 story. Some room phones. Pets accepted. Children over 10 years only. Complimentary full breakfast. Check-out 11 am, check-in 2 pm. TV; VCR (free movies). Game room. Pool. Lawn games. Free airport transportation. Concierge services. House built in 1866. Totally nonsmoking. **$**

★ ★ **ISAIAH CLARK HOUSE.** *1187 Main St (02631). Phone 508/896-2223; toll-free 800/822-4001; fax 508/896-2138. www.isaiahclark.com.* 7 rooms, 2 story. Children over 10 years only. Complimentary full breakfast; afternoon refreshments. Check-out 11 am, check-in 2-5 pm. TV in most rooms. Many room phones. Former sea captain's house (1780). Totally nonsmoking. **$**

★ ★ **OLD SEA PINES INN.** *2553 Main St (02631). Phone 508/896-6114; fax 508/896-7387. www.oldseapinesinn.com.* 24 rooms, 3 story. No room phones. Children over 8 years only except in family suites. Complimentary full breakfast. Check-out 11 am, check-in 2 pm. Room service. Service bar. On 3 1/2 acres. Founded in 1907 as School of Charm and Personality for Young Women. Breakfast in bed available. Totally nonsmoking. **$**

★ ★ **POORE HOUSE INN.** *2311 Main St (02631). Phone 508/896-0004; toll-free 800/233-6662; fax 508/896-0005. www.capecodtravel.com/poore.*

5 rooms, 2 story. Pets accepted. Children over 8 years only. Complimentary full breakfast. Check-out 11 am, check-in 2 pm. Built in 1837. Totally nonsmoking. **$$**

★ ★ **RUDDY TURNSTONE.** *463 Main St (02631). Phone 508/385-9871; toll-free 800/654-1995; fax 508/385-5696. www.ruddyturnstone.com.* 5 rooms, 2 story. No room phones. Children over 10 years only. Complimentary full breakfast. Check-out 11 am, check-in 1 pm. Lawn games. Concierge service. Early 19th-century Cape Cod house; antique furnishings. Totally nonsmoking. **$**

Restaurants

★ ★ ★ **BRAMBLE INN.** *2019 Main St (02631). Phone 508/896-7644; fax 508/896-9332. www.brambleinn.com.* This restaurant is located in the charming Bramble Inn, in the heart of the Historic District. Chef/owner Ruth Manchester delights guests with her creative cuisine and heartwarming hospitality. A perfect choice for a romantic dinner. Specializes in tenderloin of beef, rack of lamb, assorted seafood curry. Own baking. Hours: 6-9 pm. Closed Mon-Wed off season; also Jan-Apr. Reservations accepted. Service bar. Parking. Built in 1861; 4 dining areas, including enclosed porch. Totally nonsmoking. **$$$**

★ ★ ★ **CHILLINGSWORTH.** *2449 Main St (02631). Phone 508/896-3640; fax 508/896-7540. www.chillingsworth.com.* This 30-year-old restaurant is located on the 300 year-old Chillingsworth Foster estate that has 6 acres of lawns and gardens. The nightly 7 course table d'hote menu features creative French cuisine. Menu changes daily, emphasizing fresh native seafood, veal, pheasant. Own baking, pasta. Grows own herbs. Hours: mid-June-mid-Sept, 2 dinner sittings: 6-7:30 pm and 8-9:30 pm; mid-May-mid-June and mid-Sept-Nov, shortened week. **$$$**

D

★ ★ ★ **OLD MANSE INN AND RESTAURANT.** *1861 Main St (02631). Phone 508/896-3149; fax 508/896-1546. www.oldmanseinn.com.* The casual restaurant of this inn, located in the heart of Cape Cod's historic district, serves a world menu prepared by the chef/owners, both graduates of the Culinary Institute of America. Specialties: steamed lobster, braised lamb shank, lemon buttermilk pudding cake. Hours: 5:30-10 pm. Closed Mon; Jan-Apr. Wine list. Parking. Two dining rooms in early 19th-century inn; antiques. Romantic setting. Guest rooms available. Totally nonsmoking. **$$**

Buzzards Bay
(Cape Cod), MA

3 hours 50 minutes; 230 miles from New York City

Pop 3,549 **Elev** 10 ft **Area code** 508 **Zip** 02532

Information Cape Cod Chamber of Commerce, US 6 and MA 132, PO Box 790, Hyannis 02601-0790; 508/362-3225 or 888/33-CAPECOD

Web www.capecodchamber.org

Cape Cod is said to face "four seas": Buzzards Bay, Nantucket Sound, the Atlantic Ocean, and Cape Cod Bay. The shore is jagged and irregular, dotted with hundreds of summer resorts, public and private beaches, yacht clubs, and fishing piers.

The area of Buzzards Bay is at the west entrance to the Cape Cod Canal. Among the better-known towns on the mainland shore are Nonquit and South Yarmouth (see), west of New Bedford, and Fairhaven, Crescent Beach, Mattapoisett, Wareham, and Onset, to the east. On the Cape side are Monument Beach, Pocasset, Silver Beach, West Falmouth, Woods Hole (see), and the string of Elizabeth Islands, which ends with Cuttyhunk.

What to See and Do

Cape Cod Canal Cruises. *Onset Pier. 3 miles W via MA 6, 28. Phone 508/295-3883.* Cruises with historical narration. Also evening cocktail and entertainment cruises. (June-Oct, daily; May, Sat and Sun) **$$$$**

Porter's Thermometer Museum. *49 Zarahemla Rd. Just E of the junction of I-495 and I-195, in Onset. Phone 508/295-5504.* Heralded as the only museum of its kind in the world, the Porter Thermometer Museum in tiny Onset houses some 2,600 distinct specimens. Varieties include those used by astronauts, ones that can be worn as earrings, and temperature-telling instruments from around the world. One thermometer from Alaska can accurately record temperatures all the way down to -100 degrees! Run by former high school science teacher Richard Porter out of his house, the museum is free, as long as you call ahead. Make sure to admire the world's largest thermometer out front, which can be read from as far away as a mile. **FREE**

Motel/Motor Lodge

★ **BAY MOTOR INN.** *223 Main St (02532). Phone 508/759-3989; fax 508/759-3199. www.capecodtravel.com/baymotorinn.* 17 rooms, 1-2 story. Closed mid-Nov-Mar. Pets accepted. Check-out 11 am. TV; cable (premium). Pool. **$**

Chatham (Cape Cod), MA

4 hours 45 minutes; 273 miles from New York City

Settled 1656 **Pop** 6,625 **Elev** 46 ft **Area code** 508 **Zip** 02633

Information Chamber of Commerce, PO Box 793; 800/715-5567; or the Cape Cod Chamber of Commerce, US 6 and MA 132, PO Box 790, Hyannis 02601-0790; 508/362-3225 or 888/CAPECOD

Web www.capecodchamber.org

Chatham is among the Cape's fashionable shopping centers. Comfortable estates in the hilly country nearby look out on Pleasant Bay and Nantucket Sound. Monomoy Island, an unattached sand bar, stretches 10 miles south into the sea. It was once a haunt of "moon-cussers"—beach pirates who lured vessels aground with false lights and then looted the wrecks.

What to See and Do

Chatham Light. *Bridge and Main sts (02633).* Chatham Light is a quintessential Cape Cod lighthouse: gleaming white, with a charming keeper's house attached. Originally built with two towers to distinguish the signal from a single lighthouse farther north, the first pair—built of wood—decayed three decades later. A second pair, made of brick, fell to the beach far below when bad weather eroded the cliff on which they were built. A third pair was built inland, and one was moved to Nauset Beach and forever disconnected from her Chatham sister. Today, the lighthouse offers a superb view of the Atlantic and seals on the beach below, and the Coast Guard uses the keeper's house as its station. (Daily)

Clambake Celebrations. *1223 Main St (02633). Phone 508/945-7771. www.clambake-to-go.com.* For the easiest clam and lobster takeout on the Cape, visit Clambake Celebrations for simple packages that you steam and eat. You can also pick up complete meals with complementary side dishes, utensils, and bibs. If, after you leave, you need to taste fresh seafood again, you can have a meal for two or four people FedExed to you anywhere in the United States. (Mon-Sat 9 am-3 pm; closed Sun, Jan 1, July 4, Dec 25)

Gristmill. *Shattuck Place, off Cross St, W shore of Mill Pond in Chase Park. Phone 508/945-5158.* (1797) (Daily) **FREE**

Monomoy National Wildlife Refuge. *Monomoy Island (02633). Take Rte 6 east to State Rte 137 south to State Rte 28 east to the Coast Guard Station. Take the first left after the Chatham Lighthouse, and then take the first right. Follow signs for the refuge, which is on your left off Morris Island Road. Phone 508/945-0594 or (508) 443-4661.* The Monomoy National Wildlife Refuge is 2,750 acres of birdlover's paradise. You'll spot a wealth of shorebirds all year 'round, although the spectacle is greatest in spring, when birds exhibit bright plumage while breeding. Also visit Sandy Neck Recreation Area in Barnstable, Wellfleet Bay/Audubon Sanctuary in Brewster, Crane Reservation in Mashpee, and Beech Forest in Provincetown. **FREE**

Old Atwood House. *Chatham Historical Society. 347 Stage Harbor Rd, 1/2 mile off MA 28. Phone 508/945-2493.* (1752) Memorabilia of Joseph C. Lincoln, Cape Cod novelist. Shell collection, murals by Alice Stallknecht, "Portrait of a New England Town." China trade collection. Maritime collection. (Mid-June-Sept, Tues-Fri afternoons; Sat mornings; schedule may vary) **$$**

Railroad Museum. *Depot Rd, off Main St, MA 28* Restored "country railroad depot" houses scale models, photographs, railroad memorabilia, and relics; restored 1910 New York Central caboose. (Mid-June-mid-Sept, Tues-Sat) **DONATION**

Top Rod and Cape Cod Charters. *1082 Orleans Rd (02650). Next to Ryders Cove. Phone 508/945-2256. www.capefishingcharters.com.* Captain Joe Fitzback takes you to Cape Cod's prime saltwater fishing areas, providing tackle, bait, and anything else you need to bring in the big one. Although a day's adventure will cost you a bundle, each additional person adds little to the cost, so plan on bringing a group and splitting the fee. (May-Oct by reservation; closed Nov-Apr) **$$$$**

Special Events

Band Concerts. *Kate Gould Park. Phone 508/362-3225.* Fri evening. Late June-early Sept.

Monomoy Theatre. *776 Main St (02633). Phone 508/945-1589.* Ohio University Players in comedies, musicals, dramas, classics. Tues-Sat. Late June-late Aug.

Motels/Motor Lodges

★ **CHATHAM HIGHLANDER.** *946 Main St (02633). Phone 508/945-9038; fax 508/945-5731. www.realmass.com/highlander.* 28 rooms. Closed Dec-Apr. Check-out 10:30 am. TV. Outdoor pool. **$**

D ⊡ ⊠

★ **THE CHATHAM MOTEL.** *1487 Main St (02633). Phone 508/945-2630; toll-free 800/770-5545. www.chathammotel.com.* 32 rooms. Closed Nov-Apr. Check-out 11 am. TV; cable (premium). Pool. Lawn games. In pine grove. **$**

D ⊡ ⊠

★ **CHATHAM SEAFARER.** *2079 Main St (02633). Phone 508/432-1739; toll-free 800/786-2772; fax 508/432-8969. www.chathamseafarer.com.* 20 rooms, 7 kitchen units. Check-out 11 am. TV. Lawn games. **$**

⊠

★ **CHATHAM TIDES WATERFRONT MOTEL.** *394 Pleasant St (02659). Phone 508/432-0379. www.allcapecod.com/chathamtides.* 24 kitchen units. Check-out 11 am. TV. Some A/C. On private beach. **$**

D

★ ★ ★ **DOLPHIN OF CHATHAM INN AND MOTEL.** *352 Main St (02633). Phone 508/945-0070; toll-free 800/688-5900; fax 508/945-5945.*

Chatham (Cape Cod), MA

4 hours 45 minutes; 273 miles from New York City

Settled 1656 **Pop** 6,625 **Elev** 46 ft **Area code** 508 **Zip** 02633

Information Chamber of Commerce, PO Box 793; 800/715-5567; or the Cape Cod Chamber of Commerce, US 6 and MA 132, PO Box 790, Hyannis 02601-0790; 508/362-3225 or 888/CAPECOD

Web www.capecodchamber.org

Chatham is among the Cape's fashionable shopping centers. Comfortable estates in the hilly country nearby look out on Pleasant Bay and Nantucket Sound. Monomoy Island, an unattached sand bar, stretches 10 miles south into the sea. It was once a haunt of "moon-cussers"—beach pirates who lured vessels aground with false lights and then looted the wrecks.

What to See and Do

Chatham Light. *Bridge and Main sts (02633).* Chatham Light is a quintessential Cape Cod lighthouse: gleaming white, with a charming keeper's house attached. Originally built with two towers to distinguish the signal from a single lighthouse farther north, the first pair—built of wood—decayed three decades later. A second pair, made of brick, fell to the beach far below when bad weather eroded the cliff on which they were built. A third pair was built inland, and one was moved to Nauset Beach and forever disconnected from her Chatham sister. Today, the lighthouse offers a superb view of the Atlantic and seals on the beach below, and the Coast Guard uses the keeper's house as its station. (Daily)

Clambake Celebrations. *1223 Main St (02633). Phone 508/945-7771. www.clambake-to-go.com.* For the easiest clam and lobster takeout on the Cape, visit Clambake Celebrations for simple packages that you steam and eat. You can also pick up complete meals with complementary side dishes, utensils, and bibs. If, after you leave, you need to taste fresh seafood again, you can have a meal for two or four people FedExed to you anywhere in the United States. (Mon-Sat 9 am-3 pm; closed Sun, Jan 1, July 4, Dec 25)

Gristmill. *Shattuck Place, off Cross St, W shore of Mill Pond in Chase Park. Phone 508/945-5158.* (1797) (Daily) **FREE**

Monomoy National Wildlife Refuge. *Monomoy Island (02633). Take Rte 6 east to State Rte 137 south to State Rte 28 east to the Coast Guard Station. Take the first left after the Chatham Lighthouse, and then take the first right. Follow signs for the refuge, which is on your left off Morris Island Road. Phone 508/945-0594 or (508) 443-4661.* The Monomoy National Wildlife Refuge is 2,750 acres of birdlover's paradise. You'll spot a wealth of shorebirds all year 'round, although the spectacle is greatest in spring, when birds exhibit bright plumage while breeding. Also visit Sandy Neck Recreation Area in Barnstable, Wellfleet Bay/Audubon Sanctuary in Brewster, Crane Reservation in Mashpee, and Beech Forest in Provincetown. **FREE**

Old Atwood House. *Chatham Historical Society. 347 Stage Harbor Rd, 1/2 mile off MA 28. Phone 508/945-2493.* (1752) Memorabilia of Joseph C. Lincoln, Cape Cod novelist. Shell collection, murals by Alice Stallknecht, "Portrait of a New England Town." China trade collection. Maritime collection. (Mid-June-Sept, Tues-Fri afternoons; Sat mornings; schedule may vary) **$$**

Railroad Museum. *Depot Rd, off Main St, MA 28* Restored "country railroad depot" houses scale models, photographs, railroad memorabilia, and relics; restored 1910 New York Central caboose. (Mid-June-mid-Sept, Tues-Sat) **DONATION**

Top Rod and Cape Cod Charters. *1082 Orleans Rd (02650). Next to Ryders Cove. Phone 508/945-2256. www.capefishingcharters.com.* Captain Joe Fitzback takes you to Cape Cod's prime saltwater fishing areas, providing tackle, bait, and anything else you need to bring in the big one. Although a day's adventure will cost you a bundle, each additional person adds little to the cost, so plan on bringing a group and splitting the fee. (May-Oct by reservation; closed Nov-Apr) **$$$$**

Special Events

Band Concerts. *Kate Gould Park. Phone 508/362-3225.* Fri evening. Late June-early Sept.

Monomoy Theatre. *776 Main St (02633). Phone 508/945-1589.* Ohio University Players in comedies, musicals, dramas, classics. Tues-Sat. Late June-late Aug.

Motels/Motor Lodges

★ **CHATHAM HIGHLANDER.** *946 Main St (02633). Phone 508/945-9038; fax 508/945-5731. www.realmass.com/highlander.* 28 rooms. Closed Dec-Apr. Check-out 10:30 am. TV. Outdoor pool. **$**

D ⌧ ⌧

★ **THE CHATHAM MOTEL.** *1487 Main St (02633). Phone 508/945-2630; toll-free 800/770-5545. www.chathammotel.com.* 32 rooms. Closed Nov-Apr. Check-out 11 am. TV; cable (premium). Pool. Lawn games. In pine grove. **$**

D ⌧ ⌧

★ **CHATHAM SEAFARER.** *2079 Main St (02633). Phone 508/432-1739; toll-free 800/786-2772; fax 508/432-8969. www.chathamseafarer.com.* 20 rooms, 7 kitchen units. Check-out 11 am. TV. Lawn games. **$**

⌧

★ **CHATHAM TIDES WATERFRONT MOTEL.** *394 Pleasant St (02659). Phone 508/432-0379. www.allcapecod.com/chathamtides.* 24 kitchen units. Check-out 11 am. TV. Some A/C. On private beach. **$**

D

★ ★ ★ **DOLPHIN OF CHATHAM INN AND MOTEL.** *352 Main St (02633). Phone 508/945-0070; toll-free 800/688-5900; fax 508/945-5945.*

www.dolphininn.com. 38 rooms, 3 kitchen units. Check-out 10 am. TV. Restaurant. Heated pool, whirlpool. **$$**

D ⚓ ⛱

★ **THE HAWTHORNE.** *196 Shore Rd (02633). Phone 508/945-0372. www.thehawthorne.com.* 26 rooms, 10 kitchen units. Closed mid-Oct-mid-May. Check-out 11 am. TV. On private beach. **$**

Resorts

★ ★ ★ **CHATHAM BARS INN.** *297 Shore Rd (02633). Phone 508/945-0096; toll-free 800/527-4884; fax 508/945-6785. www.chathambarsinn.com.* Built in 1814, this grand and elegant Cape Cod landmark has managed to maintain all of the historic charm of a bygone era. Beauty and allure are reflected in the charmingly appointed guestrooms, some of which offer private decks along with breathtaking views of Pleasant Bay. With well maintained gardens and a private beach just steps away, guests can not help but find serenity and peace of mind amidst the luxurious setting. 205 rooms, 1-3 story. No elevator. Check-out 11 am, check-in 3 pm. TV; VCR available (free movies). In-room modem link. Dining room, bar; entertainment (in season). Room service. Free supervised children's activities (Mid-June-Labor Day); ages 4-12. In-house fitness room. Heated pool. Outdoor tennis. Lawn games. Complimentary boat shuttle. Concierge. Spacious cottages. Some A/C. On 22 acres; private beach. **$$**

D 🏃 ⚓ 🛅

★ ★ ★ **PLEASANT BAY VILLAGE RESORT.** *1191 Orleans Rd (02633). Phone 508/945-1133; toll-free 800/547-1011; fax 508/945-9701. www. pleasantbayvillage.com.* From the exquisitely arranged rock garden, where a waterfall bravely cascades its way down into a stone edged pool and offers guests a delighted view of colorful and flashing koi, to the lavishly appointed gardens, this woodland retreat welcomes guests to a place of timeless tranquility. 58 rooms, 20 kitchen units. Closed mid-Oct-mid-May. Check-out 11 am. TV. In-room modem link. Restaurant. Room service. Heated pool, poolside service. Lawn games. On 6 landscaped acres. **$$**

⚓ ⛱

★ ★ ★ **WEQUASSETT INN.** *On Pleasant Bay (02633). Phone 508/432-5400; toll-free 800/225-7125; fax 508/432-5032. www.wequassett.com.* Enjoy the warmth and elegance of this lovely inn located on Chatham's picturesque waterfront. From the quiet luxury of the rooms and suites charmingly furnished in a country house style to the extensive leisure excursions offered, this inn offers a delightful stay and memorable visit. 98 rooms, 1-2 story. Closed mid-Nov-mid-Apr. Check-out 11 am, check-in 3 pm. TV; cable (premium), VCR available. Dining room. Room service. Supervised children's activities (in season); ages 3-12 years. In-house fitness room, massage. Heated pool, poolside service. Tennis, pro. Lawn games; bocce, croquet, shuffleboard. Sailboats, windsurfing, deep-sea fishing charters, whale-watching cruises. Airport, bus depot transportation available. Business center. **$$**

D 🏃 ⚓ 🛅 ⛱ 🏃

B&B/Small Inns

★ ★ ★ **CAPTAIN'S HOUSE INN.** *369-377 Old Harbor Rd (02633). Phone 508/945-0127; toll-free 800/315-0728; fax 508/945-0866. www.captains houseinn.com.* Once a sea captain's estate, this charming inn captivates guests with the exquisite period wallpapers, Williamsburg antiques, and elegantly refined Queen Anne chairs. Some of the charmingly appointed guestsrooms are named after the ships the captain skippered. 16 rooms, 2 story. Complimentary full breakfast. Check-out 11 am, check-in 2 pm. TV in some rooms; VCR available. Fireplaces. Health club privileges. Outdoor pool. Lawn games. Bicycles. Concierge service. Greek Revival house built 1839; Williamsburg-style antiques and period pieces. Totally nonsmoking. **$$**

D ☒ ⅍ ⊠

★ ★ ★ **CHATHAM TOWN HOUSE INN.** *11 Library I.n (02633). Phone 508/945-2180; toll-free 800/242-2180; fax 508/945-3990. www.chathamtown house.com.* This former sea captain's estate has undergone many transformations over the years, yet has still maintained the elegance and style of yesterday. Guests will find some of the old hemlock floors as well as some of the original woodwork characterizing the harpoon and oar motifs still in place. The attractively furnished guestrooms offer a picturesque water or garden views, as well as romantic canopies and private balconies. 29 rooms, 2 story. Complimentary full breakfast. Check-out noon, check-in 3 pm. TV; cable (premium). Fireplace in cottages. Heated pool, whirlpool, poolside service. In Chatham historical district. Totally nonsmoking. **$**

D ☒ ⊠

★ ★ ★ **CRANBERRY INN.** *359 Main St (02633). Phone 508/945-9232; toll-free 800/332-4667; fax 508/945-3769. www.cranberryinn.com.* Built in 1830, and nestled in the heart of the village historic district, this elegant inn offers guests all the comforts of home. Relax in one of the charmingly appointed guestrooms, or enjoy the picturesque view of a windmill while lazying away in one of the Kennedy rocking chairs set along the expansive front porch. 18 rooms, 2 story. Children over 12 years only. Complimentary breakfast buffet. Check-out 11 am, check-in 2 pm. TV. Some fireplaces. Totally nonsmoking. **$**

⊠

★ ★ ★ **MOSES NICKERSON HOUSE INN.** *364 Old Harbor Rd (02633). Phone 508/945-5859; toll-free 800/628-6972; fax 508/945-7087. www.mosesnickersonhouse.com.* 7 rooms, 2 story. Children over 14 years only. Complimentary full breakfast. Check-out 10:30 am, check-in 2:30 pm. TV available. Lawn games. Built 1839. Totally nonsmoking. **$**

⊠

★ ★ **OLD HARBOR INN.** *22 Old Harbor Rd (02633). Phone 508/945-4434; toll-free 800/942-4434; fax 508/945-7665. www.chathamoldharbor inn.com.* 8 rooms, 2 story. No room phones. Children over 14 years only. Complimentary breakfast buffet. Check-out 11 am, check-in 3 pm. Fireplace in parlor. Concierge services. Built 1933; former residence of prominent doctor. Renovated and furnished with a blend of antiques and modern conveniences. Outside deck. Totally nonsmoking. **$**

★ ★ **PORT FORTUNE INN.** *201 Main St (02633). Phone 508/945-0792; toll-free 800/750-0792. www.portfortuneinn.com.* 12 rooms, 2 story. 2 rooms with shower only. Children over 8 years only. Complimentary continental breakfast. Check-out 11 am, check-in 2 pm. TV in some rooms. Built in 1910. Totally nonsmoking. **$$**

★ ★ ★ **QUEEN ANNE INN.** *70 Queen Anne Rd (02633). Phone 508/945-0394; toll-free 800/545-4667; fax 508/945-4884. www.queenanneinn.com.* 34 rooms, 3 story. Closed Jan. Complimentary continental breakfast. Check-out 11 am, check-in 3 pm. TV; VCR available. Restaurant. Heated pool, whirlpool. Outdoor tennis. Lawn games. Boats for excursions. Built in 1840. Rooms feature antique furniture. Totally nonsmoking. **$**

Restaurants

★ ★ **CHATHAM SQUIRE.** *487 Main St (02633). Phone 508/945-0945; fax 508/945-4708. www.thesquire.com.* Seafood menu. Lunch, dinner. Bar. Children's menu. **$$**

★ ★ **CHRISTIAN'S.** *443 Main St (02633). Phone 508/945-3362; fax 508/945-9058. www.christiansrestaurant.com.* Seafood menu. Lunch, dinner. Bar. Built 1819. Outdoor dining. Two-level dining. **$$**

★ ★ **IMPUDENT OYSTER.** *15 Chatham Bars Ave (02633). Phone 508/945-3545; fax 508/945-9319.* Seafood menu. Lunch, dinner. Bar. Children's menu. Reservations required. Cathedral ceilings, stained-glass windows. **$$**

Dennis (Cape Cod), MA

4 hours 30 minutes; 262 miles from New York City

Settled 1639 **Pop** 15,973 **Elev** 24 ft **Area code** 508 **Zip** 02638

Information Chamber of Commerce, 242 Swan River Rd, 508/398-3568

Web www.dennischamber.com

Dennis heads a group, often called "The Dennises," that includes Dennisport, East Dennis, South Dennis, West Dennis, and Dennis. It was here, in 1816, that Henry Hall developed the commercial cultivation of cranberries. Swimming beaches are located throughout the area.

What to See and Do

Jericho House and Historical Center. *Old Main St and Trotting Park Rd, West Dennis. Phone 508/394-6114.* (1801) Period furniture. Barn museum contains old tools, household articles, model of salt works, photographs. (July-Aug, Wed and Fri) **DONATION**

Josiah Dennis Manse. *77 Nobscusset Rd. Phone 508/385-3528.* (1736) and **Old West School House** (1770). Restored home of minister for whom town was named; antiques, Pilgrim chest, children's room, spinning and weaving exhibit, maritime wing. (July-Aug, Tues and Thurs) **DONATION**

Special Events

Cape Playhouse. *820 Main St (02638). Phone 508/385-3911. www.cape playhouse.com.* The Cape Playhouse offers opportunities to watch both established Broadway stars and up-and-coming actors for two-week runs of musicals, comedies, and other plays. Putting on performances since 1927, the Playhouse is the oldest professional summer theater in the United States—you can sometimes take a backstage tour of this historic facility. On Friday mornings during summer, attend the special children's performance that includes puppetry, storytelling, and musicals. The Playhouse complex also houses the Cape Museum of Fine Arts, the Playhouse Bistro, and the Cape Cinema. (Late June-Labor Day) **$$$$**

Festival Week. *Phone 508/398-3568.* Canoe and road races, antique car parade, craft fair, antique show. (Late Aug)

Motels/Motor Lodges

★ **BREAKERS MOTEL.** *61 Chase Ave, Dennisport (02639). Phone 508/398-6905; toll-free 800/540-6905; fax 508/398-7360. www.capecodtravel.com/breakers.* 36 rooms, 4 kitchen units, 2 story. Closed mid-Oct-Apr. Continental breakfast. Check-out 11 am. TV; cable (premium). Heated pool. On beach. **$**

★ **COLONIAL VILLAGE RESORT.** *426 Lower County Rd, Dennisport (02639). Phone 508/398-2071; toll-free 800/287-2071; fax 508/398-2071. www.sunsol.com/colonial village.* 49 rooms, 29 kitchen units, 1-2 story. Closed mid-Oct-mid-May. Check-out 11 am. TV. Fireplaces. Sauna. Indoor pool, outdoor pool, whirlpool. **$**

★ **CORSAIR OCEANFRONT MOTEL.** *41 Chase Ave, Dennisport (02639). Phone 508/398-2279; toll-free 800/889-8037; fax 508/760-6681. www.corsaircrossrip.com.* 25 kitchen units, 2 story. Closed Dec-Mar. Complimentary continental breakfast. Check-out 11 am. TV; cable (premium), VCR available. Laundry services. Supervised children's activities (in season); ages 5-14. Indoor pool, outdoor pool, whirlpool. Lawn games. **$$**

★ **THE GARLANDS.** *117 Old Wharf Rd, Dennisport (02639). Phone 508/398-6987.* 20 air-cooled rooms, 2 story. Closed mid-Oct-mid-Apr. Children over 5 years only. Check-out 10 am. TV. No Credit Cards Accepted **$**

★ **SEA LORD RESORT MOTEL.** *56 Chase Ave, Dennisport (02639). Phone 508/398-6900. www.sunsol.com/sealord.* 27 rooms, 1-3 story. Closed Nov-Apr. Check-out 11 am. TV. Beach opposite. **$**

★ **SEA SHELL MOTEL.** *45 Chase Ave, Dennisport (02639). Phone 508/398-8965; toll-free 800/698-8965; fax 508/394-1237. www.virtualcapecod.com/market/seashellmotel.* 17 rooms, 5 kitchen units, 1-2 story. Complimentary continental breakfast. Check-out 11 am. TV. Some A/C. **$**

★ **SESUIT HARBOR.** *1421 Main St, East Dennis (02641). Phone 508/385-3326; toll-free 800/359-0097; fax 508/385-3326. www.capecod.net/sesuit.* 20 rooms, 3 kitchen units, 1-2 story. Complimentary continental breakfast. Check-out 10:30 am. TV. In-room modem link. Pool. **$**

★ ★ **SOUDINGS SEASIDE RESORT.** *79 Chase Ave, Dennisport (02639). Phone 505/394-6561; fax 508/374-7537. www.thesoundings.com.* 100 rooms, 15 kitchen units, 1-2 story. Closed mid-Oct-late-Apr. Check-out 11 am. TV; cable (premium). In-room modem link. Restaurant. Sauna. Indoor pool, outdoor pool, poolside service. **$**

★ ★ **SPOUTER WHALE MOTOR INN.** *405 Old Wharf Rd, Dennisport (02639). Phone 508/398-8010; fax 508/760-3214. www.spouterwhale.com.* 38 rooms, 6 kitchen units, 2 story. Closed late-Oct-Mar. Check-out 11 am. TV. Beachside breakfast bar. Health club privileges. Heated pool, whirlpool. On ocean; private beach. Totally nonsmoking. No Credit Cards Accepted **$**

★ ★ **THREE SEASONS MOTOR LODGE.** *421 Old Wharf Rd, Dennisport (02639). Phone 508/398-6091; fax 508/398-3762. www.threeseasons motel.com.* 61 rooms, 2 story. Closed Nov-late May. Check-out 11 am. TV. Restaurant. On private beach. **$**

Resorts

★ ★ **EDGEWATER BEACH RESORT.** *95 Chase Ave, Dennisport (02639). Phone 508/398-6922; fax 508/760-3447. www.edgewatercapecod .com.* 86 rooms, 1-2 story. Closed mid-Nov-mid-Mar. Check-out 11 am. TV; VCR (movies). In-house fitness room, sauna. Indoor pool, outdoor pool, whirlpool. Lawn games. **$**

★ ★ **LIGHTHOUSE INN.** *1 Lighthouse Rd, West Dennis (02670). Phone 508/398-2244; fax 508/398-5658. www.lighthouseinn.com.* 63 rooms. Closed mid-Oct-late-May. Check-out 11 am. TV; VCR available. Restaurant, bar; entertainment. Room service. Supervised children's activities (July-Aug); ages 3-10. Heated pool. Miniature golf. Outdoor tennis. Lawn games. Business center. Large private beach. **$$**

[D] [icons]

B&B/Small Inns

★ ★ **BY THE SEA GUESTS.** *57 Chase Ave, Dennisport (02639). Phone 508/398-8685; toll-free 800/447-9202; fax 508/398-0334. www.bytheseaguests.com.* 12 rooms, 1 A/C, 3 story. Complimentary continental breakfast. Check-out 11 am, check-in 2 pm. TV. Lawn games. Concierge. On private beach. **$**

[D] [icon]

★ ★ **FOUR CHIMNEYS INN.** *946 Main St (02638). Phone 508/385-6317; toll-free 800/874-5502; fax 508/385-6285. www.fourchimneysinn.com.* 8 air-cooled rooms, 3 story. No room phones. Complimentary full breakfast. Check-out 11 am, check-in 3pm. TV in sitting room; cable (premium). Restaurant nearby. Lawn games. **$**

[icon]

★ ★ **ISAIAH HALL BED AND BREAKFAST INN.** *152 Whig St (02638). Phone 508/385-9928; toll-free 800/736-0160; fax 508/385-5879. www.isaiahhallinn.com.* 10 rooms, 2 story. No room phones, Nov-mid-Apr, Children over 7 years only. Complimentary continental breakfast. Check-out 2-9:30 pm, check-in 2 pm. TV; VCR. Restaurant nearby. Lawn games. Farmhouse built 1857. Totally nonsmoking. **$**

[icon]

Restaurants

★ ★ **CAPTAIN WILLIAM'S HOUSE.** *106 Depot St, Dennisport (02639). Phone 508/398-3910.* Seafood menu. Closed Jan-Mar. Dinner. Bar. Children's menu. **$$**

[D]

★ ★ ★ **RED PHEASANT INN.** *905 Main St (02638). Phone 508/385-2133; fax 508/385-2112. www.redpheasantinn.com.* This charming restaurant is situated in a converted 200-year-old barn in the historic part of town. Dinner. Bar. Valet parking available. Totally nonsmoking. **$$$**

[D]

★ ★ **SCARGO CAFE.** *799 MA 6A (02638). Phone 508/385-8200; fax 508/385-6977. www.scargocafe.com.* Continental menu. Closed Thanksgiving, Dec 25. Lunch, dinner. Bar. Children's menu. Former residence (1865); opposite nation's oldest stock company theater. Totally nonsmoking. **$$**

[D]

★ **SWAN RIVER.** *5 Lower County Rd (02639). Phone 508/394-4466; fax 508/398-3201. www.swanriverseafoods.com.* Closed mid-Sept-late May. Lunch, dinner. Bar. Children's menu. **$$**

D

Eastham (Cape Cod), MA

4 hours 45 minutes; 276 miles from New York City
See also Orleans

Settled 1644 **Pop** 5,453 **Elev** 48 ft **Area code** 508 **Zip** 02642

Information Chamber of Commerce, PO Box 1329; 508/240-7211 or 508/255-3444 (summer only); or visit the Information Booth at MA 6 and Fort Hill

Web www.easthamchamber.com

On the bay side of the Cape, in what is now Eastham town, the *Mayflower* shore party met their first Native Americans. Also in the town is a magnificent stretch of Nauset Beach, which was once a graveyard of ships. Nauset Light is an old friend of mariners.

What to See and Do

Eastham Historical Society. *190 Samoset Rd (02642). Just off US 6. For hours, phone 508/255-0788.* 1869 schoolhouse museum; Native American artifacts; farming and nautical implements. (July-Aug, Mon-Fri afternoons) **DONATION** The society also maintains the

> **Swift-Daley House.** *On US 6. Phone 508/255-1766.* (1741) Cape Cod house contains period furniture, clothing, original hardware. (July-Aug, Mon-Fri afternoons or by appointment) **FREE**

Eastham Windmill. *Windmill Green, in town center. Phone 508/240-7211.* Oldest windmill on the Cape (1680); restored in 1936. (Late June-Labor Day, daily) **DONATION**

Motels/Motor Lodges

★ ★ **BLUE DOLPHIN INN.** *5950 Rte 6, North Eastham (02651). Phone 508/255-1159; toll-free 800/654-0504; fax 508/240-3676. www.capecod.net/ bluedolphin.* 49 rooms. Closed late-Oct-Mar. Pets accepted. Check-out 11 am. TV; cable (premium). Restaurant. Pool, poolside service. Lawn games. On 7 wooded acres. **$**

D

★ **CAPTAIN'S QUARTERS.** *Rte 6, North Eastham (02651). Phone 508/255-5686; toll-free 800/327-7769; fax 508/240-0280. www.captains-quarters.com.* 75 rooms. Closed mid-Nov-mid-Apr. Complimentary continental breakfast. Check-out 11 am. TV. Health club privileges. Heated pool. Outdoor tennis. Lawn games. Bicycles. **$**

D

★ **EAGLE WING GUEST MOTEL.** *960 Rte 6 (02642). Phone 508/240-5656; toll-free 800/278-5656; fax 508/240-5657. www.eaglewingmotel.com.* 19 rooms. Closed Nov-May. TV; cable (premium). Pool. Totally nonsmoking. **$**

⊠ ⊠ SC

★ **EASTHAM OCEAN VIEW MOTEL.** *Rte 6 (02642). Phone 508/255-1600; toll-free 800/742-4133; fax 508/240-7104. www.easthamoceanviewmotel .com.* 31 rooms, 2 story. Closed Nov-mid-Feb. Check-out 11 am. TV. Health club privileges. Heated pool. **$**

⊠ ⊼ ⊠

★ ★ **FOUR POINTS BY SHERATON.** *3800 Rte 6 (02642). Phone 508/255-5000; toll-free 800/533-3986; fax 508/240-1870. www.fourpoints.com.* 107 rooms, 2 story. Check-out 11 am. TV; cable (premium). In-room modem link. Restaurant, bar. Room service. In-house fitness room, sauna. Health club privileges. Game room. Indoor pool, outdoor pool, whirlpool, poolside service. Outdoor tennis. **$$**

D ⊀ ⊠ ⊼ ⊠ SC

★ **MIDWAY MOTEL & COTTAGES.** *5460 Rte 6 (02651). Phone 508/255-3117; toll-free 800/755-3117; fax 508/255-4235. www.midwaymotel.com.* 11 rooms, 3 kitchen units. Closed Nov-Feb. Check-out 11 am. TV; cable (premium), VCR available. Lawn games. Bicycle rentals. **$**

★ ★ **TOWN CRIER MOTEL.** *3620 Rte 6 (02642). Phone 508/255-4000; toll-free 800/932-1434; fax 508/255-7491. www.towncriermotel.com.* 36 rooms. Check-out 11 am. TV; cable (premium). Restaurant. Indoor pool. **$**

⊠ ⊠ SC

★ **VIKING SHORES RESORT.** *Rte 6 (02651). Phone 508/255-3200; toll-free 800/242-2131; fax 508/240-0205. www.vsp.cape.com/~viking.* 40 rooms. Closed early-Nov-mid-Apr. Complimentary continental breakfast. Check-out 11 am. TV; cable (premium). Heated pool. Outdoor tennis. Lawn games. **$**

D ⊀ ⊠ ⊠

B&B/Small Inns

★ ★ **OVERLOOK INN OF CAPE COD.** *3085 County Rd (Rte 6) (02642). Phone 508/255-1886; fax 508/240-0545. www.overlookinn.com.* 10 rooms, 3 story. Complimentary full breakfast; afternoon refreshments. Check-out 11 am, check-in 2 pm. Health club privileges. Lawn games. **$$**

⊠ SC

★ ★ **PENNY HOUSE INN.** *4885 County Rd (Rte 6) (02642). Phone 508/255-6632; toll-free 800/554-1751; fax 508/255-4893. www.pennyhouseinn.com.* 12 rooms, 2 story. Children over 8 years only. Complimentary full breakfast. Check-out 11 am, check-in 2 pm. TV; cable (premium), VCR (free movies). Lawn games. Audubon Society bird sanctuary, bicycle trails nearby. Totally nonsmoking. **$$**

⊠

Falmouth (Cape Cod), MA

4 hours 10 minutes; 248 miles from New York City

Settled circa 1660 **Pop** 32,660 **Elev** 10 ft **Area code** 508 **Zip** 02540

Information Cape Cod Chamber of Commerce, US 6 and MA 132, PO Box 790, Hyannis 02601-0790; 508/362-3225 or 888/CAPECOD

Web www.capecodchamber.org

What to See and Do

Ashumet Holly & Wildlife Sanctuary. *Massachusetts Audubon Society. Ashumet Rd, off Currier Rd; just N of MA 151. Phone 508/362-1426.* A 45-acre wildlife preserve with holly trail; herb garden; observation beehive. Trails open dawn to dusk. (Tues-Sun) **$$**

Falmouth Historical Society Museums. Julia Wood House. *55 Palmer Ave. Phone 508/548-4857.* (1790) and **Conant House** (circa 1740). Whaling collection; period furniture; 19th-century paintings; glassware; silver; tools; costumes; widow's walk; memorial park; colonial garden. (Mid-June-mid-Sept, Mon-Thurs; rest of year, by appointment) Katharine Lee Bates exhibit in Conant House honors author of "America the Beautiful." (Mid-June-mid-Sept, Mon-Thurs) On village green. **$$**

Island Queen. *Phone 508/548-4800.* Passenger boat trips to Martha's Vineyard; 600-passenger vessel. (Late May-mid-Oct)

Special Events

Arts & Crafts Street Fair. *Main St (02540). Phone 508/548-8500.* On a midsummer Wednesday each year in Falmouth, more than 200 painters, weavers, glassworkers, woodworkers, potters, and others artisans set up booths along Main Street. The Arts & Crafts Street Fair is a classic summer festival, with food and entertainment for the entire family. The Falmouth Artists Guild also hosts a fundraising art auction during the fair. Mid-July. **FREE**

Barnstable County Fair. *1220 Nathan Ellis Hwy (02536). 8 miles N on MA 151. Phone 508/563-3200.* Horse and dog shows, horse-pulling contest; exhibits. Last week in July.

College Light Opera Company at Highfield Theatre. *Depot Ave (02540). Phone 508/548-2211. Phone 508/548-0668 (after June 15).* Nine-week season of musicals and operettas with full orchestra. Mon-Sat. Late June-Labor Day.

Falmouth Road Race. *790 E Main St (race headquarters) (02540). Phone 508/540-7000. www.falmouthroadrace.com.* Starting in scenic Woods Hole and winding back into Falmouth Heights, this hilly and hot course takes you past some of the best scenery in the country. This 7.1-mile race has been called the "Best USA Road Race" by *Runner's World* magazine. The entry is a lottery, which means that far more people try to enter than are allowed in.

Your best bet is to join the over 70,000 spectators who line the course. If you want to race and don't get in, check the Internet for at least a dozen other summer road races on Cape Cod. Third Sun in Aug. **$$$**

Music on the Green. *Main St, Peg Noonan Park (02540). Phone 508/362-0066. www.artsfoundationcapecod.org.* Professional musicians from the Cape Cod area take part in the Music on the Green series, held on the town green in Falmouth. You'll enjoy rock, swing, marches, and folk music, all performed in the breezy park, and you're encouraged to bring a picnic and beach chair or blanket. The town of Hyannis also offers a Jazz by the Sea concert in early August on its town green. Early July-late Aug. **FREE**

Motels/Motor Lodges

★ ★ **ADMIRALTY INN.** *51 Teaticket Hwy, Rte 28 (02541). Phone 508/ 548-4240; fax 508/457-0535. www.vacationinnproperties.com.* 98 rooms, 3 story. Check-out 11 am. TV; cable (premium), VCR. Restaurant, bar. Supervised children's activities (seasonal); ages 5-12. Indoor pool, outdoor pool, whirlpool, poolside service. **$**

D ⌖

★ **BEST WESTERN FALMOUTH MARINA TRADEWINDS.** *26 Robbins Rd (02541). Phone 508/548-4300; toll-free 800/341-5700; fax 508/ 548-6787. www.bestwestern.com.* 63 rooms, 2 story. Closed Nov-Feb. Check-out 11 am. TV; cable (premium). Pool. Overlooks Falmouth Harbor. **$**

⌖ ⌖

★ **MARINER MOTEL.** *555 Main St (02540). Phone 508/548-1331; toll-free 800/233-2939; fax 508/457-9470. www.marinermotel.com.* 30 rooms. Check-out 11 am. TV; VCR available. Pool. **$**

⌖ ⌖

★ ★ **RAMADA INN.** *40 N Main St (02540). Phone 508/457-0606; toll-free 800/272-6232; fax 508/457-9694. www.ramada.com.* 72 rooms, 2 story. Check-out 11 am. TV; VCR (movies). In-room modem link. Restaurant, bar. Indoor pool. Business center. **$**

D ⌖ ⌖

★ **RED HORSE INN.** *28 Falmouth Hts Rd (02540). Phone 508/548-0053; toll-free 800/628-3811; fax 508/540-6563. www.redhorseinn.com.* 22 rooms, 2 story. Check-out 11 am. TV; cable (premium). In-room modem link. Outdoor pool. **$**

D ⌖ ⌖

Hotel

★ ★ ★ **NEW SEABURY RESORT AND CONFERENCE CENTER.** *Rock Landing Rd, New Seabury (02649). Phone 508/477-9111; toll-free 800/999-9033; fax 508/477-9790. www.newseabury.com.* This resort, con- ference center, and residential community sits on 2,000 recreation-filled acres and offers rentals from March 3rd to January 8th. The resort's villa development began in 1962 and consists of two golf courses, 16 tennis courts, and private beaches. 160 rooms, some A/C. Crib $10. Check-out 10 am, check-in 4 pm. TV; cable (premium), VCR (movies). In-room modem link. Balconies. Private patios. Coin laundry. Dining room 7 am-10 pm. Bar noon-1 am; entertainment in season. Supervised children's activities (July-Aug). Exercise room. Sports director. Seaside freshwater pool, wading pool. Miniature golf. Two 18-hole golf courses, pro, putting green, driving range. 16 all-weather tennis courts, pro. Bike trails. Sailboats. Trips to islands, whale watching, deep sea fishing available. Wind surfing. Airport transportation. Business center, convention center/facilities. On 2,300 acres. **$**

Resort

★ ★ **SEA CREST RESORT.** *350 Quaker Rd, North Falmouth (02556). Phone 508/540-9400; toll-free 800/225-3110; fax 508/548-0556. www.seacrest-resort.com.* 266 rooms, 1-3 story. Check-out 11 am, check-in 3 pm. TV. In-room modem link. Laundry services. Restaurant, bar; entertainment. Room service. Free supervised children's activities (in season); ages over 3. In-house fitness room, sauna. Game room. Indoor pool, outdoor pool, whirlpool, poolside service. Outdoor tennis. Lawn games. Windsurfing. Business center. Concierge. **$$**

B&B/Small Inns

★ ★ **BEACH HOUSE AT FALMOUTH HEIGHTS.** *10 Worcester Ct (02540). Phone 508/457-0310; toll-free 800/351-3426; fax 508/548-7895. www.capecodbeachhouse.com.* 8 rooms, 2 story. 6 rooms with shower only. No room phones. Closed Nov-May. Children over 12 years only. Complimentary continental breakfast. Check-out 11 am, check-in 3-6 pm. Pool. Hand-painted murals and furniture; unique theme rooms. Totally nonsmoking. **$**

★ ★ ★ **CAPT. TOM LAWRENCE HOUSE.** *75 Locust St (02540). Phone 508/540-1445; toll-free 800/266-8139; fax 508/457-1790. www.captaintomlawrence.com.* Vaulted ceilings, hardwood floors and a spiral staircase add to the romantic, old-world charm of this intimate inn located within walking distance of the town's historic main street. 7 rooms, 1 apt., 2 story. No room phones. Complimentary full breakfast. Check-out 11 am, check-in 3 pm. TV. Island ferry tickets available. Whaling captain's home (1861). Totally nonsmoking. **$$**

★ ★ **ELM ARCH INN.** *26 Elm Arch Way (02540). Phone 508/548-0133; fax www.elmarchinn.com.* 24 rooms, 2 story. No room phones. Check-out 11 am, check-in noon. TV in some rooms; cable (premium). Bombarded by British in 1814; dining room wall features cannonball hole. Pool. Built 1810; private residence of whaling captain. Screened terrace. No Credit Cards Accepted **$**

★ ★ ★ **GRAFTON INN.** *261 Grand Ave S (02540). Phone 508/540-8688; toll-free 800/642-4069; fax 508/540-1861. www.graftoninn.com.* 10 air-cooled rooms, 3 story. No room phones. Children over 16 years only. Complimentary full breakfast. Check-out 11 am, check-in 2-6 pm. TV; cable (premium). Former home of sea captain; built in 1850. On Nantucket Sound. Totally nonsmoking. Free transportation. **$$**

★ ★ **INN ON THE SOUND.** *313 Grand Ave (02540). Phone 508/457-9666; toll-free 800/564-9668; fax 508/457-9631. www.innonthesound.com.* 10 air-cooled rooms, 2 story. No room phones. Children over 16 years only. Complimentary full breakfast. Check-out 11 am, check-in 3-6 pm. TV. Built in 1880. Overlooking Vineyard Sound. Totally nonsmoking. **$$**

★ ★ ★ **LAMAISON CAPPELLARI AT MOSTLY HALL.** *27 Main St (02540). Phone 508/548-3786; fax 508/548-5778. www.mostlyhall.com.* This 1849 plantation-style house, which is the only one of its kind on Cape Cod, offers a secluded location in the heart of the town's historic district. Guests will enjoy the wraparound porch and rooms that feature canopy beds and ceiling fans. 6 rooms, 3 story. Shower only. No room phones. Closed Nov-mid-May. Children over 16 years only. Complimentary full breakfast. Check-out 11 am, check-in 3 pm. TV in sitting room. Bicycles. Concierge service. Totally nonsmoking. **$**

★ ★ ★ **THE PALMER HOUSE INN.** *81 Palmer Ave (02540). Phone 508/548-1230; toll-free 800/472-2632; fax 508/540-1878. www.palmerhouseinn.com.* Perched at the upper end of Cape Cod, this Queen Anne-style inn and guesthouse welcomes visitors year-round. Beaches, the Shining Sea Bikeway, and ferries to the islands are all nearby. 16 rooms, 3 story. Complimentary full breakfast. Check-out 11 am, check-in 3-9 pm. Some TVs. Concierge service. Queen Anne-style inn built in 1901. Totally nonsmoking. **$$**

D ☒ SC

★ ★ ★ **WILDFLOWER INN.** *167 Palmer Ave (02540). Phone 508/548-9524; toll-free 800/294-5459; fax 508/548-9524. www.wildflower-inn.com.* Conveniently located near Martha's Vineyard, guests will enjoy the relaxing and peaceful atmosphere offered at this bed-and-breakfast. 6 rooms, 3 story. No room phones. Complimentary breakfast. Check-out 11 am, check-in 3-6 pm. TV; cable (premium). Restaurant nearby. Game room. Lawn games. Concierge. Built in 1898; wraparound porch. **$$**

Restaurants

★ **THE FLYING BRIDGE.** *220 Scranton Ave (02540). Phone 508/548-2700; fax 508/457-7675. www.capecodrestaurants.org.* Seafood menu. Lunch, dinner. Bar. Entertainment Fri. Children's menu. Valet parking. Outdoor seating. **$$$**

D

★ **GOLDEN SAILS CHINESE.** *143-145 Main St (02536). Phone 508/548-3526.* Chinese menu. Closed Thanksgiving Day. Lunch, dinner. Bar. **$**

D SC

Harwich (Cape Cod), MA

4 hours 30 minutes; 266 miles from New York City

Settled circa 1670 **Pop** 12,386 **Elev** 55 ft **Area code** 508 **Zip** 02646

Information Harwich Chamber of Commerce, PO Box 34; 508/432-1600; or the Cape Cod Chamber of Commerce, US 6 and MA 132, PO Box 790, Hyannis 02601-0790, 508/362-3225 or 888/CAPECOD

Web www.capecodchamber.org

Harwich, whose namesake in England was dubbed "Happy-Go-Lucky Harwich" by Queen Elizabeth, is one of those towns made famous in New England literature. It is "Harniss" in the Joseph C. Lincoln novels of Cape Cod. A local citizen, Jonathan Walker, was immortalized as "the man with the branded hand" in Whittier's poem about helping escaped slaves; Enoch Crosby of Harwich was the Harvey Birch of James Fenimore Cooper's novel *The Spy*. Today, summer people own three-quarters of the land.

What to See and Do

Brooks Free Library. *739 Main St, Harwich. Phone 508/430-7562.* Houses 24 John Rogers' figurines. (Mon-Sat; closed holidays) **FREE**

⭐ **Cape Cod Baseball League.** *11 North Rd (02645). Phone 508/432-3878. www.capecodbaseball.org.* The Cape Cod Baseball League is baseball as you remember it: local, passionate, affordable, and played only with wooden bats. The ten teams are all drawn from college players from around the country, who live with host families for the summer, visit schools to interact with kids, and host a summer baseball clinic. Spectators sit on wooden benches, pack a picnic lunch or dinner, and cheer for their favorite players during each of the 44 games played each season at venues throughout Cape Cod. Mid-June-mid-Aug. **FREE**

Harwich Historical Society. *80 Parallel St, at Sisson Rd, in Harwich Center. Phone 508/432-8089.* Includes Brooks Academy Building and Revolutionary War Powder House. Native American artifacts, marine exhibit, cranberry industry articles, early newspapers and photographs. Site of one of the first schools of navigation in US. (Usually mid-June-mid-Sept, Tues-Fri; schedule may vary) **DONATION**

Red River Beach. *Deep Hole and Uncle Venies rds (02646). Off MA 28, S on Uncle Venies Rd in South Harwich. Sticker fee per weekday.* A fine Nantucket Sound swimming beach (water 68° to 72°F in summer).

Saquatucket Municipal Marina. *715 Main St. Phone 508/432-2562.* Boat ramp for launching small craft. (May-mid-Nov) **$$$**

Special Events

Cranberry Harvest Festival. *Rte 58 N and Rochester Rd (02645).* Family Day, antique car show, music, arts and crafts, fireworks, carnival, parade. One weekend in mid-Sept.

Harwich Junior Theatre. *105 Division St, West Harwich (02671). Phone 508/432-2002.* Plays for the family and children through high school age. Reservations required. (July-Aug, daily; Sept-June, monthly)

Motels/Motor Lodges

★ **COACHMAN MOTOR LODGE.** *774 Main St, Harwich Port (02646). Phone 508/432-0707; toll-free 800/524-4265; fax 508/432-7951. www.coachman motorinn.com.* 28 rooms. Closed mid-Nov-Apr. Check-out 11 am. TV; cable (premium). Restaurant. Pool. **$**

★ **SEADAR INN.** *Bank St Beach, Harwich Port (02646). Phone 508/432-0264; fax 508/430-1916. www.seadarinn.com.* 20 rooms, 1-2 story. No A/C. Closed mid-Oct-late-May. Complimentary continental breakfast. Check-out 11 am. TV; VCR. In-room modem link. Lawn games. Main building is an old colonial house (1789). Early American décor; some rooms with bay windows. Near beach. **$**

★ **WYCHMERE VILLAGE.** *767 Main St (Rte 28), Harwich Port (02646). Phone 508/432-1434; toll-free 800/432-1434; fax 508/432-8904. www.wychmere.com.* 25 rooms. Check-out 11 am. TV. Heated pool. Lawn games. **$**

B&B/Small Inns

★ ★ **AUGUSTUS SNOW HOUSE.** *528 Main St, Harwich Port (02646). Phone 508/430-0528; toll-free 800/320-0528; fax 508/432-6638. www.augustussnow.com.* 5 rooms, 2 story. Children over 12 years only. Complimentary full breakfast. Check-out 11 am, check-in 2 pm. TV; cable. Fireplaces. Beach. Free airport transportation. Concierge service. Built in 1901; Victorian décor. Totally nonsmoking. **$$**

★ ★ **CAPE COD CLADDAGH INN.** *77 Main St, West Harwich (02671). Phone 508/432-9628; toll-free 800/356-9628; fax 508/432-6039. www.capecod claddaghinn.com.* 8 rooms, 3 story. No room phones. Closed Jan-Mar. Pets accepted. Complimentary breakfast. Check-out 10:30 am, check-in 2 pm. TV; cable (premium). Dining room. Pool. Parking. Former Baptist parsonage (circa 1900). **$**

★ ★ **COUNTRY INN.** *86 Sisson Rd, Harwich Port (02646). Phone 508/432-2769; toll-free 800/231-1722; fax 508/430-1455. www.countryinncapecod.com.* 6 rooms, 2 story. No room phones. Complimentary continental breakfast. Check-out noon, check-in 2 pm. TV. Dining room (reservations required). Pool. Built in 1780; colonial décor. On 6 acres. Use of private beach. **$**

★ ★ ★ **DUNSCROFT BY THE SEA.** *24 Pilgrim Rd, Harwich Port (02646). Phone 508/432-0810; toll-free 800/432-4345; fax 508/432-5134. www. dunscroftbythesea.com.* Guests will enjoy the white-sand beach, just steps away, as well as such nearby activitites as shopping, miniature golf, fishing, water sports, clambakes, and whale watching. 8 rooms, 2 story. Children over 12 years only. Complimentary breakfast. Check-out 11 am, check-in 2 pm. Restaurant nearby. Whirlpool. Near mile-long beach on Nantucket Sound. **$$**

★ **SEA HEATHER INN.** *28 Sea St, Harwich Port (02646). Phone 508/432-1275; toll-free 800/789-7809. www.seaheather.com.* 20 rooms, 1-2 story. Children over 10 years only. Complimentary continental breakfast. Check-out 11 am, check-in 2 pm. TV. Lawn games. Early American décor; porches. Near beach. Totally nonsmoking. **$**

Restaurant

★ ★ **BISHOP'S TERRACE.** *MA 28, West Harwich (02671). Phone 508/432-0253.* Dinner, Sun brunch. Bar. Entertainment. Children's menu. Restored colonial house. Outdoor seating. **$$**

Hyannis (Cape Cod), MA

4 hours 20 minutes; 255 miles from New York City
See also Martha's Vineyard, South Yarmouth

Settled 1639 **Pop** 14,120 **Elev** 19 ft **Area code** 508 **Zip** 02601

Information Chamber of Commerce, 1481 Rte 132; 508/362-5230 or 877/HYANNIS

Web www.hyannis.com

Hyannis is the main vacation and transportation center of Cape Cod. Recreational facilities and specialty areas abound, including tennis courts, golf courses, arts and crafts galleries, theaters, and antique shops. There are libraries, museums, and the Kennedy Memorial and Compound. Candle-making tours are available. Scheduled airliners and Amtrak stop here, and it is also a port for boat trips to Nantucket Island and Martha's Vineyard. More than 6 million people visit the village every year, and it is within an hour's drive of the many attractions on the Cape.

What to See and Do

Auto Ferry/Steamship Authority. *Ocean St. Phone 508/477-8600. www. steamshipauthority.com.* Woods Hole, Martha's Vineyard, and Nantucket Steamship Authority conducts trips to Nantucket from Hyannis (year-round); departs from South St dock.

Cape Cod Crusaders. *35 Winter St (02601). Games are played at Dennis-Yarmouth High School: Take Rte 6 to exit 8, turn right off the ramp, and the stadium is about 2 miles down on your left. Phone 508/790-4782. www.cape codcrusaders.com.* If you want to see a professional sports team on Cape Cod, the Crusaders are the only team to watch. As members of the USISL (United States Independent Soccer League), the Crusaders play about 12 home games throughout late spring and summer. The Crusaders are the farm team for the New England Revolution, which means that Crusaders' players are often recruited from around the world and start out in Cape Cod. **$$**

Cape Cod Melody Tent. *21 W Main St (02601). Phone 508/775-9100. www.melodytent.com.* Looking for top-notch musical acts? The Cape Cod Melody Tent draws top musicians from around the country—mostly easy listening and country music—plus comedians. The venue is a huge white tent that's been hosting concerts on Cape Cod for over 50 years. Wednesday mornings in July and August bring theater and musical productions for kids. Call or visit the Web site for all concert dates and times, and if you want to be sure you get tickets, purchase them the day they go on sale. You may be able to pick up tickets left behind by no-shows just before performances begin. (Late May-mid-Sept)

Cape Cod Potato Chip Company. *100 Breed's Hill Rd (02601). Phone 508/775-7253. www.capecodchips.com.* Cape Cod Potato Chips, which are now sold all over the world, may be Cape Cod's most recognizable food prod-uct (although Nantucket Nectars, a local brand of juices available on the island and around the world, may take issue with that assessment). Perhaps the best part about taking the ten-minute self-guided tour of the facility is tasting the free samples, although seeing the unique kettles in which these crunchy chips are cooked is a close second. (Mon-Fri 9 am-5 pm, also Sat 10 am-4 pm Jul-Aug; closed Sun, holidays) **FREE**

Hyannis-Nantucket or Martha's Vineyard Day Round Trip. *Hy-Line, Pier #1, Ocean St Dock. Phone 508/778-2600.* (May-Oct) Also hourly sightseeing trips to Hyannis Port (Late Apr-Oct, daily); all-day or 1/2-day deep-sea fish-ing excursions (late Apr-mid-Oct, daily).

John F. Kennedy Hyannis Museum. *397 Main St, in Old Town Hall. Phone 508/790-3077.* Photographic exhibits focusing on President Kennedy's relationship with Cape Cod; 7-minute video presentation. Gift shop. (Mon-Sat, Sun afternoons) **$$**

John F. Kennedy Memorial. *Ocean St.* Circular fieldstone wall memorial 12 feet high with presidential seal, fountain, and small pool honors late president who grew up nearby.

Pufferbellies Entertainment Complex. *183 Rear Iyanough Rd (02601). Phone 508/790-4300. www.pufferbellies.com.* Pufferbellies is a unique collection of nightclubs and places to eat. On four separate dance floors, you'll dance the night away to swing, disco, country, and Top 40 music. If you have two left feet, be sure to take an on-site dance lesson. The sports bar entertains you with three big-screen TVs, dart boards, pool tables, and basketball machines, and a beach volleyball court in the Jimmy Buffet Parrothead Bar extends the fun outdoors. (Fri, Sat; closed Sun-Thurs) **$$$**

Swimming. Craigville Beach. 141 Basset Ln. Phone 508/790-6345. SW of town center. **Sea St Beach.** Sea St. Overlooking Hyannis Port harbor, bathhouse. **Kalmus Park.** Ocean St, bathhouse. **Veteran's Park.** Ocean St. Picnicking at Kalmus and Veteran's parks. Parking fee at all beaches.

Special Events

Cape Cod Oyster Festival. *20 Independence Dr (02601). Phone 508/778-6500. www.capecodoysterfestival.com.* What you get at the Cape Cod Oyster Festival is oysters—as many as you care to eat—accompanied by wine from local vineyards. Sample raw, baked, and roasted oysters, and also taste oyster stew. Held at the Naked Oyster restaurant under a big tent, the Oyster Festival draws locals and tourists alike. Late Oct. **$$$$**

Fleet Pops By the Sea. *Town Green (02601). Phone 508/362-0066. www.artsfoundationcapecod.org.* In early August, the Boston Pops makes its way from Boston to Cape Cod for a once-a-year concert on the Hyannis town green. You'll enjoy classics, pops, and Sousa marches. Each year brings a new Celebrity Guest Conductor, from actors to poets to famous chefs. The performance serves as a fundraiser that supports the Arts Foundation of Cape Cod. **$$$$**

Hyannis Harbor Festival. *Waterfront at Bismore Park. Phone 508/362-5230 or 508/775-2201.* Coast Guard cutter tours, sailboat races, marine displays, food, entertainment. Weekend in early June.

Motels/Motor Lodges

★ **BUDGET HOST INN.** *614 Rte 132 (02601). Phone 508/775-8910; toll-free 800/322-3354; fax 508/775-6476. www.capecodtravel.com/hyannismotel.* 41 rooms, 2 story. Check-out 11 am. TV; cable (premium). Pool. **$**

D ⛵ 🏊

★ ★ **CAPE CODDER RESORT.** *1225 Iyanough Rd (02601). Phone 508/771-3000; toll-free 888/297-2200; fax 508/771-6564. www.capecodder*

resort.com. 261 rooms, 2 story. Check-out 11 am. TV; cable (premium), VCR available. In-room modem link. Restaurant, bar; entertainment. Room service. In-house fitness room. Game room. Heated pool, whirlpool. Outdoor tennis. Airport transportation. **$**

[D] [≈] [≈] [⅄] [≈]

★ **CAPTAIN GOSNOLD VILLAGE.** *230 Gosnold St (02601). Phone 508/ 775-9111; fax 508/790-9776. www.captaingosnold.com.* 36 rooms. Closed Dec-mid-Apr. Check-out 10:30 am. TV; VCR available (free movies). Pool. Lawn games. **$**

[≈] [SC]

★ **COMFORT INN.** *1470 Rte 132 (02601). Phone 508/771-4804; fax 508/ 790-2336. www.comfortinn-hyannis.com.* 104 rooms, 3 story. No elevator. Complimentary continental breakfast. Check-out noon. TV; cable (premium). Health club privileges. Sauna. Indoor pool, whirlpool. **$**

[D] [≈] [⅄] [≈] [SC]

★ **DAYS INN.** *867 Rte 132 (02601). Phone 508/771-6100; toll-free 800/368-4667; fax 508/775-3011. www.daysinn.com.* 99 rooms, 2 story. Complimentary continental breakfast. Check-out 11 am. TV. In-room modem link. In-house fitness room. Indoor pool, outdoor pool, whirlpool. **$**

[D] [≈] [⅄] [≈] [SC]

★ ★ **HERITAGE HOUSE HOTEL.** *259 Main St (02601). Phone 508/775-7000; toll-free 800/352-7189; fax 508/778-5687. www.heritagehousehotel.com.* 143 rooms, 3 story. Check-out 11 am. TV; cable (premium). Restaurant. Sauna. Indoor pool, outdoor pool, whirlpool. **$**

[≈] [≈] [SC]

★ ★ **RAMADA.** *1127 Rte 132 (02601). Phone 508/775-1153; fax 508/ 775-1169. www.ramada.com.* 196 rooms, 2 story. Check-out 11 am. TV. Restaurant, bar. Room service. Game room. Indoor pool. Concierge. **$**

[D] [≈] [≈]

Hotel

★ ★ ★ **INTERNATIONAL INN.** *662 Main St (02601). Phone 508/775-5600; toll-free 877/588-3353; fax 508/775-3933. www.cuddles.com.* With a trademark like "cuddle and bubble," it's obvious romance is the distinguishing feature of this Cape Cod inn conveniently located within walking distance of town and ferries. Geared toward happy couples, each room or suite has a Jacuzzi built for two. 141 rooms, 2 story. Check-out 11 am. TV; VCR. In-room modem link. Restaurant, bar. Sauna. Indoor pool, outdoor pool. **$**

[D] [♨] [≈] [≈]

Resort

★ ★ ★ **SHERATON HYANNIS RESORT.** *West End Cir (02601). Phone 508/775-7775; toll-free 800/598-4559; fax 508/778-6039. www.sheraton.com.* The 224 rooms and 30,000 square feet of meeting space at this Cape Cod resort usually attract business travelers or visitors of the on-site golf course. The property is conveniently located at the island's center, and is within walking distance of shops and restaurants. 224 rooms, 2 story. Check-out 11 am, check-in 4 pm. TV. In-room modem link. Social director; entertainment, movies. Dining room, bar. Room service. Supervised children's activities (in season); ages 4-13. In-house fitness room, spa, sauna, steam room. Game room. Indoor pool, outdoor pool, whirlpool, poolside service. 18-hole par 3 golf, pro, putting green. Greens fee $20-$30. Outdoor tennis, lighted courts. Lawn games. Airport transportation. Business center. Concierge. **$**

B&B/Small Inns

★ ★ **SEA BREEZE INN.** *270 Ocean Ave (02601). Phone 508/771-7213; fax 508/862-0663. www.seabreezeinn.com.* 14 rooms, 2 story. Complimentary continental breakfast. Check-out 10:30 am, check-in 2 pm. TV. Concierge. Near beach; some rooms with ocean view. **$**

★ ★ **SIMMONS HOMESTEAD INN.** *288 Scudder Ave (02647). Phone 508/778-4999; toll-free 800/637-1649; fax 508/790-1342. www.simmons homesteadinn.com.* 14 rooms, 2 story. No room phones. Pets accepted, some restrictions; fee. Complimentary full breakfast. Check-out 11 am, check-in 1 pm. TV in sitting room. Health club privileges. Lawn games. Bicycles. Concierge. Restored sea captain's home built in 1820; some canopied beds. Unique décor; all rooms have different animal themes. **$$**

Restaurants

★ **EGG & I.** *521 Main St (02601). Phone 508/771-1596; fax 508/778-6385.* Specializes in crow's nest eggs, original breakfasts. Hours: 11am-1 pm. Closed Dec-Feb; weekends only Mar, Nov. Breakfast. Children's menu. Reservations accepted. Street parking. Family dining. **$**

★ **ORIGINAL GOURMET BRUNCH.** *517 Main St (02601). Phone 508/771-2558; fax 508/778-6052. www.theoriginalgourmetbrunch.com.* Hours: 7 am-3 pm. Closed Thanksgiving, Dec 25. Breakfast, lunch. Casual dining spot. **$**

★ ★ **PADDOCK.** *20 Scudder Ave (02601). Phone 508/775-7677; fax 508/771-9517. www.paddockcapecod.com.* Seafood menu. Closed mid-Nov-Apr 1. Lunch, dinner. Bar. Children's menu. Victorian décor. Valet parking. **$$**

★ ★ **PENGUINS SEA GRILL.** *331 Main St (02601). Phone 508/775-2023; fax 508/778-6999.* Closed Thanksgiving, Dec 25. Dinner. Bar. Children's menu. **$$**

★ ★ **RISTORANTE BAROLO.** *297 North St (02601). Phone 508/778-2878; fax 508/862-8050.* Italian menu. Closed Jan 1, Dec 25. Dinner. Bar to 1 am. Reservations required. Outdoor dining. **$$**

D

★ ★ **ROADHOUSE CAFE.** *488 South St (02601). Phone 508/775-2386; fax 508/778-1025. www.roadhousecafe.com.* Continental menu. Closed Dec 24-25. Dinner. Bar. Entertainment. In 1903 house. Valet parking. **$$**

D

★ **SAM DIEGO'S.** *950 Hyannis Rd (MA 132) (02601). Phone 508/771-8816. www.caperestaurantassociation.com.* Mexican menu. Closed Easter, Thanksgiving, Dec 25. Lunch, dinner. Bar. Children's menu. Outdoor seating. **$$**

D

★ **STARBUCKS.** *668 Rte 132 (02601). Phone 508/778-6767; fax 508/790-0036. www.starbuckscapecod.com.* Mexican menu. Closed Dec 25. Dinner. Bar. Entertainment. Children's menu. Outdoor seating. **$$$**

D

Orleans (Cape Cod), MA

4 hours 38 minutes; 273 miles from New York City

Settled 1693 **Pop** 6,341 **Elev** 60 ft **Area code** 508 **Zip** 02653

Information Cape Cod Chamber of Commerce, US 6 and MA 132, PO Box 790, Hyannis 02601-0790; 508/362-3225 or 888/CAPECOD

Web www.capecodchamber.org

Orleans supposedly was named in honor of the Duke of Orleans after the French Revolution. The settlers worked at shipping, fishing, and salt production. Its history includes the dubious distinction of being the only town in America to have been fired upon by the Germans during World War I. The town is now a commercial hub for the summer resort colonies along the great stretch of Nauset Beach and the coves behind it. A cable station, which provided direct communication between Orleans and Brest, France, from 1897 to 1959, is restored to its original appearance and open to the public.

What to See and Do

Academy of Performing Arts. *120 Main St. Phone 508/255-1963.* Theater presents comedies, drama, musicals, dance. Workshops for all ages.

French Cable Station Museum. *41 S Orleans Rd (02653). MA 28 and Cove Rd. Phone 508/240-1735.* Built in 1890 as American end of transatlantic cable from Brest, France. Original equipment for submarine cable communication on display. (July-Labor Day, Tues-Sat afternoons) **$$**

Nauset Beach. *44 Main St (02643). About 3 miles E of US 6 on marked roads. Phone 508/255-1386.* One of the most spectacular ocean beaches on the Atlantic Coast is now within the boundaries of Cape Cod National Seashore. Swimming, surfing, fishing; lifeguards. Parking fee.

Motels/Motor Lodges

★ **THE COVE.** *13 State Rte 28 (02653). Phone 508/255-1203; toll-free 800/ 343-2233; fax 508/255-7736. www.thecoveorleans.com.* 47 rooms, 1-2 story. Check-out 11 am. TV; VCR. Heated pool. Lawn games. Float boat rides available. Business center. On town cove. **$**

★ **NAUSET KNOLL MOTOR LODGE.** *237 Beach Rd (02643). Phone 508/255-3348; fax 508/247-9184. www.capecodtravel.com.* 12 rooms. No room phones. Crib free. Check-out 11 am. TV; cable. Picnic tables. Overlooks ocean, beach. **$**

D

★ **OLDE TAVERN MOTEL AND INN.** *151 MA 6A (02653). Phone 508/255-1565; toll-free 800/544-7705. www.capecodtravel.com/oldetavern.* 29 rooms. Closed Dec-Mar. Complimentary continental breakfast. Check-out 11 am. TV; cable (premium). Heated pool. Main building is restored inn and tavern visited by Thoreau in 1849, Daniel Webster and other personalities of the day. 18 deck rooms. **$**

★ **RIDGEWOOD MOTEL AND COTTAGES.** *10 Quanset Rd (02662). Phone 508/255-0473. www.ridgewoodmotel.com.* 12 rooms. No room phones. Complimentary continental breakfast. Check-out 10 am. TV. Pool. Lawn games. Totally nonsmoking. **$**

★ **SEASHORE PARK MOTOR INN.** *24 Canal Rd (02653). Phone 508/ 255-2500; toll-free 800/772-6453; fax 508/255-9400. www.seashoreparkinn.com.* 62 rooms, 24 kitchen units, 2 story. Closed Nov-mid-Apr. Complimentary continental breakfast. Check-out 11 am. TV. Sauna. Indoor pool, outdoor pool, whirlpool. Totally nonsmoking. **$**

★ **SKAKET BEACH MOTEL.** *203 Cranberry Hwy (02653). Phone 508/ 255-1020; toll-free 800/835-0298; fax 508/255-6487. www.skaketbeachmotel .com.* 46 rooms, 6 kitchen units, 1-2 story. Closed Dec-Mar. Complimentary continental breakfast. Check-out 11 am. TV; cable (premium). Laundry services. Heated pool. Lawn games. **$**

B&B/Small Inns

★ ★ **KADEE'S GRAY ELEPHANT.** *216 Main St (06243). Phone 508/255-7608.* 10 rooms, 2 story. Complimentary breakfast. Check-out 10:30 am, check-in 3 pm. TV; VCR available. Restaurant, bar. Parking lot. **$**

🏷️ 🐾 🛎️ 🖼️ ✈️ 🌐

★ ★ **THE PARSONAGE INN.** *202 Main St (02643). Phone 508/255-8217; toll-free 888/422-8217; fax 508/255-8216. www.parsonageinn.com.* 8 rooms, 2 story. No room phones. Children over 6 years only. Complimentary full breakfast. Check-out 11 am, check-in 2 pm. TV. Originally a parsonage (1770) and cobbler's shop. Totally nonsmoking. **$**

🌐

★ ★ **SHIPS KNEES INN.** *186 Beach Rd (02643). Phone 508/255-1312; fax 508/240-1351. www.capecodtravel.com/shipskneesinn.* 8 suites, 2 story. No room phones. Children over 12 years only. Complimentary continental breakfast. Check-out 10:30 am, check-in 1 pm. TV. Pool. Tennis. Rooms individually decorated in nautical style; many antiques, some 4-poster beds. Restored sea captain's house (circa 1820). Near ocean, beach. Totally nonsmoking. **$**

🏃 🏖️ 🌐

Restaurants

★ ★ **BARLEY NECK INN.** *5 Beach Rd, East Orleans (02653). Phone 508/255-0212; fax 508/255-3626. www.barleyneck.com.* Continental menu. Dinner. **$$**

🄳

★ ★ ★ **CAPTAIN LINNELL HOUSE.** *137 Skaket Beach Rd (02653). Phone 508/255-3400; fax 508/255-5377. www.linnell.com.* Chef-owner Bill Conway delivers a delightful dining experience at this charming and romantic restaurant. Take a walk out to the Victorian gazebo and enjoy the smell of lavender and the refreshing ocean breeze, then settle in for a cozy candlelit dinner. Seafood menu. Dinner. Children's menu. Outdoor seating. Totally nonsmoking. **$$$**

🄳

★ **DOUBLE DRAGON INN.** *MA 6A and MA 28 (02653). Phone 508/255-4100.* Chinese, Polynesian menu. Closed Thanksgiving. Lunch, dinner. **$$**

🄳

★ **LOBSTER CLAW.** *MA 6A (02653). Phone 508/255-1800. www.capecod.com/lobclaw.* Closed mid-Nov-Mar. Lunch, dinner. Bar. Children's menu. Former cranberry packing factory. **$$**

🄳 SC

★ ★ **NAUSET BEACH CLUB.** *222 E Main St, East Orleans (02643). Phone 508/255-8547; fax 508/255-8872. www.nausetbeachclub.com.* Regional Italian menu. Closed Sun, Mon off-season. Dinner. Bar. Totally nonsmoking. **$$$**

★ ★ **OLD JAILHOUSE TAVERN.** *28 West Rd (02653). Phone 508/255-5245. www.legalseafoods.com.* Seafood menu. Closed Thanksgiving, Dec 25. Lunch, dinner. Bar. Part of old jailhouse. **$$$**

D

Provincetown (Cape Cod), MA

5 hours 30 minutes; 300 miles from New York City

Settled circa 1700 **Pop** 3,431 **Elev** 40 ft **Area code** 508 **Zip** 02657

Information Chamber of Commerce, 307 Commercial St, PO Box 1017; 508/487-3424

Web www.capecodaccess.com/provincetownchamber

Provincetown is a startling mixture of heroic past and easygoing present. The Provincetown area may have been explored by Leif Ericson in AD 1004. It is certain that the *Mayflower* anchored first in Provincetown Harbor while the Mayflower Compact, setting up the colony's government, was signed aboard the ship. Provincetown was where the first party of Pilgrims came ashore. A bronze tablet at Commercial Street and Beach Highway marks the site of the Pilgrims' first landing. The city attracts many tourists who come each summer to explore the narrow streets and rows of picturesque old houses.

What to See and Do

Commercial Street. To view a shopping district that's steeped in history and still thriving today, visit Provincetown's Commercial Street. Stretching more than 3 miles in length, the narrow street sports art galleries, shops, clubs, restaurants, and hotels. When the street was constructed in 1835, the houses that backed up to it all faced the harbor, which was the principle area of business activity. As you tour the street, note that many of those homes were turned 180 degrees to face the street or had a new "front" door crafted in the back of the house.

Expedition Whydah's Sea Lab & Learning Center. *16 MacMillan Wharf. Phone 508/487-7955.* Archaeological site of sunken pirate ship *Whydah*, struck by storms in 1717. Learn about the recovery of the ship's pirate treasure, the lives and deaths of pirates, and the history of the ship and its passengers. (Apr-mid-Oct, daily; mid-Oct-Dec, weekends and school holidays)

★ **Pilgrim Monument & Museum.** *High Pole Hill. Phone 508/487-1310. www.pilgrim-monument.org.* A 252-foot granite tower commemorating the Pilgrims' 1620 landing in the New World; provides an excellent view. (Summer, daily) **$$$** Admission includes

Provincetown Museum. *Phone 508/487-1310.* Exhibits include whaling equipment, scrimshaw, ship models, artifacts from shipwrecks; Pilgrim Room with scale model diorama of the merchant ship *Mayflower;* Donald MacMillan's Arctic exhibit; antique fire engine and firefighting equipment; theater history display. (Summer, daily)

Provincetown Art Association & Museum. *460 Commercial St. Phone 508/487-1750.* Changing exhibits; museum store. (Late May-Oct, daily; rest of year, weekends) **DONATION**

Recreation. Swimming at surrounding beaches, including town beach, west of the village, Herring Cove and Race Point, on the ocean side. Tennis, cruises, beach buggy tours, and fishing available.

Town Wharf (MacMillan Wharf). *Commercial and Standish sts.* Center of maritime activity.

Portuguese Princess Whale Watch. *Phone 508/487-2651 or 800/442-3188 (New England).* 100-foot boats offer 3 1/2-hour narrated whale watching excursions. Naturalist aboard. (Apr-Oct, daily)

Whale Watching. *306 Commercial St (02657). Dolphin Fleet of Provincetown. Phone 508/349-1900 or (800) 826-9300.* Offers 3 1/2-4-hour trips (Mid-Apr-Oct, daily). Research scientists from the Provincetown Center for Coastal Studies are aboard each trip to lecture on the history of the whales being viewed. **$$$$**

Special Event

Provincetown Portuguese Festival. *MacMillian Wharf (02657). Phone 508/487-3424.* Provincetown's fisherman of Portuguese ancestry started this enduring festival over 50 years ago. Each year in late June, the local bishop says Mass at St. Peter's Church and then leads a procession to MacMillan Wharf, where he blesses a parade of fishing boats. The festival that follows features fireworks, concerts, dancing, Portuguese art, and delightful food choices. If you aren't in town for the Provincetown Blessing, check out similar events in Falmouth (July 4) and Hyannis (early July). Last week June.

Motels/Motor Lodges

★ **BEST WESTERN CHATEAU MOTOR INN.** *105 Bradford St W (02657). Phone 508/487-1286; fax 508/487-3557. www.bwprovincetown.com.* 54 rooms, 1-2 story. Closed Nov-Apr. Complimentary continental breakfast. Check-out 11 am. TV; cable (premium). In-room modem link. Heated pool. Harbor view. **$**

★ **BLUE SEA MOTOR INN.** *696 Shore Rd (02657). Phone 508/487-1041; toll-free 888/768-7666. www.blueseamotorinn.com.* 43 rooms, 1-2 story. Closed Nov-Apr. Check-out 10 am. TV. In-room modem link. Laundry services. Indoor pool, whirlpool. **$**

Resorts

★ ★ BEST WESTERN TIDES BEACHFRONT MOTOR INN.
837 Commercial St (02657). Phone 508/487-1045; fax 508/487-3557. www.bwprovincetown.com. 64 rooms, 1-2 story. Closed mid-Oct-mid-May. Check-out 11 am. TV; cable (premium). In-room modem link. Laundry services. Restaurant. Heated pool. On private beach. **$**

★ ★ THE MASTHEAD RESORT.
31-41 Commercial St (02657). Phone 508/487-0523; toll-free 800/395-5095; fax 508/481-9251. www.capecodtravel.com/masthead. 10 rooms, 2 story. Check-out 10 am. TV. In-shore and deepwater moorings; launch service. On private beach. **$**

★ ★ PROVINCETOWN INN.
1 Commericial St (02657). Phone 508/487-9500; toll-free 800/942-5388; fax 508/487-2911. www.provincetowninn.com. 100 rooms, 1-2 story. Complimentary continental breakfast. Check-out 11 am. TV. Restaurant, bar. Heated pool. Private beach. **$**

All Suite

★ ★ WATERMARK INN.
603 Commercial St (02657). Phone 508/487-0165; fax 508/487-2383. www.watermark-inn.com. 10 rooms, 2 story. Check-out 11 am, check-in 3 pm. TV. In-room modem link. On beach. **$**

B&B/Small Inns

★ ★ FAIRBANKS INN.
90 Bradford St (02657). Phone 508/487-0386; toll-free 800/324-7265; fax 508/487-3540. www.fairbanksinn.com. 14 rooms, 2 story. No room phones. Children over 15 years only. Complimentary continental breakfast. Check-out 11 am, check-in 2 pm. TV; cable (premium). Concierge. Built 1776; courtyard. Totally nonsmoking. **$**

★ ★ ★ SNUG COTTAGE.
178 Bradford St (02657). Phone 508/487-1616; fax 508/487-5123. www.snugcottage.com. 8 rooms, 1-2 story. Complimentary breakfast. Check-out 11 am, check-in 3 pm. TV; VCR (free movies). Fireplaces. Built in 1820. **$$**

★ ★ SOMERSET HOUSE.
378 Commercial St (02657). Phone 508/487-0383; toll-free 800/575-1850; fax 508/487-4746. www.somersethouseinn.com. 13 rooms, 2-3 story. Complimentary full breakfast. Check-out 11 am, check-in 3 pm. TV; cable. Opposite beach. Restored 1850s house. Totally nonsmoking. **$$**

★ ★ **WATERSHIP INN.** *7 Winthrop St (02657). Phone 508/487-0094; toll-free 800/330-9413. www.watershipinn.com.* 15 rooms, 3 story. Some A/C. No room phones. Complimentary continental breakfast. Check-out 11:30 am, check-in 2 pm. TV. Lawn games. Built in 1820. **$**

★ ★ **WHITE WIND INN.** *174 Commercial St (02657). Phone 508/487-1526; toll-free 888/49wind; fax 508/487-4792. www.whitewindinn.com.* 12 rooms, 3 story. 8 rooms with shower only. No elevator. No room phones. Pets accepted. Complimentary continental breakfast. Check-out 11 am, check-in 2 pm. TV; VCR available (movies). Concierge service. Built in 1845; former shipbuilder's home. Opposite harbor. Totally nonsmoking. **$**

Restaurants

★ ★ **CAFÉ EDWIGE.** *333 Commercial St (02657). Phone 508/487-2008.* Closed Oct 31; also late May. Breakfast, dinner. Reservations accepted (dinner). Outdoor dining. Totally nonsmoking. Cathedral ceilings, skylights. **$$**

★ ★ **DANCING LOBSTER CAFE.** *373 Commercial St (02657). Phone 508/487-0900.* Mediterranean menu. Closed Mon; also Dec-May. Dinner. Bar. **$$**

D

★ ★ **FRONT STREET.** *230 Commercial St (02657). Phone 508/487-9715.* Italian, continental menu. Closed Jan-Apr. Dinner. Bar. Totally nonsmoking. **$$**

D

★ ★ **LOBSTER POT.** *321 Commercial St (02657). Phone 508/487-0842; fax 508/487-4863.* Closed Jan. Lunch, dinner. Bar. Lobster and chowder market on premises. **$$**

D

★ ★ **NAPI'S.** *7 Freeman St (02657). Phone 508/487-1145; fax 508/487-7123.* Continental, Vegetarian menu. Dinner. Bar. Children's menu. **$$**

D

★ **PUCCI'S HARBORSIDE.** *539 Commercial St (02657). Phone 508/487-1964.* Seafood menu. Closed Nov-mid-Apr. Lunch, dinner. Bar. **$$**

D

★ ★ ★ **RED INN RESTAURANT.** *15 Commercial St (02657). Phone 508/487-0050; fax 508/487-6253.* Located on the edge of the harbor, this historic inn features Continental cuisine with an emphasis on seafood and prime beef. The views are stunning and the service is friendly. Continental menu. Closed Dec 25. Lunch, dinner, Sun brunch. Three dining rooms in restored colonial building. **$$**

D

★ ★ **SAL'S PLACE.** *99 Commercial St (02657). Phone 508/487-1279; fax 508/487-1279. www.salsplaceprovincetown.com.* Southern Italian menu. Closed Nov-Apr. Dinner. Children's menu. Outdoor seating. **$$**

[D]

Sandwich (Cape Cod), MA

4 hours 10 minutes; 241 miles from New York City

Settled 1637 **Pop** 20,136 **Elev** 20 ft **Area code** 508 **Zip** 02563

Information Cape Cod Canal Region Chamber of Commerce, 70 Main St, Buzzards Bay 02532; 508/759-6000

Web www.capecodcanalchamber.org

The first town to be settled on Cape Cod, Sandwich made the glass that bears its name. This pressed glass was America's greatest contribution to the glass industry.

What to See and Do

★ **Heritage Plantation.** *67 Grove St (02563). Phone 508/888-3300. www.heritageplantation.org.* The Heritage Plantation offers an eclectic mix of beautiful gardens, folk art, antique cars, and military paraphernalia. Visit the Old East Windmill from 1800 and the restored 1912 carousel that's great fun for young and old. Call ahead to find out about unique exhibits, displays, and concerts. Note that the Heritage Plantation is located in the town of Sandwich, the oldest town on the Cape. (Daily mid-May-mid-Oct) **$$**

Hoxie House & Dexter Gristmill. *Water St. Phone 508/888-1173.* Restored mid-17th-century buildings. House, operating mill; stone-ground corn meal sold. (Mid-June-mid-Oct, daily)

Sandwich Glass Museum. *129 Main St (02563). Phone 508/888-0251.* Internationally renowned collection of exquisite Sandwich Glass (circa 1825-1888). (Apr-Oct, daily) **$$**

Scusset Beach. *3 miles NW on MA 6A across canal, then 2 miles E at junction MA 3 and US 6. Phone 508/362-3225.* Swimming beach, fishing pier; camping (fee). **$$**

Shawme-Crowell State Forest. *42 Main St (02563). 3 miles W on MA 130, off US 6. Phone 508/888-0351.* Approximately 2,700 acres. Primitive camping.

Motels/Motor Lodges

★ **COUNTRY ACRES MOTEL.** *187 Rte 6A (02563). Phone 508/888-2878; toll-free 888/860-8650; fax 508/888-8511.* 17 rooms. Check-out 11 am. TV; cable (premium). Pool. Lawn games. **$**

★ **EARL OF SANDWICH MOTEL.** *378 Rte 6A (02537). Phone 508/888-1415; toll-free 800/442-3275; fax 508/833-1039. www.earlofsandwich.com.* 24 rooms. Pets accepted. Complimentary continental breakfast. Check-out 11 am. TV. Tudor motif. **$**

D 🐾 ⊠

★ **OLD COLONY MOTEL.** *436 Rte 6A (02537). Phone 508/888-9716; toll-free 800/786-9716.* 10 rooms. Higher rates: holidays (2-day minimum), mid-May-mid-June; lower rates mid-Sept-Nov, Mar-mid-May. Crib free. Complimentary continental breakfast. Check-out 11 am. TV. Refrigerators. Restaurant nearby. Playground. Pool. Picnic tables. Lawn games. **$**

⊇ ⊠

★ **SANDY NECK MOTEL.** *669 Rte 6A (02537). Phone 508/362-3992; toll-free 800/564-3992; fax 508/362-5170. www.sandyneck.com.* 12 rooms. Lower rates Feb-mid-June and after Labor Day-Dec. Closed rest of year. Crib free. Complimentary coffee. Check-out 11 am. TV; cable (premium). Refrigerators. Restaurant nearby. **$**

⊠

★ **SHADY NOOK INN & MOTEL.** *14 Old Kings Hwy (02563). Phone 508/888-0409; toll-free 800/338-5208; fax 508/888-4039. www.shadynookinn.com.* 30 rooms, 7 kitchen units. Check-out 11 am. TV; cable (premium). In-room modem link. Laundry services. Heated pool. **$**

⊇ ⊠

★ **SPRING HILL MOTOR LODGE.** *351 Rte 6A (02537). Phone 508/888-1456; toll-free 800/646-2514; fax 508/833-1556.* 24 rooms, 2 kitchen units. Check-out 11 am. TV; cable (premium). Heated pool. Tennis. **$**

🎿 ⊇ ⊠

B&B/Small Inns

★ ★ ★ **BAY BEACH BED & BREAKFAST.** *3 Bay Beach Ln (02563). Phone 508/888-8813; toll-free 800/475-6398; fax 508/888-5416. www.baybeach.com.* Overlooking Cape Cod Bay, this private beachfront bed-and-breakfast offers guests a quiet haven from their busy lives. Visitors will enjoy the elegant guest room amenities such as fresh flowers, wine and cheese, and fresh fruit in their refrigerator. 6 rooms, 3 story. Closed Nov-mid-May. Children over 16 years only. Complimentary full breakfast. Check-out noon, check-in 2-6 pm. TV; cable (premium). In-house fitness room. Concierge service. On beach. Totally nonsmoking. **$$$**

🧍 ⊠

★ ★ **THE BELFRY INN & BISTRO.** *6-8 Jarves St (02563). Phone 508/ 888-8550; toll-free 800/844-4542; fax 508/888-3922. www.belfryinn.com.* 3 story. No elevator. Children over 10 years only. Complimentary full breakfast. Check-out 11 am, check-in 3 pm. TV in common room; cable (premium), VCR available (movies). In-room modem link. Fireplaces. Restaurant 5-11 pm. Room service 24 hours. Lawn games. Business center. Concierge service. Former rectory built 1882; belfrey access. Totally nonsmoking. **$$**

D ⊠ 介

★ ★ **CAPTAIN EZRA NYE HOUSE BED & BREAKFAST.** *152 Main St (02563). Phone 508/888-6142; toll-free 800/388-2278; fax 508/833-2897. www.captainezranyehouse.com.* 6 rooms, 2 story. No A/C. No room phones. Children over 10 years only. Complimentary full breakfast. Check-out 11 am, check-in 2 pm. TV in sitting room. Built in 1829. Totally nonsmoking. **$**

⊠

★ ★ ★ **THE DAN'L WEBSTER INN.** *149 Main St (02563). Phone 508/ 888-3622; toll-free 800/444-3566; fax 508/888-5156. www.danlwebsterinn.com.* 54 rooms, 1-3 story. Check-out 11 am, check-in 3 pm. TV; cable (premium). In-room modem link. Dining room (see THE DAN'L WEBSTER INN). Bar; entertainment. Room service. Health club privileges. Pool. Whirlpool in suites. Modeled on an 18th-century house. **$$**

➤ 介 ⊠

★ ★ ★ **ISAIAH JONES HOMESTEAD.** *165 Main St (02563). Phone 508/888-9115; toll-free 800/526-1625; fax 508/888-9648. www.isaiahjones.com.* An American flag and flower-lined porch beckon guests inside this 1849 Victorian home. The guest rooms, decorated with antiques and country-patterned fabrics, are a great resting stop when visiting this Cape Cod town's many historic sites. 7 rooms, 2 story. No A/C. No room phones. Children over 16 years only. Complimentary full breakfast. Check-out 11 am, check-in 3-6 pm. TV in sitting room. Concierge service. Restored Victorian house built 1849. Totally nonsmoking. **$**

⊠

★ ★ **VILLAGE INN.** *4 Jarves St (02563). Phone 508/833-0363; toll-free 800/922-9989; fax 508/833-2063. www.capecodinn.com.* 8 rooms, 3 story. No A/C. No room phones. Children over 8 years only. Complimentary full breakfast. Check-out 11 am, check-in 3-6 pm. Federal-style house (1837) with wrap-around porch, gardens. Totally nonsmoking. **$**

⊠

Restaurants

★ **BOBBY BYRNE'S PUB.** *Rte 6A and Tupper Rd (02563). Phone 508/ 888-6088; fax 508/833-1614. www.bobbybyrnes.com.* Seafood, steak menu. Closed Thanksgiving, Dec 25. Lunch, dinner. Bar. Children's menu. **$$**

D

★★ **BRIDGE RESTAURANT.** *21 MA 6A, Sagamore (02561). Phone 508/888-8144. www.capecodmenus.com.* Continental, Italian, seafood menu. Closed Thanksgiving, Dec 25. Lunch, dinner. Bar. Children's menu. **$**

D

★★★ **THE DAN'L WEBSTER INN.** *149 Main St (02563). Phone 508/888-3623; fax 508/888-5156. www.danlwebsterinn.com.* Dinner in the dining room of the historic Cape Cod inn is a romantic affair, complete with candlelight and a wood-burning fireplace. The updated Continental menu ranges from prime rib and filet mignon to pan-seared monkfish. Don't miss the award-winning wine list, or indulgent desserts like the white chocolate macadamia nut blondie. Seafood menu. Breakfast, lunch, dinner, Sun brunch. Bar. Children's menu. Valet parking. Conservatory dining overlooks garden. Reproduction of 1700s house. **$$**

D

★ **HORIZON'S.** *98 Town Neck Rd (02563). Phone 508/888-6166; fax 508/888-9209.* Seafood, steak menu. Closed Jan-Apr. Lunch, dinner. Bar. Entertainment Sat. Children's menu. Outdoor seating. **$**

D

South Yarmouth (Cape Cod), MA

4 hours 25 minutes; 260 miles from New York City

Pop 11,603 **Elev** 20 ft **Area code** 508 **Zip** 02664

Information Yarmouth Area Chamber of Commerce, PO Box 479; 800/732-1008 or the Cape Cod Chamber of Commerce, US 6 and MA 132, PO Box 790, Hyannis 02601-0790; 508/362-3225 or 888/CAPECOD

Web www.capecodchamber.org

Much of the area of the Yarmouths developed on the strength of seafaring and fishing in the first half of the 19th century. South Yarmouth is actually a village within the town of Yarmouth. Well-preserved old houses line Main Street to the north in Yarmouth Port, architecturally among the choicest communities in Massachusetts. Bass River, to the south, also contains many fine estates.

What to See and Do

Captain Bangs Hallet House. *11 Strawberry Ln. Off MA 6A, near Yarmouth Port Post Office. Phone 508/362-3021.* Early 19th-century sea captain's home. (June-Oct, Thurs-Sun afternoons; rest of year, by appointment) Botanic trails (all year; donation). Gate house (June-mid-Sept, daily). **$$**

Swimming. *265 Sisson Rd (02645). Phone 508/430-7553.* Nantucket Sound and bayside beaches. Parking fee.

Winslow Crocker House. *250 Rte 6A (02675). On Old King's Hwy, US 6A, in Yarmouth Port. Phone 508/362-4385.* (circa 1780) Georgian house adorned with 17th-, 18th-, and 19th-century furnishings collected in early 20th century. Includes furniture made by New England craftsmen in the colonial and Federal periods; hooked rugs, ceramics, pewter. (June-mid-Oct, Tues, Thurs, Sat, and Sun) **$$**

Motels/Motor Lodges

★ ★ **ALL SEASON MOTOR INN.** *1199 Rte 28 (02664). Phone 508/394-7600; toll-free 800/527-0359; fax 508/398-7160. www.allseasons.com.* 114 rooms, 2 story. Check-out 11 am. TV; cable (premium), VCR (movies). Laundry services. Restaurant. In-house fitness room, sauna. Game room. Indoor pool, outdoor pool, whirlpool. **$**

[D] [⇌] [⚂] [⛾]

★ **AMERICANA HOLIDAY MOTEL.** *99 Main St (02673). Phone 508/775-5511; toll-free 800/445-4497; fax 508/790-0597. www.americanaholiday.com.* 153 rooms, 2 story. Closed Nov-Feb. Check-out 11 am. TV. Sauna. Game room. Indoor pool, outdoor pool, whirlpool. Lawn games. **$**

[D] [⇌] [⛾] [SC]

★ **BEACH N TOWNE MOTEL.** *1261 Rte 28 (02664). Phone 508/398-2311; toll-free 800/987-8556. www.sunsol.com/beachntowne.* 21 rooms. Closed Jan. Check-out 11 am. TV. Pool. Lawn games. **$**

[⇌] [⛾]

★ ★ **BEST WESTERN BLUE ROCK MOTOR INN.** *39 Todd Rd (02664). Phone 508/398-6962; fax 508/398-1830. www.bestwestern.com.* 44 rooms, 1-2 story. Closed late-Oct-Mar. Check-out 11 am. TV. Restaurant, bar. Heated pool, whirlpool. Overlooks golf course. Greens fee $31. Outdoor tennis. **$**

[D] [⚄] [⛿] [⇌] [⛾]

★ ★ **BEST WESTERN BLUE WATER ON THE OCEAN.** *291 S Shore Dr (02664). Phone 508/398-2288; toll-free 800/367-9393; fax 508/398-1010. www.bestwestern.com.* 106 rooms, 1-2 story. Check-out 11 am. TV. Restaurant, bar; entertainment Fri-Sat. Free supervised children's activities (July-Labor Day); ages 6-15. Sauna. Indoor pool, outdoor pool, whirlpool, poolside service. Outdoor tennis. Lawn games. On 600-foot private ocean beach. **$$**

[D] [⛿] [⇌]

★ **CAVALIER MOTOR LODGE.** *881 Main St (02664). Phone 508/394-6575; toll-free 800/545-3536; fax 508/394-6578. www.cavaliermotorlodge.com.* 66 rooms, 1-2 story. Closed Nov-late-Mar. TV; VCR available (movies). Sauna. Game room. Indoor pool, outdoor pool, children's pool, whirlpool. Lawn games. **$**

[⇌] [⛾]

★ ★ **GULL WING SUITES.** *822 Main St (Rte 28) (02664). Phone 508/394-9300; fax 508/394-1190. www.ccrh.com.* 136 rooms, 2 story. Check-out

11 am. TV; cable (premium). Sauna. Game room. Indoor pool, outdoor pool, whirlpool. **$**

D ▭ ▭ SC

★ **HUNTERS GREEN MOTEL.** *553 Main St (Rte 28) (02673). Phone 508/771-1169; toll-free 800/775-5400. www.capecodmotel.com.* 74 rooms, 2 story. Closed Nov-mid-Apr. Check-out 11 am. TV; cable (premium). Indoor pool, outdoor pool, whirlpool. Lawn games. **$**

D ▭

★ **LEWIS BAY LODGE.** *149 Rte 28 (02673). Phone 508/775-3825; toll-free 800/882-8995; fax 508/778-2870. www.lewisbaylodge.com.* 68 rooms, 2 story. Closed Nov-late-Apr. Complimentary continental breakfast. Check-out 11 am. TV; cable (premium). In-house fitness room. Indoor pool, outdoor pool, whirlpool. **$**

D ▭ ⚀ ▭

★ **MARINER MOTOR LODGE.** *573 Rte 28 (02673). Phone 508/771-7887; toll-free 800/445-4050; fax 508/771-2811. www.mariner-capecod.com.* 100 rooms, 2 story. Continental breakfast. Check-out 11 am. TV; cable (premium). Sauna. Game room. Indoor pool, outdoor pool, whirlpool. **$**

D ▭ ▭ SC

★ ★ ★ **RED JACKET BEACH.** *1 S Shore Dr (02664). Phone 508/398-6941; toll-free 800/672-0500; fax 508/398-1214. www.redjacketbeach.com.* Found steps away from the coast, this Cape Cod oceanfront resort has private balconies or porches so that guests may enjoy the view. Indoor and outdoor heated pools and complete recreation facilities including spas, sailing, and tennis are available. 150 rooms, 1-2 story. Closed late-Oct-Mar. Check-out 11 am. TV. Laundry services. Restaurant, bar. Room service. Supervised children's activities (July-Labor Day); ages 4-12. In-house fitness room, sauna. Game room. Indoor pool, outdoor pool, whirlpool, poolside service. Outdoor tennis. Lawn games. Sailing. **$$**

D ⚑ ▭ ⚀ ▭

★ **TIDEWATER MOTOR LODGE.** *135 Main St (02673). Phone 508/775-6322; fax 508/778-5105. www.tidewaterml.com.* 100 rooms, 1-2 story. Check-out 11 am. TV. Sauna. Game room. Indoor pool, outdoor pool, whirlpool. Lawn games. On 4 acres; view of Mill Creek Bay. **$**

▭ ▭

Resorts

★ ★ **RIVIERA BEACH RESORT–BASS RIVER.** *327 S Shore Dr, Bass River (02664). Phone 508/398-2273; toll-free 800/CAPECOD; fax 508/398-1202. www.redjacketinns.com/riviera.* 125 rooms, 2 story. Lower rates mid-Apr-June, early Sept-late Oct. Closed Nov-Mar. Crib free. Check-out 11 am. TV; VCR available (movies). Balconies. Refrigerators. Some in-room whirlpools. Restaurant 7:30-11 am, noon-2 pm. Bar noon-8 pm. Free supervised children's activities (July-Labor Day); ages 4-11. Two pools, one indoor, whirlpool. Lawn games. Sailing, waterbikes, sailboards in season. On 415-foot private beach.

`D` `≕` `N`

★ ★ **YARMOUTH RESORT.** *343 Rte 28 (02673). Phone 508/775-5155; fax 508/790-8255. www.yarmouthresort.com.* 138 rooms, 2 story. Check-out 11 am. TV. In-room modem link. Sauna. Game room. Indoor pool, outdoor pool, whirlpool. **$**

`D` `≕` `N`

B&B/Small Inns

★ ★ ★ **CAPTAIN FARRIS HOUSE BED & BREAKFAST.** *308 Old Main St, Yarmouth (02664). Phone 508/760-2818; toll-free 800/350-9477; fax 508/398-1262. www.captainfarris.com.* With it's beautifully landscaped lawns and breathtaking views, this bed-and-breakfast will surely please everyone. Guests can enjoy sailing, canoeing, kayaking, and windsurfing. Antique shopping, birdwatching and The John F. Kennedy Museum are also nearby. 10 rooms. Children over 10 years only. Complimentary full breakfast. Check-out 11 am, check-in 3 pm. TV; VCR. In-room modem link. Fireplaces. Dining room by reservation. Whirlpool. Lawn games. Concierge service. Two buildings (1825 and 1845). Near Bass River. **$**

`N`

★ ★ ★ **INN AT LEWIS BAY.** *57 Maine Ave (02673). Phone 508/771-3433; toll-free 800/962-6679; fax 508/790-1186. www.innatlewisbay.com.* Located in a quiet seaside neighborhood just one block from Lewis Bay, this Dutch colonial bed and breakfast offers guests a relaxing place to vacation. A bountiful breakfast is served each morning, and afternoon refreshments each afternoon. 6 rooms, 2 story. No room phones. Children over 12 years only. Complimentary full breakfast. Check-out 11 am, check-in 3-8 pm. Lawn games. Concierge service. Beach house built in the 1920s. Totally nonsmoking. **$**

`N`

★ ★ ★ **LIBERTY HILL INN.** *77 Main St (MA 6A) (02675). Phone 508/362-3976; toll-free 800/821-3977; fax 508/362-6485. www.libertyhillinn.com.* Built in 1825, this charming bed-and-breakfast features individually appointed rooms, all unique in their decor and feel; many feature fireplaces and canopy beds to ease guests through their stays. 9 rooms, 3 story. No room phones. Complimentary breakfast. Check-out 11 am, check-in 3-9 pm. TV. Free airport transportation. Concierge. Totally nonsmoking. **$**

`N`

Restaurants

★ ★ **ABBICCI.** *43 Main St, Yarmouth (02675). Phone 508/362-3501; fax 508/362-7802. www.abbiccirestaurant.* Italian menu. Dinner. Bar. **$$$**

`D`

★ ★ **RIVERWAY LOBSTER HOUSE.** *MA 28 (02664). Phone 508/398-2172.* Seafood menu. Closed Dec 25. Dinner. Bar. Children's menu. **$**

D

★ **SKIPPER RESTAURANT.** *152 S Shore Dr (02664). Phone 508/394-7406; fax 508/394-0627. www.skipper-restaurant.com.* Seafood, steak menu. Closed Oct-Mar. Breakfast, lunch, dinner. Bar. Children's menu. A/C upstairs only. **$$**

D

★ ★ **YARMOUTH HOUSE.** *335 Main St, West Yarmouth (02673). Phone 508/771-5154; fax 508/790-2801. www.yarmouthhouse.com.* Seafood menu. Closed Dec 25. Lunch, dinner. Bar. Children's menu. 3 dining rooms; working water wheel. **$$**

D

If you want to spend a little more time away from the City that Never Sleeps, take a long weekend trip to Lake Placid, Martha's Vineyard, Nantucket Island, or Saranac Lake. All will rejuvenate your soul and senses. After a few days in one of these places you should be ready to face and enjoy the manic pace of NYC.

Lake Placid

5 hours; 296 miles from New York City
See also Saramac Lake

Pop 2,638 **Elev** 1,882 ft **Area code** 518 **Zip** 12946

Information Essex County Visitors Bureau, Olympic Center, 216 Main St; 518/523-2445 or 800/447-5224

Web www.lakeplacid.com

Mount Marcy, the highest mountain in New York State (5,344 feet) rises in the Adirondack peaks that surround the town. On Lake Placid, the village also partly surrounds Mirror Lake. This is one of the most famous all-year vacation centers in the East and the site of the 1932 and 1980 Winter Olympics. The Intervale Olympic Ski Jump Complex has 229-foot and 296-foot ski jumps constructed for the 1980 games, now open to the public and used for training and competition.

What to See and Do

John Brown Farm Historic Site. *2 John Brown Rd, 2 miles S, 1 mile off NY 73. (12946). Phone 518/523-3900.* Brown's final home; graves of the noted abolitionist, two sons, and ten others who died in the struggle to end slavery. (Late May-late Oct, Mon, Wed-Sun) **$**

Lake Placid Center For the Arts. *91 Saranac Ave at Fawn Ridge. Phone 518/ 523-2512 for ticket prices.* Concerts, films, art exhibits. Gallery (Tues-Sun). **FREE**

Lake Placid Marina. *Mirror Lake Dr and NY 86, 1 mile N on NY 86 to Mirror Lake Dr. (12946). Phone 518/523-9704.* One-hour scenic cruises. (Mid-May-mid-Oct) **$$$**

Olympic Arena and Convention Center. *218 Main St (12946). Phone 518/ 523-1655.* Built for the 1932 Winter Olympics and renovated for the 1980 Winter games. Winter and summer skating shows, family shows, hockey; public skating, concerts.

Olympic Sports Complex (Mount Van Hoevenberg Recreation Area). *7 miles SE on NY 73. Phone 518/523-1655.* Site of 1980 Winter Olympic Games. Bobsled, luge, cross-country, biathlon events. Championship bobsled and luge races most weekends in winter. Cross-country trails (33 miles) open to the public when not used for racing. Bobsled rides (mid-Dec-early Mar, Tues-Sun; fee); luge rides (mid-Dec-early Mar, weekends; fee).

Uihlein Sugar Maple Research-Extension Field Station. *Bear Cub Rd. Phone 518/523-9337.* 4,000-tap sugar bush; maple syrup demonstrations, exhibits in Sugar House. Owned and operated by NY State College of Agriculture at Cornell University. (July-Labor Day, Tues-Fri; mid-Sept-mid-Oct, Fri; closed July 4) Schedule may vary. **FREE**

Motels/Motor Lodges

★ **ALPINE AIR MOTEL.** *99 Saranac Ave (12946). Phone 518/523-9261; toll-free 800/469-3663; fax 518/523-9273.* 24 rooms, 2 story. Check-out 10:30 am. TV. Heated pool. Downhill ski 8 miles, cross-country ski 1 mile. **$**

★ **ALPINE MOTOR INN.** *Rte 86 (Wilmington Rd) (12946). Phone 518/ 523-2180; fax 518/523-1724. www.alpine-inn.com.* 18 rooms, 2 story. Check-out 11 am. TV; cable (premium). Restaurant 5-9:30 pm. Bar 3 pm-midnight. 45-hole golf privileges opposite. Downhill ski 8 miles, cross-country ski 1 mile. **$**

★ **ART DEVLINS OLYMPIC MOTOR INN.** *348 Main St (12946). Phone 518/523-3700; fax 518/523-3893. www.artdevlins.com.* 40 rooms, 2 story. Pets accepted. Complimentary continental breakfast. Check-out 11 am. TV. Pool, children's pool. Downhill ski 8 miles, cross-country ski 2 miles. Airport transportation. **$**

★ **THE BARK EATER INN.** *Alstead Hill Rd (12942) Phone 518/576-2221; toll-free 800/232-1607; fax 518/576-2071. www.barkeater.com.* 19 rooms, 7 share baths, 3 buildings, 1-2 story. No room phones. Crib free. TV in living room; cable (premium). Complimentary full breakfast. Dining room 8-9 am, dinner (1 sitting) 7 pm. Box lunches. Setups. Check-out 11 am, check-in 1 pm. Business services available. Downhill ski 15 miles; cross-country ski on site, rentals. Picnic tables, grills. Former stagecoach stop built in early 1800s; antiques. Spacious farm with 5-acre pond. Horse stables. Polo field. Family-owned since 1936. Totally nonsmoking. **$**

★★ **BEST WESTERN GOLDEN ARROW HOTEL.** *150 Main St (12946). Phone 518/523-3353; toll-free 800/582-5540; fax 518/523-8063. www.golden-arrow.com.* 130 rooms, 4 story. Pets accepted; fee. Check-out 11 am. TV. In-room modem link. Some fireplaces. Restaurant, bar; entertainment. Exercise room, sauna. Indoor pool, children's pool, whirlpool. Downhill ski 9 miles, cross-country ski on site. Paddle boats, canoes, racquetball. Free airport transportation. **$**

★★ **HOLIDAY INN.** *1 Olympic Dr (12946). Phone 518/523-2556; toll-free 800/874-1980; fax 518/523-9410. www.lakeplacidresort.com.* 199 rooms, 4 story. Pets accepted. Check-out 11 am. TV. In-room modem link. Restaurant, bar. Room service. Exercise room, sauna. Heated pool, whirlpool. Tennis. **$**

★ **HOWARD JOHNSON.** *90 Saranac Ave (12946). Phone 518/523-9555; toll-free 800/858-4656; fax 518/523-4765. www.hojo.com.* 92 rooms, 2 story. Pets accepted. Check-out noon. TV; cable (premium). Restaurant, bar. Indoor pool, whirlpool. Outdoor tennis. Downhill ski 10 miles, cross-country ski on site. Lawn games. **$**

★★ **RAMADA.** *8-12 Saranac Ave (12946). Phone 518/523-2587; fax 518/523-2328. www.ramada.com.* 90 rooms, 3 story. Pets accepted, some restrictions. Check-out noon. TV; VCR available. In-room modem link. Restaurant, bar. Exercise equipment. Game room. Indoor pool, whirlpool. Downhill ski 10 miles, cross-country ski 1 mile. **$**

Hotels

★★ **ADIRONDACK INN BY THE LAKE.** *217 Main St (12946). Phone 518/523-2424; toll-free 800/556-2424; fax 518/523-2425. www.lakeplacid. com/adkinn.* 49 rooms, 2 story. Check-out 11 am. TV. Restaurant, bar.

Exercise equipment, sauna. Indoor pool, whirlpool. Downhill ski 8 miles, cross-country ski 1 mile. Opposite Olympic Arena and Convention Hall. **$**

D ⬛⬛⬛⬛⬛

★ ★ ★ ★ **LAKE PLACID LODGE.** *Whiteface Inn Rd (12946). Phone 518/523-2700; fax 518/523-1124. www.lakeplacidlodge.com.* Nestled on the wooded shores of Lake Placid with majestic views of Whiteface Mountain, Lake Placid Lodge may be the most restful spot around. The lodge is a celebration of the simple beauty of the Adirondacks. The rooms, suites, and log and timber cabins from the 1920s reflect the region's unique style with twig and birch bark furniture and one-of-a-kind decorative accents. Every piece of artwork and furniture is attributed to a local artist or craftsman, adding to the lodge's individual style. Stone fireplaces and deep-soaking tubs further enhance the rustic sophistication of the accommodations, and discriminating diners praise the restaurant's refined new American cuisine. The lakeside setting makes it ideal for water sports; during the winter months, ice skating, snowshoeing, and cross-country skiing are popular activities. The pristine setting is often experienced from the comfortable seat of a lakefront Adirondack chair. 17 cabins. No elevator, Pets accepted; fee. Complimentary full breakfast. Check-out noon. In-room modem link. Some fireplaces. Restaurant, bar. Game room. Downhill skiing 10 miles, cross-country skiing on site. Concierge. **$$$$**

D ⬛⬛⬛⬛⬛⬛

Resorts

★ ★ ★ **HILTON LAKE PLACID RESORT.** *1 Mirror Lake Dr (12946). Phone 518/523-4411; toll-free 800/755-5598; fax 518/523-1120. www.lphilton.com.* With 179 rooms, all with a private balcony or patio overlooking the mountains or lake, this hotel offers it all, summer or winter. Two indoor and two outdoor pools, 72 championship holes of golf and nearby skiing/snowboarding are just a few reasons to stay. 176 rooms, 5 story. Pets accepted. Check-out noon. TV. Restaurant, bar; entertainment. Room service. Exercise equipment. Game room. Four pools, two indoor, poolside service. Downhill ski 8 miles, cross-country ski 1 mile. Boats. **$**

D ⬛⬛⬛⬛⬛⬛⬛⬛ SC

★ ★ ★ **MIRROR LAKE INN RESORT AND SPA.** *5 Mirror Lake Dr (12946). Phone 518/523-2544; fax 518/523-2871. www.mirrorlakeinn.com.* Walnut floors, marble, antiques and stone fireplaces build a warm atmosphere in this traditional inn that also offers its guests all the amenities of a modern inn. A complete health spa and exercise facilities can be found at this property. 4 story. Check-out noon. TV. Fireplaces. Dining room, bar. Exercise equipment, sauna. Two heated pools; one indoor; children's pool, whirlpool. Outdoor tennis. Downhill ski 10 miles, cross-country ski 1 mile. Row boats, paddle boats, canoeing. On 8 acres. **$$**

D ⬛⬛⬛⬛⬛⬛⬛

B&B/Small Inn

★ **PLACID BAY INN ON LAKE PLACID.** *70 Saranac Ave (12946). Phone 518/523-2001; fax 518/523-2001. www.placidbay.com.* 20 rooms, 8 kitchen units, 2 story. Check-out 11 am. TV. Heated pool. Paddleboats, canoes. Fishing charters and guide service. **$**

D 🛟 ⚡ 🏊 ⛷ SC

Restaurants

★ ★ ★ **AVERIL CONWELL DINING ROOM.** *5 Mirror Lake Dr (12946). Phone 518/523-2544. www.mirrorlakeinn.com.* Located in the Mirror Lake Inn, this restaurant offers both views of the lake and the mountains. A special dinner series features theme nights including wine dinners and many international meals. American menu. Breakfast, dinner. Bar. Children's menu. Outdoor seating. Totally nonsmoking. **$$$**

D

★ ★ ★ **LAKE PLACID LODGE.** *Whiteface Inn Rd (12946). Phone 518/ 523-2700; fax 518/523-1124. www.lakeplacidlodge.com.* The emphasis is on the upscale eclectic at the inn's dining room, where guests may find anything from duck consomme to lobster and sweetbread ravioli. There's even a tempting vegetarian option: toasted tomato cannelloni with sage and goat cheese. Contemporary American menu. Dinner. Bar. Outdoor seating. **$$$$**

D

Martha's Vineyard, MA

5 hours 20 minutes; 264 miles from New York City
See also Falmouth, Nantucket Island

Settled 1642 **Pop** 12,690 **Elev** 0-311 ft **Area code** 508

Information Chamber of Commerce, Beach Rd, PO Box 1698, Vineyard Haven 02568; 508/693-0085

Web www.mvy.com

This triangular island below the arm of Cape Cod combines moors, dunes, multicolored cliffs, flower-filled ravines, farmland, and forest. It is less than 20 miles from west to east and 10 miles from north to south.

There was once a whaling fleet at the island, but Martha's Vineyard now devotes itself almost entirely to being a vacation playground, with summer houses that range from small cottages to elaborate mansions. The colonial atmosphere still survives in Vineyard Haven, the chief port; Oak Bluffs; Edgartown; West Tisbury; Gay Head; and Chilmark.

Gay Head is one of the few Massachusetts towns in which many inhabitants are of Native American descent.

What to See and Do

Aquinnah Cliffs. *State Rd (02535).* These cliffs—a national landmark—are the most popular and most photographed tourist attraction on Martha's Vineyard because of the stunning view they offer. The 150-foot, brilliantly colored cliffs were formed over millions of years by glaciers; today, the cliffs are owned by the Wampanoag Indians, who hold them sacred. (Previous names of the cliffs include Dover Cliffs, so named by settlers in 1602, and Gay Head Cliffs, a name that originated from British sailors. Gay Head was the official name of this area of Martha's Vineyard until 1998.) On top of the Cliffs stands Aquinnah Light lighthouse, which was commissioned by President John Adams in 1844 to protect ships from the treacherous stretch of sea below and built with clay from the cliffs.

Chicama Vineyards. *Stoney Hill Rd (02545). Phone 508/693-0309. www. chicamavineyards.com.* Martha's Vineyard was once awash in winemaking; today Chicama Vineyards is reviving the practice. The European grapes are used to produce a variety of wines, including Merlot, Chardonnay, and Cabernet. You'll also find other foodstuffs for sale, including vinegars and salad dressings, mustards and chutneys, and jams and jellies. Tours and wine tasting are available, but hours vary with the day and season. (Hours vary; call ahead) **FREE**

East Beach. *Chappaquiddick Rd (02539). Take your four-wheel drive car on the On Time ferry from Martha's Vineyard to Chappaquiddick Island. From the ferry dock, take Chappaquiddick Road until a sharp right turn, where the road becomes Dike Bridge Road. Park near the bridge or obtain an oversand vehicle permit to drive on the beach. Phone 508/627-7689.* East Beach is the popular name for two adjoining beaches: Wasque Reservation and Cape Pogue Wildlife Refuge. You'll go to a lot of trouble to get to this rustic beach that has no restrooms or concessions, but the quiet, beautiful stretch of shoreline makes the preparation and trip worthwhile. Chances are, you'll have this stunning beach all to yourself. (Daily) **$$**

Featherstone Meeting House for the Arts. *Barnes Rd, Oak Bluffs (02568). Phone 508/693-1850. www.featherstonearts.org.* This unique arts center offers tourists the hourly use of artists' studios and also features classes in photography, woodworking, pottery, weaving, and stained glass. Nestled on a former horse farm on 18 acres, the Meeting House also includes a gallery of works from local artists. Call for details about a summer art camp for kids. (Daily; call for studio availability)

Felix Neck Sanctuary. *3 miles from Edgartown off Edgartown-Vineyard Haven Rd. Phone 508/627-4850. www.massaudubon.org/Nature_Connection/ Sancturaries/Felix_Neck.* This 350-acre wildlife preserve is a haven for kids and bird lovers alike. Six miles of trails (guided or self-guided) meander through the sanctuary's meadows, woods, salt marshes, and beaches. The visitors center offers unique exhibits along with a more traditional gift shop. In summer, consider enrolling the kids in Fern & Feather Day Camp at the Sanctuary. (Daily June-Sept 8 am-4 pm; Oct-May Tues-Sun 8-4) **$**

Flying Horse Carousel. *33 Circuit Ave, Oak Bluffs (02557). Phone 508/693-9481.* Whether you're traveling with a youngster who loves horses (but is too young to ride them for real) or want to hop on for yourself, Flying Horse Carousel is a treat not to be missed. This carousel, the oldest in the country and a national historic landmark, looks nothing like modern carousels you may have seen in malls or shopping centers. Instead, Flying Horse features gorgeous, hand-carved, lifelike horses that glide to festive music. Try to grasp the brass ring in the center to earn your next ride free.

Hyannis-Martha's Vineyard Day Round Trip. *Phone 508/778-2600.* Passenger service from Hyannis (May-Oct).

Menemsha Fishing Village. *North St (02552).* Take a shuttle bus or bike ferry from Aquinnah. Menemsha is a picturesque fishing village, which means you'll see plenty cedar-sided fishing shacks, fishermen in waterproof gear, and lobster traps strewn about. The movie *Jaws* was filmed here, and if you saw it, you may have haunting flashbacks while you're here! You'll find quaint shopping areas in the village, as well.

Mytoi. *Dike Rd (02539). Phone 508/693-7662; 508/627-6789.* Although Martha's Vineyard may not be a logical location for a Japanese garden, Mytoi has won praises for its breathtaking mix of azaleas, irises, dogwood, daffodils, rhododendron, and Japanese maple for nearly 50 years. You'll spy goldfish and koi swimming in a pond that's the centerpiece of the garden; you can visit the small island at the pond's center via the ornamental bridge. Take an easy 1-mile hike that weaves through the gardens and into forested area and salt marshes. Allow from an hour to a half-day. (Daily) **FREE**

Oak Bluffs. In 1835, this Methodist community served as the site of annual summer camp meetings for church groups. As thousands attended these meetings, the communal tents gave way to family tents, which in turn became wooden cottages designed to look like tents. Today, visitors to the community may see these "Gingerbread Cottages of the Campground."

Recreation. Swimming. *Phone 508/693-3057; 508/693-0600 (Mink Meadows).* Many sheltered beaches, among them public beaches at Menemsha, Oak Bluffs, Edgartown, and Vineyard Haven. Surf swimming on south shore. **Tennis.** Public courts in Edgartown, Oak Bluffs, West Tisbury, and Vineyard Haven. **Boat rentals** at Vineyard Haven, Oak Bluffs, and Gay Head. **Fishing.** Good for striped bass, bonito, bluefish, weakfish. **Golf** at Farm Neck Club.

Steamship Authority. *1494 E Rodney French Blvd (02744). Phone 508/477-8600 or 508/693-9130. www.steamshipauthority.com.*

> **New Bedford-Martha's Vineyard Ferry.** Daily passenger service (mid-May-mid-Sept) to New Bedford. Same-day round-trips available. Also bus tours of the island. Schedule may vary; contact Steamship Authority. **$$$$**
>
> **Woods Hole, Martha's Vineyard & Nantucket Steamship Authority.** *Phone 508/477-8600. www.islandferry.com.* Conducts round-trip service to Martha's Vineyard (all year, weather permitting).

⭐ **Vincent House.** *Pease's Point Way (02539). Main St in Edgartown. Phone 508/627-4440.* Oldest known house on the island, built in 1672. Carefully restored to allow visitors to see how buildings were constructed 300 years ago. Original brickwork, hardware, and woodwork. (June-early Oct, daily; rest of year, by appointment) **FREE** Also on Main St is

Old Whaling Church. *89 Main (02539). Phone 508/627-4442.* Built in 1843, this is a fine example of Greek Revival architecture. Now a performing arts center with seating for 500.

Vineyard Haven and Edgartown. *Phone 508/693-0085. www.mvy.com/shopping.* Vineyard Haven is where most of Martha's Vineyard's year-round residents live, so its shops are a bit less upscale than those in ritzy Edgartown, where you could spend an afternoon or even an entire day. In both areas, you'll find clothing (both casual and upscale), books, jewelry, home-decorating items, and goodies to eat (fudge, candy, and jams). Vineyard Haven is perhaps best known as the location of the Black Dog General Store (along with the Black Dog Bakery and Black Dog Tavern) that sell T-shirts and other goods bearing the logo of its now-famous black Lab. Edgartown, the island's first colonial settlement, and the location of stately white Greek Revival houses built by whaling captains, is also home to an astounding number of art galleries.

Vineyard Museum. *8 Cooke St, Edgartown (02539). Phone 508/627-4441.* Four buildings dating back to pre-Revolutionary times join together to form the Vineyard Museum. Thomas Cooke House, an historic colonial home, specializes in antiques and folk art; Foster Gallery displays exhibits from the whaling industry; Pease Galleries specializes in Native American exhibits, and Gale Huntington Library is a useful tool for genealogy. A Cape Cod museum wouldn't be complete without displaying a huge Fresnel (lighthouse) lens—view it just outside the front doors. **$**

The Yard. *Middle Rd (02535). Phone 508/645-9662. www.dancetheyard.com.* For 30 years, The Yard has hosted dance performances throughout the summer. The theater is intimate, with just 100 seats available, and makes its home in a renovated barn nestled in the Chilmark woods. The Yard also offers community dance classes, and free performances for children and senior citizens. (Mid-Oct-mid-June) **$$$**

Event

Striped Bass & Bluefish Derby. *1A Dock St, Edgartown (02539). Phone 508/693-0085. www.mvderby.com.* Just after midnight on the first day of the Derby, fishing enthusiasts seek out their favorite fishing holes and cast off, hoping to land the big one during the following month. Whenever contestants haul in striped bass, bluefish, bonito, or false albacore, the catch is weighed and measured at Edgartown Harbor. Prizes are awarded daily for the largest fish; a grand prize awaits the contestant who nets the largest fish caught during the tournament. Watching the weighing in at the Harbor is a unique Cape Cod treat. Mid-Sept-mid-Oct.

Hotels

★ ★ ★ **HARBOR VIEW HOTEL OF MARTHA'S VINEYARD.** *131 N Water St, Edgartown (02539). Phone 508/627-7000; toll-free 800/225-6005; fax 508/627-8417. www.harbor-view.com.* Built in 1891, this resort is another prime example of the heritage of Martha's Vineyard. Overlooking Egartown Harbor, guests can relax in a rocking chair on one of the verandahs, stroll among the beautifully maintained gardens, enjoy a swim in the heated outdoor pool, or even practice their backhand at a game of tennis. 124 rooms, 14 kitchen units, 1-4 story. Check-out 11 am. TV; cable (premium). Fieldstone fireplace in lobby. Restaurant (see COACH HOUSE), bar. Heated pool, poolside service. Outdoor tennis. Concierge. Overlooks harbor; view of lighthouse. In operation since 1891. Beach opposite. **$**

★ ★ ★ **KELLEY HOUSE.** *23 Kelly St, Edgartown (02539). Phone 508/627-7900; fax 508/627-8142. www.kelleyhouse.com.* 53 rooms, 1-3 story. No elevator. Complimentary continental breakfast. Check-out 11 am. TV; cable (premium). Pool. Concierge. In operation since 1742. **$$**

Resort

★ ★ **ISLAND INN.** *Beach Rd, Oak Bluffs (02557). Phone 508/693-2002; toll-free 800/462-0269; fax 508/693-7911. www.islandinn.com.* 51 kitchen units, 1-2 story. Check-out 11 am. TV. In-room modem link. Restaurant 6-11 pm. Bar 4 pm-midnight. Pool. Tennis. Bicycle path adjacent. Near beach. **$**

B&B/Small Inns

★ ★ **THE ARBOR INN.** *222 Upper Main St, Edgartown (02539). Phone 508/627-8137; toll-free 888/748-4383. www.mvy.com/arborinn.* 10 air-cooled rooms, 2 story. No room phones. Closed Nov-Apr. Children over 12 years only. Complimentary continental breakfast. Check-out 11 am, check-in 2 pm. Concierge. Built 1880; antiques. **$$**

★ ★ **ASHLEY INN.** *129 Main St (02539). Phone 508/627-9655; toll-free 800/477-9655; fax 508/627-6629.* 10 rooms, 3 story. Children over 12 years only. Complimentary continental breakfast. Check-out 11 am, check-in 2 pm. TV. Fireplaces. Totally nonsmoking. **$**

★ **THE BEACH HOUSE.** *Pennacook and Seaview aves, Oak Bluffs (02557). Phone 508/693-3955. www.beachhousemv.com.* 9 rooms, 3 story. No room phones. Children over 10 years only. Complimentary continental breakfast. Check-out 11 am, check-in 1 pm. TV. Built in 1899; front porch. Opposite ocean. **$**

★ ★ ★ **BEACH PLUM INN.** *50 Beach Plum Ln, Menemsha (02552). Phone 508/645-9454; toll-free 877/645-7398; fax 508/645-2801. www. beachpluminn.com.* This Martha's Vineyard inn sits on a hilltop overlooking the ocean and boasts one of the islands most well-regarded restaurants. A stone drive and garden-like path lead to the main house, and several other cottages dot the 7-acre property. 11 rooms, 2 story. Complimentary full breakfast. Check-out 11 am, check-in 2 pm. TV; cable (premium), VCR (movies). In-room modem link. Restaurant. Tennis. Lawn games. Concierge service. Built 1890 from salvage of shipwreck. **$$**

★ ★ ★ ★ **CHARLOTTE INN.** *27 S Summer St, Edgartown (02539). Phone 508/627-4751; fax 508/627-6452.* The Charlotte Inn extends open arms to guests seeking a quintessentially New England experience. This charming inn enjoys a central location among Edgartown's quaint streets and stately sea captains' homes. Convenient to the village, the Charlotte Inn is the perfect place to enjoy the many delights of Martha's Vineyard. A wrought-iron fence stands guard over the manicured grounds of this irresistible Colonial inn. Inside, a romantic English country style dominates the public and private rooms. Artwork, antiques, and other decorative objects lend a hand in creating a historical flavor in the bedrooms. Individually designed, some rooms feature four-poster beds. Spread throughout the main house, Carriage House, and Coach House, the rooms and suites are simply delightful. Light French cuisine enhanced by American and French wines is served in the restaurant, where candlelit dinners are particularly unforgettable. 25 rooms. Children over 14 only. TV; cable (premium), VCR available. Restaurant. Parking available. Concierge. Afternoon tea. **$$**

★ ★ **COLONIAL INN OF MARTHA'S VINEYARD.** *38 N Water St, Edgartown (02539). Phone 508/627-4711; toll-free 800/627-4701; fax 508/627-5904. www.colonialinnmvy.com.* 43 rooms, 1-4 story. No elevator. Closed Jan-mid-Apr. Complimentary continental breakfast. Check-out 11 am. TV; cable (premium), VCR available (free movies). In-room modem link. Restaurant. **$**

★ ★ **DAGGETT HOUSE.** *59 N Water St, Edgartown (02539). Phone 508/627-4600; fax 508/627-4611. www.mvweb.com/daggett.* 31 rooms, 10 kitchen units, 2 story. Check-out 11 am, check-in 3 pm. TV. Restaurant. Open hearth, antiques in dining room, part of historic tavern (1660). Private pier. New England atmosphere. Totally nonsmoking. **$$**

★ ★ ★ **DOCKSIDE INN.** *Circuit Ave Ext, Oak Bluffs (02557). Phone 508/693-2966; toll-free 800/245-5979; fax 508/696-7293. www.vineyard.net/ inns.* This gingerbread-style inn overlooks the harbor in the seaside village of Oak Bluffs and is walking distance to many attractions, miles of beaches, and shopping areas. 22 rooms, 5 kitchen units, 3 story. Crib free. Complimentary continental breakfast. Check-out 11 am, check-in 2-7 pm.

TV. In-room modem link. Balconies. Refrigerators. Restaurant nearby. Game room. Business services. Concierge service. Colorful gingerbread-style inn opposite docks. Totally nonsmoking. **$$**

D ⊠

★ ★ **THE EDGARTOWN INN.** *56 N Water St, Edgartown (02539). Phone 508/627-4794; fax 508/627-9420. www.edgartowninn.com.* 12 rooms, 1-3 story. Closed Nov-Mar. Check-out 11 am, check-in 2 pm. TV in some rooms. Dining room. Historic (1798) sea captain's home. Inn since 1820; colonial furnishings and antiques in rooms. **$**

⊠

★ ★ **GREENWOOD HOUSE.** *40 Greenwood Ave (02568). Phone 508/693-6150; toll-free 866/693-6150; fax 508/696-8113. www.greenwoodhouse.com.* 5 rooms, 3 story. Complimentary full breakfast. Check-out 10 am, check-in 2 pm. TV. In-room modem link. Lawn games. Concierge service. Built 1906. Totally nonsmoking. **$$**

⊠

★ ★ ★ **THE HANOVER HOUSE.** *28 Edgartown Rd, Vineyard Haven (02568). Phone 508/693-1066; toll-free 800/339-1066; fax 508/696-6099. www.hanoverhouseinn.com.* Set on a half acre of land, this cozy bed-and-breakfast is walking distance to the ferry, shopping, restaurants, and the library. Shuttles are available for travel to Edgartown and Oak Bluffs. 15 rooms, 3 suites, 2 kitchen units, 2 story. No room phones. Complimentary continental breakfast. Check-out 10 am, check-in 2 pm. TV. Built 1920; gardens, enclosed sitting porch. Totally nonsmoking. **$$**

⊠

★ ★ ★ **HOB KNOB INN.** *128 Main St, Edgartown (02539). Phone 508/627-9510; toll-free 800/696-2723; fax 508/627-4560. www.hobknob.com.* 16 rooms, 3 story. Complimentary full breakfast. Check-out 11 am, check-in 2 pm. TV. In-room modem link. In-house fitness room, massage, sauna. Bicycles. Concierge service. Inn built 1860; many antiques. Totally nonsmoking. **$$**

D 🏃 ⊠

★ ★ **LAMBERT'S COVE COUNTRY INN.** *Lambert's Cove Rd, Vineyard Haven (02568). Phone 508/693-2298; fax 508/693-7890. www.lambertscoveinn.com.* 15 rooms, 2 story. No room phones. Complimentary full breakfast. Check-out 11 am, check-in 2 pm. TV in sitting room. Dining room (public by reservation) 6-9 pm. Outdoor tennis. **$$**

🏌

★ ★ ★ **MARTHA'S PLACE B&B.** *114 Main St, Vineyard Haven (02568). Phone 508/693-0253. www.marthasplace.com.* This Greek Revival home offers the perfect location: across from Owen Park Beach overlooking Vineyard Haven Harbor and just one block from the ferry, restaurants, and shops. All guestrooms feature down comforters and Egyptian cotton linens. 7 rooms, 2 story. 3 rooms with shower only. No room phones. Complimentary continental breakfast. Check-out 10 am, check-in after noon. TV in some rooms. Built in 1840, restored Greek Revival mansion. Totally nonsmoking. **$$**

★ ★ ★ **THE OAK HOUSE.** *Seaview and Pequot aves, Oak Bluffs (02557). Phone 508/693-4187; fax 508/696-7385. www.vineyard.net/inns.* 10 rooms, 9 with shower only, 3 story, 2 suites. No elevator. Closed Mid-Oct-mid-May. Children over 10 years only. TV; cable, VCR available. Complimentary continental breakfast; afternoon refreshments. Check-out 11 am, check-in 4 pm. Street parking. Some balconies. Picnic tables, grills. Opposite beach. 1872 summer home for MA governor. Antique furnishings in rooms. Totally nonsmoking. **$$**

★ ★ **OUTERMOST INN.** *171 Lighthouse Rd, Chilmark (02535). Phone 508/645-3511; fax 508/645-3514. www.outermostinn.com.* 7 rooms, 2 story. No A/C. Lower rates mid-Apr-mid-June, mid-Sept-Oct. Children over 12 years only. TV. Complimentary full breakfast; afternoon refreshments. Dining room 6-8 pm. Check-out 11 am, check-in 2 pm. Luggage handling. Concierge service. Business services available. Balconies. Picnic tables. Picture windows provide excellent views of Vineyard Sound and Elizabeth Islands. Totally nonsmoking. **$$**

★ ★ **PEQUOT HOTEL.** *19 Pequot Ave, Oak Bluffs (02557). Phone 508/693-5087; toll-free 800/947-8704; fax 508/696-9413. www.pequothotel.com.* 29 rooms, 25 with shower only, 3 story. No elevator. No room phones. Higher rates July 4. Closed Nov-Apr. Crib $25. TV in some rooms. Complimentary continental breakfast. Restaurant nearby. Check-out 11 am, check-in 3 pm. Street parking. Picnic tables. Built in 1920s. **$**

★ ★ **POINT WAY INN.** *104 Main St, Edgartown (02539). Phone 508/627-8633; toll-free 888/711-6633; fax 508/627-3338. www.pointway.com.* 14 rooms, 1-3 story. Pets accepted, some restrictions; fee. Complimentary continental breakfast. Check-out 11 am, check-in 2 pm. TV. Totally nonsmoking. **$$**

★ ★ **SHIRETOWN INN.** *44 N Water St, Edgartown (02539). Phone 508/627-3353; fax 508/627-8478. www.shiretowninn.com.* 35 rooms, 1-3 story. Some A/C. Closed mid-Oct-Apr. Complimentary continental breakfast. Check-out 11 am, check-in 2 pm. TV. Dining room, bar. 18th-century whaling house. **$**

★ ★ ★ **THORNCROFT INN.** *460 Main St (02568). Phone 508/693-3333; toll-free 800/332-1236; fax 508/693-5419. www.thorncroft.com.* Secluded on a tree-lined, 3-acre peninsula, this charming, white-shuttered home houses 14 romantic guestrooms, some with hot tubs and fireplaces. A full country breakfast can be enjoyed in the dining room or requested for "breakfast in bed" delivery. 14 rooms, 2 story. Complimentary full breakfast. Check-out 11 am, check-in 3-9 pm. TV. In-room modem link. Totally nonsmoking. **$$$**

D ⊠

Restaurants

★ ★ ★ **COACH HOUSE.** *131 N Water St, Edgartown (02539). Phone 508/627-7000; fax 508/627-8417. www.harbor-view.com.* Part of the Harbor View Hotel, this spacious dining room has beautiful views of the harbor. The menu features updated New England classics. Breakfast, lunch, dinner, Sun brunch. Bar. Children's menu. Totally nonsmoking in restaurant. New England cuisine. **$$$**

D

★ ★ **HOME PORT.** *512 North Rd, Menemsha (02552). Phone 508/645-2679; fax 508/645-3119.* Specializes in seafood, lobster. Outdoor clam bar. Hours: 5-10 pm. Closed mid-Oct-mid Apr. Reservations required. No A/C. Setups. Children's menu. Parking. On harbor; scenic view; nautical atmosphere. **$$**

D

★ ★ **LE GRENIER FRENCH RESTAURANT.** *82 Main St, Vineyard Haven (02568). Phone 508/693-4906; fax 508/693-5008. www.legrenier restaurant.com.* French provincial menu. Dinner. **$$$**

★ **LOUIS' TISBURY CAFE.** *350 State Rd, Vineyard Haven (02568). Phone 508/693-3255.* Italian, seafood menu. Closed most major holidays. Dinner. Children's menu. Totally nonsmoking. **$$**

D

★ ★ **THE NAVIGATOR.** *2 Lower Main St, Edgartown (02539). Phone 508/627-4320; fax 508/627-3544.* Seafood menu. Closed mid-Oct-mid-May. Lunch, dinner. Bar. Children's menu. Outdoor seating. **$$$**

D

★ ★ **SQUARE RIGGER.** *225 State Rd, Edgartown (02539). Phone 508/627-9968; fax 508/627-4837.* Seafood menu. Hours: 5:30-10 pm. Dinner. Bar. Children's menu. Totally nonsmoking. **$$**

D SC

★ ★ **WHARF & WHARF PUB.** *Lower Main St, Edgartown (02539). Phone 508/627-9966.* Seafood menu. Closed Thanksgiving, Dec 24-25. Lunch, dinner. Bar. Entertainment Wed-Sun. Children's menu. **$$**

D

Nantucket Island, MA

7 hours 30 minutes; 287 miles from New York City
See also Hyannis

Settled 1659 **Pop** 6,012 **Elev** 0-108 ft **Area code** 508 **Zip** 02554

Information Chamber of Commerce, 48 Main St; 508/228-1700. General information may also be obtained at the Information Bureau, 25 Federal St; 508/228-1700

Web www.nantucketchamber.org

This is not just an island; it is an experience. Nantucket Island is at once a popular resort and a living museum. Siasconset (SCON-set) and Nantucket Town remain quiet and charming despite heavy tourism. Nantucket, with 49 square miles of lovely beaches and green moors inland, is south of Cape Cod, 30 miles at sea. The island was the world's greatest whaling port from the late 17th century until New Bedford became dominant in the early 1800s. Whaling prosperity built the towns; tourism maintains them.

There is regular car ferry and passenger service from Hyannis. If you plan to take your car, make advance reservation by mail with the Woods Hole, Martha's Vineyard & Nantucket Steamship Authority, PO Box 284, Woods Hole 02543; phone 508/477-8600. A great variety of beaches, among them the Jetties, north of Nantucket Town (harbor), and Surfside, on the south shore of the island (surf), offer swimming. Tennis, golf, fishing, sailing, and cycling can be arranged.

What to See and Do

Actors Theatre of Nantucket. *2 Centre St (02554). Phone 508/228-6325. www.nantuckettheatre.com.* The Actors Theatre of Nantucket has staged comedies, dramas, plays, and dance concerts since 1985. Both professionals and amateurs make up the company, which offers between six and ten performances during the summer. When purchasing tickets, ask whether family matinees are offered for that performance. **$$$$**

Altar Rock. *Off Polpis Rd to the south on unmarked dirt road.* Climb up Altar Rock, which rises 90 feet above sea level, and you're afforded stunning views of Nantucket and the surrounding Cape. Go at first or last light (dawn or dusk) for the best views. The Moors surrounding Altar Rock offer a chance to hike on the trails or two-track dirt roads. Few tourists make the trek, which makes for unexpected solitude on Nantucket.

Barrett's Tours. *Phone 508/228-0174.* Offers 1 1/2-hour bus and van tours (Apr-Nov).

Bartlett's Ocean View Farm. *33 Bartlett Farm Rd (02584). Phone 508/228-9403. www.bartlettsoceanviewfarm.com.* Nurturing Nantucket's largest farm, the Bartlett family has tilled this land for nearly 200 years. Stop by for fresh vegetables, milk, eggs, cheese, freshly baked bread, and cut flowers. If you're looking for prepared dishes, taste the farm kitchen's salads, entrees (including several that are vegetarian), pies, snacks, jams, chutneys, and other farm delights. Also visit the East Coast Seafood market, less than a mile away, for fresh fish and seafood to complete your meal. (Daily 8 am-6 pm)

Bass Hole Boardwalk and Gray's Beach. *End of Centre St (02675). Take Route 6A to Church St. Bear left onto Centre St and follow to the end.* This honest-to-goodness elevated boardwalk—stretching 860 feet—offers delightful scenery as it meanders through one of Cape Cod's finest marshes to the beach. Kids enjoy playing on the beach or adjoining playground; the whole family can walk the beach and into the bay at low tide.

Boat Trips. Hyannis-Nantucket Day Round Trip. *22 Channel Point Rd (02601). Phone 508/778-2600.* Summer passenger service from Hyannis. **$$$$**

Cisco Brewers. *5 Bartlett Farm Rd (02584). Phone 508/325-5929. www.ciscobrewers.com.* If you enjoy beer, visit Cisco Brewers and taste the delicious locally made brews. From Whale's Tales Pale Ale and Bailey's Ale to Moor Porter, Cap'n Swain's Extra Stout, Summer of Lager, and Baggywrinkle Barleywine, just about every variety of beer is represented at Cisco. Stop by for the daily guided tour ($10; times vary) that includes a walk through the brewery (including taste testing), as well as a tour of the Triple Eight Distillery and Nantucket Vineyard next door. Allow one-and-a-half hours for the entire tour. (Summer: Mon-Sat 10 am-6 pm; Fall-Spring: Sat 10 am-5 pm) **FREE**

Claire Murray. *11 S Water St (02554). Phone 508/228-1913. www.claire murray.com.* Even if you've seen Claire Murray's delightful rug designs elsewhere in the country, visit the store where she got her start. Nantucket winters don't bring many visitors, and Claire Murray, who used to run a bed-and-breakfast, started hooking rugs to pass the time during these months. She soon began designing and selling rugs full-time around the world. Today, her store in Nantucket sells both finished rugs and kits and also offers classes. Around the Cape, look for three other locations in West Barnstable, Osterville, Mashpee, and Edgartown (on Martha's Vineyard). (Mon-Sat 10 am-9 pm, Sun 11 am-7 pm)

★ *Endeavor* Sailing Adventures. *Straight Wharf (02554). Phone 508/228-5585. www.endeavorsailing.com.* U.S. Coast Guard Captain James Genthner built his sloop, named the *Endeavor,* and has been sailing it for over 20 years. Take a 90-minute sail around Nantucket Sound and let the good captain and his wife, Sue, acquaint you with Nantucket's sights, sounds, and history. No sailing experience is necessary, and you can bring a picnic lunch. A special one-hour kids tour sails at 11:30 daily. (May-Oct; closed Nov-Apr) **$$$$**

First Congregational Church & View. *62 Centre St (02554). Phone 508/228-0950.* Also called Old North Church, the First Congregational Church offers Nantucket's best view of the island and surrounding ocean. Climb 94 steps to the 120-foot-tall steeple, and you're amply rewarded with a view from the top of the world. While you're at the church, take in the historical display that shows photos of the church as has looked throughout its long history. (Mon-Sat, mid June-mid Oct) **$**

Gail's Tours. *Departs from Information Center at Federal and Broad sts. Phone 508/257-6557.* Narrated van tours (approximately 1 3/4 hours) of area. Three tours daily. Reservations recommended.

Jetties Beach. *Take North Beach Rd to Bathing Beach Rd; from there, take a shuttle bus (June 15–Labor Day), walk, or bike, the distance (just over a mile) to the beach.* You won't find better amenities for families with kids than Jetties Beach. Besides the convenient restrooms, showers, changing rooms, and snack bar, the beach employs life guards, offers chairs for rent, provides a well-equipped playground, maintains volleyball and tennis courts, and offers a skateboarding park. You can also rent kayaks, sailboards, and sailboats through Nantucket Community Sailing (508/228-5358), which maintains an office at the beach. Look for occasional concerts and a July 4th fireworks display. (Daily)

The Lifesaving Museum. *158 Polpis Rd (02554). Phone 508/228-1885. www. nantucketlifesavingmuseum.com.* The building that houses the museum is a recreation of the original 1874 lifesaving station that was built to assist mariners from the oft-times deadly seas. Museum exhibits include lifesaving surfboats, large and intricate lighthouse lenses, historical objects from the *Andria Doria* (which sank off the coast of Nantucket Island), demonstrations, stories of rescues, and action photos. **$**

Loines Observatory. *59 Milk St (02554). Phone 508/228-8690. www.mmo.org.* Part of the Maria Mitchell Association (MMA)—named for the first professional female astronomer—the Loines Observatory gives you a chance to peek through a fine old telescope and view the magnificent, star-filled Cape Cod skies. Also visit the MMA's other observatory on Vestal Street, which includes an outdoor true-to-scale model of the solar system, an astronomy exhibit, and a sundial. Kids may prefer the attractions at The Vestal Street Observatory, which is noted for its work with young scientists. (Mon, Wed, Fri evenings in summer, Sat evenings year-round; closed Tues, Thurs, Sun in summer, Sun-Fri year-round) **$$**

★ **Main Street.** *15 Broad St. Phone 508/228-1894. www.chathamcapecod.org.* Main Street offers shoppers such a plethora of choices—from paintings, glass, pottery, and antique furniture to clothing, jewelry, and yummy taste treats—that many consider this street to offer the best shopping on Cape Cod. For a similar shopping experience without having to ride the ferry to Nantucket or Martha's Vineyard (which are also delightful havens for shoppers), visit Commercial Street in Provincetown.

1800 House. *Mill St, off Pleasant St. Phone 508/228-1894.* Home of sheriff, early 19th century. Period home and furnishings; large, round cellar; kitchen garden.

Folger-Franklin Seat & Memorial Boulder. *Madaket Rd, 1 mile from W end of Main St.* Birthplace site of Abiah Folger, mother of Benjamin Franklin.

Hadwen House. *Main and Pleasant sts.* (1845) Greek Revival mansion; furnishings of whaling period; gardens. **$$**

⭐ **Jethro Coffin House (Oldest House).** *16 Sunset Hill Ln (02554). N on North Water to West Chester, left to Sunset Hill. Phone 508/228-1894.* Built in 1686, Oldest House is, true to its name, one of the oldest houses you'll ever visit in the United States, and the oldest on Nantucket. The house was a wedding present given to the children of two feuding families (the Gardners and the Coffins) by their in-laws, who reconciled after the happy event. In 1987, after lightening struck Oldest House, it was fully restored to its original beauty. This colonial saltbox and spare furnishings exude classic Nantucket style and charm. (Seasonal; call for dates and times) **$**

Museum of Nantucket History (Macy Warehouse). *2 Whalers Ln (02554). Straight Wharf. Phone 508/228-1894.* Exhibits related to Nantucket history; diorama; craft demonstrations. **$$**

Old Fire Hose Cart House. *Gardner St off Main St.* (1886) Old-time fire-fighting equipment. **FREE**

Old Gaol. *Vestal St. Phone 508/228-1894.* (1805) Unusual two-story construction; used until 1933. **FREE**

Old Mill. *South Mill and Prospect sts (02554). Phone 508/228-1894.* This Dutch-style windmill is impressive in its beauty and sheer size (50 feet high), but it was built for function—to grind grain brought by local farmers—and it remains functional today. Believed to be the oldest windmill in the United States, it was built in 1746 with salvaged oak that washed up on shore from shipwrecks and after many owners, eventually came to belong to the Nantucket Historical Society. (Daily June-Aug; call for off-season hours) **$**

Research Center. *Broad St, next to Whaling Museum. Phone 508/228-1655.* Ships' logs, diaries, charts, and Nantucket photographs; library. (Mon-Fri)

Whaling Museum. *12 Broad St, near Steamboat Wharf (02554). Phone 508/228-1736.* Outstanding collection of relics from whaling days; whale skeleton, tryworks, scrimshaw, candle press. **$$**

Miacomet Golf Course. *12 W Miacomet Rd (02554). Phone 508/228-9764.* Nantucket's only public golf course offers 9 holes—including two par-5 holes—that you can play twice for a par-74 round. Winds off the ocean make for interesting play. Reserve a tee time at least a week in advance; your chances of playing without a reservation are zero during summer. (Daily) **$$$$**

Murray's Toggery. *62 Main St (02554). Phone 508/228-0437. www.nantucketreds.com.* Murray's Toggery was the first store in Nantucket to sell Nantucket Reds—casual red pants that eventually fade to a decidedly pink hue—a products that defines both Cape Cod and the preppy look. Murray's also sells oxford shirts, jackets, sweaters, shoes, hats, coats and jackets for both men and women. (Mon-Sat 9 am-7 pm, Sun 10 am-6 pm; winter: Mon-Sat 9 am-5 pm; closed Sun in winter)

Nantucket Gourmet. *4 India St (2554). Phone 508/228-4353. www.nantucket gourmet.com.* Nantucket Gourmet offers a well-balanced blend of cookware and other culinary tools, and condiments to take back home with you (including marmalades, jams, mustards, and vinegars), and ready-to-eat deli foods for your lunch on the island. You'll find great gifts for any food-lover. (Summer: daily 10 am-6 pm; Winter: Mon-Fri 10 am-4 pm; closed holidays)

Nantucket Maria Mitchell Association. *1 Vestal St. Phone 508/228-9198 or 508/228-0898 in summer. Combination ticket available for museum, birthplace and aquarium.* Birthplace of first American woman astronomer; memorial observatory (1908). Scientific library has Nantucket historical documents, science journals and Mitchell family memorabilia. Natural science museum with local wildlife. Aquarium at 28 Washington St. (Mid-June-Aug, Tues-Sat; library also open rest of year, Wed-Sat; closed July 4, Labor Day) **$$**

Nantucket Town. *The areas between Main, Broad, and Centre sts. Phone 508/228-1700. www.nantucketchamber.org/directory/merchants.* Nantucket Town is a shopper's dream, with narrow cobblestone streets that wind past hundreds of shops. You'll find items for your home (furniture, rugs, throws and blankets, baskets, prints, soaps, and so on), your boat (including all manner of weather-predicting equipment), and yourself (from preppy and upscale clothing, hats, shawls, jewelry, and everything in between). In about 20 stores, you'll find the famous Nantucket baskets (also called lightship baskets), which are handmade through a time-consuming process. You'll also come across numerous art galleries, antiques shops, and craft stores.

Nantucket Whaling Museum. *13 Broad St (02554). Phone 508/228-1894. www.nha.org.* To really understand Nantucket, you have to understand whaling, the industry that put Nantucket on the map. The Nantucket Whaling Museum—housed in a former factory that produced candles from whale oil—shows you a fully rigged whale boat (smaller than you may think), rope and basket collections, scrimshaw (whale-bone carving) exhibits, a huge lighthouse Fresnel lens, a skeleton of a finback whale, and maritime folk art. Enjoy to one of three daily lectures offered by the museum staff. Visit in December to see the Festival of Trees, which includes 50 decorated Christmas trees. **$$**

Rafael Osona Auctions. *21 Washington St (02554). At the American Legion Hall. Phone 508/228-3942.* If you like antiques, you'll love Rafael Osona. The auctioneers host estate auctions on selected weekends (call for exact dates and times) that feature treasured pieces from both the US and Europe. If an auction isn't planned while you're in town, visit the two dozen other antique stores on the island, plus many more around Cape Cod. (Late May-early Dec)

Siasconset Village. *East end of Nantucket Island (02554).* The Siasconset Village—known locally as 'Sconset—lies 7 miles from Nantucket Town, and can by traveled by bicycle or shuttle bus. This 18th-century fishing village features quaint cottages, grand mansions, restaurants, a few shops, and a summer cinema. Visit Siasconset Beach and the paved biking path that meanders through the area.

Something Natural. *50 Cliff Rd (2554). Phone 508/228-0504. www.something natural.com.* If you're looking for a casual breakfast or lunch—perhaps even one to take with you on a bike ride or island hike—check out Something

Natural for healthy sandwiches, breads and bagels, salads, cookies, and beverages. The eatery has also established a second location at 6 Oak St (508/228-6616). (May-Oct)

The Straight Wharf. *Straight Wharf (02554). On the harbor, next to the ferry* Built in 1723, the Straight Wharf is Nantucket's launching area for sailboats, sloops, and kayaks, but it's also a great shopping and eating area. Loaded with restaurants and quaint, one-room cottage shops selling island fare, the wharf also features an art gallery, a museum, and an outdoor concert pavilion.

Strong Wings Summer Camp. *Phone 508/228-1769. www.strongwings.com.* Open for just one month every year, the Strong Wings Summer Camp offers more excitement and activity for kids than you're likely to find anywhere else on the Cape. Kids ages 5 to 15 attend three-day or five-day sessions, where they explore the natural attributes of the area, mountain bike, hike, kayak, snorkel, rock climb, and boogie board (as appropriate for each age group). Older kids even learn search-and-rescue techniques. (Daily, late June-late Aug; closed Sept-mid-June) **$$$$**

The Sunken Ship. *12 Broad St (02554). Phone 508/228-9226. www.sunkenship.com.* The Sunken Ship is a full-service dive shop that offers lessons and rentals. When the *Andrea Doria* sank off the coast of Nantucket in the middle of the last century, the area invited divers from around the world to investigate the sunken ship, hence the name of this shop. The general store offers an eclectic array of dive and maritime goods. (Daily; call for closures) **$$$$**

Windswept Cranberry Bog. *Polpis Rd, Siasconset (02554).* Cranberries are an important industry to Nantucket; in town, you can purchase jars of cranberry honey, and Northland Cranberries harvests berries from Nantucket to make its well-known juices. To see how cranberries are grown and harvested, visit this 200-acre cranberry bog during the fall harvest (late September through October from dawn to dusk), when bogs are flooded so that machines can shake off and scoop up the individual berries. (Mid-October also brings the Nantucket Cranberry Festival.) Even at other times of year, the bog is peaceful and beautiful—a good place to walk and bike and spend half a day. Another nearby cranberry bog is the Milestone Bog (off Milestone Rd west of Siasconset). (Daily dawn-dusk)

Special Events

Christmas Stroll. *Phone 508/228-1700.* First weekend in Dec.

Daffodil Festival. *Siasconset Village (02564). Phone 508/228-1700. www.nantucket.net/daffy.* The Daffodil festival celebrates the budding of millions of daffodils on the main roads of Nantucket. A parade of antique car classics kicks off the well-attended event, which also includes open houses, garden tours, and a lively picnic in 'Sconset that offers great food and live entertainment. Late Apr. **FREE**

Harborfest. *Phone 508-228-1700.* Early June.

Nantucket Arts Festival. *Various venues. Phone 508/325-8588.* This week-long festival celebrates a full range of arts on the island: films, poetry and fiction readings, acting, dance performances, and exhibits of paintings, photography, and many other art forms. Look for the wet-paint sale in which you can bid on works completed just that day by local artists. Early Oct. **FREE**

Nantucket County Fair. *Tom Nevers Navy Base (02554). Phone 508/325-4748.* Looking for an old-fashioned county fair? Head to Nantucket for down-home family fun and entertainment. At the Nantucket County Fair, an event that began over 150 years ago, you'll find pies, breads, pastries, jams, jellies, fresh fall fruits, and concessions of all types. You'll also see and experience tractor displays and rides, a petting zoo and pet show, a flea market, quilt displays and sales, hay rides, concerts, and square dancing. Third weekend in Sept. **$$**

Nantucket Film Festival. *Various venues. Phone 508/228-6648. www.nantucket filmfestival.org.* Like other film festivals worldwide, Nantucket's festival screens new independent films that may not otherwise garner attention. You'll be joined by screenwriters, actors, film connoisseurs and, occasionally, big-name celebrities at the festival's seminars, readings, and discussions. A daily event call Morning Coffee showcases a panel of directors, screenwriters, and actors participating in Q&A with festival-goers, who sip coffee and munch on muffins. Mid-June. **$$$$**

Nantucket Wine Festival. *Phone 508/228-1128. www.nantucketwinefestival .com.* This is a wine festival like no other: take in a wine symposium, a variety of food and wine seminars, a wine auction, and many other events. The Great Wine in Grand Houses event allows you to visit a private mansion, sip fine wines drawn from nearly 100 wineries, and dine on food prepared by some of the world's finest chefs. Reservations are required and should be made as soon as you know you'll be visiting the island. Mid-May. **$$$$**

Sand Castle Contest. *Phone 508/228-1700.* Third Sat Aug.

Motel/Motor Lodge

★ ★ **HARBOR HOUSE VILLAGE.** *S Beach St (02554). Phone 508/228-1500; toll-free 866/325-9300; fax 508/228-7639. www.nantucketislandresorts .com.* 104 rooms, 2-3 story. No elevator. Check-out 11 am, check-in 3 pm. TV; cable (premium). In-room modem link. Restaurant, bar; entertainment. Room service. Heated pool, poolside service. Concierge. Public beach opposite. **$**

D ⇌ ⬩

Hotels

★ ★ ★ **VANESSA NOEL HOTEL.** *5 Chestnut St (03554). Phone 508/ 228-5300. www.vanessanoel.com.* 8 rooms, 3 story. Complimentary continental breakfast. Check-out 11 am, check-in 1 pm. TV; cable (premium). Internet access. Restaurant, bar. Room service. **$$$**

D ⬩

★ ★ ★ **WHITE ELEPHANT RESORT.** *50 Easton St (02554). Phone 508/228-2500; toll-free 800/475-2637; fax 508/325-1195. www.whiteelephant resort.com.* Step back in time for a game of croquet on a sweeping, manicured lawn at this Harbor-front resort. 80 rooms, 1-3 story. No elevator. Closed Nov-Apr. Check-out 11 am, check-in 3 pm. TV; cable (premium). In-room modem link. Restaurant, bar; entertainment. Heated pool, whirlpool, poolside service. Beach nearby; boat slips for guests only. Concierge. **$$$**

⊡ ⊠ SC

B&B/Small Inns

★ ★ **CARLISLE HOUSE INN.** *26 N Water St (02554). Phone 508/228-0720; fax 781/639-1004. www.carlislehouse.com.* 17 rooms, 3 story. No room phones. Closed early Dec-Mar. Children over 10 years only. Complimentary continental breakfast. Check-out 11 am, check-in 2 pm. Street parking. Restored whaling captain's house (1765). Totally nonsmoking. **$**

⊠

★ **THE CARRIAGE HOUSE.** *5 Ray's Ct (02554). Phone 508/228-0326. www.carriagehousenantucket.com.* 7 rooms, 2 story. No A/C. Complimentary continental breakfast. Check-out 11 am, check-in 1 pm. Victorian décor. Center of Old Historic District; near ferries. Totally nonsmoking. No credit cards accepted. **$**

⊠

★ ★ ★ **CENTERBOARD GUEST HOUSE.** *8 Chester St (02554). Phone 508/228-9696. www.nantucket.net/lodging/centerboard.* 8 rooms, 3 story. Closed Jan-Feb. Complimentary continental breakfast. Check-out 11 am, check-in 3 pm. TV. In-room modem link. Street parking. Restored Victorian residence (1885). Totally nonsmoking. **$**

⊠

★ ★ **CENTRE STREET INN.** *78 Centre St (02554). Phone 508/228-0199; toll-free 800/298-0199; fax 508/228-8676. www.centrestreetinn.com.* 14 rooms, 3 story. No room phones. Closed Jan-Apr. Children over 8 years only. Complimentary continental breakfast. Check-out 11 am, check-in 3 pm. Concierge service. Colonial house built in 1742; some antiques. Totally nonsmoking. **$**

⊠

★ ★ **COBBLESTONE INN.** *5 Ash St (02554). Phone 508/228-1987; fax 508/228-6698.* 5 rooms, 3 story. Closed Jan-Mar. Complimentary breakfast. Check-out 11 am, check-in 2 pm. TV. Fireplace in library. Lawn games. Concierge. Built in 1725. Totally nonsmoking. **$**

⊠

★ ★ ★ **JARED COFFIN HOUSE.** *29 Broad St (02554). Phone 508/228-2400; fax 508/228-8549. www.jaredcoffinhouse.com.* 60 rooms, 3 story.

Check-out 11 am, check-in after 3 pm. TV. In-room modem link. Restaurant, bar. Concierge service. Historical objets d'art. Restored 1845 mansion. **$**

D ⊠

★ ★ **MARTIN HOUSE INN.** *61 Centre St (02554). Phone 508/228-0678. www.nantucket.net/lodging/martinn.* 13 rooms, 3 story. No A/C. No elevator. No room phones. Closed Jan-Feb. Complimentary continental breakfast. Check-out 11 am, check-in 3 pm. TV in common room; cable (premium). In-room modem link. Restaurant. Street parking. Built in 1803. Totally nonsmoking. **$**

⊠

★ ★ **ROBERTS HOUSE INN.** *11 India St (02554). Phone 508/228-0600; toll-free 800/872-6830; fax 508/325-4046. www.robertshouseinn.com.* 45 rooms, 3 story. Complimentary continental breakfast. Check-out 11 am, check-in 2 pm. TV. Concierge. Built in 1846; established 1883. **$**

D ⊠

★ ★ **SEVEN SEA STREET INN.** *7 Sea St (02554). Phone 508/228-3577; fax 508/228-3578. www.sevenseastreetinn.com.* 11 rooms, 2 story. Children over 5 years only. Complimentary continental breakfast. Check-out 11 am, check-in 3 pm. TV; VCR. Whirlpool. View of Nantucket Harbor. Totally nonsmoking. **$$**

⊠

★ ★ ★ **SHERBURNE INN.** *10 Gay St (02554). Phone 508/228-4425; toll-free 888/577-4425; fax 508/228-8114. www.nantucket.net/lodging/sherburne.* 8 rooms, 3 story. Children over 6 years only. Complimentary continental breakfast. Check-out 11 am, check-in 2 pm. Street parking. Concierge service. Built in 1835 as a silk factory; period antiques, fireplaced parlors. Totally nonsmoking. **$**

⊠

★ ★ **SHIPS INN.** *13 Fair St (02554). Phone 508/228-0040; fax 508/228-6254. www.nantucket.net/lodging/shipsinn.net.* 12 rooms, 4 story. No A/C. Closed Nov-Apr. Complimentary continental breakfast. Check-out 10 am, check-in 2 pm. TV. Dining room, bar. Built in 1831 by sea captain; many original furnishings. Totally nonsmoking. **$$**

⊠

★ ★ **TUCKERNUCK INN.** *60 Union St (02554). Phone 508/228-4886; toll-free 800/228-4886; fax 508/228-4890. tuckernuckinn.com.* 20 rooms, 2 story. Check-out 11 am, check-in 3 pm. TV; cable (premium), VCR. Laundry services. Dining room. Lawn games. Totally nonsmoking. **$**

⊠

★ ★ ★ ★ **THE WAUWINET.** *120 Wauwinet Rd (02584). Phone 508/228-0145; toll-free 800/426-8718; fax 508/228-6712. www.wauwinet.com.* Nearly

30 miles out to sea, the idyllic island of Nantucket is a place where crashing waves wash away everyday cares. The Wauwinet embodies the perfect getaway on this magical island. Tucked away on a private stretch of beach, The Wauwinet leads its guests to believe that they have been marooned on a remote island, yet this delightful hotel remains close to the town's charming cobblestone streets, a complimentary jitney ride away. Built in 1876 by ship captains, The Wauwinet's rooms and suites have a sophisticated country style blended with the services of a posh resort. Private beaches fronting the harbor and the Atlantic Ocean are spectacular, and clay tennis courts challenge guests to a match. Whether diners choose to arrive by foot or by sunset cruise on the 26-foot *Wauwinet Lady,* Topper's restaurant (see also TOPPER'S) promises to be an exceptional event. With a 20,000-bottle wine cellar and an impressive menu, it is an epicurean's delight. *Secret Inspector's Notes:* One of the most enjoyable ways to enjoy the fabulous Nantucket sunsets is with a signature pitcher of martinis or a glass of Champagne on the outdoor terrace at the back of the hotel or in an Adirondack chair at the base of the lawn. 36 rooms, 1-3 story. Closed Nov-early May. Complimentary full breakfast. Check-out 11 am, check-in 4 pm. TV; VCR (movies). In-room modem link. Dining room. Room service. Outdoor tennis. Lawn games. Bicycles. Sailboats, rowboats. Totally nonsmoking. **$$$$**

D ⛆ ⊠

Restaurants

★ ★ ★ **21 FEDERAL.** 21 Federal St (02554). Phone 508/228-2121; fax 508/228-2962. Seafood menu. Menu changes daily. Closed Jan-Mar. Dinner. Bar. Outdoor seating. **$$$**

D

★ ★ ★ **AMERICAN SEASONS.** 80 Center St (02554). Phone 508/228-7111; fax 508/325-0779. Regional American menu. Closed Jan-Apr. Dinner. Bar. Outdoor seating. **$$$**

D

★ **ATLANTIC CAFE.** 15 S Water St (02554). Phone 508/228-0570; fax 508/228-8787. www.atlanticcafe.com. Mexican, seafood menu. Closed late Dec-early Jan. Dinner. Bar. Children's menu. **$$**

D

★ ★ **BLACK EYED SUSAN'S.** 10 India St (02554). Phone 508/325-0308. Eclectic/International menu. Closed Sun; Nov-Apr. Breakfast, dinner. Casual attire. Outdoor seating. **$$**

★ ★ ★ **BOARDING HOUSE.** 12 Federal St (02554). Phone 508/228-9622; fax 508/325-7109. www.nantucketrestaurants.com. Contemporary American Menu. Dinner. Bar. Outdoor seating. **$$$**

★ ★ **BLUE FIN.** 15 S Beach St (02554). Phone 508/228-2033. www.nantucketbluefin.com. Eclectic/International menu. Closed Jan-Apr. Dinner. Bar. Children's menu. Casual attire. **$$**

D

fiction readings, acting, dance performances, and exhibits of paintings, photography, and many other art forms. Look for the wet-paint sale in which you can bid on works completed just that day by local artists. Early Oct. **FREE**

Nantucket County Fair. *Tom Nevers Navy Base (02554). Phone 508/325-4748.* Looking for an old-fashioned county fair? Head to Nantucket for down-home family fun and entertainment. At the Nantucket County Fair, an event that began over 150 years ago, you'll find pies, breads, pastries, jams, jellies, fresh fall fruits, and concessions of all types. You'll also see and experience tractor displays and rides, a petting zoo and pet show, a flea market, quilt displays and sales, hay rides, concerts, and square dancing. Third weekend in Sept. **$$**

Nantucket Film Festival. *Various venues. Phone 508/228-6648. www.nantucket filmfestival.org.* Like other film festivals worldwide, Nantucket's festival screens new independent films that may not otherwise garner attention. You'll be joined by screenwriters, actors, film connoisseurs and, occasionally, big-name celebrities at the festival's seminars, readings, and discussions. A daily event call Morning Coffee showcases a panel of directors, screenwriters, and actors participating in Q&A with festival-goers, who sip coffee and munch on muffins. Mid-June. **$$$$**

Nantucket Wine Festival. *Phone 508/228-1128. www.nantucketwinefestival .com.* This is a wine festival like no other: take in a wine symposium, a variety of food and wine seminars, a wine auction, and many other events. The Great Wine in Grand Houses event allows you to visit a private mansion, sip fine wines drawn from nearly 100 wineries, and dine on food prepared by some of the world's finest chefs. Reservations are required and should be made as soon as you know you'll be visiting the island. Mid-May. **$$$$**

Sand Castle Contest. *Phone 508/228-1700.* Third Sat Aug.

Motel/Motor Lodge

★ ★ **HARBOR HOUSE VILLAGE.** *S Beach St (02554). Phone 508/228-1500; toll-free 866/325-9300; fax 508/228-7639. www.nantucketislandresorts .com.* 104 rooms, 2-3 story. No elevator. Check-out 11 am, check-in 3 pm. TV; cable (premium). In-room modem link. Restaurant, bar; entertainment. Room service. Heated pool, poolside service. Concierge. Public beach opposite. **$**

D ⩤ ⩥

Hotels

★ ★ ★ **VANESSA NOEL HOTEL.** *5 Chestnut St (03554). Phone 508/ 228-5300. www.vanessanoel.com.* 8 rooms, 3 story. Complimentary continental breakfast. Check-out 11 am, check-in 1 pm. TV; cable (premium). Internet access. Restaurant, bar. Room service. **$$$**

D ⩥

★ ★ ★ **WHITE ELEPHANT RESORT.** *50 Easton St (02554). Phone 508/228-2500; toll-free 800/475-2637; fax 508/325-1195. www.whiteelephant resort.com.* Step back in time for a game of croquet on a sweeping, manicured lawn at this Harbor-front resort. 80 rooms, 1-3 story. No elevator. Closed Nov-Apr. Check-out 11 am, check-in 3 pm. TV; cable (premium). In-room modem link. Restaurant, bar; entertainment. Heated pool, whirlpool, poolside service. Beach nearby; boat slips for guests only. Concierge. **$$$**

D ⌷ SC

B&B/Small Inns

★ ★ **CARLISLE HOUSE INN.** *26 N Water St (02554). Phone 508/228-0720; fax 781/639-1004. www.carlislehouse.com.* 17 rooms, 3 story. No room phones. Closed early Dec-Mar. Children over 10 years only. Complimentary continental breakfast. Check-out 11 am, check-in 2 pm. Street parking. Restored whaling captain's house (1765). Totally nonsmoking. **$**

⌷

★ **THE CARRIAGE HOUSE.** *5 Ray's Ct (02554). Phone 508/228-0326. www.carriagehousenantucket.com.* 7 rooms, 2 story. No A/C. Complimentary continental breakfast. Check-out 11 am, check-in 1 pm. Victorian décor. Center of Old Historic District; near ferries. Totally nonsmoking. No credit cards accepted. **$**

⌷

★ ★ ★ **CENTERBOARD GUEST HOUSE.** *8 Chester St (02554). Phone 508/228-9696. www.nantucket.net/lodging/centerboard.* 8 rooms, 3 story. Closed Jan-Feb. Complimentary continental breakfast. Check-out 11 am, check-in 3 pm. TV. In-room modem link. Street parking. Restored Victorian residence (1885). Totally nonsmoking. **$**

⌷

★ ★ **CENTRE STREET INN.** *78 Centre St (02554). Phone 508/228-0199; toll-free 800/298-0199; fax 508/228-8676. www.centrestreetinn.com.* 14 rooms, 3 story. No room phones. Closed Jan-Apr. Children over 8 years only. Complimentary continental breakfast. Check-out 11 am, check-in 3 pm. Concierge service. Colonial house built in 1742; some antiques. Totally nonsmoking. **$**

⌷

★ ★ **COBBLESTONE INN.** *5 Ash St (02554). Phone 508/228-1987; fax 508/228-6698.* 5 rooms, 3 story. Closed Jan-Mar. Complimentary breakfast. Check-out 11 am, check-in 2 pm. TV. Fireplace in library. Lawn games. Concierge. Built in 1725. Totally nonsmoking. **$**

⌷

★ ★ ★ **JARED COFFIN HOUSE.** *29 Broad St (02554). Phone 508/228-2400; fax 508/228-8549. www.jaredcoffinhouse.com.* 60 rooms, 3 story.

Check-out 11 am, check-in after 3 pm. TV. In-room modem link. Restaurant, bar. Concierge service. Historical objets d'art. Restored 1845 mansion. **$**

D 🔄

★ ★ **MARTIN HOUSE INN.** *61 Centre St (02554). Phone 508/228-0678. www.nantucket.net/lodging/martinn.* 13 rooms, 3 story. No A/C. No elevator. No room phones. Closed Jan-Feb. Complimentary continental breakfast. Check-out 11 am, check-in 3 pm. TV in common room; cable (premium). In-room modem link. Restaurant. Street parking. Built in 1803. Totally nonsmoking. **$**

🔄

★ ★ **ROBERTS HOUSE INN.** *11 India St (02554). Phone 508/228-0600; toll-free 800/872-6830; fax 508/325-4046. www.robertshouseinn.com.* 45 rooms, 3 story. Complimentary continental breakfast. Check-out 11 am, check-in 2 pm. TV. Concierge. Built in 1846; established 1883. **$**

D 🔄

★ ★ **SEVEN SEA STREET INN.** *7 Sea St (02554). Phone 508/228-3577; fax 508/228-3578. www.sevenseastreetinn.com.* 11 rooms, 2 story. Children over 5 years only. Complimentary continental breakfast. Check-out 11 am, check-in 3 pm. TV; VCR. Whirlpool. View of Nantucket Harbor. Totally nonsmoking. **$$**

🔄

★ ★ ★ **SHERBURNE INN.** *10 Gay St (02554). Phone 508/228-4425; toll-free 888/577-4425; fax 508/228-8114. www.nantucket.net/lodging/sherburne.* 8 rooms, 3 story. Children over 6 years only. Complimentary continental breakfast. Check-out 11 am, check-in 2 pm. Street parking. Concierge service. Built in 1835 as a silk factory; period antiques, fireplaced parlors. Totally nonsmoking. **$**

🔄

★ ★ **SHIPS INN.** *13 Fair St (02554). Phone 508/228-0040; fax 508/228-6254. www.nantucket.net/lodging/shipsinn.net.* 12 rooms, 4 story. No A/C. Closed Nov-Apr. Complimentary continental breakfast. Check-out 10 am, check-in 2 pm. TV. Dining room, bar. Built in 1831 by sea captain; many original furnishings. Totally nonsmoking. **$$**

🔄

★ ★ **TUCKERNUCK INN.** *60 Union St (02554). Phone 508/228-4886; toll-free 800/228-4886; fax 508/228-4890. tuckernuckinn.com.* 20 rooms, 2 story. Check-out 11 am, check-in 3 pm. TV; cable (premium), VCR. Laundry services. Dining room. Lawn games. Totally nonsmoking. **$**

🔄

★ ★ ★ ★ **THE WAUWINET.** *120 Wauwinet Rd (02584). Phone 508/228-0145; toll-free 800/426-8718; fax 508/228-6712. www.wauwinet.com.* Nearly

30 miles out to sea, the idyllic island of Nantucket is a place where crashing waves wash away everyday cares. The Wauwinet embodies the perfect getaway on this magical island. Tucked away on a private stretch of beach, The Wauwinet leads its guests to believe that they have been marooned on a remote island, yet this delightful hotel remains close to the town's charming cobblestone streets, a complimentary jitney ride away. Built in 1876 by ship captains, The Wauwinet's rooms and suites have a sophisticated country style blended with the services of a posh resort. Private beaches fronting the harbor and the Atlantic Ocean are spectacular, and clay tennis courts challenge guests to a match. Whether diners choose to arrive by foot or by sunset cruise on the 26-foot *Wauwinet Lady,* Topper's restaurant (see also TOPPER'S) promises to be an exceptional event. With a 20,000-bottle wine cellar and an impressive menu, it is an epicurean's delight. *Secret Inspector's Notes:* One of the most enjoyable ways to enjoy the fabulous Nantucket sunsets is with a signature pitcher of martinis or a glass of Champagne on the outdoor terrace at the back of the hotel or in an Adirondack chair at the base of the lawn. 36 rooms, 1-3 story. Closed Nov-early May. Complimentary full breakfast. Check-out 11 am, check-in 4 pm. TV; VCR (movies). In-room modem link. Dining room. Room service. Outdoor tennis. Lawn games. Bicycles. Sailboats, rowboats. Totally nonsmoking. **$$$$**

D ⛷ ⊠

Restaurants

★ ★ ★ **21 FEDERAL.** *21 Federal St (02554). Phone 508/228-2121; fax 508/228-2962.* Seafood menu. Menu changes daily. Closed Jan-Mar. Dinner. Bar. Outdoor seating. **$$$**

D

★ ★ ★ **AMERICAN SEASONS.** *80 Center St (02554). Phone 508/228-7111; fax 508/325-0779.* Regional American menu. Closed Jan-Apr. Dinner. Bar. Outdoor seating. **$$$**

D

★ **ATLANTIC CAFE.** *15 S Water St (02554). Phone 508/228-0570; fax 508/228-8787. www.atlanticcafe.com.* Mexican, seafood menu. Closed late Dec-early Jan. Dinner. Bar. Children's menu. **$$**

D

★ ★ **BLACK EYED SUSAN'S.** *10 India St (02554). Phone 508/325-0308.* Eclectic/International menu. Closed Sun; Nov-Apr. Breakfast, dinner. Casual attire. Outdoor seating. **$$**

★ ★ ★ **BOARDING HOUSE.** *12 Federal St (02554). Phone 508/228-9622; fax 508/325-7109. www.nantucketrestaurants.com.* Contemporary American Menu. Dinner. Bar. Outdoor seating. **$$$**

★ ★ **BLUE FIN.** *15 S Beach St (02554). Phone 508/228-2033. www.nantucketbluefin.com.* Eclectic/International menu. Closed Jan-Apr. Dinner. Bar. Children's menu. Casual attire. **$$**

D

★ ★ ★ **CHANTICLEER.** *9 New St (02564). Phone 508/257-6231; fax 508/ 257-4154. www.thechanticleerinn.com.* Owner/chef Jean-Charles Berruet delights his guests with his expertly prepared food and perfectly professional service. The main dining room is cozy and romantic with a crackling fireplace, fresh flowers and a view of the famous rose garden. Take a stroll through the rose and herb gardens during a visit here and drink up all of the beauty of the place. French menu. Closed Mon; also late Oct-mid-May. Dinner. Bar. Reservations required. Outdoor seating. **$$$**

D

★ ★ ★ **CLUB CAR.** *1 Main St (02554). Phone 508/228-1101. www.theclubcar.com.* Lunch and dinner at the Club Car are elegant, but the atmosphere remains casual. The Club Car lounge is housed in a renovated club car from a train that used to run between Steamboat Wharf and Siasconset Village, so the décor is fascinating. The restaurant offers seats for people-watching along Main Street and the waterfront, and a pianist performs nightly. French, continental menu. Closed Nov-late May. Dinner. Bar. Piano. Turn-of-the-century décor. Reservations required. **$$$**

★ ★ ★ **COMPANY OF THE CAULDRON.** *7 India St (02554). Phone 508/228-4016.* Eclectic/International menu. Closed Mon; also Mid-Dec-May. Dinner. Harpist Wed, Fri, Sun. Totally nonsmoking. **$$$**

D

★ ★ ★ **LE LANGUEDOC.** *24 Broad St (02554). Phone 508/228-2552; fax 508/228-4682. www.lelanguedoc.com.* The upstairs of this French spot features a romantic setting. Downstairs is a casual cafe and a "fun" place to go. French, American menu. Closed Feb-Mar. Dinner. Bar. Early 1800s building in heart of historic district. Outdoor seating. **$$$**

★ ★ ★ **ORAN MOR.** *2 S Beach St (02554). Phone 508/228-8655.* International menu. Closed Dec 25. Dinner. Bar. Casual attire. **$$**

D

★ **ROPE WALK.** *1 Straight Wharf (02554). Phone 508/228-8886; fax 508/ 228-8740. www.theropewalk.com.* Seafood menu. Closed mid-Oct-mid-May. Dinner. Bar. Children's menu. Outdoor seating. **$$**

D

★ ★ ★ **SUMMER HOUSE.** *17 Ocean Ave (02554). Phone 508/257-9976.* American menu. Closed Mid-Oct-mid-May. Dinner. Bar. Children's menu. Casual attire. Outdoor seating. **$$**

D

★ ★ ★ **TOPPER'S.** *120 Wauwinet Rd (02554). Phone 508/228-0145; fax 508/325-0657. www.wauwinet.com.* Located near the Great Point Lighthouse in the Wauwinet Inn, this romantic, sophisticated restaurant is filled with flowers, art, and the island's upper-crust clientele. The food, service, and wine list are all first rate. American menu. Closed late Oct-early May. Dinner, Sun brunch. Bar. Outdoor seating. Totally nonsmoking. **$$$**

D

★ ★ **WEST CREEK CAFE.** *11 W Creek Rd (02554). Phone 508/228-4943.* Contemporary American menu. Closed Tues; also Jan 1, July 4, Dec 25. Dinner. Bar. Outdoor seating. Totally nonsmoking. **$$$**

Saranac Lake, NY

5 hours 30 minutes; 305 miles from New York City

Settled 1819 **Pop** 5,041 **Elev** 1,534 ft **Area code** 518 **Zip** 12983

Information Chamber of Commerce, 30 Main St; 518/891-1990 or 800/347-1997

Web www.saranaclake.com

Surrounded by Adirondack Park, the village of Saranac Lake was first settled in 1819 when one Jacob Moody, who had been injured in a sawmill accident, retired to the wilderness, built a log cabin at what is now Pine and River streets, and raised a family of mountain guides. The qualities that attracted Moody and made the town a famous health resort in the 19th century continue to lure visitors in search of fresh, mountain air and a relaxing environment.

What to See and Do

Fishing. More than 130 well-stocked ponds and lakes plus 600 miles of fishing streams.

Meadowbrook State Public Campground. *4 miles E on NY 86, in Adirondack Park. Phone 518/891-4351.* Tent sites, picnicking. (Mid-May-mid-Oct) **$$$**

Mount Pisgah Veterans Memorial Ski Center. *3 miles NE on NY 86. Phone 518/891-0970. www.saranaclake.com/pisgah.* Five slopes, T-bar; patrol, school, snowmaking; snacks. Longest run 1,800 feet, vertical drop 300 feet. (Mid-Dec-mid-Mar, Thurs-Sun) **$$$$**

Robert Louis Stevenson Memorial Cottage. *11 Stevenson Ln (12983). Phone 518/891-1462.* Where Robert Louis Stevenson lived while undergoing treatment for what is believed to have been tuberculosis, 1887-1888; mementos. (July-mid-Sept, Tues-Sun) Schedule may vary. **$**

Six Nations Indian Museum. *On Buck Pond Rd, off NY 3, in Onchiota. Phone 518/891-2299.* Indoor and outdoor exhibits portray the life of the Native American, with a council ground, types of fires, ancient and modern articles; lecture on Native American culture and history. (July-Aug, Tues-Sun) **$**

Special Events

Adirondack Canoe Classic. *30 Main St (12983). Phone 518/891-2744; toll-free 800/347-1992. www.saranaclake.com/acc.shtml.* Ninety-mile, three-day race from Old Forge to Saranac Lake for 250 canoes, kayaks, and guideboats. Early Sept.

Willard Hanmer Guideboat, Canoe, and War Canoe Races. *Lake Flower and Saranac River. Phone 518/891-1990.* Early July.

Winter Carnival. *30 Main St # 2. Phone 518/891-1990.* Parade; skating, ski, snowshoe, and snowmobile racing. Early Feb.

Motel/Motor Lodge

★ **SARA PLACID MOTOR INN.** *120 Lake Flower Ave (12983). Phone 518/891-2729; toll-free 800/794-2729; fax 518/891-5624. sara-placid.com.* 18 rooms. Complimentary breakfast. Check-out 11 am. TV; cable (premium), VCR available. Outdoor tennis. Cross-country ski on site. Paddle boats. Ice-skating. **$**

D 🐾 ⚡ ✈ 🏊 SC

Hotel

★ ★ **HOTEL SARANAC OF PAUL SMITH'S COLLEGE.** *101 Main St (12983). Phone 518/891-2200; toll-free 800/937-0211; fax 518/891-5664. www.hotelsaranac.com.* 92 rooms, 6 story. Check-out 11 am. TV; VCR available (movies). Restaurant, bar. Cross-country ski 2 miles. Historic hotel (1927); lobby replica of foyer in Danvanzati Palace in Florence, Italy. **$**

D ✈ 🏊

Resort

★ **SARANAC INN GOLF & COUNTRY CLUB.** *125 County Rte 46 (12983). Phone 518/891-1402; fax 518/891-1309. www.saranacinn.com.* 10 rooms. Closed rest of year. Check-out 11 am. TV. Restaurant, bar. 18-hole golf, greens fee $50, putting green, driving range. **$$**

🐾 ⛳ 🏊

B&B/Small Inn

★ ★ ★ ★ ★ **THE POINT.** *HC1, Box 65, NY 30 (12983). Phone 518/891-5674; toll-free 800/255-3530; fax 518/891-1152. www.thepointresort.com.* Well-heeled travelers seeking a gentleman's version of "roughing it" head straight for The Point. This former great camp of William Avery Rockefeller revives the spirit of the early 19th century in the Adirondacks, when the wealthy came to rusticate in this sylvan paradise. No signs direct visitors to this intimate and discreet country house hotel, and a decidedly residential ambience is maintained. The resort enjoys a splendid location on a 10-acre peninsula on Upper Saranac Lake. Adirondack twig furnishings, regional decorative objects, and antiques finish the rustic yet sophisticated décor in the accommodations. From snowshoeing and cross-country skiing to water sports and trail hikes, a variety of outdoor activities beckon. Thoughtful touches include morning bread baskets delivered to guests' doors; everyone feels cosseted here. Gourmet dining figures largely in the experience, and with a nod to the patrician past, guests don black-tie attire twice weekly. 11 rooms, 1 story. No room phones. Pets accepted. Adults only. Restaurant, bar. Cross country skiing. **$$$$**

Restaurant

★ ★ **A.P. SMITH.** *101 Main St (12983). Phone 518/891-2200; fax 518/891-5664. www.hotelsaranac.com.* Dinner, brunch. Bar. Children's menu. Totally nonsmoking. College-operated as training facility. **$$**

D

Index

Notes

Notes

Notes

Notes

Notes

Notes

Notes